Citizenship from Below

NEXT WAVE: **NEW DIRECTIONS**
IN WOMEN'S STUDIES

*A series edited by Inderpal Grewal,
Caren Kaplan, and Robyn Wiegman*

CITIZENSHIP FROM BELOW

Erotic Agency and

Caribbean Freedom

MIMI SHELLER

DUKE UNIVERSITY PRESS
Durham & London 2012

© 2012 Duke University Press
All rights reserved

Printed in the United States of America
on acid-free paper ∞
Designed by Jennifer Hill
Typeset in Minion Pro by
Keystone Typesetting, Inc.

*Library of Congress
Cataloging-in-Publication Data appear on
the last printed page of this book.*

Unless noted otherwise, images are from
the Alexander Dudgeon Gulland
photographic album of Jamaica, 1865,
Graphic Arts Collection, Department of
Rare Books and Special Collections,
Princeton University Library.

For the people of Haiti

Without new visions
we don't know what to build,
only what to knock down.

ROBIN D. G. KELLEY,
Freedom Dreams

CONTENTS

ACKNOWLEDGMENTS   xi

INTRODUCTION   1

ONE   History from the Bottom(s) Up   19

TWO   Quasheba, Mother, Queen   48

THREE   Her Majesty's Sable Subjects   89

FOUR   Lost Glimpses of 1865   114

FIVE   Sword-Bearing Citizens   142

SIX   "You Signed My Name, but Not My Feet"   166

SEVEN   Arboreal Landscapes of Power and Resistance   187

EIGHT   Returning the Tourist Gaze   210

NINE   Erotic Agency and a Queer Caribbean Freedom   239

NOTES   281
WORKS CITED   305
INDEX   339

ACKNOWLEDGMENTS

The material that has gradually been incorporated into this book began during the period of my dissertation research, from 1993 to 1996, and extended across time and space, catching wide-ranging empirical and theoretical currents as I moved many times across the Atlantic. Some of the chapters began as journal articles that refused to fit within the confines of my doctoral dissertation, which was published in 2000 as *Democracy after Slavery: Black Publics and Peasant Radicalism in Haiti and Jamaica*. In 1988, a conference on "The Meaning of Freedom" was held at the University of Pittsburgh, coinciding with the one hundred fiftieth anniversary of emancipation in the British Caribbean and the one hundredth anniversary of emancipation in Brazil. This led to the publication of *The Meaning of Freedom: Economics, Politics, and Culture after Slavery* (1992), edited by Frank McGlynn and Seymour Drescher. Contributors to that volume such as O. Nigel Bolland focused on the activities of formerly enslaved people and their descendants, particularly how they conceived freedom and defined it for themselves. This included attention to ongoing struggles over land, labor, political rights, and wider cultural issues. My doctoral work was inspired by this turn toward a historiography of emancipation that rejected the simple dichotomy between slavery and freedom, began to note some of the continuities from the era of slavery into the period of emancipation, and recognized emancipation as a long-term process rather than as a single event.

Yet many aspects of my daily life, including gender relations, sexualities, and embodied interactions, still seemed inaccessible to historians due to archival and conceptual limitations. So this book emerged slowly as a kind of shadow dissertation that was percolating below the skin of my thesis, not yet ready to surface. Now, finally, this more slowly gestating text complements its elder sibling, and thanks are owed again to those who made that initial research possible. My research in Jamaica in 1993 was supported by the New School's Janey Program in Latin America and the Caribbean; research in England and France in 1994–95 was supported by an Elinor Goldmark Black dissertation fellowship from the New School for Social Research and by the MacArthur Program in Global Change and Liberalism in 1995–96. I thank the many helpful archivists and librarians at the National Library of Jamaica; the Jamaica Archives; the British Library; the British Public Record Office; the Angus Library at Regents College, Oxford; the French National Archives; and the French Ministry of Foreign Affairs.

I thank my dissertation committee at the New School for Social Research for encouraging my initial work on the Caribbean and for ongoing support over the years: the late Charles Tilly and William Roseberry, both of whom strongly influenced my understanding of the Caribbean past, and my greatest supporter, Mustafa Emirbayer, who inspired my interest in publics and in social theory. I also appreciate my external examiner, Harrison White, who complained that I had not left enough bones sticking out of the text/carcass for him to pick apart. Well, Harrison, here is the untidy pile of bones that I have been gnawing on ever since. I also thank the many other excellent teachers in the New School's Graduate Faculty of Political and Social Science in the 1990s who also influenced my work and gave me inspiration: Janet Abu-Lughod, Andrew Arato, Seyla Benhabib, Jean Cohen, Diane Davis, Bill Hanagan, Eric Hobsbawm, Antonio Lauria Pericelli, Deborah Poole, Rayna Rapp, and Louise Tilly. Fellow graduate students were incredibly supportive and inspiring, with special thanks to Ann Mische and Joel Stillerman.

A postdoctoral fellowship from the Center for African and Afro-American Studies at the University of Michigan enabled me to work further on the article that is incorporated into chapter 2 and to benefit from conversations with Rebecca Scott, Frederick Cooper, Julius Scott, and Margaret Somers. I especially thank my cohort there for conversation and support, especially the historian Laurent Dubois, whose ongoing work on the French West Indies and Haiti has been inspirational, and the groundbreaking anthropologist Gina Athena Ulysse, who has remained a friend, interlocutor, and provocateur over many years.

I joined the Society for Caribbean Studies (SCS) in the United Kingdom in 1996 and eventually served as vice-chair (2002–2003) and acting chair (2003–2004) of the society, whose members I cannot thank enough for their welcome, intellectual curiosity, generosity of spirit in sharing their work, and camaraderie. In particular, I extend thanks to Gad Heuman, who first supported my involvement in the SCS through a visiting scholar's position at the Centre for Caribbean Studies at Warwick University; Marjorie Davies, our tireless administrator; and all of my close collaborators on the SCS Committee, including Sandra Courtman, Ruth Minott Eggleston, David Howard, Cecily Jones, David Lambert, Diana Paton, Christer Petley, and Tracey Skelton. Diana Paton especially has helped me in the conceptualization of some of the chapters in this book, and her friendship and the example of her work have kept me on track at times when I might have strayed. And many thanks to the illustrious company of Jean Besson, O. Nigel Bolland, Richard Hart, Janet Momsen, Jean Stubbs, and the other SCS stalwarts who took me into the fold. Some sections of this work also draw on research that was supported by the British Academy (1999) and the Arts and Humanities Research Board (2001), which extended a sabbatical from Lancaster University while I completed my second book, *Consuming the Caribbean: From Arawaks to Zombies* (2003), which also inadvertently laid the groundwork for some of the ideas about agency, embodiment, postcoloniality, and counter-power developed here.

While I am neither located in nor originally from the Caribbean, I hope my thoughts are a contribution to an intellectual community that is being built and shaped by scholars in the Caribbean, as well as those in the wider Atlantic worlds I inhabit and that have been continuously touched by Caribbean histories, migrants, and cultures. I envision my home city of Philadelphia as part of a Caribbean diaspora, and the areas of New York (Flatbush Avenue, Brooklyn) and London (Dalston) in which I have lived over the years had significant influence from Caribbean migrants. This has made Caribbean culture—from the music and language in my ears to the books, politics, fashion, festivals, carnivals, and cuisine—a crucial part of my world. Over the past fifteen years, I have attended many conferences in the field of Caribbean studies and met remarkable Caribbean scholars from many countries. I have tried to contribute to building networks of Caribbean scholarship by attending conferences in the Caribbean, inviting Caribbean scholars to speak at conferences I have organized, citing Caribbean authors and teaching their work, and collaborating in founding a

Caribbean research network (in 2000) that spanned northern England and Scotland and continues to this day.

I owe special thanks to the many brilliant historians, anthropologists, and social theorists from the Caribbean and its diasporas who have discussed my work with me or whose own work on gender and racial or sexual relations has directly or indirectly influenced me over the years. They include especially M. Jacqui Alexander, Hilary Beckles, Natalie Bennett, Carolle Charles, Carolyn Cooper, Esther Figueroa, Lyndon Gill, Aaron Kamagusha, Kamala Kempadoo, Linden Lewis, Patricia Mohammed, Melanie Newton, Agostinho Pinnock, Shalini Puri, Rhoda Reddock, Patricia Saunders, Verene Shepherd, Faith Smith, Deborah Thomas, Alissa Trotz, Gina Athena Ulysse, Amar Wahab, and Gloria Wekker. Aaron Kamagusha especially gave me final pep talks to complete this book. For the ultimate flourish of inspiration via his doctoral dissertation, I especially thank Lyndon Gill, who has embarked on his own important work on erotic subjectivity—a topic in which the two of us found unexpected resonance in our work.

Alongside these comrades in Caribbean studies, I must also thank my many close friends at Lancaster University who supported my work and expanded my intellectual horizons in so many ways. I owe much of my ongoing interest in learning about new approaches to race, gender, and sexuality to my wonderful colleagues at Lancaster University, especially Sara Ahmed, Anne-Marie Fortier, Sarah Franklin, Maureen McNeil, Jackie Stacey, Divya Tolia-Kelly, and Imogen Tyler. Special thanks to John Urry for continuing collaborations and conversations. When I moved back to my hometown of Philadelphia in 2005, with thanks to my friend Ann Mische, I found a welcoming haven as a visiting associate professor in the Department of Sociology and Anthropology at Swarthmore College, where I am grateful especially to Robin Wagner-Pacifici, Miguel Diaz-Barriga, and Sarah Willie for supporting my work and to Rose Maio for her invaluable administrative support.

When I took up a new position as professor of sociology and director of the Center for Mobilities Research and Policy at Drexel University in 2009, I thought I had finally completed this project, but a chance discovery of a photo album from Jamaica in 1865 gave me pause once again. An even greater pause struck with the earthquake in Haiti on 12 January 2010. I want to thank my colleagues Franco Montalto, Michael Piasecki, Patrick Gurian, and Jennifer Britton for enabling me to revisit Haiti in the midst of its recovery from the shocking devastation. While flying to Port-au-Prince as part of a research team funded by the National Science Foundation in the spring and summer of 2010, I could not help but think of the hundreds of thousands of people who had perished beneath the rubble, the million more who had lost their homes and were described as living "down in the mud," and those who looked up at the airplanes passing overhead but could not leave the island. Beneath the rubble of Port-au-Prince there is much to learn about the struggles for citizenship from below. I thank the many people of Léogâne who shared their experiences and views of the future, including those who answered survey questions, participants in workshops who gave us a full day to share their views on water and sanitation. Above all, I thank the spirited Haitian and diaspora colleagues who made our visits possible in so many ways and from whom we learned so much: Jean de Vernet, Joseph (Lavaud) Vernet, Yves Rebecca, and Marie Yoleine Gateau, and the many students and assistants recruited along the way. We hope to return soon and continue the work you started in rebuilding your country from the ground up.

Because this work has evolved over many years, it requires a relatively detailed bibliographic history to record its emergence. I want to give some sense of the trajectory of presentations and publications that eventually crystallized into this book, because the input of so many commentators and critics has been crucial to its genesis. Each of the chapters here takes a substantially new form but one that, in many cases, is grounded in earlier conference papers and publications.

My reflections on the methodology that informs this project, now found in the introduction, began in a presentation to the workshop "Breaking Methods in Historical Research" at the Institute for Commonwealth Studies, London, in March 2000. It was revised for the "Things That Can't Quite Speak" workshop at the Centre for Science Studies, Lancaster University, in February 2003, and later iterations were presented to the London Group of Historical Geographers, Institute of Historical Research, University of London, in March 2005, and at the University of Toronto in January 2005, whose participants I thank for their comments. Parts of chapter 1 and chapter 9 appear in "Work That Body: Sexual Citizenship and Embodied Freedom" (Sheller 2007b). These chapters were also influenced by ongoing conversations with many colleagues, especially Sara Ahmed, Divya Tolia-Kelly, Imogen Tyler, Gina Athena Ulysse, and more recently by exposure to the work of Caribbean scholars such as Angelique Dixon, Lyndon Gill, and Agostinho Pinnock.

An early version of chapter 2 was presented at the Annual Meeting of the American Sociological Association in New York in August 1996 and to the Center for African and Afroamerican Studies Faculty Colloquium at the University of Michigan in October 1997, where it was printed in the Working Paper Series no. 42 (1997). It was eventually published as "'Quasheba, Mother, Queen': Black Women's Public Leadership and Political Protest in Post-emancipation Jamaica, 1834–1865" (Sheller 1998). A slightly earlier version of chapter 3 appeared as "'Her Majesty's Sable Subjects': Citizenship and Subaltern Masculinities in Post-Emancipation Jamaica" (Sheller 2005b), and another version was published as "Acting as Free Men: The Performance of Masculinity among Free and Indentured Men in Post-emancipation Jamaica" (Sheller 2005a). Chapter 4 was originally written for the *Princeton Library Chronicle* (Sheller 2011b), at the suggestion of Julie Melby in the Firestone Library's Rare Books and Manuscripts Division. Here I especially thank Gretchen Oberfrank, who did wonderfully careful and helpful editing and kindly helped me make use of the remarkable photographic album from 1865.

An early version of chapter 5, "Nationhood, Brotherhood, and Manhood in the Republic of Haiti in the Nineteenth Century," was presented at the 20th Annual Conference of the Society for Caribbean Studies in London in July 1996 and was awarded the David Nicholls Memorial Prize. It was later published as "Sword-Bearing Citizens: Militarism and Manhood in Nineteenth-Century Haiti" (Sheller 1997). I thank Hilbourne Watson, Alissa Trotz, and Gad Heuman for helpful suggestions and give special thanks to Kevin Yelvington for his timely encouragement of its publication. Chapter 6 arose out of the workshop "Control and Resistance in Post-emancipation Societies," sponsored by the Centre for Caribbean Studies at University of Warwick, in July 2000 and was later published as "'You Signed My Name but Not My Feet': Paradoxes of Peasant Resistance and State Control in Post-Revolutionary Haiti" (Sheller 2005c).

Chapter 7 extends and builds on my chapter "Arboreal Landscapes of Power and Resistance" in *Caribbean Land and Development Revisited* (Sheller 2007a). I thank that volume's editors, Janet Momsen and Jean Besson, for their helpful comments. I thank Insomniac Press for granting me permission to use Olive Senior's poem "Plants" in chapter 7; the poem was published in Senior's book *Gardening in the Tropics* (2005). Chapter 8 has not been published in any form previously; however, versions were presented to the Centre for Caribbean Studies, University of Warwick, in October 2002; the American Sociological Association's Annual Meeting in

San Francisco in August 2004; the Latitudes Group, Department of English, University of Pennsylvania, in December 2004; and the University of Toronto in January 2005, where I especially thank Jacqui Alexander, Aaron Kamagusha, Kamala Kempadoo, Melanie Newton, Mary Nyquist, Alyssa Trotz, Amar Wahab, and Derek Williams for their feedback.

Finally, for reading and discussing several parts of the manuscript, I thank Shalini Puri for a reading group she organized at the University of Pittsburgh in 2010 and O. Nigel Bolland for offering constructive and deeply informed commentary and for graciously reminding me of the original contexts for my work, which arose out of *The Meaning of Freedom*. These final encouragements helped me step back and reflect on the book as a whole. Many thanks to Caren Kaplan and Inderpal Grewal for providing intellectual support, inviting this book for their series, and having the vision to see it as a contribution to women's studies, and to my editor Ken Wissoker at Duke University Press for his infinite patience, eye for readability, and insistence on the final touches.

Finally, there are no words to express my thanks to all of my family for putting up with my work over the years, taking an interest in it, never questioning my choices, and supporting me in every way possible. I would not be here without you. To my nearest and dearest, a big thanks for welcoming me back to Philadelphia with open arms and warm hearts; you all know how much I owe you and how much I love being home. To Alexandra Liberty, my sweet angel, thanks for always making me happy. To Eve Adeline, my little sassy girl, thanks for always making me laugh. And love to Dan, for appearing at the crossroads as a "cosmos mariner" to join me in a journey of winter nights toasting marshmallows on the fire, welcoming the spring with windows and doors thrown open, filling summer days to the brim picking the bounty of the garden, and awakening to crisp fall mornings with the precious world at our fingertips.

The patterns of highly uneven distribution of human suffering, poverty, and violence found in many parts of the Caribbean and the wider Americas are closely related to the histories of colonialism, slavery, and exclusion that formed the contemporary world. It is this shared history, and the ongoing injustices arising from it, that first drew me into studying the connections and relations that bridge the Caribbean and Atlantic worlds. My sense of the unequal exposure of people to violence, poverty, and sheer human suffering began from personal experience of places like Philadelphia, where I grew up and now live, and New York, where I began my research on the Caribbean in the mid-1990s. I also encountered it in starker form in the Caribbean, as a tourist and while conducting long-term research in Jamaica and Haiti, as well as more briefly while attending conferences throughout the region. The astounding disparities of social violence emerge most starkly in the confrontation with the present-day realities of Haiti since the earthquake in January 2010. In the earthquake's aftermath we have all been faced with the continuing homelessness of hundreds of thousands of people; the reported rapes of women and children in camps that are supposed to offer shelter, including by United Nations peacekeepers; the violent halting of food aid to, and evictions of people from, those camps; and the ongoing interception of Haitian refugees at sea and their enforced return to Haiti and the detention of "illegal" migrants at borders such as U.S. airports (Center for Human Rights and Global Justice 2011; Schuller 2010). These are all instances of the lingering violence of life in the post-slavery Atlantic world.

People of African descent throughout the Americas continue to be especially vulnerable to environmental disasters, health threats, state violence, and neighborhood violence. The sudden upheaval of the earthquake in Haiti compounded the slow-motion social disaster that was already unfolding in the everyday interpersonal and international systems of violence that created desperately poor slums, denuded mountainsides, flooding rivers, and an unsustainable state squeezing the life out of its own population and thus creating its vulnerability to forces of nature. The precarious circumstances of the people in Haiti who still have nowhere to rebuild their lives, no means of living, and no safety or security are an outcome of the failures of modern citizenship and the mockery it makes of freedom.

Racial, class, and gender boundaries continue to delineate the inequitable distribution of rights, freedom, protection, and justice, both within cities (whether Philadelphia, Port-au-Prince, Kingston, or London) and across nations, and these inequities and injustices reiterate and reinforce those boundaries that differentiate humans from one another. A differential valuing of white and black bodies, as well as of socially acceptable forms of male and female bodies, is one of the most enduring legacies of slavery, and my work ultimately aims to contest some of the continuing privileges and protections of whiteness and sexual normativity in the post-slavery Caribbean and Atlantic worlds. But I also understand these embodied subjectivities as formed in relation to spatial settings and performed within specific material contexts, which resonate with and against bodies. This book itself must be situated in relation to its spatial and material context, just as I am situated as a researcher and writer outside of the Caribbean.

As much as transatlantic and pan-Caribbean connections and journeys make up the shared world that this work inhabits, I always remain aware of my own location as a white(ish) heterosexual academic located in the United States with access to various kinds of capital (financial, social, cultural, and network). I repeatedly question the aims of my work and the institutional structures in which it is produced, circulated, and legitimated. For generations, Caribbean historians, anthropologists, theorists, and teachers have raised crucial epistemological questions concerning historical methodology, authorial position, and power through their explorations of the institutions of historiography (Higman 2000; Nettleford 1978); the potential uses of oral history (Price 1983; Sistren Theatre Collective 1986); popular memory and commemoration (Wilmot 2009); the "silencing of the past" (Trouillot 1995); and the color, class, and gender performances of the researcher (Ulysse 2002, 2008). A key methodological premise of this book is that power operates precisely through unmarked but situated knowledge, which marks others as objects of knowledge. Rather than simply presenting archival evidence on Caribbean histories, I repeatedly ask myself: What do we know about the Caribbean past(s), and how do we know it? Who can make claims to knowledge, with what license and legitimation? How does a researcher's location inside or outside the Caribbean, and within or outside particular fields of power, matter in writing history? While they do not arrest my research, these questions give me pause to reflect on its purpose, context, methods, and audience.

The Haitian American anthropologist Michel-Rolph Trouillot sensitively explored how the power relations that shape the production of history may lead to a silencing of the past. He memorably argued that "any historical narrative is a particular bundle of silences. . . . Silences enter the process of historical production at four crucial moments: the moment of fact creation (the making of *sources*); the moment of fact assembly (the making of *archives*); the moment of fact retrieval (the making of *narratives*); and the moment of retrospective significance (the making of *history* in the final instance)" (Trouillot 1995: 26). The effort to reconstruct and tell Caribbean histories, then, must always grapple with the various levels of silencing that are intrinsic to the production of history. Insofar as "power is constitutive of the story" (Trouillot 1995: 28), we can say that silences "are inherent in history because any single event enters history with some of its constituting parts missing. Something is always left out while something else is recorded. . . . Thus whatever becomes fact does so with its own inborn absences, specific to its production" (Trouillot 1995: 49). Identifying those absences may be an important element of the historian's task. Simply finding more or "better" facts by enlarging the empirical base is not sufficient (though in many cases, it is welcome). Writers of historical narrative must also attend to its silences and examine the processes by which these yawning gaps in historicity are produced, whether in the sources, in the archives, in the narratives, or in the making of history itself.

One of the greatest silences in Caribbean historiography is the invisibility of queer subjectivities (Gill 2010; Glave 2005, 2008; Silvera 1991). Existing approaches to nineteenth-century Caribbean history have largely ignored the methodological problems raised by subaltern studies, postcolonial theory, and, especially, queer theory. While reflexive ethnographers of the contemporary Caribbean have more willingly reflected on their own gender, racial, and national positioning (e.g., Besson 2002; Gill 2010; Skelton 2004; Ulysse 2002), most professional histories of colonialism, slavery, emancipation and post-emancipation transitions continue to be written on the basis of archival research carried out by an "objective" researcher trained to write in the neutral, self-effacing, and disembodied yet authoritative voice of social science and political history. Issues of power and positionality in the research and writing of history are thus often sidestepped by historians who write Caribbean history, especially those from outside the Caribbean (although for some exceptions, see Lambert 2004; Petley 2004; Sheller 2003). Even if anthropologists have more effectively grappled with their relation to "the field," the larger problem of historical methodologies for studying non-elite, non-normative, and silenced social histories remains an open issue. Before proceeding, then, it is necessary to pause for some methodological considerations.

The French historian Marc Bloch wrote in 1940 that "knowledge of all human activities in the past, as well as of the greater part of those in the present, is . . . a knowledge of their tracks; . . . what do we really mean by document, if it is not a 'track,' as it were—the mark, perceptible to the senses, which some phenomenon, in itself inaccessible, has left behind?" (Bloch 1953: 54–55). By carefully cross-examining the evidence before us, Bloch argued, we can draw out not only witnesses to the past but also the more elusive "witnesses in spite of themselves"—unintentional traces left in the sands of time. But where are the tracks of the most marginal, such as the enslaved and the very poor, the derided sexual outlaw, or the persecuted ethnic minority? What counts as a track and what counts as an archive, and who determines the authority of different kinds of evidence? There are always "dimensions of institutional control here which limit access to historical materials and therefore define boundaries of historical research" (Hallam 2000: 273). A great deal of Caribbean historiography traditionally has depended on colonial sources, such as government archives, missionary archives, and the writings of white colonists and visitors. As Rex Nettleford (1978: 58) argued, "It is the written records of the literate scribal masters which determined the substance of much of the recorded history of the Caribbean people." Even today we might observe that the process of producing silences continues. In post-earthquake Haiti, for example, the business of disaster relief and decision making about reconstruction takes place almost exclusively in French and English. At the levels of the Haitian government; the United Nations clusters working on shelter, water, sanitation, and hygiene; and the many meetings of dozens of nongovernmental organizations, no one bothers to provide Kreyòl translation. Thus, not only the Haitian people but also their local organizations and local government representatives are excluded from the process of fact creation, as I saw during research trips there in May–June 2010 and July–August 2010.[1]

It is imperative therefore to ask: How are those who are barred from political personhood, along with their forms of local and embodied knowledge, made present within academic, legal, governmental, and other official discourses? What dilemmas of representation face historians of slavery and emancipation—or of any field more generally in which the subjects of history cannot "speak" or be represented in official evidentiary terms? And how can historiography both find these sources beneath the surface and tap into non-representational dimensions of the past, the embodied, spatial, and affective aspects that escape archival record? The emergence of subaltern studies in the 1980s (Guha and Spivak 1988) and feminist standpoint theories and ideas of situated knowledge in the 1990s (Harding 1991) made traditional archival and literate textual sources increasingly less palatable insofar as they represented only one perspective: that of the ruling class. The existence of romanticized, righteous, struggling subaltern subjects—however problematic—became the basis of much research on resistance, counter-publics, social movements, and radical politics. History "from below," representing subaltern perspectives, continues to seek non-elite actors to tell the story of their struggles in their own voices, even as it struggles with the paradoxes of representation as posed by Gayatri Spivak's famous query, "Can the Subaltern Speak?" What this approach needs now is a far more savvy contextualization of when, how, and where subaltern subjects appear, or are silenced, and a better understanding of how and why they, too, despite everything, sometimes reproduce the "hegemonic" perspectives of the ruling regime, exclude "other others," and leave their own silences.

If it were not for the historians who first recognized the importance of freed people's vision of freedom, we would not even be in a position to ask such questions. In his essay "The Politics of Freedom in the British Caribbean" (1991), for example, Nigel Bolland made crucial contributions to the realization that the formerly enslaved people of the Caribbean and their descendants had a non-market-oriented and non-state-oriented understanding of freedom that was defined instead by their relations to one another, including forms of kinship and egalitarianism. Pamela Scully (2005: 39–41) also makes an important intervention in post-emancipation histories, however, when she observes: "An investigation into freedmen's understanding and representations of citizenship necessarily involves us in a consideration of the production of knowledge in the postemancipation era. . . . The historian trying to uncover or analyze slaves' perspectives on slavery, emancipation, and gender and racial ideologies has to press the limits of the evidence. . . . Freedmen appear in the archives already to some extent bound and constructed by power relations of colonial knowledge." Thus, historians of colonial societies have sought to uncover "different perspectives of the colonized through attention to practices, through the use of oral history, and through skilful reading between the lines to find evidence of subaltern views" (Scully 2005: 41). Yet anyone who has engaged in this process quickly comes up against the "unresolved ambiguity" of many sources, the impossibility of establishing truth, and the frequent silences of the past: "Embracing the ambiguity of the archives means acknowledging our limitations as historians. It also means acknowledging the political agency of freedpeople" (Scully 2005: 41). But where is such political agency located?

In my view, the historian of freedom who seeks traces of subaltern agency must also look beneath conventional definitions of political agency and of citizenship and seek out the unexcavated field of embodied (material and spiritual) practices through which people exercise and envision freedom in a domain that I will define later as "erotic agency." Indeed, it requires us to question the very categories within which we operate, as well as foundational concepts such as "freedom," "citizenship," and "agency," which Trouillot (2003) has so astutely analyzed as seductive "North Atlantic Fictions" that hide the marks of their own provenance. Just as the publication of slave narratives in the nineteenth century was caught within the skeins of abolitionist viewpoints, publicity networks, and modes of textual and visual representation (Sheller 2011a), more recent efforts to decolonize Caribbean history raise further methodological questions about the framing of the subject who may speak in the name of the people, the control of historical narratives and their interpretation, the deployment of symbolic capital by state institutions, and the seductive fictions of freedom and citizenship that often hide certain kinds of complicity. Oral histories, for example, are a narrative framework in which the past is constantly retold, revised, and reconstructed; thus, they depend on very different conceptualizations of what the past is, how we come to know it, and for what purposes it is remembered.[2] Yet projects of recovery and reconstruction may "give voice to the voiceless" by allowing them voice only in very circumscribed ways, often as representative national subjects who serve particular nationalist or postcolonial histories.

It is difficult for any reclamation of the African or Afro-Caribbean roots of Caribbean national cultures to avoid entanglement in deeply seated colonial *and* postcolonial ideologies of gendered, ethnic, and heteronormative boundary drawing and exclusion. In the post-independence period in the British West Indies, for example, projects of nation building insisted that popular histories and African Studies in particular were "vital for the preservation and development of key cultural values like self-confidence and a sense of heritage among the masses of people in Jamaica and the [wider] Caribbean" (Nettleford 1978: 61). Nevertheless, these projects of decolonization raised thorny questions of who owns national history (or histories) and who is excluded. Where an aspiring black middle-class and governing elite controlled the definition and production of national history, it remained as exclusionary as ever. As Deborah Thomas (2004: 5) argues for post-independence Jamaica, "While the government's legitimation of aspects of Jamaica's African cultural heritage broadened the public space in which notions of national identity could be debated, the actual process of privileging particular elements of Jamaica's African cultural heritage also marginalized alternative visions . . . [Efforts at] revalorizing rural Afro-Jamaican cultural practices neither tended to appreciably alter the structural position of rural Afro-Jamaicans, nor to significantly reinvent the ideological systems through which modern 'progress' had been measured and 'development' evaluated." Thus, the national cultural projects, the new educational initiatives, and the reclamation of the folk traditions of a "respectable" Afro-Jamaican independent peasantry by the nation-building middle classes, however progressive and anticolonial, nonetheless placed limits on national belonging. Heritage projects maintained colonial gender hierarchies and marginalized popular urban culture while simultaneously reinforcing deeply heteronormative moral orders.

Whether using colonial sources, nationalist historiography, or popular oral histories, one must always interrogate how subaltern subjects who are barred from political personhood (and how illegitimate or "vulgar" topics such as sexuality) are made present within academic, legal, and other official discourses, including historical studies such as this one. In some of the chapters that follow, therefore, I will write against the grain of both mainstream academic histories and nationalist popular histories of freedom and emancipation. I will ask thorny questions about the romantic conventions and heroes of subaltern history, embracing instead the anti-romance (Francis 2010). Jean-Jacques Dessalines and Toussaint Louverture in Haiti or George W. Gordon and Paul Bogle in Jamaica might be transformed from "Arch-Traitors" to "National Heroes," but what modes of national masculinity are they called on to uphold, and why have Jamaicans forgotten Letitia Geoghagan? How are the Maroons romanticized as an authentic African Caribbean roots culture, even as their violent protection of the white colonial state is conveniently forgotten? How are Indo-Caribbean people silenced in post-independence nationalist histories of nation building? And where would marginal characters ranging from the Jewish Jamaican Sidney Levien to the queer Caribbean subject, as discussed in later chapters, fit into these national mythologies and historiographies? Can historians dare to ask how queer sexualities and "erotic subjectivities" (Gill 2010) might trouble our telling of nationalist histories of emancipation, freedom, and citizenship?

Beneath the official histories of post-emancipation political struggles—peopled with valiant laborers and hardy peasants, wicked colonial elites and imperious foreign powers, military mobilizations and noble popular resistance—lies an equally relevant domain of sexual and spiritual struggles, gendered and queer meanings, and a deeper undertow of erotic politics (described more fully throughout this book) that have been silenced in Caribbean history and in our conceptualization of the making of modern freedom. While some may feel this is an abandonment of the more acceptable traditions of social and political historiography, and a departure from my work in *Democracy after Slavery* (Sheller 2000), which dealt with explicitly state-oriented political publics and repertoires of contention, I feel it is a continuation and broadening of that project, with a deeper understanding of the challenges and limitations not only of sources, archives, and the making of facts, but also of citizenship and freedom itself and of the kinds of narratives we tell about them. Others may feel that I am unlicensed to tread this ground because of my own social positioning, which, I make explicit here, is neither queer nor Caribbean.[3] Yet I beg their indulgence (as many have already generously given me) to embrace an emerging field of queer Caribbean studies that is already at large in the world and speaking for itself, though some do not want to listen.

At the annual conference of the Caribbean Studies Association (csa) in Kingston in 2009, for example, panels included the roundtable "Contending Forces: Politics of Respectability and the Caribbean Sexual Imaginary," organized by Angelique Nixon, and the panels "Centering Sexuality in Caribbean Studies," organized by Kamala Kempadoo; "Caribbean Sexualities: Work, Risk and Identity"; and "Queerness and the Jamaican Nation," organized by Esther Figueroa. A concurrent workshop was also held on gender and leadership, which brought together lgbtq activists from across the region who joined the International Research Network (IRN), as well as a series of panels sponsored by the Masculinities Network. The IRN then sponsored a very dynamic and well-attended series of panels at the CSA conference in 2010 in Barbados, established a Sexualities Working Group within the CSA, and launched an LGBT oral history collection and Jamaica Gay Freedom Movement digital archive.[4] This vibrant field of exchange spans established scholars and doctoral candidates, academics and activists, artists and poets, regionally based and diasporic participants, all of whom are building a safe space for discussions, dialogue, debate, and political intervention in the realm that I call "citizenship from below." It has been through such spaces that I have been able to meet incredibly attuned and attentive researchers who have encouraged my interventions in this field (even though I am something of an outsider) through listening to and encouraging my work and graciously sharing their own work.

OVERVIEW OF THE BOOK

Chapter 1, "History from the Bottom(s) Up," introduces theories of citizenship, performativity, and sexual citizenship, developing a new understanding of "embodied freedom" as a key concept informing the book as a whole. Especially during the post-slavery period known as "emancipation" —in which we in the Atlantic world arguably continue to exist—bodies, sexualities, and sexual orientations remain the most contested yet crucial terrains for the elaboration of freedom. When slavery ended, techniques and practices of sexual domination and biopolitical power remained entrenched. Violence against the body continued to be exercised in corporeal forms of private and public embodiment that reproduced racial, gender, sexual, and class hierarchies. As the chapters that follow suggest, people freed from slavery in both Jamaica and Haiti (and throughout the Americas) were also being more deeply inscribed into particular gender, racial, and moral orders, even as they tried to challenge them. As postcolonial theorists note, subaltern claims for political inclusion and attempts to exercise their rights are a double-edged sword, since the expression of political subjectivity is also always a further inscription into the state order (cf. Scully and Paton 2005).

This study locates the Caribbean in a wider realm of "inter-embodiments" that informed the entire Atlantic world and its African diasporas. At stake here is how one deploys the body's sexual and erotic potential in a context of constrained freedom, social inequality, and state regulation of deviance. In taking up positions as free subjects, freed men and women at times had to (indeed, wanted to) perform normative scripts of sexual citizenship such as the good mother, the respectable woman, the worthy Christian, or the father of a family. Yet there was always a tension within these performances, which involved the harnessing and simultaneous disavowal of the erotic potential of the body, including its spiritual dimensions. The book therefore addresses African-Caribbean practices of *embodied freedom* and *sexual citizenship* in post-slavery Haiti and Jamaica, which generally have been neglected in mainstream historiography. It shows how the formation of free subjects in this period connects to a postcolonial feminist and queer theory of embodied freedom and erotic agency that still has implications today.

Comparisons of differing post-slavery contexts stretching across more than one linguistic region and empire are still rare within Caribbean historiography, yet they can enrich our understanding of the different forms of embodied freedom that were provided by different contexts of social and political action. Freedom was not uniformly experienced; nor do we have access to the same kinds of archival records of different times and places. I begin from colonial and missionary archives to find examples of the actions and words of lower-class rural and urban people in Jamaica, including their petitions, reported words of challenge to authorities, and accounts of their actions in public spaces such as courthouses and streets and during riots. This part of the book shows how attention to forms of racial and gendered language within archival sources is crucial to post-emancipation studies of embodied freedom, yet it also has some limitations due to the nature of the inequality of "facticity" and how facts are assembled, archived, and recalled (Trouillot 1995). Based largely on written evidence gathered from public texts, newspapers, petitions, and official correspondence, the history presented here is shaped in part by the sources; however, in chapter 3, another kind of source is introduced, in the form of a photographic album that troubles conventional historical facticity and leads into wider methodological departures later in the book.

Chapter 2, "Quasheba, Mother, Queen," surveys evidence for the leadership of Afro-Jamaican women in political protest under the system of slavery, during the transition to apprenticeship, and in the immediate post-emancipation situation. The ending of slavery in the British colonies in 1834 did not lead immediately to freedom. Instead, a system known as apprenticeship existed during which the sugar plantations were wracked by labor disputes. Prominent in these disputes were events described as "petticoat rebellions," uprisings of "nursing mothers," and work stoppages or strikes by women who proclaimed their rights as mothers. The discursive and enacted positions of "Mother" and "Queen" became crucial public personas for black women and went on to have great significance in subsequent popular religious and political movements in Jamaica. Building on theories of the formation of black counter-publics, this chapter addresses not only the ways in which freed women were excluded from citizenship in post-slavery contexts but, more important, the ways they found to claim gendered rights and exercise personal freedom. Contrary to critiques of the constitutive gender exclusions of the bourgeois public sphere in Western Europe, chapter 2 demonstrates that black Jamaican women played a very visible and audible part in subaltern counter-publics, through which they challenged the gender and racial inequalities that delimited freedom. The chapter foregrounds subaltern women's voices and actions as found in the existing archive and explores the possibilities for recovering an anticolonial and anti-patriarchal history submerged in official sources. It also suggests some of the ways in which black women manipulated existing gendered and sexual identities to position themselves in liberal Christian political discourse and competently enter public spheres from which their bodies generally were barred, including public spaces such as church meetings, courthouses, and street protests.

Chapter 3, "Her Majesty's Sable Subjects," turns to the construction of subaltern masculinities in post-emancipation Jamaica. As freed men increasingly exercised civil and political rights from the 1840s to the 1860s, they, too, framed a collective identity as Christian, as fathers of families, and as free subjects, emphasizing particular forms of masculinity as the foundation for claims to citizenship. However, I argue that it is crucial to consider not only how masculine citizenship reinforced the patriarchal domestication of women and the formation of a "manly" public sphere, but also how discourses of black Jamaican freedom excluded indentured men and foreigners, such as the recently arrived Africans "liberated" from Spanish slaving vessels. Whereas previous studies of colonial gender orders have emphasized elite perspectives and the black–white divide, I turn to evidence of subaltern gender formations and relations between various marginalized groups, including emancipated plantation workers and indentured laborers from Africa and India. There have been very few studies of the relation between Creolized Caribbean people and those of African and Indian origin in the nineteenth century, and this chapter contributes significant new archival findings on popular discourses about race, ethnicity, and gender. I show how forms of subaltern masculinity were often in competition not only with elite white masculinity, but also with one another. This involved moral claims about appropriate gender norms, sexualities, and familial forms. This kind of exclusionary masculine nationalism has significant implications for the contemporary positioning of black Jamaican heteronormative masculinity today.

In Chapter 4, "Lost Glimpses of 1865," I revisit the history of the Morant Bay Rebellion in Jamaica through the use of a recently discovered rare photo album. When the Firestone Library at Princeton University acquired the previously unknown album containing images of Jamaica in 1865–66 in 2009, it sent a ripple of excitement through the scholarly community. The photographs have never been published, and few people have seen them until now. They provide a remarkable new resource to complement the extensive written archival records and printed sources from this period. Photographs printed in the mid-nineteenth century, using a collodion process on albumen paper, provide a rare glimpse into the material worlds, buildings, clothing, landscapes, and faces of the period. They seem to catch something of the spirit of the times, the ephemeral atmosphere of place. Even though photographs are framed and manipulated to represent a particular point of view, photography nevertheless records certain fleeting details of materiality that words alone cannot convey. Photographs add a depth to our historical imagination even as they make acute the absence of that which is beyond apperception, lost to the archives and to time. Albums also incorporate modes of ordering and making sense, while the photographs themselves are carefully framed, selected, printed, and organized to tell us something about the social and cultural context in which they were produced. I use the album to explore other approaches to the narrative of the events of 1865 and suggest surprising interpretations of the alignments of color, class, and politics.

In the next chapters, I turn to performances of citizenship in Haiti, which offers a very different political context for examining intersections of gender, race, nation, citizenship, and sexuality in the aftermath of slavery. I report archival evidence of the actions of both literate elites and lower-class rural and urban people in Haiti, including their involvement in rebellions. However, the sources are limited, and "giving voice" to subalterns is never straightforward or even desirable. Thus, I emphasize that the articulation of claims to citizenship in post-independence Haiti (as in post-emancipation Jamaica) implicated the citizen in racialized, gendered, and sexually embodied performances, often reproducing colonial forms of symbolic capital and colonial structures of domination and exclusion.

Again, these histories of formations of masculinity, sexuality, and spirituality all left legacies that continue to inform forms of embodied freedom and erotic agency in Haiti.

Chapter 5, "Sword-Bearing Citizens," explores militarism, manhood, and the gendering of black citizenship in Haiti through a discourse analysis of the language of masculine republicanism and the feminine nation in the early nineteenth century. Despite the paucity of archival evidence on women's lives in Haiti in this period, I argue that crucial aspects of the gender order still can be uncovered by paying attention to public discourses of masculinity. For example, Haitian writers described their republic, founded in 1804 after more than a decade of revolution, as the "mother of African liberty," whose male citizens were rallied as fathers, husbands, and sons to protect her. The chapter shows how freedom is performed through scripts of gender and sexuality that inform genres of citizenship and national belonging. I argue that the militarization of masculinity in the Haitian construction of republican citizenship undermined the revolutionary promise of freedom, especially for women. However, rather than attributing women's subordination to a misogynistic culture (as some have done), I also argue that alternative masculinities were circulating within Haitian culture and that black women also held positions of relative power, even though both subaltern men and women were generally excluded from political power.

Chapter 6 begins with the Haitian saying "You signed my name, but not my feet," to examine issues of historiographical absences or silences in any attempt to account for embodied freedom and agency in Haiti in the nineteenth century. After a brief review of forms of elite economic and political control, the chapter identifies some evidence of popular practices of embodied resistance, focusing in particular on women's involvement in marketing and their use of public space, as well as evidence of their involvement in armed struggle and crucial public protests. It also highlights the period of the Piquet Rebellion of 1844, in which rural men and women were mobilized in a democratization movement that included religious forms of solidarity, and links this to evidence of women's political participation. Nevertheless, the chapter acknowledges the problems of evidence in the Haitian case and the limits of "facticity" when trying to reconstruct citizenship from below, a challenge for the entire methodology of narrative history.

Precisely because of these methodological problems in seeking out subaltern voices and subjects, the final chapters of the book turn instead to non-verbal and non-textual evidence. This part of the book shifts the prism of Caribbean history to refract its stories in new ways. The central questions about citizenship and embodied freedom remain the same, but here the main emphasis is on material and mobile inter-bodily encounters. Freedom and control are achieved through a variety of spatial formations, and one fundamental relation between bodies and spatial forms concerns the very question of who can define spatial form in the first place. How is space controlled and structured and by whom? How are structural forms fixed in place and with what effects on the disposition of bodies? Here I consider the limitations of conventional historical methods in addressing the silencing of the past and the absence of subaltern subjects from many archival records, highlighting issues that have propelled the shift from second-wave to third-wave historical sociology and that instigated my departure from traditional comparative and historical sociology into more interdisciplinary fields that encompass visual analysis, material culture, and the analysis of spatiality and mobility.

Turning to cultural geographies of space and place, material cultures, visual histories, and the geography of place and embodiment, I draw on evidence such as the living landscape, the vernacular meanings of nature, and the local reaction against tourism as ways to gauge aspects of history from below that are otherwise silenced. This wider sense of bodily relations extends out into the surrounding environments, whether of the plantation, the peasant plot, or the tourist resort, while continuing to engage with questions of agency, sexuality, spirituality, and embodiment. This also demands that we interrogate more carefully the scale at which citizenship is imagined. Citizenship regimes may be particular to specific states, and the form of the state and of citizenship certainly differed immensely in Haiti and Jamaica. Yet claims to embodied freedom may also burrow beneath the state apparatus into more local concerns, or they may expand outward to a transnational or even transcendental vision of belonging that challenges the containment of the nation-state. Here I seek to show how the lived materiality of Caribbean freedom both embeds itself in small localities and expands into a transnational critique of European land possession and communal dispossession across the African diaspora and its subsequent Caribbean offspring.

Chapter 7, "Arboreal Landscapes of Power and Resistance," explores the spatial arrangement of agency and resistance in the Caribbean from a starting point grounded in the physical environment. Through a study of human interrelations expressed with and through trees, I develop a spatial methodology for tracking citizenship from below in modes that burrow beneath human interactions to encompass interactions with natural and sacred places, non-human spirits and entities. This contributes to rethinking silences in the historical record not only through attention to material culture, lived spatiality, and embodied interaction, but also sacred spaces and immaterial worlds. To understand the physicality and performativity of a politics from below, in other words, I choose to begin from the ground up, literally: roots, plants, gardens, plots of land. Land and its uses have been a key site of social struggle in post-slavery societies. Social relations of power and resistance are inscribed into living landscapes of farming, dwelling, and cultivation. Drawing on historical archives, literary sources, and visual imagery mainly from the Anglophone and Francophone Caribbean, chapter 7 examines how trees in particular have been used to identify, symbolize, demarcate, and sustain various Caribbean places, meanings, and lives. I build on anthropological approaches to the study of family land within the plot–plantation nexus but also draw on recent approaches in cultural geography to develop a cultural geography of trees and land in the Caribbean. I focus especially on the contestation of colonial arboreal landscapes of power by Afro-Caribbean agents who reclaim particular trees for their projects of survival and meaning making— sacred ancestral trees, liberty trees, family land trees, gathering-place trees. Drawing on histories of landscape, political economies of land use, and theorists of the social production of space such as Henri Lefebvre, I suggest that multiple superimposed orderings of space are evident in the historical and contemporary landscapes of Caribbean post-plantation societies and that these include sacred and spiritual dimensions. This notion of superimposed orderings is important to understanding the ongoing dynamics of agency and resistance that are explored throughout the book.

Chapter 8, "Returning the Tourist Gaze," draws on postcolonial literary theory to address some of the silences or absences in the historical record by reading the bodily politics hinted at within Caribbean travel writing. Here I concentrate on gendered and racialized embodied encounters in the late-nineteenth-century Caribbean as seen through the prism of travel writing and the incipient tourist industry. Chapter 8 thus provides a link from the concerns of the immediate post-emancipation period to the place of the Caribbean today in (sexualized) global networks of travel and tourism. The analysis focuses on issues of embodiment and the gaze in relation to European and North American travelers' objectification of "exotic" bodies and the countering of that objectification by the return of the gaze, the appropriation of the gaze, and making counter-use of being the subject of another's gaze. Thus, it moves into more recent theoretical debates concerning the operation of gender performances and the racial marking of bodies and poses alternative ways to think through questions of agency and freedom using problematic archives. In both chapters 7 and 8, I show how forms of embodied resistance are subtly intertwined with practices of reproduction, sexual-economic transaction, and the building of resistant networks of kin and community, which ultimately provide the resources for citizenship from below.

Freedom of movement is one of the key ways that individuals can experience freedom as spatial and can enact physical existence as a form of freedom. The constraint of movement is conversely one of the key ways in which states exercise spatial control over populations and deprive individuals of their freedom (e.g., slaves, prisoners, detainees). Tourists especially have exercised certain kinds of freedom of mobility across Caribbean space, in which they use the power of the tourist gaze as a way to encounter and control people, places, sites, and sights (Urry 1990, Urry and Larsen 2011). When local people come face to face with the tourist, a moment of spatial dissonance is registered in the return of the tourist gaze. In chapter 8, I trace these moments of tense encounter, which can highlight the uneven distribution of certain embodied freedoms and the social inequalities inherent within spatial formations and mobilities across them. This offers another methodological departure for thinking about where we might find traces of a counter-hegemonic perspective on embodied freedom.

Finally, chapter 9, "Erotic Agency and a Queer Caribbean Freedom," carries forward my analysis of the techniques and practices of racial, gendered, and sexual differentiation into the late twentieth century and begins to explore the repercussions of post-slavery embodied freedom for inter-embodiments today. It opens up a new field of analysis emerging at the intersection of Caribbean studies, black studies, women's studies, and queer studies that focuses on sexual citizenship and erotic agency as central concerns for a renewed theory of embodied freedom, countering the exercise of erotic domination within contemporary world economies. I seek to show how Caribbean forms of erotic agency address fundamental political issues regarding the praxis of embodied freedom. Building on recent black feminist theorizations of sexual politics and the emerging field of black queer anthropology (Allen 2011; Gill 2010), chapter 9 contributes to a theory of erotic agency as a basis for resisting the forms of sexual violence and erotic domination through which racial, ethnic, and sexual inequalities are sustained and reproduced within local, regional, national, and transnational contexts. Above all, it examines the meanings and practices of embodied freedom, erotic agency, and erotic subjectivity in the world today. I argue that understandings of citizenship must encompass not only discursive practices, but also the full sexual, sensual, and erotic agency of an embodied freedom. This is why I pay attention not only to public political claim making and political movements, but also to a kind of everyday politics of what I call "inter-embodiments" and interactional spaces. This includes practices of family formation and their embedding in landholding institutions; forms of bodily assertion through contesting the power and gaze of others; and performative practices such as music, dance, and worship. All of these practices are relevant to erotic agency and em- bodied freedom, and thus to citizenship from below.

Citizenship from Below explores how freedom is exercised and enacted as a complex set of embodied relations in diverse contexts of activation— bodies not simply marked by race, sex, and class, as described in many social-constructivist accounts, *but active inter-embodiments that bring dif- ferent bodies to the social (and political) surface through their intimate rela- tions to each other in both private and public encounters.* The organization of the book as a whole moves forward chronologically and widens its concerns spatially from very specific case studies in Jamaica and Haiti to more loosely located transnational questions that foreground diasporic cultural practices and performativity. In examining the production and performance of freedom with both historical depth and contemporary relevance, *Citizenship from Below* poses the following questions: How does racialization (and its associated normative sexualities) affect Caribbean men's and women's access to public arenas and public spaces in different ways? How are femininity and masculinity racially, ethnically, and sexually marked in different private and public, national and transnational, arenas, and with what consequences? How are class, ethnicity, and nationality marked or elided in the creation of categories of citizenship and belonging, and how does gaining the status of citizen depend on certain kinds of performance of gender, race, and sexuality? How do national historiogra- phies contribute to producing racial, ethnic, and gender formations? How do transnational historiographies redeploy such formations, and what role can alternative methodologies play in undoing the restrictions of given moral orders? And, finally, where do heteronormative performances of whiteness fit within this unfolding transnational political landscape?

Once such embodied struggles come into focus as a key aspect of the making of freedom, and of its historical narration, we can also begin to see how embodied agents may find ways to engage in transgressive, disruptive, or redemptive performances. How might people use their embodied performances to infiltrate public space, exposing and possibly transforming assumptions about who is a free person, a citizen, or even a human being? How might we practice new kinds of inter-embodiment that challenge or undermine the prevailing racial, gender, or sexual order and hence transform citizenship and freedom? How do people use the energy of sexuality, spirituality, and investments of eroticism not just to reclaim their citizenship, but also to assert their humanity in, sadly, all-too-frequent contexts of dehumanization and physical violence? In beginning to answer these questions, I hope this book will contribute to emerging directions in Caribbean studies and that it will have implications for a wider field of feminist and queer studies of (post)colonial citizenship and human freedom. I also hope it will provide a guide to some of the emerging new directions in historical sociology, postcolonial feminist and queer studies, and critical geography. Efforts to re-think the past can help us to generate new understandings of the present postcolonial modernity in which freedom, liberty, and democracy are so widely claimed as universal values yet are so problematically enacted and so fleetingly lived.

CHAPTER ONE

History from the
Bottom(s) Up

Although the dismantling of the Atlantic system of slavery is crucial to the political processes by which citizenship was remade from below, the post-slavery Caribbean has yet to have a major presence in the literature on subaltern practices of citizenship. The study of post-emancipation social relations in the Caribbean is a key area in recent British and North American historiography, but historians still remain largely focused on elite discourses and ideologies (in part because of the nature of the archives available) and do not engage directly with questions of embodiment, performativity, and sexual subjectivities as crucial to politics.[1] To truly write a history of embodied freedom, and to understand its contemporary limitations and possibilities, we need better accounts of the emergence of inter-bodily relations in the aftermath of slavery.[2] Although some very interesting work is grappling with the meaning and practice of freedom in the Caribbean, both retrospectively and prospectively (Wilmot 2009), it mostly fails to address directly the complex intersections of gender, race, ethnicity, and sexuality. The number of monographs on women and slavery in the Caribbean is growing, and several landmark edited collections on gender and race in Caribbean history have been published, but still surprisingly few monographs addressing more subtle forms of "biopower" in the making of freedom in a theoretically rigorous and extended treatment of the complexities of the Caribbean.[3]

The close relationship between intimacy, violence, citizenship, and the state must come to the fore in studies of slavery and emancipation, which can no longer avoid the ironies that "riddled the event of emancipation," as Saidiya Hartman (1997: 126) puts it: "How does one narrate a story of freedom when confronted with the discrepant legacy of emancipation and the decidedly circumscribed avenues available to the freed? What does autonomy mean in a context of coercion, hunger, and uncertainty?" As she has shown, aspects of manhood, domesticity, and responsible productivity and reproduction were all crucially at stake in the fashioning of free subjects. This book is offered as a contribution to an emerging historical analysis and critical theory of embodied freedom, sexual citizenship, and erotic agency in post-slavery societies.[4] Indeed, the intersectionality of these dimensions is arguably the prime theoretical paradigm driving the analysis of black diaspora cultural and political formations generally (Collins 2000, 2004; Spelman 1990). The time is overdue for Caribbean historiography to revisit histories of emancipation in relation to more recent understandings of sexual citizenship and the sexual state.[5] In contrast to the existing mainstream of post-emancipation historiography and studies of post-slavery freedom, this book pays more attention to subaltern discourses and interventions in the public sphere and explores the relations between multiple subaltern positions. Most importantly, it reclaims the disavowed realms of the vulgar, including the lower regions of the body politic and the excluded realms of the bodily, the sexual, and the spiritual, which Lyndon Gill (2010: 301) has so usefully theorized as "erotic subjectivity." This is an "interpretive frame that highlights the spectacular and quotidian interworking of the political, the sensual and the spiritual"—a topic to which I return later.

There is a growing need to bridge understandings of citizenship derived from the "second-wave" historical sociology that focused on "authoritative state power," on the one hand, and "third-wave" (Foucauldian) approaches that attend to "disciplinary power dispersed throughout the social landscape," on the other hand (Adams et al. 2005: 12).[6] In the late 1980s and early 1990s historical sociologists and theoretically oriented historians began to develop a more practice-oriented framework for citizenship studies that began "recognizing popular social practices as expressions of citizenship identities" (Somers 2005: 463). Margaret Somers (2005) builds on T. H. Marshall's triad of civil, political, and social rights to highlight the prehistory of citizenship *before* juridically defined rights and obligations exist. Thus, she argues that citizenship is an "instituted process," showing how in specific local contexts within Britain (and, we might add, its colonies) there were varying "community capacities for participatory association" that interacted with the national legal structure to produce different political cultures of citizenship and different potentially available structures and capacities for appropriating public institutions (Somers 1993, 1994). In line with broader shifts within socio-legal studies, it is not sufficient to look at the letter of the law alone, or at the formal constitution of the state-citizen relation, without also understanding its situated practice, including among colonial and enslaved populations.[7] This more cultural and discursive model of citizenship as a locally instituted practice—spread across the metropolitan and colonial worlds—can be fruitfully combined with performative models of gender, racial, ethnic, and sexual subjectivity.

One of the key arguments of this book is that to act and make claims as a free citizen, political subjects must first position themselves as raced, gendered, national, and sexual subjects of particular kinds (i.e., as free men, or heads of patriarchal families, or good mothers, or British subjects, or loyal soldiers) in discursive performances that always rest on the exclusion or repulsion of others.[8] Thus, the very performativity of citizenship is one of the crucial ways in which political subjectivity translates into differentiated embodiments. Citizenship can be understood as a set of intertwined practices and collective repertoires for defining, legitimating, and exercising the rights of some bodies against others: who can occupy public space, who can speak in public, who can bear arms, who can vote? Who does the state have an obligation to protect, and who is empowered to judge, punish, and imprison others? Who can own property, protect their privacy, or make contracts, oaths, and wills? And just as significant, who can marry whom, who can be a legal parent or guardian of a child? Who can have sex with whom, and what sex acts are proscribed? To answer such questions is not simply a matter of mapping these distinctions onto pre-existing social cleavages. Rather, in answering these practical yet morally charged questions, we can begin to see how states and citizens applied a set of techniques and practices of differentiation that both united and divided a population along particular lines. It is through these "institutionally embedded practices" and local "contexts of activation" of citizenship, as Somers (1993) puts it, that the surface effects (and deeper reiterations) of corporeal difference are relationally performed.

At the same time, the focus on embodied performance and spatial relations alerts us to the extra-discursive and non-representational forces on which exercises of citizenship are always grounded: bodies in motion and in contact, gazes and counter-gazes, intimate gestures, and attractions and repulsions just below the surface of formal interaction. The body as a colonial "contact zone" (Pratt 1992) has been taken up as a way and a method "to see with particular vividness the variety of somatic territories that modern states have identified as the grounds for defining and policing the normal, the deviant, the pathological, and, of course, the primitive" (Ballantyne and Burton 2005: 406). Focusing on the discursive and performative mobilization of citizenship as an embedded practice in various post-slavery settings, I explore how intimate bodily encounters within disciplined workplaces (including domestic ones), organized public and semipublic spaces, and counter-spaces of performance and counter-performance can sometimes reproduce governing ideals of respectability yet can also deploy sexual and erotic agency to undo the gender, racial, and sexual inequalities that uphold normative orders. Race, ethnicity, gender, and sexuality are bodily practices of differentiation that surface at the intersections of multiple forms of state ordering, moral regulation, self-discipline, and the systems of governance that endorse and make possible regimes of free citizenship. My overall aim is to show not only that we need to attend to sexuality and the body within the study of citizenship but, even more crucially, that we need to broaden our understandings of the underlying meanings of Caribbean freedom and emancipation by recognizing that intimate inter-bodily relations are the fundamental basis for human dignity and thus for freedom in its widest sense.

This historical study of post-slavery citizenship moves from the archival traces of the past toward the heterogeneous present, tracing how such practices of embodied freedom continue to inform the contemporary national, racial, and sexual geographies that arose out of post-slavery transitions in state power. I draw on feminist theory, postcolonial theory, and critical race theory to explore the making of gender, racial, and sexual formations in the colonial and postcolonial Caribbean, with special (though not exclusive) emphasis on Haiti and Jamaica, although wider Caribbean and transatlantic political formations also come into play. Unlike some studies that have been framed mainly in the tradition of women's history, my focus is on the making of men and masculinity as much as women, on formations of race and ethnicity as much as gender, and on transnational as much as national histories. Thus, this book tracks broader epistemological and methodological shifts—from women's history to gender history, from social history to cultural history, and from national history to transnational history—while always maintaining an appreciation of earlier approaches. Going beyond liberal accounts of the gradual yet seemingly inevitable extension of civil, political, and social rights to ever wider circles of inclusion, my approach to citizenship from below instead addresses the deeper constitutive struggles over embodied freedoms and embodied constraints within unequal interpersonal and international relations. In doing so, it calls into question the boundaries of national histories and isolated accounts of citizenship regimes, which ignore the comparative, transregional, and transnational relations through which freedom is exercised. The bodily politics of freedom extend both below and beyond the state.

In following the embodied tracks that people left on their journeys out of Africa, out of India, out of Europe—into the Americas, away from enslavement or indenture, into and around the Caribbean, into the diaspora, and back to many different homes, both physical and spiritual—this book tries to unearth a different kind of political history. It is a history etched by everyday actions, scrubbed by washerwomen's hands, dug into small plots of land, sewn into new fashions, danced to sacred rhythms honoring ancestral spirits. It is about all of the collective processes, public spaces, aesthetic forms, and material cultures that were mobilized in the struggles between erotic subjugation and erotic knowledge, both by those who were seeking to make the abolition of slavery into a living reality and by those who continue in their footsteps today. This is not to deny the importance of the state or of state-centered politics, which have so long been the subject of citizenship studies and of emancipation studies, but it is a broadening of our understanding of the grounds for political action, inspiration, and organization. It demands a larger vision of what citizenship in its fullest sense might mean. It challenges us to think about the limitations imposed on how we think about "freedom" and how this narrow idea of freedom has stunted our historical imaginations. And it brings into view the full humanity of gnarled hands and hardened feet, dusty earth and ancient trees, and the erotic actions (in the full meaning of the term "erotic," which I discuss later) of walking, dancing, writing, speaking, singing, drumming, and serving the spirits.

History is a kind of listening for traces of other lives beneath the frequencies of the present, for the past is not just an absence; it is below us, the grounding of the now. The past reaches up from below the waves of history, telling us something again and again, if only we can hear it. But often the volume is turned too low, and those who are living are too loud. Beneath the dominant citizenship regimes of liberalism and republicanism and the noisy politics of the public sphere are hints of an alternative Caribbean ideology of freedom, one grounded in the living sensual body as a more fully rounded, relationally connected, erotic, and spiritual potential.

IMAGINING CITIZENSHIP FROM BELOW

In what sense is citizenship made (or remade) from below? Citizenship from below not only refers to the struggles for state recognition by excluded subaltern groups who exist "below" the level of the citizen, as non-citizens or second-class citizens (i.e., the enslaved, foreign immigrants, women in many cases), but also alerts us to questions of embodiment, corporeality, and the "vulgar" (cf. Cooper 1993). It brings into focus the everyday aspects of physical life, the disavowed, and the abject (low class, low life, low brow, low down) that are usually excluded from the "high" political realm (high class, high politics, high minded, high and mighty).[9] In this disavowed realm of Arendtian necessity and "bare life" (Agamben 1998), human being (or being human) takes shape through the intimacy of inter-bodily relations, spatial arrangements, and material exchanges. Nancy Stepan (2000: 65) argues that "the political questions of liberal rights and universalism always occur in a subtle exchange with that of anatomy," so that political and ethical arguments about individual rights are always converted into biological arguments about group differences. "The history of embodiment," she continues, "must be seen as part of the story of citizenship and its limits; and that it is no accident that 'race' and 'sex,' in their modern, primarily naturalized or biological meaning, emerged in the eighteenth century, when the new political concept of the individual self and the individual bearer of rights was being articulated." These bodily matters, anatomies, and necessities press up against the disembodied realms of high politics and constitutional law and lay bare the limits of civil, political, and social rights.

Recent Caribbean feminist research addresses questions of sex and sexuality in relation to gender, race, ethnicity, and nationality in innovative and compelling ways, suggesting new empirical and theoretical questions around histories of embodied freedom, sexuality, legal regulation, and the state (e.g., Alexander 1994, 1997, 2005; Kempadoo 2004; Lewis 2003; Mohammed 2002). Yet the gathering significance of this body of knowledge has not been fully recognized, in part because it is scattered across diverse disciplinary fields, historical periods, and area studies. By integrating these critical approaches into an empirically grounded historical study of the Caribbean, this book aims to pose new questions about citizenship and freedom in post-slavery contexts. In doing so, it also explores how the complex historical intersections and inter-embodiments of race, gender, and sexuality in the Caribbean region might inform a theory of embodied freedom and erotic agency in wider contemporary contexts of the neo-colonial restructuring of citizenship, sovereignty, and power across both national and transnational terrains.

The creation of an increasingly universal complex of citizenship through-out the world today can be seen as the outcome of long historical struggles in which enslaved and indentured workers, women and sexual minorities, indigenous peoples, peasants, migrants, and refugees have both challenged regimes of exclusionary citizenship and negotiated with states and with existing citizenries for inclusion. In so doing, they have transformed (and continue to contest) the meaning and practice of citizenship today. As many feminist theorists and historians have argued, the category of citizen historically excluded women, dependents, slaves, former slaves, and servants precisely because their bodies were stigmatized as overly sexual, emotional, and incapable of the higher rationality of disembodied objectivity, which was understood as a bourgeois, white, and heterosexual masculine trait (see, e.g., Fraser 1992; Glenn 2002; Landes 1988; Lloyd 1984; MacKinnon 1989; Pateman 1988; Ryan 1990, 1992, 1997; Smith 1997). In taking up positions as citizens and claiming fundamental human rights, many formerly enslaved, indentured, and otherwise undocumented people—and their descendants—have played a crucial part in contesting these exclusions, broadening the scope of freedom, and performing new embodiments of freedom.

The fundamental questions driving this work concern the *political* relationship between differently gendered, raced, ethno-national, and sexualized bodies and the performative exclusions inherent in differing citizenship regimes and their associated *forms of intimacy*. As Elizabeth Povinelli (2006: 17) argues, "The intimate couple is a key transfer point between, on the one hand, liberal imaginaries of contractual economics, politics, and sociality and, on the other, liberal forms of power in the contemporary world." Movements for citizenship, performances of citizenship, and the spatial relations that arise from contestations over citizenship are irrevocably grounded in the intimate domains of bodily practice. This is especially true during the extended and difficult transitions from systems of slavery toward polities and cultures of announced democratic freedom in the modern Americas. How do some bodies come to be excluded from the rights and protections of citizenship? How do performances of citizenship and state regimes of citizenship shape the categories of gender, race, ethnicity, and sexuality into forms of inclusion, as well as exclusion? And how have these exclusions been challenged by alternative performances that come from below—in the many senses of that word that are entertained throughout this book—to remake the contours of embodied freedom?

This book aims to demonstrate some of the specific ways in which gendered, racial, ethnic, and sexual discourses, practices, and inter-bodily relations were contested and reshaped during particular located struggles over freedom in post-slavery Caribbean societies, especially in Jamaica and Haiti. Recent work on gender and emancipation emphasizes the centrality of these constructions of the embodied person in shaping post-slavery moral orders, legal systems, state practices, and everyday interaction. Historical studies of the Atlantic world suggest that ideas and practices "of masculinity and femininity [not only] shaped slaves' and abolitionists' understanding of the wrongs of slavery, [but also] consolidated notions of contract and liberalism, contributed to the organization of postemancipation wage labor and political economies, and influenced freedpeoples' dreams of freedom and family in racially charged postemancipation landscapes" (Paton and Scully 2005: 1). Gender and sexuality, in other words, were not peripheral concerns; they were *central* to the practice of slavery, to antislavery movements, and to the reorganization of post-slavery societies. At each step along the way, gender and sexuality were also racially and ethnically charged, electrifying daily conflicts, sparking collective protests, and adding voltage to armed struggle.

Citizenship, especially in post-slavery contexts, is profoundly implicated in what Michel Foucault (1997) called the "biopolitics" of racialization, sexual normalization, and national procreation. To become a citizen is also to become a gendered, racialized, and sexed subject; thus, citizenship is fundamentally connected to the discursive history and scientific understanding of the human body and how the state regulates such bodies (Stepan 2000). Forms of national participation are tightly linked to state policies governing sexuality, fertility, and reproduction, which are crucial elements in the production and reproduction of racially and ethnically differentiated populations (see Anthias and Yuval-Davis 1992; Enloe 1990; Glenn 2002; Mosse 1985; Nagel 2003; Parker et al. 1992). Thus, an embodied theory of citizenship insists (following Judith Butler [2003]) that "bodies matter." Gender, sexuality, color, ethnicity, and class not only enter the public sphere, but they are performed and discursively constituted precisely in public arenas of civic, political, and social interaction that are erotically and sexually charged across "ethnosexual frontiers" of many kinds (Nagel 2003). Thus, racial, ethnic, gendered, and sexual claims to citizenship in the post-slavery Caribbean emerge as attempts to institute specifically embodied masculinities and femininities that are always in tension with state efforts to control and discipline sexuality, fertility, and labor relations. The claiming and performance of citizenship is at its core a negotiation of freedom that is based on how bodies are used (one aspect of personal freedom), how bodies are socially interrelated with other bodies (one aspect of civic freedom), and how state practices regulate and legislate the uses of and relations between bodies (one aspect of sovereign freedom), with the regulation of sexualities being key here.[10]

Drawing from these theoretical wells, this book aims to show how post-emancipation performances of racialized, gendered, and sexualized citizenship responded to and reshaped the inter-bodily relations, spatial arrangements, and material inequalities inherent in systems of enslavement *and* emancipation in the Caribbean. Focusing on the discursive and performative mobilization of citizenship as an embedded practice in various post-slavery settings (in both the Caribbean and its diasporas), I argue that intimate bodily encounters within disciplined work places (including domestic spaces of reproductive labor), organized public and semipublic spaces (including plots of land and tourist resorts), and counter-spaces of performance (including the riotous street, the spirit realm, and the dancehall) are crucial to understanding the national and transnational formation of free subjectivities across the post-slavery Atlantic world. I draw on traditions of history from below, the study of subaltern counter-publics, and black feminist and queer theorizations of sexual citizenship and erotic agency to develop an understanding of citizenship from the "bottom(s) up," taking on different connotations throughout the book. And I consider the ways in which counter-performances of citizenship can sometimes deploy sexual and erotic agency to undo the gender, racial, and sexual inequalities that uphold normative moral orders, legal systems, and state practices, both national and transnational.

Recent approaches to gender, sexuality, race, and ethnicity have moved away from essentialist or primordialist models of biological determinism in which bodies in any simple way pre-exist social or cultural contexts (even as these models are being strongly resurrected in sociobiology, evolutionary biology, and human genomics). The histories of citizenship that I offer here contribute evidence to the argument that gendered, racial, ethnic, and sexual categories are always contingent and contextual: They do not precede social interaction but arise as meaningful only out of social interaction yet form into long-term "durable inequalities" (Tilly 1999). If race making "take[s] place in the interplay between bodies and their mobile habits of gesture, dress and speech" (Knowles 2003: 101), then the governance and regulation of racial, gender, and sexual etiquettes, norms of dress, public demeanor, forms of respectability, speech acts, symbolic violence, and obscenity are all crucial aspects of embodied freedom. Citizenship (like race) is performative in the sense of constituting the identity that it purports to be: In claiming to be a citizen, one is enacting citizenship, and only in acting as a citizen can one become a citizen. Acknowledging this performativity recognizes that to become a free citizen requires one to act as a particular kind of subject before the law, one who is always positioned as a gendered, racialized, and sexed subject in the legal discourse. Insofar as freedom is an embodied performance that requires racial, ethnic, gender, and sexual boundaries to be marked and articulated in public ways, any exercise of autonomy or agency is always in tension with state efforts to control sexuality, reproduction, family formation, kinship systems, landholding, and labor systems.

In moving away from a history in which it is assumed that black and white; male and female; or African, European, and Indian are unproblematic natural categories, my approach highlights the public performances and marking of bodies as political and cultural projects of generative ordering. The formation of the colonial bourgeois masculine body, of the emancipated black British subject, of the respectable Afro-Jamaican mother, of the indentured Coolie worker, or of the Haitian soldier-citizen are always located, relational identities, specific to a time and place; they are what Sara Ahmed (2000: 48) refers to as "inter-embodiments" produced at "sites of differentiation." As she asks:

> How do "bodies" become marked by difference? How do bodies come to be lived precisely through being differentiated from other bodies, whereby the differences in other bodies make a difference to such lived embodiment? Such questions require that we consider how the very materialisation of bodies in time and space involves techniques and practices of differentiation. . . . To examine the function of cultural difference and social antagonism in the constitution of bodily matters is not to read difference on the surface of the body (the body as text), but to account for the very effect of the surface, and to account for how bodies come to take certain shapes over others, and in relation to others. (Ahmed 2000: 42–43)

What is called for, then, is a history of the techniques and practices of differentiation that produce differently marked bodies in particular relations with others. Citizenship in its everyday public forms is one such practice of differentiation. My close analysis of public (and counter-public) discourses of gender, race, and ethnicity in the post-slavery period shows how a vision of citizenship that connects family, race, and nation makes the regulation and governance of family formation (and, hence, reproduction and sexuality) central aspects of both the nation-state *and* the international system of colonial states and empires (Collins 2000). For example, I will point to the ways in which we might locate contemporary forms of Jamaican popular and elite homophobia in relation to histories of state formation and practices of citizenship that vibrate between the local and the imperial, linking them in a circuit of historical techniques and practices of differentiation.

NEW VOICES FROM BELOW

I hope this book will serve as both a guide to the field and a summation of fifteen years of archival research and publication, offering an empirically grounded historical analysis of formations of gender, sexuality, race, class, and ethnicity in the Caribbean, as well as a compendium of recent literature, approaches, and theoretical tools being used in this field. Gender, race, and sexuality are currently at the forefront of research in Caribbean studies, especially in studies of slavery and emancipation, colonial and postcolonial governance, and citizenship and nation building, as well as in critical legal studies. Caribbean feminist research and emerging queer theory suggest new empirical questions especially around issues of embodiment and sexuality, new theoretical perspectives emerging out of the strong traditions of Caribbean theory and philosophy, and new methodologies for conducting research in the Caribbean in a way sensitive to questions of power and positionality (see, e.g., Alexander 2005; Gill 2010; Mohammed 1998; Mohanty 1991; Tinsley 2008; Ulysse 2002).

Caribbean and African American women's history and Caribbean and black feminist theory have made major contributions to our understanding of the racial and class disparities in the areas of reproduction, motherhood, family formation, and domestic and reproductive labor. Intimate inter-embodiments (including child care, marriage, family, sex, and sexual-economic transactions) and the state's governance of both sexual and domestic reproduction are fundamental to the perpetuation of racial, gendered, and sexual categories and inequalities. This history first of all alerts us to the important nexus of personal freedom with reproductive labor and the need for any history from below to take into account not only the traditional realms of labor history and the masculine public sphere, but also the domestic realm and the labor done there. Caribbean women's reproductive labor includes not only bearing and raising children and labor within their own homes and families, but also, historically, their wider reproductive labor as domestic workers engaged in raising the children of employers, nursing, cooking, cleaning, and caring for the elderly, especially as immigrants to other countries. These jobs remained the purview of black women throughout the Americas from the era of slavery until well into the twentieth century (Jones 1985). An enhanced understanding of citizenship from below must take into account not only civic freedom in the public sphere, but also the question of personal freedom within these reproductive realms and economies of caring that so often exploit sexual and racial or ethnic boundaries to compound durable inequality (Tilly 1999).

Second, I draw especially on the work of M. Jacqui Alexander to point out how property, respectability, sexualities, and citizenship have been violently intertwined since the era of slavery, with ongoing repercussions in the post-slavery period.[11] Alexander's work, Tracy Robinson argues, crucially "calls for Caribbean women's erotic autonomy to become a benchmark of our citizenship, dismantling 'the colonial connection between property ownership, respectability, and citizenship'" (Robinson 2007: 122, citing Alexander 2005: 21). These are themes I will explore throughout this book. Nevertheless, use of the language of "autonomy" and "citizenship" remains problematical as long as the basic terms of liberal political discourse continue to rest on the autonomous masculine individual as model citizen. Any theorization of citizenship must grapple with the legacies of the sexual underpinnings of slavery and the constrained forms of respectability, propriety, property, and autonomy that emancipation entailed and authorized. This means not only including alternative sexualities in our contemporary theoretical vision, but also beginning to explore how we might revisit the past with sensitivity to the variety of sexualities that people would have lived. It also means that the mainstream historiographies of slavery, emancipation, freedom, and national politics must be reconsidered in view of the erotic politics of citizenship.

To speak of citizenship from below signals not just the "lower orders," the subordinate, the common people, and the subaltern, but also the lower body, the vulgar, the sexual, the impure, and the forbidden. As Ahmed (2004: 89) observes, "Lower regions of the body—that which is below—are clearly associated both with sexuality and with 'the waste' that is literally expelled by the body." The concept of below can also be linked with Caribbean theorizations of "bass culture," which encompasses bottom-end low-frequency sound systems, downtown spaces of the dancehall, and debased sexually explicit choreography (Henriques 2008). Caribbean sacred and secular dance forms that use the lower body—the winding of the hips, the shaking of the bottom, or the stomping of the feet—all stand in opposition to the more refined movements of "high" dance forms such as ballet (Cresswell 2006). Mapping conventions, of course, place the Caribbean "below" the United States, a point not missed by critical cartographies that reverse the projection of north and south. Lower regions are further aligned with psychological theories of the subconscious and the understanding that there are things going on below our conscious perception, or subtle gestural interactions below the radar of our social attention.

Thus, "below" resonates in many ways, whether as a political or social position, as a distinction between regions of the body and their functions, as a spatial metaphor for larger geographical regions, or as a particular kind of low vibration, bodily movement, or subconscious thought. To think about what is below also means to interrogate the spatializations of power that maintain and make material such high–low distinctions and social judgments in the first place (Ulysse 2008). In addition to these bodily and profane meanings, moreover, there is a further sacred meaning within West African and Caribbean cosmologies in which the ancestral spirits are thought to dwell beneath the waves—or, as Haitians say, *en ba dlo*. Yet the sacred and the profane, the higher and the lower, are not cleanly separated realms. In the ongoing "conflation of economic, spiritual, and sexual exchange" in African diaspora cultures and New World performance cultures (Browning 1998: 7; Stanley-Niaah 2004: 115), ancestral histories press on the present, surfacing from beneath the waves, beneath our conscious understanding, to connect physical bodies in other ways to worlds that hum steadily below the noise of the present.

LABOR HISTORY FROM BELOW

To understand the wider context of thinking from below, I begin with a brief review of three streams of "history from below," or subaltern studies, that feed into my concept of citizenship from below: (1) labor history, agrarian history, and studies of peasant rebellion and revolution; (2) studies of popular public spheres, subaltern publics, and black counter-publics; and (3) the recognition of the sexual dimension of politics within feminist theory and queer theory. In the traditions of studying political power relations, there is a rich tradition of studying history "from below" in terms of processes of domination (from the top down) and resistance (from the bottom up). I briefly review each of these streams of history from below in the sections that follow, partly to distinguish what is distinctive about my understanding of citizenship from below and to highlight the original contributions it can make to histories of emancipation and critical studies of freedom that extend from the abolition of slavery until today.

Labor historians first dragged the social history of workers and women onto the terrain of political history, which had once been the purview of a mainly elite-centered historiography (e.g., Hobsbawm 1964; Thompson 1966). Later, this was expanded to include not only Europeans but also a unified world history that encompassed peasants, the enslaved, and indigenous peoples (e.g., Roseberry 1988; Wolf 1982). These historians explored the problems of domination, resistance, and hegemony, drawing selectively on Marxian and Gramscian frameworks, with an emphasis on the dignity and agency of working classes facing conditions not of their own making. Thus, a tradition emerged of studying rebellion and revolution in Latin America and the Caribbean "from the bottom up" (Gould 1990; Stern 1987; Winn 1986; Wolf 1969). Popular movements for emancipation, enfranchisement, and citizenship in the nineteenth century often had a transnational dimension that laid the groundwork for the definition and protection of broader human rights in the twentieth century. Thus, what we think of as universal citizenship and human rights today in many ways owe their existence to these historical movements, which are described as emanating alternately from the lower classes, the grassroots, the base, or the subaltern—all signaling from below. Indeed, there is a case for seeing democracy itself as an outcome of centuries of political mobilization and radicalization of the people below, including post-slavery peasant and proletarian movements in the Caribbean (see Sheller 2000).

Later, history from below took a more cultural turn as agrarian studies reformulated peasants' political agency (in Latin America and Africa especially) in terms of oppositional cultures, or "cultures of resistance," through which subaltern groups have both contested and contributed to modern state formation and capitalist development (Comaroff and Comaroff 1991; Cooper et al. 1993; Mallon 1983, 1995; Scott 1985, 1990; Stern 1987). The study of "everyday forms of state formation" also highlights the day-to-day conflicts between state routines, rituals, and technologies of power versus the popular cultures and "moral economies" (a term first used by E. P. Thompson) always emerging within and contesting national (and transnational) hegemonies (Comaroff and Comaroff 1997; Corrigan and Sayer 1985; Joseph and Nugent 1994; Thomas 2004). One of the key issues raised in this school of thought concerns the agency of the subaltern and the meaning of hegemony.

William Roseberry (who was one my dissertation advisers, along with Charles Tilly and Mustafa Emirbayer) proposed that we should use the concept of hegemony "*not* to understand consent but to understand struggle; the ways in which the words, images, symbols, forms, organizations, institutions, and movements used by subordinate populations to talk about, understand, confront, accommodate themselves to, or resist their domination are shaped by the process of domination itself. What hegemony constructs, then, is not a shared ideology but a common material and meaningful framework for living through, talking about, and acting upon social orders characterized by domination" (Roseberry 1994: 360–61). If hegemony constructs the common material and meaningful framework for action, then counter-hegemony concerns efforts to talk about and act on that underlying framework. Thus, the concept of citizenship from below is connected to forms of material struggle within hegemonic systems, as well as the quest for more culturally constituted (and constitutive) counter-hegemonic transformations, both of which have been highlighted within the fields of history from below and subaltern studies.

My approach also resembles other, related terms, especially within the field of Latino/a studies. Michael Smith and Luis Guarnizo (1998) discuss "transnationalism from below." Frances Aparicio and Susana Chavez-Silverman (1997: 12) refer to "tropicalization from below" as the processes "by which subaltern Latino and Latina subjects and communities struggle to attain power and cultural authority" in the United States. And Agustin Lao-Montes (2001: 17–18) refers to "latinization from below" as "the processes of Latino self-fashioning that arise from resistances against marginality and discrimination and as expressions of a desire for a definition of self and an affirmative search for collective memory and community." All of these approaches share the idea that there are processes of self-fashioning, culture building, and communal self-affirmation that emerge out of resistance to discrimination and that challenge hegemonic power. Nevertheless, in all of these struggles for self-definition, subaltern subjects come to be positioned in particular ways vis-à-vis state powers, ways that may be limiting and may contain their own internal silences and disavowals of internal subaltern positions (e.g., female, queer, or ethnic minorities within the group), as subaltern theory reminds us (Spivak 1988).

Insofar as the struggle against slavery required that former slaves take up positions as free men or free women (with the gendered and sexual nuances of these positions being crucial), how did it shape and enable continuing processes of colonial domination and state formation? In what ways did becoming free entail the delimitation of constricted forms of subjectivity and the disavowal of others? Diana Paton and Pamela Scully correctly observe that, although discourses "of race and their articulation with gendered ideologies and practices underwent transformations in the emancipation period," both abolitionists and freed people brought their own gender ideologies to the claiming and making of freedom. "Abolitionist gender politics, with its twin rhetorical questions 'Am I not a woman and a sister?' and 'Am I not a man and a brother?' worked to fix black people within newly defined versions of femininity and masculinity" (Paton and Scully 2005: 3; Sheller 2011a). To assert citizenship and claim political subjectivity is always already to speak the language of the state (or the language of the political opposition), to enter its "common material and meaningful framework," as Roseberry (1994: 361) puts it.

Yet this is not to deny the transformative power of such struggles, as people live through, talk about, and act on social orders characterized by domination. Many contemporary anthropological studies of "globalization from below" also pay close attention to the everyday practices by which globality is negotiated, imagined, contested, and practiced by non-elite actors (Inda and Rosaldo 2002). While not denying the powerful structuring forces unleashed by contemporary capitalist states and economies, such studies aim to show how people perform and transform globalization through specific lived relations. However much agents of the state may try to simplify, order, and control unruly populations through modes of "seeing like a state" (Scott 1999), citizens nevertheless have improvised and invented ways to dodge, escape, and trick the state with forms of power from below exercised in evolving everyday practices. In relation to Caribbean history more specifically, this power from below takes on further connotations as it resonates with the subaltern histories of enslavement and Atlantic crossings. Like the poet Kamau Brathwaite, who emphasizes the "submarine" level of memory and connectivity across submerged worlds, the Antillean theorist Edouard Glissant (1989: 62–67) embraces the "submarine roots" of Caribbean history "that is floating free, not fixed in one position in some primordial spot, but extending in all directions in our world through its network of branches." Saidiya Hartman (1997: 75) likewise redresses the pain of the "violated, dismembered, captive body" in terms of a "subterranean history of death and discontinuity [that] informs everyday practice in myriad ways," some of which are explicitly enacted in forms of dance and popular embodied memory.

COUNTER-PUBLICS ACTING FROM BELOW

This brings me to the second resource for theorizing citizenship from below: the growing historiography of "plebeian publics" and "counter-publics" as submerged networks, free spaces, or popular democratic spaces that are conceptualized as existing beneath, within, or hidden from the more formal spaces of organized politics. In *Democracy after Slavery* (Sheller 2000), I contributed to the history of the formation of black counter-publics in post-slavery Jamaica and Haiti, which bears significantly on my approach here. Indeed, much of the primary research arose out of the doctoral dissertation research that was published in that book. Yet even though I began that research fifteen years ago with a strong interest in gender and sexuality, I was not theoretically equipped (or perhaps historiographically licensed) to incorporate a combined approach to the politics of freedom, citizenship, race, class, ethnicity, gender, and sexuality. It is only as my understanding has developed over these years, informed especially by Caribbean feminist theorists and queer theorists, that I now feel sufficiently capable of returning to my earlier work and re-elaborating its fundamental concerns.

I draw on the work of M. Jacqui Alexander, Carolle Charles, Patricia Hill Collins, Carolyn Cooper, Kamala Kempadoo, Patricia Mohammed, Patricia Saunders, Gina Athena Ulysse, Gloria Wekker, and others to extend my historical analysis of post-emancipation citizenship toward the horizon they have opened for thinking through sexual citizenship and erotic agency as crucial neglected aspects of freedom in the contemporary Caribbean and circum-Atlantic world. Both feminist studies of the public–private distinction (e.g., Berlant 1997; Fraser 1992; Landes 1988, 1998; Phillips 1991; Ryan 1992, 1997) and historical studies of black exclusion and counter-publics (Black Public Sphere Collective 1995; Gilroy 1993, 2000; Higginbotham 1993; Kelley 1996) have shown the importance of racial and gender boundaries in limiting access to public spheres—and, indeed, in drawing this distinction in the first place through racialized and gendered discourses. Yet it is Caribbean theorists especially who have shown that such counter-publics are literally "below" the mainstream public in that they gather in hidden places, in the nighttime, in the dancehalls and jook joints, in the sexually suspect cultural spaces beneath the radar that occasionally emerge into broader public notice. This is where the low down meet up with those on high, where the rhythms and noise of bass culture bleed out into public space, where uptown and downtown vie for cultural power.

Critics of the Habermasian rational-critical public sphere (Habermas 1989 [1962]) emphasize the corporeal dimensions of politics (Eley 1992; Fraser 1989), the multiple free spaces of interaction (Evans and Boyte 1986; Kelley 1996), and the class and gender exclusions of the bourgeois public sphere (Calhoun 1992; Emirbayer and Sheller 1999). Historical analyses of working-class and non-literate publics, for example, emphasize outdoor assemblies, rowdy demonstrations, festivals, and the general "dispersal of the agon" (Honig 1992) in a multiplicity of counter-publics (Eley 1992; Fraser 1992; Hansen 1993; Keane 1988). Mary Ryan (1990: 131), for example, argues that in American cities of the nineteenth century, public opinion "was formed in the streets, in the struggles of political parties, and in the popular press." Focusing on "a plural and decentered public," she argues that public life in Jacksonian America flourished in outdoor, open urban spaces, and that its style of debate was raucous, contentious, and unbounded. This spatiality was crucial because, "while this rough-and-tumble life of nineteenth-century cities seems worlds apart from the Olympian notion of the public sphere as theorized by Hannah Arendt or Habermas, it nonetheless set the historical conditions for a multi-voiced, often discordant deliberation on questions that concerned the people as a whole, including women" (Ryan 1990: 131). The same could be said for Caribbean popular publics.

These critical studies of publicity also emphasize the styles of speech and behavioral norms that govern public debate. Nancy Fraser (1992: 116) influentially encapsulated a key argument that "virtually from the beginning, counterpublics contested the exclusionary norms of the bourgeois public, elaborating alternative styles of political behavior and alternative norms of public speech." Thus, she calls for an examination of processes of discursive interaction and, in particular, "the protocols of style and decorum that were themselves correlates and markers of status inequality" (Fraser 1992: 118–19). In a critique of Habermas's rational-critical ideal of the public sphere, drawing on Pierre Bourdieu's notions of distinction and class habitus, she questions "whether it is possible even in principle for interlocutors to deliberate as if they were social peers in specially designated discursive arenas when these discursive arenas are situated in a larger societal context that is pervaded by structural relations of dominance and subordination"

(Fraser 1992: 120). The cultural and class specificity of public arenas filters and frames utterances, "accommodat[ing] some expressive modes and not others" (Fraser 1992: 126). For speakers of languages that were derided as "broken" patois or allegedly simplified "creoles," this was especially the case, and throughout my archival research I have always been especially interested in finding evidence of "creole" speech contexts recorded in various ways or self-referenced by speakers and writers who excuse their incorrect modes of speaking and writing (e.g., Sheller 2000).

Thus, norms of rational-critical debate predetermine the idiom and style of expression in ways that historically have served to exclude subordinate groups and to normalize whiteness and maleness (Warner 1990). Many theorists of publicity therefore emphasize its embodied forms, including both the corporeality of speaking and a broader spectrum of speech genres such as the dramaturgical, the artistic, and the expressive. Paul Gilroy (1993: 75), for example, stresses "dramaturgy, enunciation, and gesture—the pre- and anti-discursive constituents of black metacommunication." Black feminist theory especially has emphasized the situated context of black men's and women's embodiment and sexuality in the popular cultures that inflect movements for empowerment and political protest. Critical race theory has further contributed to a performative theory of racial embodiment. Caroline Knowles (2003) usefully summarizes how this perspective is linked to studies of the "techniques of the body," such as "its postures, movement, attitudes and habits, the ways in which bodies move, sleep, sit, wash, dress, groom and eat," all of which are learned through a kind of "corporeal apprenticeship" (Roderick 1998, drawing on Mauss [1934] 1992). These techniques, habits, and inculcated performances are closely linked to the composition of space over time through architectural configurations, aesthetics, and "accumulated times" that mark past and present activity (de Certeau 1984: 108). Thus, Knowles (2003: 99) argues, through daily routines and actions, textured by ethnicity and race, social actors contribute "to the *racing* [and gendering and sexing] of space."

Thus, an idea of public space is emerging in which race and ethnicity, as well as gender and sexuality, are attached to bodies through their spatial "orientations," their ongoing relations with other bodies, and their reiterations or reorientations of habitual actions over time (Ahmed 2006; Puwar 2005). Spatial and temporal arrangements of bodies and places as legitimate versus illegitimate, respectable versus degenerate, appropriate versus inappropriate, uptown versus downtown, safe versus dangerous together carve out geographies of citizenship, public access, and social belonging. Joseph

Roach (1996: 25) argues that "genealogies of performance attend not only to 'the body,' as Foucault suggests, but also to bodies—to the reciprocal reflections they make on one another's surfaces as they foreground their capacities for interaction." Bodily interactions mobilize what he calls a kinesthetic imagination, including "patterned movements made and remembered by bodies" and other mnemonic "vortices of behavior" (Roach 1996: 26). Small acts, fleeting encounters, spatial arrangements, and qualities as transient as the atmosphere of a place can powerfully shape the processes of inclusion and exclusion, the reiterated intangibles that enable or inhibit freedom.

Crucially, though, such kinesthetic patterns are not simply intuitive or natural. They are social performances that occur in relation to wider social topographies, such that "forms of 'correct' and 'appropriate' movement are produced in relation to 'inappropriate' forms of movement through a complicated representational process" and through normative regulation (Cresswell 2006: 142). As Tim Cresswell argues, the codification and regulation of ballroom dancing in the United Kingdom was based on the eradication of "degenerate" and "freakish" dance movements that were associated with Africa and Latin America, with jazz clubs, and with overly sexual moves. From the opposite side, Sonjah Stanley-Niaah identifies a "performance geography" that extends from the limbo dance of the slave ship to the ghetto dance cultures of African American blues, Kingston's dancehall, and South Africa's Kwaito, which are not simply unconscious kinesthetic memories spread over a diaspora but are elaborated spatial categories, philosophies, and systems that engage with forms of social exclusion, marginalization, and claims to citizenship (Stanley-Niaah 2008; Stanley-Niaah and Hope 2009). This has profound implications for the performativity of acts and claims of citizenship, which overflow beyond the formal political realm, explaining why the analysis of citizenship from below ultimately must engage with popular cultures of dance and performance as aspects of embodied freedom as politicized erotic agency.

Recent ethnographies also emphasize the complex relations between different colors, classes, ethnic groups, and multiple diasporic "blacknesses" (Thomas 2004), which helps to complicate the meaning of the body by drawing attention to the symbolic weight attached to features such as hair, skin, and forms of what Bourdieu would call bodily hexis (see, e.g., Barnes 2000; Cooper 1993; Ulysse 1999, 2002). In a symbolic sense, then, citizenship from below also refers to being positioned at the bottom of a racialized hierarchy, as noted by Linda Basch, Nina Glick Schiller, and Cristina Szanton Blanc with reference to the work of James Baldwin: "The social location of blackness as a marker of the bottom of society has been frequently noted by African-American writers [such as Baldwin and Nora Zeale Hurston]. James Baldwin described the meaning of blackness in America through the imagery of social location. 'In a way the Negro tells us where the bottom is: because he is there, and where he is, beneath us, we know where the limits are and how far we must not fall. We must not fall beneath him. We must never allow ourselves to fall that low'" (quoted in Basch et al. 1994: 40). Baldwin observes the subordinate location of blackness vis-à-vis whiteness within U.S. racial formations and global racial formations, a subordination embodied in the very act of inhabiting a black body that is stigmatized. This bottom is both a racial location and a spatial location inasmuch as racial distinctions become symbolically marked in spatial forms such as segregated housing, schools, and neighborhoods or racially demarcated national identities, institutions, and borders.

The move toward history from below, I have so far argued, requires a recognition of everyday struggles for political, civil, and social rights across a wide range of social sites and discursive fields that are "beneath" formal politics. Second, it is joined by a theorization of counter-publics and the racialization of space, which broadens understandings of the forms and styles of embodied political discourse, including its performativity, whether in speech, in habit, in dance, or simply in bodily comportment and verbal and non-verbal expressivity. These two moves alone, however, while extremely productive in expanding the field of political history, have yet to acknowledge the sexual dimensions of being at the bottom, being positioned quite literally beneath those with more power. It is also necessary to turn to feminist and queer theories of citizenship to grasp the full implications of citizenship from below. Caribbean historiography has begun to incorporate the lessons of history from below and subaltern political theory, but it is only just beginning to recognize the implications of a sexual theory of citizenship. Placing sexuality (and erotic agency) at the center of our understanding of what freedom means and how it might be embodied and performed offers a breathtaking revision of traditional political histories of slavery and freedom.

SEXUALITY AS "BOTTOM(S) UP" HISTORY

The third element crucial to what I am calling citizenship from below is the recognition of the connection between sexuality, embodiment, and politics. This begins from the feminist articulation of a core theory that the personal is political, which was extended into an entire corpus of political philosophy on questions of gender, sexuality, race, and embodiment (for overviews, see Butler and Scott 1992; Landes 1998; Young 1990). Iris Marion Young (1998 [1987]: 433) usefully outlines how, in the creation of the modern separation between the public and private spheres, the public virtues of reason, impartiality, and rationality were set apart from the needs, desires, sentiment, and affect of the private familial realm. "Impartial civilized reason characterizes the virtue of the republican man who rises above passion and desire," she argues, but instead of "cutting bourgeois man entirely off from the body and affectivity, . . . this culture of the rational public confines them to the domestic sphere," where sentiment, passions, and particularity are associated with female bodies and racialized bodies. She argues that Habermas's model of communicative action and discourse ethics "expels and devalues difference: the concreteness of the body, the affective aspects of speech, the musical and figurative aspects of all utterances . . . the specifically bodily aspects of speech [such as] gesture, facial expression, tone of voice, rhythm" (Young 1998 [1987]: 437–38), all of which are crucial elements of communication in its full sense. Thus, Young calls for a heterogeneous public life in which the "affective and bodily dimensions of meaning" have full play, and no people, groups, or topics are excluded. While she may have had in mind feminist politics in the U.S. context, if we add to this theory both a Caribbean dimension and a queer dimension, it becomes even more compelling.

Making both homosexuality and heteronormativity topics of public debate are a crucial element of this feminist ethics, and of queer theories of sexual citizenship. Michael Warner (2002: 86) argues that counter-publics embody "not merely a different or alternative idiom, but one that in other [public] contexts would be regarded with hostility or with a sense of indecorousness." Insofar as the public sphere is governed by modes of heteronormative, bourgeois sexual mores, queer publics seek to deploy "sociability, affect and play" in alternative "world-making projects," according to Warner (2002: 88), "in which intimate relations and the sexual body can in fact be understood as projects for transformation among strangers." The practice of sexual citizenship, however, is always in tension with ceding too much to the state. When such indecorous (or lewd) publics start to act as more formal state-oriented social movements, he observes, "they acquire agency in relation to the state" in ways that force them "to adapt to the performatives of rational-critical discourse" and to "cede the original hope of transforming, not just policy, but the space of public life itself" (Warner

2002: 89). Thus, in the "very struggle toward enfranchisement and democ-ratization," argues Judith Butler (1992: 14), "we might adopt the very mod-els of domination by which we were oppressed, not realizing that one way that domination works is through the regulation and production of sub-jects." Just as earlier theorists of history from below realized, recognition by the state and the granting of rights comes at the price of ever deeper inscription into the hegemonic social order (Agamben 1998; Butler 2002). The question, then, is whether a radical sexual politics can short-circuit such ordering hegemonies by intervening directly in the material disposi-tion of bodies in ways that disrupt the normalizing structures of everyday-ness. Even while sexual citizenship may be self-disciplining and normaliz-ing, it nevertheless remains "ambivalent, producing new and contested fissures in subjectivities and their governance" (Cossman 2007: 3).

A theory of sexual citizenship begins from the placement of the body at the core of political analysis—a kind of shift of attention from the body politic to a "body politics" (Bordo 1993), and a concern with the relation between the two. To conjoin a politics of sex and citizenship is to insist not only on the primacy of inter-bodily relations as the basis for human dignity and freedom, but also on the importance of those esthetic forms—whether poetry, music, dance, fashion, or style—that "encourage awareness of the political character of sexuality" and offer "the possibility of understanding the social contradictions [people] embodied and enacted in their lives" (Davis 1998a: 179). Sexual citizenship is not just about personal rights or individual empowerment; nor is it simply about state recognition of cer-tain kinds of privacy, although it includes all of these. It is also concerned with collective processes, public spaces, and forms of interrelatedness that are sexual or sexualized. Thus, it is a politics that is closely linked to public performances and to the performativity of public actions and, hence, a politics in which bodies are central and cannot be ignored or bracketed as in classical liberal theory. As I shall show in the empirical chapters that follow, public performances of claims to citizenship depend for their ef-ficacy on the political subject's assertion of particular racial, gendered, and sexual positions—especially those that uphold the racially homologous patriarchal heterosexual family.

We can turn here to the work of Lauren Berlant, which emerges at the confluence of feminist theory and queer theory but is also in dialogue with African American women's literature and political theory. Berlant (1993: 178) traces the fatal "dialectic between abstraction [the disembodied 'per-son' in the language of law] in the national public sphere and the surplus of corporeality of racialized and gendered subjects" and tracks "its discursive expressions, its erotic effects, its implications for a nationalist politics of the body." A crucial question for Berlant (1993: 176) concerns the "complex relation between local erotics and national identity" and, hence, the possibilities for corporeal enfranchisement in the American body politic. Berlant is right that the failure of emancipation and suffrage "to solve the relation between the body and the state in the United States" remains central to U.S. politics; only counter-public discourses of citizenship can "break the sanitizing silences of sexual privacy in order to create national publics trained to think, and thus to think differently, about the corporeal conditions of citizenship" (Berlant 1993: 239).[12] Like the theorists of subaltern counter-publics discussed earlier, Berlant valorizes "everyday forms of assertive and contesting speech" that "violate norms of class decorum" to argue "that the transgression of a gentility that pretends social relations are personal and private rather than public, political, and class-based must be central to any liberation politics" (Berlant 1993: 224).

Several Caribbean and black diasporic theorists also link the (corpo)realities of sexuality directly to questions of agency and freedom in contemporary contexts. Cooper examines the role of "slackness" and what she calls the "vulgar" in Jamaican popular culture; Noble discusses black lower-class women's sexual agency within dancehall culture; Alexander explores questions of embodied freedoms in terms of what she calls erotic autonomy; Stanley-Niaah looks at the wider culture of dancehall and its embodied performances as a space of both celebration and critique of Western domination; and Kempadoo explores the sexual agency of working-class women, each of which I shall discuss more fully in chapter 9. While many historians have engaged in bottom-up history, Cooper's tongue-in-cheek, yet serious, call for "bottoms-up history" (Cooper 1993: x) reminds us of the "pubic" that is the root of the word "public" and of the "sexualised representation of the potent female bottom in contemporary Jamaican dancehall culture" (Cooper 1993: xi)—these nether regions that are not spoken of in polite/political society (cf. Collins 2004). In a controversial reading of slackness (sexually explicit lyrics, performance, dress, and dance) as "erotic play in the dancehall," Cooper argues that, "liberated from the repressive respectability of a conservative gender ideology of female property and propriety, these women lay proper claim to the control of their own bodies" (Cooper 1993: 11). Nevertheless, it remains hotly debated whether this sexual performance is liberatory or not. The "Bottoms Up!" of Rabelaisian carnival, as Mikhail Bakhtin (1984) observed, was beyond the law, above the law, and even against the law. Yet in other times and places, "Carnival and the law conspire together to craft a contingent margin of behavior that remains easily within the laws' reach, if need be, but hovers provisionally outside its grasp" (Roach 1996: 252).[13]

What does it mean to lay claim to one's own body? And how is this connected to state practices of citizenship, (il)legality, and the problem of agency and autonomy within hegemonic processes? What are we to make of anthems of slack excess such as Trey Songz's "Bottoms Up" (2010), featuring Nicki Minaj, for example, in which his doubled calls for bottles of alcohol and bottoms-up girls is met with her demand that he not only buy her drinks (Remy, Coke, Henny, margarita on the rock rock rocks) but also hand over "keys to the Benz" if he likes her body. The drunken ode dissolves into violence: "If a bitch try to get cute, I'ma stuff her/Throw a lot of money at her, then yell fucka, fucka, fucka." Just as claims to citizenship from below may inscribe political subjects more deeply into state governmentalities, as Foucault (1991) argued, claims to sexual agency (especially heterosexual agency) evidently risk deeper inscription/insertion into the legalities and violently heteronormative cultures of contemporary sexuality. For Afro-Caribbean, Indo-Caribbean, and multiracial Caribbean men and women in particular, the debased racialized histories of colonial and postcolonial hypersexuality (hooks 1994; Kempadoo 2004) often seem to over-determine any forms of sexual agency and to already defuse any efforts to "folk up theory."

What scope is there, then, for agency and autonomy in negotiating these pitfalls? As Collins (2004: 35) observes, "Sexualized Black bodies seem to be everywhere in contemporary mass media, yet within African American communities, a comprehensive understanding of sexual politics remains elusive. In a social context that routinely depicts men and women of African descent as the embodiment of deviant sexuality, African American politics has remained curiously silent on issues of gender and sexuality." This goes doubly for Caribbean and Caribbean diaspora sexual politics—wherein, for example, Minaj's precarious position as a diasporic Indo/Afro-Trinidadian launching attacks on other black women performers triggered vehement backlashes against her, especially across black social media networks. Such interethnic tensions speak to the traces of histories of citizenship still played out on Caribbean bodies, as do the raging debates about homosexuality in the region. But perhaps it is here that some of the protocols of silence are beginning to be breached.

One important locus for the broaching of subjects of sexuality within

Jamaica especially involves a series of local and international actions concerning the homophobic violence that has come to be associated with dancehall culture. This began with international boycotts and protests against artists such as Buju Banton, Beenie Man, Bounty Killer, Capleton, and Sizzla and in certain media coverage that associated Jamaican culture with violent homophobia (including a *Time* magazine cover that proclaimed Jamaica "The Most Homophobic Place on Earth").[14] A report by Human Rights Watch in 2004 suggested a connection between the violent lyrics of dancehall music, the general disavowal of homosexuality within Jamaican culture, and actual acts of violent attack and murder.[15] Jamaican activists have been working to call attention to the human-rights violations occurring in Jamaica through web blogs, Internet chats, and organizations such as the Jamaican Forum for Lesbians, All-Sexuals, and Gays (J-FLAG), an advocacy group founded in 1998.[16] Inside Jamaica, a decision was taken in 2009 to ban sexually explicit dancehall music lyrics from radio play, partly in reaction to the song "Rampin' Shop" by Vybz Kartel, which was associated with the dance known as daggering. This was not a response to violence and homophobia, but it was indicative of an "Uptown" conservative backlash against lower-class "Downtown" slack culture in the name of protecting children. Nevertheless, debates about dancehall music have generated space for discussion on radio, in newspapers, and in public settings about cultures of sexuality and violence and the role of the state in their regulation.

There has also been a major series of reports on homophobia and HIV/AIDS in Jamaica, produced in 2009 by the Pulitzer Center on Crisis Reporting in partnership with WNET's *Worldfocus* program.[17] The series, "The Glass Closet," offers in-depth interviews with a range of Jamaicans representing those who are suffering from HIV infection and from violent homophobic attacks; social workers, advocates, anthropologists, health managers, educators and others who are working to address these problems; and some of the political and religious leaders who continue to advocate anti-gay views and to strongly support Jamaica's anti-sodomy laws. The debate about sexuality and citizenship is particularly acute in Jamaica today because of the lethal combination of the criminalization of sodomy; the subsequent driving underground of men who have sex with men, which has contributed to high HIV infection rates in this population (up to 30 percent, according to one study by the Ministry of Health); and the high levels of violence in the poor slum areas of Kingston, which in some ways have normalized violent attacks on gay men. In a population of about 2.8 million, there were 1,600 murders in 2008. At the same time, human-rights groups view the nature of violence against gay men as particularly extreme. Since the United States began to allow asylum on the basis of sexual persecution, seventeen of the fifty-five successful gay asylum cases have been Jamaicans.

The Caribbean as a whole has the second-highest rate of new HIV infection in the world, with 230,000 people living with HIV and AIDS. But countries with anti-sodomy laws that criminalize men who have sex with men appear to have disproportionately high rates of infection, and Jamaica in particular is singled out for driving gay men underground and toward unsafe sexual practices. Because public gay identities are banned, even health advocacy groups have been attacked and must work underground in Jamaica. Some sexually conservative Jamaicans perceive LGBTQ human-rights advocates as a foreign imposition and draw on biblical teachings to insist on upholding Jamaica's anti-sodomy laws and homophobic culture. However, issues of queer citizenship and human rights in the Caribbean should not be understood simply as a conflict between a supposedly traditional "native" heteronormativity that rejects all things queer and a supposedly modern "foreign" homonormativity that attempts to impose "acceptable" queer ideas and practices from outside. Instead, I argue in this book, we need a better appreciation of the existence of diverse Caribbean sexual subjectivities (including queer ones), a better knowledge of the histories of sexual citizenship that have produced the current situation, and a capacity to learn from the Caribbean theoretical projects that offer an autochthonous critical discourse for unraveling the complex knots of racial-sexual-national subjectivities that are producing multiple forms of violence within countries such as Jamaica.

It is the complex, long-term interaction of popular cultures of freedom with colonial state power, forms of citizenship, and forms of spirituality that requires our attention. The "formidably material character of the state's power" means not only that "popular culture is not a thoroughly autonomous domain" (Joseph and Nugent 1994: 20–21), but also that forms of embodiment, bodily knowing, and sexuality are deeply organized social forms. Cresswell (2006: 145) puts it well when he observes, "Power is not simply about control and regulation through denial, but about the production of pleasure itself. As Bourdieu, among others, was eager to show, it is exactly the process of the internalization of the social in the body that produces the strongest adherence to established norms. This adherence is at its most successful when it is experienced as pleasure." In explor-

ing further the relation between forms of domination and resistance, popular cultures of pleasure, and spaces for the performance of freedom, I
suggest that a bottoms-up history can teach us a great deal about the
processes of racialized gender formation and gendered racial formation
(interacting with moral economies of class, color, and sexuality) that were
crucial to post-emancipation democratic citizenship, public and private
spheres, subaltern politics, state formation, and the relation of all of these
to personhood and freedom in the Caribbean and beyond.

Finally, there are other powers beyond the material, as Alexander's *Pedagogies of Crossing* (2005) has most forcefully argued from a Caribbean
feminist perspective. Especially when Christianity is being mobilized in
Jamaica and other parts of the Caribbean for the criminalization of some
sexualities, and even for condoning the occurrence of violence against gay
men and women, it is necessary and urgent to encompass religion and
spirituality in any discussions of freedom and citizenship. Kate Ramsey, for
example, has recently explored the historical relation between Vodou and
the state in Haiti in her book *The Spirits and the Law: Vodou and Power in
Haiti* (2011). She poses the question of how nineteenth-century penal laws
against "le vaudoux" specifically targeted the rural population, asking: "to
what extent and in which ways did the prohibition of many family- and
temple-based ritual practices classified as *sortileges* [sorcery] and *pratiques
superstitieuses* [superstitions] contribute to the political marginalization,
economic exploitation, and social stigmatization of this population over
the course of the nineteenth and twentieth centuries?" (2011: 3). Beliefs in
sorcery and spirits are not a remnant of backward, superstitious peasant
cultures, she argues, but are produced in conjunction with state projects of
modernization and control.

Only with such expansive understandings of the spiritual realm are we
equipped to address citizenship from below. Secular intellectuals often dis-
miss religion as the "opium of the masses," as Karl Marx called it, and see
some of the fast-spreading forms of Protestant evangelicalism and self-help
theology as depoliticizing; thus, they entirely reject any serious engagement with religious discourse as a grounds for politics. Religious thinkers,
on the other hand, often are uncomfortable discussing the politics around
issues of sexuality and popular culture and their relation to forms of agency
and freedom, except insofar as sexuality must be repressed and morally
regulated. While the work of the spiritual only tangentially enters into the
empirical chapters that follow, this final resonance of what a project of

history from below might entail insists—without political embarrassment or moral qualms—that the concept of erotic agency that informs this work also offers alternative ways to think about the deep-seated relation between the self, the social, and the sacred; agency, structure, and the metaphysical; autonomy, subordination, and divinity; and the body, the state, and the spirit.

CHAPTER TWO

Quasheba, Mother, Queen

Nearly two decades of reassessments of Caribbean women's political roles both during and after slavery suggest that their leadership was crucial to popular collective action, contrary to an earlier historiography that had focused on male actors and masculine narratives of armed struggle and rebellion. Many scholars have come to see women as "central to the Afro-Caribbean peasant cultures of resistance, rooted in the tradition of slave resistance, which emerged in response to colonialism and the plantation system" (Besson 1993: 30). For the period of slavery, there emerged in the 1990s a strong interest in women's contributions to slave resistance, including both violent opposition and what James Scott (1990: 198) calls "everyday forms of resistance."[1] This built on the groundbreaking work of Lucille Mathurin Mair, who was one of the first to argue that "motherhood with its biological and customary social applications is frequently perceived as a conservative force which imposes constraints on female activism. It became, however," amongst female fieldworkers in Jamaica during slavery, "a catalyst for much of women's subversive and aggressive strategies directed against the might of the plantation" (Mair 1987: 11–12, quoted in Mohammed 1995: 32–33).

For the post-emancipation period, attention turned to women's participation in labor protest, as well as in more diffuse community organization and cultural resistance (Heuman 1994; Momsen 1993; Olwig 1985; Reddock 1985, 1994; Wilmot 1995). Comparative syntheses in the field demonstrate that, "despite the sexism and racism which initially denied black and coloured women the legal right to vote, the lack of the franchise did not exclude women from active participation in the public world of politics during slavery and in the post-slavery Caribbean" (Shepherd et al. 1995: xix). Like disfranchised people elsewhere, Afro-Caribbean women turned everyday activities into sites of resistance and ordinary space into theaters for collective action. In the case of Jamaica, one is confronted head-on with the unexpected but crucial participation of women not only in behind-the-scenes cultural resistance, but also in *public* activities such as collective labor protest, petitioning, demonstration, and riot.

This chapter contributes to research on African Jamaican women's public leadership by examining three arenas of women's involvement in protest and political mobilization between 1834 and 1865:

1 Labor protest on sugar plantations in the mid-1830s to early 1840s, when female workers not only drew on traditions of slave resistance, but also quickly grasped new political opportunities to challenge overseers and landowners.

2 Challenges to white men's control of religion through efforts to democratize the dissenting (Baptist, Methodist) churches and, more radically, through indigenous forms of Afro-Christian Revival and the practice known as Myalism.

3 Political contention targeting police, courthouses, and other symbols of the colonial state, based in a developing urban popular culture in which women played a highly visible role in the markets, streets, yards, and rioting "mobs" and often suffered the full brunt of official reaction and repression.

As Swithin Wilmot (1995: 292) concludes, "Though patriarchy ruled supreme, the Jamaican freed women resisted their banishment from the public sphere and played an important part in the politics of the black community, thereby maintaining the tradition that they had established in slave society as 'persistent rebels.'"

Yet we would be remiss to read such actions in an overly simplistic fashion. As Diana Paton (2004: 159) points out, "In some Jamaican historiography the focus on post-emancipation riots and rebellions has been at the expense of a broader understanding of the dynamics of daily life, with the result that we end up with a portrait of heroic but uncomplicated people" and "false assumptions of both the ease with which opposition can be organized and the unproblematic nature of what might be put in place of the status quo." The historiography of African Jamaican women as "natural rebels" (Beckles 1989) also rests on a problematic legacy of Romantic nationalism invoked by Caribbean writers, poets, and politicians, in which peasant women are linked to the colonized landscape and idealized as mothers of the nation, sources of native culture, and conduits for authentic folkways (Stitt 2007).[2] Furthermore, a slippage between the nature of women's political resistance and the normative models of the reproductive heterosexual family tends to inscribe African Jamaican women as "national heroes" (such as Nanny of the Maroons in Jamaica) and the black family as a proto-nationalist incubator of postcolonial independence. As Saidiya Hartman (1997: 157) warns, "While the ability to forge and maintain familial relations must not be minimized, neither should the family be naturalized as the measure of racial progress [because] the articulation of black politics at the site of the family is often consistent with the regulatory efforts of the state. Therefore, the domestic articulation of a politics of racial uplift risks displacing the political, endorsing a repressive moral economy, and privileging the family as a site for the reproduction of racial values." How, then, can we recognize women's political agency without reducing them to "natural" mothers of the nation?

Despite this welcome spate of historiographical attention to African Jamaican women's political activism, it remains to be explained, on the one hand, why they took the kinds of actions they did, how their collective action differed from men's, and how their gender-specific uses of public space challenged white elites and the colonial state, and on the other hand, how their specific deployments of gendered identities interacted with colonial discourses to produce delimited political subjectivities. Beyond the simple (though still necessary) point that, yes, women were in public and made their voices heard in protest, a more complex understanding is emerging of the interplay between gendered discourses and state power (Paton 2004; Scully 1997; Scully and Paton 2005). Drawing on both secondary sources and new primary evidence on African Jamaican women's collective action and political participation, this chapter presents the growing evidence not only that many individual women and groups of women acted publicly, but also that they drew on particular kinds of gendered discourses to build a distinctive repertoire of embodied freedom and claims to citizenship. I explore the social contexts that encouraged women's political activism and consider how such activists drew on their intersecting racial, class, and gender identities to become leaders and spokespeople for their communities. Yet at the same time, this analysis also bears witness to the processes of discursive regulation and heteronormative presumption that framed practices of subaltern citizenship, as well as later accounts of those practices.

What specific "repertoires of contention" and styles of collective action did African Jamaican women use? To which authorities or audiences did they address their claims? What language of protest and weapons of opposition did they wield, and how did holders of power and state agents respond? Key findings are first that African Jamaican women cited familial responsibilities to justify protest and recognized that the role of motherhood carried special moral weight in making claims aimed at a British Christian public. The articulation between Christian discourses of motherhood, British colonial practices of citizenship, and a local embodied sense of freedom produced a distinctive gendered political culture in postemancipation Jamaica. Second, groups of women brought together by workplace relationships or other shared activities often acted in concert and supported each other's claims. While men and women sometimes acted together, there are also clear patterns of single-sex cohorts mobilizing explicitly gendered claims to rights. And third, ties of kinship could be important mobilizing factors in communitywide demonstrations or riots.

I also suggest that there have been long-term continuities in the forms and styles of African Jamaican women's political participation and leadership, with possible parallels to other African diaspora communities. Reveling in the prevalent colonial stereotype of the proud and independent slave woman (often called "Quasheba"), generations of black women reenacted and sustained their communities' empowering leadership personae, whether as African Queen Mothers, Jamaican Mothers, Revival Queens, Church Mothers, or Queens of the Rebels. It is important to note that these political and religious roles were not necessarily based on reproductive (biological) motherhood or Christian bourgeois monogamous familial structures. Rather, they explicitly expanded the signifier "Mother" to serve a symbolic purpose of social or community mothering as a form of women's leadership, much as happens among some transgendered and queer familial groupings today.

Having established that women drew on their embodied experience to engage in public politics, this chapter will also examine how the politics of post-emancipation reproduction contributes to a general theory of embodied freedom. Caribbean and African American women's history and black feminist theory have made major contributions to our understanding of the racial and class disparities in the areas of reproduction, motherhood, family formation, and domestic and reproductive labor (Clarke 1957; Spillers 1987). Black feminist theorists have extensively analyzed the field of reproduction and "mother work" in ways that challenge traditional understandings of the universality of motherhood and bring differences of race, class, and nation to the fore (Collins 1990, 1994, 1999, 2000, 2004; Roberts 1997). At the same time, questions of reproduction are central to a number of feminist theorizations of citizenship (Pateman 1988; Young 1990), placing the problem of reproduction at the heart of politics. From other directions, transnational studies of health and medicine highlight the racial, class, and ethnic structuring of health care, including the uneven medicalization of pregnancy and childbirth, the unequal circumstances in which women of color can or cannot gain access to health care, and the impact of broader movements such as eugenics and population control on black motherhood (Ginsburg and Rapp 1995; Martin 1987). With regard to reproduction, abortion, and infanticide, historical sociologists argue that reproductive politics in the United States of the mid-nineteenth century (and, by extension, the wider British colonial world) "were part of an Anglo-Saxon racial project" (Beisel and Kay 2004: 499), which was reinforced and extended in subsequent "racial hygiene" and eugenics movements in the twentieth century, a topic I discuss further in chapter 9.

Issues of reproduction, procreation, and non-procreation are crucial to the exercise of citizenship and central to the very definition of the citizen and to policing of the boundaries of the nation. I therefore pay attention to African Jamaican women's specific relation to what I here call reproductive freedom. Caribbean women's history alerts us to the important nexus of personal freedom with reproductive labor and the need for any history from below to take account not only of the traditional realms of labor history and the masculine public sphere, but also the domestic realm and the labor done there. Elaborating on the Marxian notion of production, reproduction refers to both the gendered housework that goes into keeping all people cleaned, fed, nursed, and ready for work each day and the sexual labor that goes into pregnancy, childbirth, wet nursing, and the overall genesis of children as new laboring bodies to replace those that are used up, so to speak. When we speak of the history of New World black women's reproductive labor, then, we must consider several different dimensions, including not only their reproductive labor in bearing and raising children and their reproductive labor within their own homes and families, but also their wider reproductive labor as domestic workers engaged in raising the children of employers, nursing, cooking, cleaning, washing clothes, and caring for the elderly. Some theorists also include the reproduction of sustainable natural ecologies as another aspect of women's reproductive labor.

An enhanced understanding of citizenship from below must take into account not only civic freedom in the public sphere, but also the question of personal freedom within these reproductive realms. Feminist historians, philosophers, and political theorists have shown how civil society, the civic realm, and the practice of citizenship have been constructed and enabled by a constitutive exclusion of the personal, the sexual, and the domestic (and hence, of women). As Nicola Beisel and Tamara Kay (2004: 504) argue, the politics of reproduction and abortion are "simultaneously racial and gender politics" that bring together two aspects of racial reproduction: "reproduction of the cultural categories of race, and reproduction of children, which generally entails control over the (racially inscribed) bodies and sexuality of adults." What has less commonly been noted is the extent to which it is through the struggle for reproductive freedom (in its widest sense) that women—especially enslaved women, freed women, and racially subordinated women—have claimed citizenship. When a Jamaican historian such as Mair argued that enslaved women in Jamaica deliberately depressed their fertility rates and withheld their labor and that of their children at crucial moments specifically to frustrate "the planter's hopes for a self-reproducing labour force" (Mohammed 1995: 33), she was recognizing these women's own awareness of the intimate connections between production and reproduction played out through their bodies and the bodies of their children—a point missed by many white, male historians.

After the abolition of slavery apprenticed women's and freed women's efforts to reclaim not only their own labor time for rearing children but also their *identities as mothers* was crucial to building both a public subjectivity and a private space for remaking a familial realm. Indeed, the whipping and mutilation of women—especially while pregnant—became the marker and symbol for what was wrong with the apprenticeship system and hastened its abolition, just as lurid accounts of the injuries wrought by whipping and other forms of punishment of the flesh helped to mobilize the antislavery movement. "Abolitionists condemned all flogging of slaves," notes Paton (2004: 6), "but found the flogging of women particularly offensive, as much because it led to the exposure of enslaved women's bodies as because of its violence and brutality." Hortense Spillers (1987: 77) examines some of the perverse effects of the de-gendering of enslaved black women, the denial of kinship and motherhood, and their vulnerability to a "gigantic sexualized repertoire," which informs the "incestuous, interracial genealogy" of slavery in the United States—and, we could add, the Caribbean. These twisted genealogies and their multiple forms of violence mark the psycho-geography of racialized, gendered, and sexualized subject positions today. Yet the history of black women's efforts to counter these perversities also offers important resources for ongoing practices of embodied freedom grounded in the struggle for citizenship from below.

THE RIGHTS AND WRONGS OF MOTHERHOOD: BRITISH PUBLICS AND PLANTATION PROTEST

The feisty female slave was commonly caricatured in Jamaican publications of the early nineteenth century with a character called Quasheba, who was known as an independent and outspoken troublemaker. The eighteenth-century ode to the "Sable Venus," for example, refers to the "pleasure" and "raptures" the poet would seek in "gentle Phibia . . . artful Benneba . . . wanton Mimba . . . sprightly Cuba . . . Or grave in sober Quasheba I still shall find thee out."[3] This none-too-subtle threat to rape the least willing "Sable Queen" alludes to her spirit of defiance and resistance. A Wesleyan Methodist pamphlet lamenting the absence of marriage among the slaves observed that "Quasheba, in fact, showed no signs of subjection and demonstrated great pride in her economic independence" (quoted in Turner 1982: 74). In this case, the caricature hinges on the slave woman's lack of both husband and Christian shame. Such satire belittled black women's economic independence and reduced their acts of political resistance to individual willfulness. The historical record, to the contrary, indicates that slave women's activism emerged in the context of the supportive networks of families, communities, and collective work groups (and helped to sustain those very contexts). Quasheba, it should be noted, is a West African day name used for girls born on Sunday, thus indicating a community that had maintained its African cultural traditions even in Creole contexts.

A woman being punished in the Spanish Town workhouse in 1791 is recorded as "Quasheba, a creole, to Williken's estate, marked W, HD on left shoulder, 5 feet 6½ inches high" (quoted in Paton 2004: 11). Paton argues that the act of branding people like Quasheba combines the deliberate infliction of pain—supposedly characteristic of premodern forms of power, according to Michel Foucault (1995)—with a form of legibility that belongs to processes of surveillance and normalization that are characteristic of modern forms of discipline. "Instead of seeing Jamaica's experience as deriving from either its backwardness or its specifically colonial status," Paton (2004: 12) argues, "it demonstrates a problem in the binary conception of premodernity–modernity itself," because "violence and pain are fully part of modern power." The corollary to this, I argue, is that forms of personal autonomy, control of one's own body, and resistance to bodily exploitation are absolutely foundational to modern forms of freedom. The ongoing violence of modern disciplinary power is exercised in the most extreme forms on the kinds of unregulated public spheres that I examine later. Elizabeth Povinelli (2006: 163) points out that such "unregulated public spheres are often sites where the state exerts repressive, coercive power," citing Habermas's view that unregulated spaces are more "vulnerable to the repressive and exclusionary effects of unequally distributed social power, structural violence, and systematically disturbed communication" (Habermas 1998: 307). Therein lies the genesis of the modern Caribbean as a space of vulnerability and social exclusion, at least for some.

Against the forces of a world economy that commodified enslaved human beings and the personal relations of domination that inflicted extreme violence on black flesh (as Spillers puts it), resistance has long taken the form of staking a claim in one's own body. Studies of slavery first of all suggest that women (of all colors) traded on sexuality (including converting it into forms of either "respectability" or "reputation") to better their condition. Thus, deployments of sexuality play a highly strategic part in post-slavery societies. Barbara Bush (1990: 110) argues that, despite black women's sexual subordination under slavery, "Sexuality constitutes a 'particularly dense transfer point for relations of power,' allowing for many varied strategies," such that "there are innumerable, diverse points of resistance which may even involve a temporary inversion of power relations." She reads the sexual relationships between enslaved black women and slaveowning and other white men, in particular, as "ambivalent" and the sexual power exercised within them as "not purely repressive" (Bush 1990: 110). Kamala Kempadoo (2004: 53) likewise points out that the "exchange of sex for material benefits or money has been evident in the Caribbean region for several centuries. Under slavery such transactions were lodged at the nexus of at least two areas of women's existence: as an extension of sexual relations (forced or otherwise) with white men and as an income-generating activity for both slave and 'free colored' women."

The history of women's public leadership in Jamaica, beginning under slavery, demonstrates a consciousness, among working women, of gender and sexuality as tangled points of power and resistance. The phrase "petticoat rebellions" was used by the Jamaican slaveowner Matthew Gregory Lewis, who wrote in 1816 that on his plantation "the women, one and all, refused to carry away the [cane] trash [and] in consequence, the mill was obliged to be stopped; and when the driver on that station insisted on their doing their duty, a little fierce young devil of a Miss Whaunica flew at his throat, and endeavoured to strangle him" (Lewis 1834: 139). Resistance like this was risky. There was safety neither in numbers nor in gender for enslaved women. A trial in 1828, for example, found that the complaint of "severe and illegal floggings" by a group of slaves was "totally void of foundation and completely frivolous and vexatious"; the "principal ring-leaders," named as Eliza Bighie, Selina Wallace, Ruthe Thomas, Bridget Elmslie, Mary Phillips, and Ithe Stewart, were sentenced to thirty-nine lashes, three months' hard labor in the workhouse, and another thirty-nine lashes on their release.[4] Later that year, an enslaved woman was sentenced to thirty-nine lashes for "use of the most obscene, filthy and gross language." Even after emancipation, in 1839, the Buff Bay Court was still notorious for injustice, and in one instance the stipendiary magistrates "were not only received with violent language, but were pelted with stones by some of the most turbulent of the party, amongst whom," according to the governor, "the women were the most conspicuous" (quoted in Wilmot 1995: 283). Female laborers had to stick by one another in agreements to stop work and in facing the violence of plantation personnel and courts of law and were prepared to do the same after slavery ended.

Women in the post-emancipation period not only drew on deep-rooted traditions of slave resistance to challenge coercive labor policies. They also quickly grasped new political opportunities to confront overseers directly and to state their cases before special magistrates. Several studies of plantation conflict during the apprenticeship period (1834–38) recognize the prominence of women as spokespeople and leaders of labor protest in Jamaica. Wilmot (1995: 287) observes that, despite patriarchal definitions of "public actors" as male, "Any balanced discussion of politics in the immediate post-slavery period in Jamaica must take into account the extent to which women never accepted that legal marginalisation." Among the "more striking features of all of these [plantation] disturbances," writes Thomas Holt (1992: 64) about the post-emancipation period, "was the solidarity of the workers and the prominence of women among the activists and leaders." Yet we still lack convincing explanations of this phenomenon of female leadership. Holt (1992: 64) suggests that it is explicable "since women made up a disproportionate share of the field labor force on sugar estates." Beyond sheer numbers at the bottom of the labor hierarchy, however (which in itself does not explain the emergence of women as leaders), one must also consider how freed women were able to exploit politically their dual roles—and identities—as agricultural workers and mothers. Accounts of women's leadership of plantation conflicts demonstrate that it was their conscious awareness and strategic exploitation of this duality that enabled them to become mainsprings of collective action in the post-emancipation era.

Although the tension between "productive" and "reproductive" demands on slave women's time have been identified as a central structural contradiction within the slave system (Higman 1984; Morrissey 1989; Olwig 1985; Reddock 1985),[5] many historians overlook the ways in which formerly enslaved women *themselves* capitalized on their special position as caregivers. The pro-natalist policies of the "amelioration" period in the 1820s, when slaveowners sought to increase slaves' birthrate, would have made such ideological contradictions in the system of slavery perfectly evident, and enslaved women appear to have exploited this vulnerability. From the earliest days of European contact with Africa, colonizers deployed a discourse of African women's "fecundity," "propensity for easy birth and breastfeeding," and "mechanical and meaningless childbearing" (Morgan 2005: 61–62). Under the dehumanizing system of slavery, the sellers and buyers of human beings had a fundamental economic interest in acquiring more laboring bodies, and control over enslaved women's fertility was one crucial way of "breeding slaves." Paton (2008) notes the remarkable statistic that by 1830, up to one-third of enslaved women in the British Caribbean had no children, despite supposedly pro-natalist policies of slaveowners; thus, there was a hyper-politicization of both maternity and non-maternity. Historians of women and slavery have shown how African, African Caribbean, and African American women's bodies were appropriated in multiple ways, as laboring bodies, serving bodies, reproductive bodies, and punished bodies, and how resistance to slavery required a fundamental reclaiming of the body (Beckles 1989; Bush 1996).[6] This could take the form of avoiding exploitation of one's labor power by running away, taking one's time, or retaking the products of one's labor; it could take more extreme forms, such as self-mutilation, abortion, suicide, and infanticide; and it could take more existential forms, such as bodily transcendence into music, dance, and the spiritual realm. The corporeality of existence and procreation (and its utter constraint by enslavement) have thus been crucially linked to the question of how freedom has been practiced, imagined, and theorized in the modern Atlantic world—including by women who themselves were in law enslaved and later emancipated.

Orlando Patterson (1991: xiii, xv), one of the foremost historical sociologists of slavery and freedom, has eloquently argued that the core Western value of freedom "was generated from the experience of slavery" and, to his surprise, "women played a decisive role in the Western social invention of *personal* freedom" and "continued to play a critical role in the history of this element of freedom, continuously reconstructing a distinctively feminine version of the value." Various readings of the famous "Ar'n't I a Woman?" speech of 1851 by Sojourner Truth, for example, underline how she performed her embodiment as a black woman through the display of her powerful laboring arm and used her "inappropriate/d" body to challenge the exclusions of the existing gender and racial order that denied black working women access to the category of (white) "woman" (Giddings 1984; Haraway 1992; hooks 1981). During the transition from slavery to freedom, African Jamaican women also used their positions as working mothers to challenge ongoing exploitation and protect their customary rights. The feminist theorization of women's "double burden" must be understood not simply as a structural contradiction, but also as a lived reality, which in some circumstances could be empowering. Unlike their male counterparts, female field laborers made claims for improved working conditions not simply as free workers, but specifically as mothers who were struggling to support their families. In the initial stages of apprenticeship and emancipation, freed women clearly took advantage of well-known British views of femininity to press their claims against local male authorities, with an eye to allies in the powerful metropolitan public sphere and abolitionist movement, as well.

Assertions of special prerogatives for women and criticism of the abuse of women had extra resonance in the British Victorian setting, with its sharp delineation of a boundary between the masculine public world and the feminine private sphere of domesticity (Davidoff and Hall 1987; cf. Ryan 1990). If the existence of hard labor by women on the sugar plantations did not alone move abolitionists, then reports of the cruel punishments inflicted on slave women for their resistance activities did. Such reports, along with intimations of immoral concubinage, prostitution, and lurid images of naked women being whipped, fed the antislavery press in both England and America (Bush 1990; Wilberforce 1823). Jean Yellin (1989: 12) has shown that the emblem of the female supplicant slave with the words "Am I Not a Woman and a Sister" was probably designed by British women and was certainly exported by them to help move middle-class American women to action. Publications such as the *Westminster Review* "ran lead articles urging British women to redouble their abolition-ist efforts and detailing the violence inflicted on female slaves in Jamaica and the Bahamas." British mobilization against apprenticeship built on this earlier antislavery literature and highlighted the mistreatment (and pun-ishment) of female apprentices as important signifiers of the immorality of this "experiment" in half-freedom. Public debate kept returning to the unacceptability of physical punishment of women (Paton 2004), especially mothers, who were depicted as simply trying to care for their children and families, as good mothers should.[7]

Thus, the development of a Christian female antislavery public in Brit-ain mirrored and fed off African Jamaican women's leadership of high-risk protest. As the "cult of domesticity" took on increasing salience for British middle-class abolitionists, freed women began to articulate their own "rights of motherhood" in relation to the white philanthropists who claimed to speak for them. As Catherine Hall (1992: 211) has shown, be-tween the early 1830s and the late 1840s, "There was a never-ending flow of words and people between England and Jamaica, attempting to secure the on-going politics of emancipation. Reports in the missionary press and in the anti-slavery press, public meetings, lecture tours, fund-raising cam-paigns, books, pamphlets, private letters designed to be read in part at missionary prayer meetings or abolitionist gatherings, all fueled the fires of the emancipatory public and kept the issue of Jamaica at the forefront of public conscience." Although represented to the English public as voice-less victims, Afro-Jamaican women came into public notice precisely be-cause they refused to suffer silently. They exploited not only an indigenous "moral economy" of claims on planters' paternalism but also Christian morality, with its rhetoric of domestic motherhood and the mother's duty to protect her children.[8] The evidence for this exists in both the records of actions taken by women to protest against the system of apprenticeship and the political use made of those records in England, where the issue of women's treatment in Jamaica was explicitly laid before Parliament and the general public. The point is not simply that motherhood is a natural site of political conflict under slavery (although it is that in many particular in-stances), but that it was *discursively constructed as such* by female agents who understood its symbolic resonance even as they struggled against the multiple forms of personal and social violence that infiltrated the famil-ial realm.

PROTESTING APPRENTICESHIP:
THE POLITICS OF WOMEN'S FREEDOM

Female apprentices were punished in large numbers for trying to assert and protect the limited rights they had won as mothers of the slave labor force during the period of so-called amelioration (an attempt to raise the birthrate among slaves following abolition of the slave trade). Conflicts brought before special magistrates during the apprenticeship period in Jamaica revolved significantly around issues concerning women, including the rights of pregnant women; the time allowed to mothers to nurse infants, feed children, and attend sick family members; the special allowances for elderly matriarchs who had raised large families; and the question of physical punishment of women (cf. Paton 2008). While British abolitionists focused on the cruel treatment of women, Jamaican women themselves took a major part in protesting the conditions in which they found themselves supposedly free. "The most militant resistance to the apprenticeship regime came from women workers," Holt (1992: 64) argues, "and eventually the method used to tame them—the treadmills at the houses of correction—created a scandal discrediting the whole apprenticeship system and paving the way for its abolition." Speeches made during the debate in the House of Lords on ending apprenticeship focused on the loss of "customary indulgences" to mothers with children, as well as on the brutal and indecent flogging of women in the workhouses.[9]

John Sturge and Thomas Harvey, prominent Quaker philanthropists and promoters of immediate full emancipation, highlighted the abuse of female apprentices in their widely distributed publications. Representing the condition of women was a crucial part of their publicity project, tying in to other efforts aimed at gaining sympathetic supporters in Britain, especially the middle-class women who had already been mobilized in the campaigns of antislavery petitioning, fundraising, and boycotting of imports produced by slaves. They toured several islands to interview apprentices both on the estates and in the workhouses. They found that general complaints "include flagrant instances of the frauds of time which are committed on the apprentices, of the enforcement of extra labor in and out of crop time for little or no remuneration, of the neglect of the sick, oppression of nursing mothers, pregnant women, and mothers of six children who were exempt during slavery from field labor." The stipendiary magistrates who were responsible for settling labor disputes worried that "symptoms of rebellion" were appearing "particularly amongst the women" (Sturge and Harvey 1838: 231, 217).[10]

In one case reported by Sturge and Harvey, "a strong body of police" had to be sent to the Lansquinet Estate near Falmouth "to quell, we presume, by their presence, a rebellion among the nursing mothers," a notion they seemed to find oxymoronic. Ten of the women were sent to the Falmouth workhouse with their infants and stated to Sturge and Harvey that

> on Friday morning last, as it was very wet, and they were obliged to carry their children into the field with them, they did not turn out before breakfast. For this they were taken to the Special Magistrate on Monday, who sentenced them to pay six Saturdays. They told them they could not, as their mountain grounds were six miles distant, as they were deprived of their half Fridays and out of their salt-fish, and received now no sugar or flour for the children; that without their Saturdays, they had no means of obtaining subsistence. For their contumacy, they were sent to the workhouse for three days, and will still have to work the six Saturdays. (Sturge and Harvey 1838: 217–18)

Anti-apprenticeship campaigners used information like this to demonstrate that plantations were exploiting female apprentices in particular, since they had the added responsibility of caring for and feeding children. The incident demonstrates the women's concerted efforts to resist the plantation labor regime by stopping work, presenting justifications in terms of their need to protect and feed their children, and protesting their lack of subsistence and free time, both of which they had formerly depended on to support families. After lifelong resistance to slavery, such protesters seemed well aware of which narratives of grievance would be most effective in an English court and in an account given to curious white men: the "suffering mother" genre.[11]

Sturge's and Harvey's report was backed up by a litany of unfair cases against female apprentices. When Sally Hutchinson, an apprentice at the Treadways Estate, spoke up for her gang to say they were not being paid enough for extra labor, the landowner responded, "I don't want to hear a word. . . . Woman, hold your tongue," and when she persisted, he ordered her to be confined for a week in a dark room. She was then sentenced by a court to six days in the "house of correction," while the gang itself lost five alternate Saturdays (when they normally tended their provision grounds).

In another instance, three women with more than six children each, who had been exempt from field labor before Emancipation Day on 1 August, were ordered to the field again as soon as they were "free." When they did not "turn out," a magistrate sentenced them to the workhouse. Sarah Nelson and Bessy Grant of the Phoenix Estate were sentenced to hard labor in the penal gang and twice a day on the treadmill for two calendar months for "combining and resisting work" and "insolent and disorderly conduct." Several women on the Friendship Estate refused to give up their half-Fridays, which were needed to grow provisions; Bettriss Holland, Kitty Jones, Dolly Ferguson, Christian Williams, and Ruth Allen were not allowed to speak before the magistrate and were summarily sentenced to fifteen days on the treadmill for "disobedience to orders" (Sturge and Harvey 1838: sec. 4).

   The campaign to publicize such abuses was also aided by the eyewitness account of James Williams, an apprentice who reported on horrific conditions for women in the Saint Ann's Bay Work-house. Williams described how "one old woman with grey head . . . could not dance the [tread]mill at all: she hang by the two wrist which was strapped to the bar, and the driver keep on flogging her. . . . [W]hen she come down all her back covered with blood." Two young women were flogged so severely that "they cut away most of their clothes, and left them in a manner naked; and the driver was bragging afterwards that he see all their nakedness." One woman "quite big with child" was "not able to dance good" on the spinning treadmill, "and them flog her; she complain about her stomach hurt her . . . and beg the overseer not to work her on the mill," but he persisted. Women were also reportedly sexually abused by overseers who were themselves prisoners. On their release, he stated, "them all look quite shocking when them let out, some hardly able to walk to go home . . . all mashed up with the mill" (Williams 1838: 19).[12] The attention these reports brought to West Indian prisons "both inside and outside Parliament led the Colonial Office in August 1837 to send Captain John Pringle to the West Indies in order to investigate the prisons" (Paton 2004: 116). Pringle's report arrived back in London in July 1838 and, along with a Parliamentary inquiry into Williams's report, also "focused in particular on problems in the management of gender within prisons: the possibilities for mixing of prisoners of different sexes, the flogging of women, and the sexual abuse of women in prison" (Paton 2004: 117). This led to the passage of a new West India Prisons Act, which produced consternation in Jamaica and a crisis that "brought Anglo-Jamaican relations to the brink of dissolution," including threats to institute direct rule from London, according to Paton (2004: 118).

But I want to return to the role of Jamaican women in these events. The penalties against women and the debates surrounding corporal punishment of women reflect not merely British revulsion at the system that produced them, but also, more fundamentally, the widespread collective efforts by Jamaican women to resist the plantation labor regime (often by claiming a right to family subsistence) despite harsh repression and reprisals. Working women's right to speak publicly and to make claims against employers and before magistrates became central to the transition to wage labor; the everyday verbal skills of challenge and protest—once used by the enslaved—were now turned to more overt forms of public claim making and resistance to the new order of free labor. Recognition of the prevalence of women's collective action and public protest raises new questions about the movement of women away from fieldwork following emancipation. Until recently, many historians interpreted the "withdrawal of female labor" from plantations in terms of women's supposed reluctance to engage in a detested form of hard physical labor and men's supposed desire to keep their female kin in the home. Yet as Rebecca Scott (1988: 423) argues, "Most discussions of the 'withdrawal' of women's labor tend to blur the question of choice and decision, leaving it unclear just who initiated the reallocation of work time, at what point, and in what directions." This question has important political implications: What if leaving the plantations was not simply a "withdrawal" into private domestic work but a key move in a highly public labor struggle that was also about the exercise of embodied freedom and the formation of the citizenship rights of free subjects?

Several historians have argued that the aim of many Afro-Jamaicans after emancipation was not simply to flee the estates, but to combine wage work with small landholding. There is evidence that former slaves were attached to their houses, gardens, and provision grounds, which in many cases had valuable mature trees or ripening crops, not to mention the burial places of ancestors (Besson 1979, 2002; Hall 1993 [1978]; Higman 1988). Apprentices did not choose voluntarily to leave their homes on the sugar plantations, Mary Turner (1995: 12) argues; they "were driven from the estates post-emancipation by low wages, high rents, competition from cut-rate contract workers and the discovery that to become an estate-based wage earner was to remain, in social terms, a slave. They turned to the land for want of a different option." It may therefore be more accurate to say that Jamaica's female workers moved away from plantation labor largely as a result of the super-exploitation of family labor on the plantations through both the low wages paid to women and children and the manipulative tying of wage contracts to rent payment. It was not a "flight" from the estates so much as a strategic move in a political struggle or, as Douglas Hall (1993: 62) says, "a protest against the inequities of early 'freedom.'" These inequities affected women particularly strongly, Marietta Morrissey (1989: xi) argues, since women's "lack of access to skilled agricultural work diminished their social status and authority, and gender became an increasingly salient expression of stratification." Women were excluded from skilled jobs and all of the ancillary occupations that paid higher wages, such as sugar boiler, wheelwright, cooper, blacksmith, or carpenter, and they generally had less access to land than did men (Higman 1988; Reddock 1985).

This puts in new perspective the post-emancipation debate over the linkage of rent to wages and its implications for female plantation workers. When apprenticeship ended, planters tried to tie payment of wages to the rent of houses and provision grounds, which had once been customarily distributed among slaves and even passed down through slave families (Besson 2002; Higman 1988), many of whom, not surprisingly, expected that with emancipation the land would also be given to them as a form of reparation (an issue that remains unresolved in Jamaica even today). The planters charged each family member rent, deducting it directly from wages. Thus, families who had cleared ground for planting, paid for materials, and built houses and occupied them for years, perhaps generations, suddenly found rent demanded by the property owner from every family member, and non-payment was met with notices to quit and eviction (Waddell 1970 [1863]: 148–51). As the *Morning Journal* noted in August 1838, "We understand that on an estate in St. Andrew's, and upon some others in parishes to Leeward, it is demanded that each man and woman who agrees to labour should give two days in each week in lieu of house and grounds. This is objected to by such labourers as have wives and grown up children as unreasonable, and has operated to prevent the terms offered being accepted, and the labour of the properties resumed."[13] Wilmot (1995: 280) suggests, "Confronted by the women's determination not to be tied down to the rigid demands of regular work on the plantations, the planters, in the first three months of full freedom, initiated a series of labour recruitment strategies, many of which aimed at coercing women to perform estate work, especially during crop time." Resistance to these attempts to control families by requiring rent from each person led to many violent conflicts immediately following emancipation, and several parishes were swept by work stoppages and strikes as workers bargained for higher wages and tried to control the terms of the labor contract (Holt 1992; Wilmot 1986, 1995).

Not just men but whole families were involved in these strikes. The *Morning Journal* reported, "The stand for exorbitant wages is general, and the refusal to resume work, such as to justify the opinion that the plan was preconcerted. The evil is not confined to two or three parishes, or to particular parts, or districts of a parish, but to nearly every parish in the island, and to all parts of them."[14] A complaint filed at Halfway Tree Court stated that several women had refused notices to quit and were instead planting more provisions on their grounds at the Temple Hall Estate. When constables tried to levy goods for outstanding rent on a coffee plantation in Saint George's Parish, "workers, especially females, confronted them with missiles and 'violent language.'"[15] Laborers from the Richmond Estate in Trelawny were imprisoned for resisting rent payment, but they actually won an appeal and were awarded significant damages.[16] The sympathetic *Baptist Herald and Friend of Africa* editorialized, "How any person could suppose himself justified in demanding rent from women and children, is to us astonishing, and we sincerely hope that ample redress will be afforded to those people who have been illegally imprisoned." The court's decision, the paper pointed out, showed that "the wife is not liable, nor can the husband be made to pay any extra rent, because his wife or friends are permitted to reside with him. Should any person be so foolhardy in Trelawny as to try to impose this system upon you, refuse to pay it: and let them, if they dare, enforce the unjust claim."[17] In February 1840, the *Baptist Herald* reported other instances of unfair rent arrangements. In one case, the overseer trampled the provision grounds of people who did not pay rent, and the paper advised people to leave the estate and live in Baptist free villages.[18] Some workers, trying to distinguish labor contracts from rent agreements, specifically asserted that married women should not be "required to labour unless they are so disposed to labour" (Wilmot 1995: 281). In response to the general resistance to rent arrangements, the governor issued a proclamation that "the Agricultural population of this Island labour under considerable misunderstanding as to a supposed right on their part to the houses and provision grounds which they were permitted to occupy and cultivate during slavery and the Apprenticeship." His views stirred considerable resentment, and public meetings were convened at Baptist chapels to discuss his charges and to debate the "rights and privileges" of the people.[19]

Women's withdrawal from the plantations must be placed in the context of this political struggle. Hard-won customary rights to houses and provision grounds were being directly undercut by emancipation, and deduction of rent from wages was particularly unfair to women, who earned far less than men. The planters' backlash against the customary rights of women, against families' rights to allocate their own time and labor, and against the subsistence rights of households not only directly contradicted the missionary's image of Christian families settling in villages with married housewives by every hearthside (cf. Hall 1995; Mintz 1958); it also drove workers away from the plantations.[20] Women's rejection of plantation fieldwork was not the embrace of a more "feminine" domestic role, then, but part of a broader political strategy of strikes and labor solidarity that aimed to break the planters' power to control freed families. As Carolyn Cooper (1995: 66) says of working-class Jamaican women's politics, "This is the ultimate subterfuge: to evade domesticity in the very act of seeming to embrace it." To claim the biopolitical rights of wife and mother was to assert political autonomy and community solidarity under highly disadvantageous economic conditions; nevertheless, we should not ignore the fact that it also simultaneously reinforced Christian moralistic discourses of women's respectability and reproductive heteronormativity.

Ursula Vogel identifies the legal subordination of married women as constitutive of male citizenship. Tracing European marriage law back to medieval precedents in which a husband controlled "the body, property and freedom of his wife," she shows how "a relationship reminiscent of feudal bondage" has been carried forward into natural jurisprudence and modern liberalism (Vogel 1994: 78–79). In a reading of Alexis de Tocqueville's *Democracy in America*, she argues that "de Tocqueville links the freedom and equality of citizens in the public domain to the conditions of autocratic government in the household and, in particular, to the unquestionable authority of husbands over wives" (Vogel 1994: 84). This "paradoxical nexus of citizenship and bondage, of companionship and subordination," she argues, "is rooted in the belief that the stability of political society requires the guarantee of sexual fidelity" of wives, through which property inheritance is assured from father to son (Vogel 1994: 84). Sexual control over women through marriage, even in the "softer" forms of companionate marriage that emerged in the twentieth century, continues women's civil and legal subordination at the same time that it upholds masculine egalitarianism and men's freedom to act as heads of household in the public sphere. Such patriarchal heads of households also frequently exercised legal control over slaves and servants, which also conditioned their claims as legitimate citizens. As we shall see in the next chapter, the Jamaican discourse of motherhood and women's domesticity was matched by a public discourse of free black manhood, with problematic ethnocentric elements. These gendered/racialized constructs of sexual subjectivity would influence nationalist discourses in Jamaica, explored in later chapters, that could veer toward ethnocentric, homophobic, and fundamentalist positions that have reproduced the violence of colonial biopolitics.

DEMOCRATIZING RELIGION: BLACK WOMEN'S VOICES IN DISSENT AND REVIVAL

The planters' backlash against the customary rights of women, against the family's right to allocate its own time and labor, and against the subsistence rights of households not only drove workers away from the plantations but also, as already noted, directly contradicted the missionary's image of Christian families with married housewives by every hearth, in tidy homes from which productive working men could be reproduced. Baptist missionaries took the side of the people in the wage-rent debates and promoted free villages not just because they were self-proclaimed "friends of the Negro," but also because they were interested in encouraging the formation of stable monogamous Christian families. In the free villages, as Diane Austin-Broos suggests, "a new persona emerged for the emancipated. The sober and industrious 'Christian black' replaced 'Quashie' [or Quasheba, we might add], the devious trickster slave" (Austin-Broos 1997: 38–39; cf. Patterson 1973 [1967]: 174–81). African Jamaican women, however, turned the Christian vision of women's domesticity toward their own ends by fighting coercive contracts and by trying to de-link private household decision making from enforced plantation labor. Just as they resisted the plantation labor regime, so, too, did free women resist the missionary's moral regime. While embodied freedom was being vehemently contested in the fields of secular work, it was also being forged on the terrain of sacred work.

As women left the plantations, they took their gender-specific consciousness and forms of collective action to new arenas—perhaps most important, into the very churches that had set themselves the mission of rebuilding Afro-Jamaican families in their own middle-class mold. "The religious sects and movements that follow in a chain from emancipation," argues Austin-Broos (1997: 38–39), "chart Jamaican attempts to supersede the persona of the Christian black." Although European missions played a colonizing role in many parts of the world (Comaroff and Comaroff 1992), they also inadvertently provided the material, cultural, and social basis for political movements. Religious organizations at the community level have long been recognized as a source for political leadership and organization throughout the African diaspora (Du Bois 1992 [1935]; Evans and Boyte 1986; Harding 1981, 1997 [1969]; McAdam 1982; Morris 1984). As Elizabeth Fox-Genovese suggests, "Churches and secret religious networks undoubtedly provided the institutional links between acts of individual resistance and revolts in the name of the collectivity. And women were integral members of those churches and religious associations" (cf. Brown 1995; Fox-Genovese 1986: 159; Higginbotham 1993). At the same time, though, far more attention has been paid to overtly political actions by men in Jamaica (e.g., Native Baptist leaders during the Baptist War of 1831 and the Morant Bay Rebellion of 1865) than to the thousands of women who constituted the mainstay in the day-to-day politics of the churches.

A crucial aspect of laying the foundations for subsequent oppositional cultures in Jamaica was black women's promotion of a popular "voice" within the missionary churches and, more radically, by forming their own "Afro-Christian" religious associations, and beyond that in continuing the non-Christian spiritual practices of Obeah and Myal. By extending notions of public leadership and protest beyond the overly simplistic dualism of *either* violent rebellion *or* hidden resistance, a third realm of public, non-violent *citizenship from below* emerges. Churches, as the main centers of Jamaican social life, became the terrain for this open and (usually) non-violent struggle against white domination. The politics of religious practices occurred in part within the churches, but it also spilled over into the wider political public realm. The practices of Obeah and Myal, especially, "cannot be characterized as medicine, law, religion, magic, or judicial practice; they encompassed all these areas of life but were not confined to any of them" (Paton 2004: 183), thus defying neat categorization and blending the sacred and the secular.

In regard to Christianity, on the one hand, African Jamaicans challenged the power of white missionaries and asserted control over religious congregations (which their monetary contributions and voluntary labor supported) through participation in meetings, vocal opposition to racial and gender discrimination, and insistence on the independent church principle of democratic selection of their own elders, deacons, and pastors through voting and petitioning. On the other hand, white resistance to increasingly autonomous popular decision making led black congregations to adopt strategies of forcing change either through schism or through forms of revivalism that promoted indigenous leadership, idioms, and practices. These "native" practices challenged white power and overturned the hierarchy of white, male clergy and black (often female) laity. The Revival movements and their offspring turned away from the hierarchical European churches and sought religious self-determination by blurring the boundaries between Christian and African religious beliefs, between men's and women's religious roles, and between private worship and public acts. In the process, they challenged the entire basis of religious practice in the Americas.

An early public challenge to black women's subordination in the dissenting churches occurred in the Baptist congregation of Reverend Samuel Oughton in Kingston. When Eleanor Vickars was selected to become a "class leader," Oughton opposed her election on the grounds that class leaders were required to read and write. Vickars took the unusual step of defending herself in the *Morning Journal*. "Reluctant as I am to see my name in the public papers," she wrote, "and knowing also that it is not customary for females to defend themselves before the public, I am nevertheless compelled to this step."[21] She went on to explain that for nearly twenty years she had been the leading female singer at the Text-lane and East Queen Street chapels and that she was in charge of the female inquirers and assistant leader of a class. She attributed Oughton's refusal of her nomination not to her illiteracy, but to his discrimination against women. "These facts are known to thousands; and there is not a class, I believe, in the whole society, but has two or more female leaders," she continued. "However much he may now be opposed to it, I defy him to abolish it. It has existed from the formation of the Baptist Society in this island. Mr. Oughton was desirous of informing the public that he only recognized me in the menial situation of washing the sacrament table cloth. It was certainly sent to my washing establishment, and of which I am not ashamed." Oughton's efforts to impose a requirement of literacy suggests a move toward excluding working-class women from these positions of leadership. This was part of a general movement within the Baptist and other denominations to assert white control and limit the influence of more popular Afro-Jamaican leaders. That Vickars was a lead singer, an important role in Afro-American churches (Sutcliffe and Tomlin 1986), also suggests that this was part of the missionary's "broad and rigorous ethical program that inevitably staunched the eudemonic of freedom," driving song, dance, and other African-rooted forms of religious expression from the churches (Austin-Broos 1997: 39). Moreover, her defense of washerwomen hints at a kind of solidarity with those lower-class women who made up the mass of any congregation in Jamaica.

Many women of color, including those who were illiterate, participated in activities of a public and political nature through their churches, including elections and petitioning. Even the relatively conservative Presbyterian church required every communicant to vote for elders, bringing non-white men into positions of leadership even while slavery existed (Waddell 1970 [1863]: 113). The act of petitioning may first have been practiced by many Afro-Jamaicans within their churches and only later took on a wider political character as it was used for claim making outside the churches (Sheller 2000). In several denominations, women were as likely to sign petitions as were men. In the case of the London Missionary Society (LMS) in the 1840s, for example, three petitions to the directors of the society from church members who identify themselves as "a labouring people" or "labourers with large families" have 134 names identifiable as women out of a total of 236 signatories.[22] In the case of the Wesleyan Methodist Missionary Society, a key debate emerged in the 1840s over the extent to which congregations should participate in church governance, which until then was facilitated via democratically structured meetings. The Kingston Quarterly Meeting was the most active in producing petitions, leading to controversy not so much over the content of the petitions as over the procedure by which they were "got up." A subtext of this debate was the degree of power that black women should exercise within the dissenting churches, where they served in many lay offices and participated in petitioning the district meetings and governing committee; even as white missionaries denounced complaints of racial discrimination, they increasingly argued against too much congregational independence. This can be seen as part of the wider conflict over enthusiastic revivalism and democratization of Christianity in the proliferating Protestant sects of the Americas, in which African Americans played a crucial part (Austin-Broos 1997; Hatch 1989; Raboteau 1978).

The crux of the matter was the charge by Reverend Martin Young that the Kingston Quarterly Meeting of 1847 was "a fractious proceeding" characterized by "a noisy and indecent discussion" that led many to abstain from voting. Most significantly, he suggested that this was due to the "popular character" of the meeting and, particularly, the number of *female* "class leaders" (an important elected lay office) and their energetic participation in debate and voting:

> The constitution of the Kingston Quarterly Meeting, as it appears to be established by custom, is of an unusually popular character, it being composed of an exceedingly small number of stewards, and about 300 leaders, of whom two thirds are females; *(usually forming by far the larger portion of the attendants, and as a matter of course discussing and deciding on all questions which may be brought forward;)* and probably scarcely more than one in eight or ten of whom is able either to write or read. The meeting is therefore exceedingly liable to be influenced by the representations of any person of active and restless disposition, and that to so great an extent as sometimes to be beyond the control of the ministers, and the more discreet and reflecting portion of the attendants.[23]

Popular democratic procedures and participation in meetings by illiterate women were perceived as a threat to the white English missionaries' control over the society. Young concluded his attack on democratic procedure by noting that the Kingston petitions were a kind of test case, part of a larger agitation for popular independent control of the churches, arguing that the society must clarify its stance on the "privilege of petitioning Conference." By making a formal distinction between "home" and "foreign" stations, the society sought to contain not only dangerous democratic currents, but also the black and brown women who exercised roles of leadership within their churches. A major difference between "home" and Jamaica, after all, was the degree to which women "as a matter of course" discussed and decided all questions brought forward.[24]

If petitioning and other attempts to control the churches were engagements within the terms of the system, religious revival provided an escape from the system. Above all, its rejection of the formal order of European-controlled churches (and of the limited "Christian black" persona) offered more opportunities for women's leadership. As numerous scholars have argued, creative adaptation of African-influenced religious practices, whether in the form of Native Baptist chapels or Myal revivals and Obeah, underlay an alternative "moral order" in Jamaica that had a major impact on forms of political mobilization and leadership (Austin-Broos 1997; Chevannes 1994; Schuler 1993; Stewart 1992). Even before the Baptist War of 1831, when it became clear that slaves' political networks were intimately related to religious organizations, black religion threatened white Jamaican society. A newspaper from 1829, for example, berates the "self-stiled Reverends, alias Baptist preachers" who roared out psalms and hymns one Saturday night in Port Royal, "to the great annoyance of the quiet and orderly portion of the inhabitants," until joined on Sunday morning "by a large party of female slaves, when the whole moved off in a body toward the sea, where they were well soused."[25] Black congregations were able to seize public space and use it for religious rituals of their own making.

The Myal revivals of 1842 and 1860–61 indicate radical forms of religious and spiritual self-determination in which women participated fully, often in positions of leadership.[26] Women's houses were often used for "prayer meetings" in which "the spirit of convincing power" first took hold. Women's prayer meetings, or "Mothers' meetings," were the basis for extensive networks of Revivalism outside the control of missionaries (Waddell 1970 [1863]: 169). Reverend Walter Dendy reported that independent of Sunday services in his district, "There are one hundred and twelve district prayer meetings held in the week, in connexion with the [Baptist] church." Reverend George Truman reported that "they have what is called a godmother of the revivals, the headmother or shepherd. . . . [S]he chastises the women." William Hillyer of the LMS reported "a large amount of superstition, Error, and blasphemy. Women representing themselves as the 'Virgin Mary,' men calling themselves the 'Lord Jesus Christ,' and others going from place to place saying they can give their fellow men the spirit." These activities also took place in public space. In 1842, there were reports in Cornwall of an "Attack upon the Police by the Obeah and Myalpeople" in which the crowd threw stones at police and made threats, while leaders known as "angels" visited various estates to seize and punish people accused of practicing Obeah. As Paton (2004: 187) argues, the vast majority of Jamaicans believed in Obeah, which was criminalized in Jamaican law as "pretend[ing] to any supernatural power," and plenty of evidence exists showing that "elites feared it because of its power to mobilize Afro-Jamaicans to political ends." In the 1860s, Revivalists took to the streets of Kingston, where "followed by mobs, [they] have been parading through the streets, singing and giving expression to imprecations most fearful." Revivalists in the western parishes were reportedly stockpiling sharpened spears and had leaders such as "Isabella the Comforter," who were "in the habit of prophesying the destruction of life and property."[27]

Reverend W. Holdsworth, like many other Methodists, reported that the revival of 1860 was not going as the missionaries had hoped. Although they initially gained many new and enthusiastic members, there were worrisome cases of "extravagant" behavior. His comments demonstrate his explicit connection of women's sexuality with fears of black women's empowerment: "A number of those extravagant young people are pregnant, among them, the one 'that sat as a queen' and had revelations from heaven, and saw hell without a covering, and your humble servant [Holdsworth] there, who predicted the destruction of one of our chapels by fire. She had an influence over multitudes that was astounding, she had only to say do this, and a host was ready to do it."[28] This spiritual "queen" is strongly reminiscent of figures such as Queen Cubah, a Koromantyn spiritual leader involved in the slave revolt of 1760, whose role may have been modeled on that of West African queen mothers (Aidoo 1985; Gaspar 1996: 231; Mathurin 1975; Terborg-Penn 1986: 204–6). In fact, popular organizations throughout the African diaspora, from carnival bands to collective work groups, are known to have elected female leaders who were often called queens. The Jamaican use of this politico-religious title indicates both the public ceremonial role and the political overtones of women's religious leadership. Most significantly, the veneration of a young woman who is pregnant suggests an alternative vernacular moral order, in which female sexuality and reproductive autonomy are empowering.

The 1860–61 Revival is the origin of several more recent Jamaican religious sects in which women continue to exercise central leadership roles, such as Revival Zion and Pukumina. "To a far greater extent than most people realize," argues Barry Chevannes (1994: 21), "Myal and its later manifestation, Revival, have shaped the worldview of the Jamaican people, helping them to forge an identity and a culture by subversive participation in the wider polity." Jean Besson's work has long supported this view, and she continues to argue that women are central to the evolution of Myalism and Revival as "peasant cultures of resistance" and instances of Caribbean "culture building" (Besson 2002). Female leaders in Revival Zion, Pukumina, and, more recently, Pentecostal and Holiness denominations are commonly referred to as "Mother" or "Queenie," and sacred knowledge has been passed down from mother to daughter (Barrett 1976: 54; Besson 1993: 28; Lowe 1972). Rosalyn Terborg-Penn (1986) points out similar patterns of women's leadership throughout the African diaspora, including popularly given titles, celebration of militant female warriors, the attribution of spiritual powers to female leaders, and the role of older women as strategists, advisers, and warriors. Cheryl Townsend Gilkes has pointed out from a comparative perspective that in the U.S. African American community "there are powerful and respected older women addressed by the title

'Mother.' . . . The public prestige and real power of certain elderly black women in community work diverged from dominant (white) cultural norms" (Gilkes 1997: 367, 372; cf. Higginbotham 1993). Are the African Jamaican Queens and Mothers of today direct descendants of Quasheba, the public voice of female leadership in the slave community? The tradition of black women's resistance, leadership, and participation in public protest certainly suggests some continuity from the slave plantation to the post-emancipation churches and into the modern political sphere and forms of subaltern citizenship.

It is not surprising, then, that subsequent concern over the apparent absence of heteronormative patriarchal nuclear families in Afro-Caribbean cultures became central to state policy and national debate in both the colonial and post-independence periods. As Christine Barrow (1998: 342–43) explains, "Remoulding black men and women according to these received images was integral to the colonial government's vision of a civilized social order in the post-emancipation Caribbean. The master plan for social gender reconstruction harnessed the combined forces of government, education and religion to domesticate women and to recast men as responsible, productive workers and household heads." The negative perception of "matrifocal households" (Clarke 1957; Smith 1973), alleged sexual promiscuity, high rates of "illegitimate" births, and more recent concerns over "male marginality" (Miller 1987, 1992) continue a long tradition of representing Afro-Caribbean kinship systems and reproductive practices as "abnormal" and even pathological. Indeed, following the labor rebellion of 1938, the West India Royal Commission issued a report that blamed the unrest on the "dysfunctional" family structure and sexual practices of the lower classes. The Office of Colonial Development and Welfare was created in 1941 to implement improvements in basic living conditions for the Jamaican working classes but also to foster more sexual restraint and responsible parenting within a normalized domestic sphere consisting of a male breadwinner and his domestically oriented wife. This was understood as leading to good citizenship. As in the United States, "Issues of family and domesticity emerge obliquely and in relation to issues of labor, hygiene, and discipline. The utility of the family as a mechanism in the transition to a free labor system is evidenced by the importance attached to the home" (Hartman 1997: 157). Only recently have social scientists begun to debate alternative interpretations of Caribbean kinship structures and gender roles (Barrow 1998a; Reddock 2004).

URBAN POPULAR CULTURE, RIOTOUS WOMEN, AND COLLECTIVE ACTION

"Quasheba" did not only turn to the churches; she also took to the streets. It is politically significant that black and brown women formed by far the majority of inhabitants of Jamaica's larger towns and ports in the nineteenth century. A census of Kingston taken in 1844 found a total population of 14,350 males and 18,543 females, while the island-wide census of 1861 found that in all towns there were a total of 36,805 women, compared with only 26,378 men (Higman 1980).[29] Non-white women were a permanent presence in the public spaces of towns because of their central role in marketing agricultural produce, as well as their concentration in domestic-service jobs in urban areas. Thus, they played an important part in the development of a politically active African Jamaican public in two ways: they facilitated flows of information between town and country (cf. Mintz and Hall 1960; Momsen 1988; Olwig 1985; Turner 1982), and they filled the streets and squares during popular political mobilizations or demonstrations. As Robin D. G. Kelley (1996: 75) points out for the U.S. South, "For black workers, public spaces both embodied the most repressive, violent aspects of race and gender oppression and, ironically, afforded more opportunities than the workplace itself to engage in acts of resistance." Whereas many studies have concluded that the street is the locale of masculine "reputation" in the Caribbean, with women relegated to the home, the fenced-in yard, or the "respectability" of the church, there is in fact plenty of evidence that working-class women dominated the life of the streets.[30] Above all, it is clear that black women played a highly visible part in the markets, streets, and rioting "mobs," often suffering retaliatory police attacks.

Many examples of "violent language" in the British records were spoken by women, whether during slavery and apprenticeship or in later courthouse scuffles and riots; when violence occurred, working-class women were often at the forefront, brandishing not only insults and provocation but also, quite often, weapons. By the 1850s, those words and weapons were increasingly turned not only against overseers and plantation personnel, but also against the actual representatives of the colonial state: policemen, courthouses, militias, even magistrates. Here again, women's political leadership was not simply due to sheer numbers on the lowest social rungs. Rather, it was their special economic and social position as a link between town and country, between markets and fields, and between the state and the families it tried to control, all of which enabled networks of women to facilitate crucial flows of information and to orchestrate collective action through the female-dominated public spaces of the markets.

Market women, or "higglers," brought produce from the country into the towns and carried news and information to rural districts in the process. In largely nonliterate societies, women's concentration in the towns and markets gave them an advantage in gathering oral information, while their economic and familial ties throughout the countryside enabled them to disseminate important information more quickly than even official channels. A letter to the editor of the *Watchman and Jamaica Free Press* in 1831 indicates the degree to which free black women dominated trade, often making a good profit along the way:

> Having occasion to go to the Beef Market on Sunday last, I was not a little astonished to find it infested by a number of black females, well known by the name of "Higglers" (most of them free), who monopolize every thing. The poor country negroes have scarcely time to put down their loads, before they are surrounded, and in a thousand instances robbed by these women. It is a well known fact, that these Higglers take every possible advantage of the poor negroes, who, for the advantage of a better market, and with the hope of obtaining higher prices, travel upwards of forty miles from their homes to this town, with ground provisions, etc, etc. . . . the poor country slaves are imposed upon by these unprincipled characters, and the poorer classes of the community deprived of an opportunity of procuring ground provisions, etc. immediately from the country people, and compelled to pay these monopolists a high price for whatever they purchase from them.[31]

Thus, even before slavery ended, free black urban women in Jamaica had established an entrepreneurial niche of their own, exploiting their less streetwise country cousins perhaps, but also providing them with opportunities they might not otherwise have found.[32] The importance of these internal marketing networks as channels of political communication during the period of slavery has been recognized by a number of historians (Mintz and Hall 1960; Momsen 1988; Olwell 1996; Olwig 1985; J. S. Scott 1986; Turner 1982). There has been less discussion, however, of their ongoing significance after emancipation.

Following emancipation, the markets of Jamaica continued to be run largely by women, with only minimal regulation of their organization.

Working-class women dominated the public life of the streets, especially in major market centers. As Rhoda Reddock (1994: 81) notes for Trinidad and Tobago, "For most women the street was their arena of activity. They worked there, were entertained, quarreled, fought, and even ate there. The Victorian adage that women should be seen and not heard was not applicable here, and the strict division between public and private life was not yet instituted among the working classes."[33] Given their numerical predominance in urban public spaces, black women played a special part in public disturbances and riots, where they often made up the majority of participants in contentious gatherings. Not only were women's public activities a constant challenge to the security of the class, racial, and gender identity of the white male elite, but working-class public culture often transmuted into direct verbal challenges to the authorities, sometimes turning into violent riots. Drawing on the work of Lisa Douglass (1992: 249), Richard Burton (1997: 164) points out that "the street woman par excellence—who in the West Indies is not the prostitute but the haggler (market woman)—is regarded with ambivalence by the wider society: admired for her 'manlike' autonomy and assertiveness, she is also derided on account of her often invasive physical presence, her loud dress, and her even louder demeanor and language." Thus the higgler or haggler becomes "a comical character, a caricature of a woman," who remained a figure of humoristic commentary and touristic interest, constantly represented in the accounts of travelers, images of artists, and snapshots of photographers to the present (see chapter 8).

It is a familiar caricature, updating earlier images of the independent and threatening Quasheba; urban women carried on her tradition of protest and resistance. Even when riots arose out of religious or cultural issues, the following examples show that urban disturbances were always political insofar as they demonstrated black physical power and numerical strength against representatives of the state. In a clash with police over the treatment of recaptured (then indentured) Africans in Falmouth in 1840, a woman named Mary Clarke was singled out by police: "She abused the Police frequently and we were obliged to put her back. She always retreated with reluctance, and come back again. . . . Mary Clarke was conspicuous from first to last. . . . She damned the police and asked what right they had to interfere with people in the street" (Wilmot 1995: 286). Here the street is claimed as a public space, to which the people had a "right." Newspaper reports of this incident indicate that the public disturbance arose when the Africans were handcuffed, ill treated, and, most important according to one witness, a woman was pitched into a cart, knocked on the head, and "her person exposed."[34]

After Christmas riots in Kingston in 1842, the *Morning Journal* reported that when the usual John Canoe festivities were banned by the mayor and a man was arrested simply for playing a violin, angry women assembled:

> But so soon as the people saw that one of their body who had violated no law, who had acted contrary to no order, had been taken by the police, they assembled in numbers, [four-fifths] of them women. The crowd was great, but it consisted chiefly of defenseless women. Then was it that the police committed an outrage upon the people which was unparalleled. Seeing the people thus assembled, instead of recommending them quietly to disperse, they attempted to ride them down. Remonstrance would not do—ordinary means would not do—force must be resorted to. It was resorted to. The police attempted to ride the people down—and then had the people recourse to brick-bats; then, as he was informed, began the uproar.[35]

The police were driven back and eventually opened fire on the crowd, killing three people, including one pregnant woman, and wounding several others. Although this writer foregrounds the imagery of "defenseless women," the urban crowds were in fact far more threatening than the small groups of women who had once challenged plantation personnel. As James Scott (1990: 65) suggests, "Large, autonomous gatherings of subordinates are threatening to domination because of the license they promote among normally disaggregated inferiors."

A new urban political culture was emerging on the streets of Kingston and other large towns in the mid-nineteenth century, and women were instrumental in its formation. Women of the "lower classes" were an object of fear and ridicule to elite Jamaicans who were clearly threatened by both their public presence and their domestic practices. A report by the Central Board of Health of Jamaica, presented to the legislature in 1852, reveals official views of popular urban life in which the private sphere was as much a threat to "public order" as the streets and markets. The authors wanted to establish better sanitation, housing, and medical provisions, but they contrasted the "powerful aid of science" with the "filthy" customs of the "idle" lower classes:

> The market places, situated in the most crowded thoroughfares, their sheds and buildings miserably ventilated and undrained, frequently tainted articles of food exposed for sale, contaminate the surrounding atmosphere

with their putrid effluvia. . . . [The houses are] in some places sheds, more fit for the shelter of brutes than men . . . composed of the staves of salt fish and flour barrels. . . . These small dark unventilated houses are frequently overcrowded, especially at night; within the small space of a few square feet, perhaps on the bare ground . . . a whole family of eight or nine persons, of all ages and both sexes, huddled together with the door and so called window closed. . . . The rush of pent up odours, on opening such a place, must be experienced to be understood. (*Report by the Central Board of Health of Jamaica* 1852: 98, 102, 112–14)

They go on to complain about the lack of personal hygiene, the ragged clothing, the gatherings in the open night air, the calendar of rape cases in the criminal courts, the abortions and infanticides, the quacks and unlicensed practitioners, and the "ignorant, uneducated females attending as midwives; the majority of these are aged African crones." Their recommendations for regulating both public and private life ranged from changes in diet, dress, and the layout of housing to regulation of midwives and medical dispensaries. Rather than addressing the causes of poverty, however, the report blamed the poor themselves, suggesting that the idle man should "be held up to public scorn and contumely, let him be deprived of all his rights as a citizen—let him be disfranchised." Poor men and women were, of course, already disfranchised by property and gender qualifications for voters.[36]

Disfranchisement, however, did not preclude women from participating in political movements. In a popular petitioning campaign led by the Native Baptist Reverend Charles Fletcher in 1858, for example, separate women's and juveniles' committees were formed to send petitions to the queen and to raise subscriptions. The subsequent petitions carry more than 1,000 signatures, with at least 160 identifiable as women's names.[37] During the Westmoreland Toll Gate riots of February 1859, several toll bars and tollhouses on the main roads were pulled down after petitions to have them removed were ignored. More than a hundred warrants were put out, and thirty-one people were bound over to appear at the Circuit Court. During the hearing, according to Stipendiary Magistrate D. W. Kelly, the petty court at Grange Hill was surrounded by a "large mob collected principally of Females and boys" who threatened witnesses and interrupted the proceedings. When the Circuit Court met in Savanna-la-Mar, it had to be adjourned when crowds of up to 10,000 people, "male and female," filled the streets. A group of more than 1,800 people attacked thirty policemen and stoned the police station, broke windows, and vandalized its interior. As the custos put it, "Every person, male and female, amongst the laboring population, are now sympathising with the parties concerned in this movement and from all I can learn labor is at a standstill on the estates."[38] Because women were the backbone of the internal economy, shifting goods by foot between country and towns for tiny profits, added tolls were particularly burdensome to them.

In July 1859, another riot broke out during a court case in Falmouth. The "Rabble" freed prisoners from the lockup, assailed both police and magistrates, and stoned the houses of officials. Finally, they attacked the police station and battered in every window; twenty-two policemen holed up inside opened fire, killing two women and wounding others, one of whom later died; the deaths were ruled to be justifiable homicide.[39] Trials of the rioters revealed that women were prominent, including Emily Jackson, Mary Hoad, Margaret Anderson, Wilhemina Peterkin, Jessy Simpson, Isabella Campbell, Mary Frackis, Adelaide Benarm, Elize Lyon, Rebecca Saffery, Maria Chippendale, and Mary Campbell. Crowds involved in the disturbances were described by some witnesses as "principally female." Emily Jackson was singled out in the report of the inspector of police, who stated, "Emily Jackson was also most prominent, she was armed with this stick and flourishing it, she was very violent. She and Sutherland appears to be leadings [*sic*] the whole mob. The riot began with her that morning and she was one of those rescued in the first attack and rescue at the Cage in the morning."[40] She had to be forcibly removed from court after shouting, "Da Buckra commence the war and they must take all them get. This is nothing, before the week is out you will see the whole of the Maroons down here and they will make them fly." Her father was said to be a Maroon himself.[41]

In periods of drought and economic recession such as the early 1860s, the large unemployed population of the towns became especially apparent (and threatening) to the ruling elite. Working in what was largely an informal economy of higglering, domestic work, washing, sewing, and little documented but ever present prostitution, urban women were especially vulnerable to economic downturns. As the custos of Kingston reported in 1865, "Out of a population of 27,000 persons in Kingston, nearly one-half have nothing to do. Great hulking men and women may be seen in the different yards all day long, basking in the sun and picking each other's heads, alternating the singing of psalms with ribald and obscene songs."[42] Baptist missionaries described the "very precarious existence" of Spanish

Town's tradesmen and other residents, including "nearly 1,000 domestics, not half of whom were employed; 772 seamstresses, who got occasional work before the August and Christmas holidays; 422 laundresses, who were nearly all out of work; and 163 fishermen and fisherwomen" (Hall 1959: 213). The town "was pauper-stricken, with large numbers seeking relief." The newspaper editor Sidney Levien noted, "In every town there are hundreds of females who cannot obtain work, who are actually starving unless they ply the harlot's trade, the needle lying idle because of the fatuous obstinancy of the Governor and Government."[43] Out of this urban milieu emerged the politicized population who participated in the Underhill Meetings of 1865. Given that many of the complaints in the lead-up to the Morant Bay Rebellion concerned low wages, unfair terms of employment, lack of food and clothing, and failure of the courts to provide justice, it is not surprising that women again played a prominent part in protesting a system that threatened the very existence of their families (Heuman 1994; Sheller 2000).

Protest involved the entire community and emerged out of the popular justice of the street and the market, locales populated by women as well as men. Even before the events at Morant Bay, reports of "disturbances" in the western parishes led Governor Edward Eyre to send two war vessels. A custos reported one such incident in which women participated: "On the first day of August a large body of Negroes from the neighborhood . . . determined on proceeding to Black River accompanied by their wives and the women of the Neighborhood and that the purpose was that the women should take at the stores any thing they required. . . . The People allege that they have been informed that the Queen has sent out a large sum of money to be laid out in the purchase of lands to be divided among them and that the Custos has kept it for himself."[44] Here, a popular sense of justice was asserted through the symbolic act of a procession through the streets on the 1 August, a holiday commemorating the anniversary of emancipation. Due to their special role in the "moral economy" of the market, it was the *women* who were to take from the stores what was asserted to be their due, while the supposed good intentions of the queen were used to legitimize protest against local authority.

Women were again prominent during the events at Morant Bay in October 1865, as both Gad Heuman (1994) and Wilmot (1995) have carefully documented and my research confirms (Sheller 2000). As Heuman (1994: 185) notes,

At Morant Bay [women] threw stones at the volunteers, encouraged the men to continue fighting and were responsible for the burning down of the court house. Some had scores to settle: Elizabeth Faulkner wanted to kill a black shopkeeper "because of his dishonest business practices." Mary Ward and other women implicated in the killing of Charles Price complained that he had not paid them for their work. Swithin Wilmot has suggested that "women may have had their own agenda in addition to the general ones relating to land, low wages and oppressive and partial administration of the law."

Family ties may have been one important aspect of some women's participation in the Morant Bay Rebellion, as, for example, in the case of the Geoghagan family. It was James Geoghagan who shouted out in the Morant Bay Courthouse on 7 October 1865 that the defendant should not pay the costs of 12 shillings and 6 pence; he was ordered out of the court, and when he did not go quietly, the judge ordered his arrest. A policeman named John Burnett reported that he had said to Geoghagan, "You come here to cheek me always in this Court," and as Geoghagan was leaving the court, "his sister, called Isabella Geoghagan, came up directly and said, 'Come out of the Court, let us go down in the market, and let us see if any d—d policemen come here if we don't *lick* them to hell.' "[45] Her challenge clearly demonstrates the sense of women's control over the market as a public space in which, unlike the courts, popular justice could prevail; it was a threat backed not just by profanity but also by force, because once out in the market square, an armed mob indeed rescued James from police.

Isabella was not the only family member involved in the events at Morant Bay. A woman of the same surname was described by one of the volunteer militiamen as the "guide" or "leader" at the front of the crowd that marched into Morant Bay on 11 October. She threw the first stone at the militia, initiating the rebellion:

> Afterward we saw them coming round the corner into the Parade, with guns and bayonets fixed, sticks, swords, machettes, and lances; they were advancing, blowing shells and playing drums. How near did they get to you before anything was done?—About 20 yards, and a woman named Geoghagan . . .—Is that a person now living?—No, she is dead. What did she say or do?—She first fired a stone, and several other women followed her, and then the men rushed right in. . . . Whereabouts was this woman when she threw the stone?—She was just in front of us, in the north part of the Parade. Did she come up with the people?—She was the guide and led

them; she came up in front of them. But they did not want a guide?—She was a sort of leader. Well, she threw the first stone?—Yes. Then other women threw stones?—Yes.[46]

This woman was Letitia Geoghagan, the mother of Isabella, James, and another son, Charles. The British investigators seemed uncomfortable with the idea of a female leader, but the description makes it clear that Geoghagan's role was as a leader. She was tried by court-martial and sentenced to be hanged alongside one of her sons (Heuman 1994: 139). Wilmot (1995: 291) names other women, such as Rosanna Finlayson, Caroline Grant, and Sarah Johnson, who were also found to have been directly involved in the march into Morant Bay, the raid on the police station to get weapons, and the attack on the courthouse; a policeman even described Grant as "a queen of the rebels," perhaps using a popular title.

One striking aspect of initial reports on the rebellion at Morant Bay were the repeated descriptions of women taking a particularly "fiendish" part in the violence, often spread by hearsay and third-hand reports. The custos of Kingston, Dr. Bowerbank reported: "All parties agree that the most heartless and beastly atrocities committed by the blacks were done by the women, who in many cases mutilated the dead bodies."[47] Thomas Clark of the LMS reported (falsely, as it turned out), "One minister had his tongue cut out, while he was alive, by a Woman, who held it up in fiendish triumph."[48] Governor Eyre was especially influenced by such reports. In his initial dispatches, he compared the incident at Morant Bay to the Indian mutiny and added, "Women, as usual on such occasions, were even more barbarous and brutal than the men" (quoted in Fletcher 1867: 150). He even argued, "It is not pleasant to hear of women being flogged . . . but the evidence is that in the attack upon the Court-House some furies urged on the men, and in the after raids upon the estates they are responsible for much of [the] pillage."[49] Reverend Duncan Fletcher expressed his outrage at the actions of General Luke O'Connor who, in his military dispatch, stated that he had hanged a woman as an example to others, "not because she individually had been convicted of perpetrating these atrocities, but because 'women' were supposed to have perpetrated them, and, therefore, it seems, he thought it desirable to hang her as a warning, or punishment—what shall we say?—to those other women; the fact being that these atrocities which the women were supposed to have perpetrated, had not been perpetrated at all" (Fletcher 1867: 151). Indeed, the dispersed nature of women's networks of political mobilization and communication probably made it difficult to identify leaders, and the punishment of a few did send a message to the entire black community. The official demonization of black women suggests recognition of their community leadership and fear of their pervasive political influence.

Reports of women's involvement in "atrocities" and looting during the rebellion led to their harsh treatment by troops and courts of martial law. Papers published in London by the Jamaica Committee compiled excerpts from local newspapers with numerous reports of the flogging and execution of women. The *Colonial Standard* reported in October, "Prisoners are every day brought in, and those on hand left to be tried number over two hundred—a great many women among them," and in November, "Thirteen sentenced to be hanged, among these Jessie Taylor, the woman who, it was proved, sat on the late Charles A. Price's chest with a hatchet in her hand." In the end, seven women were hanged—Sarah Francis, Mary Ward, Letitia Geoghagan, Mary Ann Francis, Ellen Dawkins, Judy Edwards, and Justina (Jessie) Taylor (Heuman 1994: 139); thousands had their property destroyed by soldiers, and perhaps two hundred or three hundred women and girls were flogged (Jamaica Committee 1866: 23, 28; see also Harvey and Brewin 1867: 11–16; Heuman 1994). Edward Bean Underhill himself wrote to a colleague, "I am afraid that our newspapers will be too delicate in reporting the atrocities of which we hear. . . . I think English women ought to know how their black and coloured sisters have been treated."[50] There was particular concern for the case of Miss Roach, whose father, an Independent Wesleyan Methodist pastor, had been arrested for involvement in public meetings in Kingston. When informed of her father's arrest, she "imprudently gave vent to her feelings, and gave utterance to language that was very improper in such times." For this, she was taken into custody in Kingston, which was not under martial law, and conveyed to a military camp, "where martial law did exist; her clothes were turned up, thus exposing the person of a young and virtuous female in the presence of soldiers, and she was flogged on her bare person."[51] In 1866, when Thomas Harvey returned to investigate complaints in Jamaica, he found nearly thirty people in Port Antonio still "under sentence of Court Martial, chiefly women, some of them mothers of families who knew not what had become of their children" (Harvey and Brewin 1867: 11–16). Once again, the punishment of women became a prominent cause of complaint in England, where the Jamaica Committee demanded an official inquiry into the suppression of the rebellion and prosecuted Governor Eyre for his part in it (C. Hall 1992; Semmel 1962).

CONCLUSION

One year after the brutal suppression of the Morant Bay Rebellion, the *Gleaner* printed a parody letter to the editor in a white approximation of working-class speech, signed "Quasheba." Under the headline "Colour fe Colour," the erstwhile slogan of the defeated rebellion, the letter supposedly concerned a recent lecture by Reverend Samuel Holt at the East Queen Street Baptist Chapel. During a visit he made to England to raise money for a Jamaican co-operative marketing association, it was said, "white ladies" there had asked him whether "any Black men in Jamaica had married white women." The fictional "Quasheba" writes to "Massa Editor" to complain that her husband is "gwine to England fe marry one Bucra lady" since they "is all fe black man now, dem no care no mo fo de Bucra man, black man is de bess." The mock letter poses as a plea for white men's help and a warning to white women about black family life: "Dem nigger man is de real good for noting nega, dem tump and trash we al'time, dem cuss we mothus, dem make we labour for dem all time. . . . Dem take all de money and go a rum shop—gamble, drink and come home drunk den dey kick up de row, beat we, buse we, flog de picaninnies, and make we house jis like a hell."[52] This white Jamaican humor, in the long tradition of Quasheba jokes, simultaneously ridicules blacks' speech, families, working-class culture, and women who noisily butt into public space with their "private" grievances. It rests on the ideology of white women as "angels in the house," whose domestic life is heaven rather than hell, and it relegates men's violence and women's uncompensated domestic labor to the realm of the "nigger" family. It uses a standard repertoire of ridicule to disarm the threatening power of the real black women who participated in the recent rebellion, to criticize black men who travel to England seeking public support, and to warn off white women who become involved in colonial politics. As I explore further in the next chapter, it employs a discourse of racialized sexuality to police citizenship.

This parody raises questions about where we find the "voices" of black working-class women in the historical record. Contrary to this mock voice, the archives considered in this chapter suggest the strength of black family solidarity, associational cohesiveness, and community self-protection—with an understanding that violence against black women came most often from the wider white society. Accounts of black women's leadership and political protest exist precisely because of the contradictory position they occupied in the colonial symbolic mapping of social order and disorder.

Their words speak for themselves, while their troubled embedding in government archives, missionaries' correspondence, and newspapers suggests their powerful impact. In contrast to this ridicule of African Jamaican women's public political interventions, we can turn to the community-building work of the Bahamian political radical Robert Love (b. ca. 1839), who went to Jamaica in the 1890s as a medical doctor, publisher of the *Jamaica Advocate* newspaper, Anglican minister, and founder of the People's Convention (1898–1903), a public event held on the 1 August (Emancipation Day) in Jamaica. Wigmoore Francis cites the important research of Joyce Lumsden, who has shown that "women played very prominent roles" in these conventions; "Love systematically included female speakers in the lineup" and "published many of their speeches in his newspaper and as separate pamphlets" (Francis 2003: 118–19; Lumsden 1987, 1995). Robert Love's work built on popular traditions of women's citizenship from below and fostered women's continuing public roles as community activists and leaders.

This chapter has shown, first, that female agricultural laborers exploited a "discourse of domesticity" and took advantage of their special position as workers and mothers to organize collective action against labor coercion and protect their household autonomy. Second, Afro-Jamaican women promoted black empowerment within the dissenting churches and led efforts both to democratize decision making in the independent congregations and to pass down the African-rooted practices of their own communities. And third, urban working-class women were at the forefront of public protests and demonstrations against injustice and social inequality and suffered heavy state repression for their trouble.

While these three aspects of Afro-Jamaican women's public leadership and political protest between 1834 and 1865 may seem unrelated, they are in fact all part of a complex culture of resistance based on the strategic manipulation of points of tensions within the social, economic, and political structures of post-slavery Jamaica, particularly those revolving around gender and sexuality. By recognizing the depth and continuity of women's activism in Jamaica in the nineteenth century, whether in the roles of Quasheba, Mother, or Queen, we are in a better position to unravel later popular political mobilization. This history forces us not only to re-evaluate prevalent conceptions of women's "respectability" in the Caribbean, but also to re-examine assumptions (developed from European and North American experiences) about the supposed "silencing" and "exclusion" of women from the bourgeois public sphere. Enslaved women in Jamaica used the persona of Quasheba and the collective mobilization of defiant nursing mothers to challenge their enslavement. Apprenticed and freed women used the public and spiritual personas of Mother and Queen to defend their familial autonomy and spiritual agency. Despite the circumscription of their capacity to act as citizens, the women discussed in this chapter nonetheless challenged colonial institutions for the governance and control of reproduction and sexuality, rejecting the social positioning of black women in situations of racial, class, gender, and sexual subordination.

Questions of "mother work," childbearing, child rearing, and birth control remain central to racial politics throughout the Americas. To place this Jamaican women's history in a wider context, we could compare it to the struggle for reproductive rights in other post-slavery societies. Donna Haraway (1992: 95) notes that white women in the United States experienced patriarchy mainly as control over the reproduction of legitimate children. Black women, in contrast, "faced a broader social field of reproductive unfreedom, in which their children did not inherit the status of human in the founding hegemonic discourses of U.S. society. The problem of the black mother in this context is not simply her own status as subject, but also the status of her children and her sexual partners, male and female." Thus, "reproductive rights" for women of color include not simply the recent movement for choice in bearing children (or not), but a wider set of freedoms from "lynching, imprisonment, infant mortality, forced pregnancy, coercive sterilization, inadequate housing" (Haraway 1992: 95). The black feminist critique of the women's liberation movement of the 1970s showed the limits of the projects of "sexual emancipation" and "choice" insofar as they addressed only white heterosexual women's sexualities and choices.

Today, the situated knowledge grounded in the embodied labor of black women remains central to black feminist theorizing. Drawing on a large body of existing scholarship, Patricia Hill Collins (1990) effectively synthesizes a "black women's standpoint" on motherhood that includes five elements: the extension of motherhood beyond biological "bloodmothers" to also include "othermothers" and extended women-centered networks; the dilemmas of the mother–daughter relationship and socialization for survival; the link between black women's experiences as othermothers and their community work and political activism; the invocation of "Motherhood" as a symbol of power within African American communities; and the high personal costs of motherhood and the struggle to protect black children. However, it would be wrong to read this as a naturalization of motherhood and to read motherhood as the only grounds for Caribbean women's politicization. Collins's point is that a black women's standpoint is a consciously attained critical construct and is linked to community work and political activism. Nevertheless, it is important to remember that not all women choose to become mothers and that this basis for community building may feed into state projects that outlaw and marginalize nonreproductive sexualities.

The rich history presented here of women's emancipatory struggles in Jamaica brings out the extent to which emancipation from slavery and the citizenship that was supposed to proceed from it were never accomplished by a single legal proclamation. They required generations of mobilization, contestation, and often violent conflict. African Jamaican women as family members, as mothers, as sexual partners, as laborers, as rioters, as rebels, and as sacred healers played a central part in theorizing and enacting an embodied sense of freedom that built on their experiences of both production and reproduction, work and family, daily life and divinity. These practices of embodied freedom continue to offer a critical perspective on the violent impositions of state power on human bodies and show the extent to which the intersections of race, gender, and sexuality continue to form a key nexus of political struggle. They also offer us a window into the local communities and social inequalities that may have been marginalized internally within these familial discourses and practices of embodied freedom. In the next chapter, I turn to the ethnic others who were placed in an antagonistic position vis-à-vis the emancipated African Jamaican community and who became a foil against which black British subjects measured their freedom.

CHAPTER THREE

Her Majesty's Sable Subjects

One of the key advances in recent historiography of the Caribbean is the realization that enslaved, emancipated, and indentured peoples' struggles to escape exploitation are crucial to the entire story of the democratic expansion of freedom, rights, and citizenship in the Western world. When the story of modern freedom is retold from the perspective of the laboring people of the Caribbean, it becomes strikingly clear that these most marginalized people—enslaved sugar workers and domestic servants, washerwomen and coffee pickers, dockworkers and indentured laborers—seized the ideology of universal rights, the language of liberty, and the repertoires of national claim making, transformed them, and made them their own. As Laurent Dubois (2004a: 28) puts it, "The movement that transformed slaves into free citizens gave new content to the universalism that was the centerpiece of Republican political culture." By claiming and fighting for the rights of citizenship before those rights were granted to or bestowed on them, the enslaved people (and later free colonial subjects and postcolonial citizens) of the Caribbean pushed colonial and imperial states toward far more radical political projects than the framers of Western democratic nation-states had originally envisioned. They made our world what it is today by showing just how freedom could and should work—for all—and, as Anthony Bogues (2009) argues, by breaking new ground in political thought through their "quest against a specific form of domination of human beings which turned human beings into things, what Aimé Césaire has called the process of 'thingification'. It is that quest which is the overarching value of radical Caribbean political thought" (see, e.g., Cooper et al. 2000; Dubois 2004a, 2004b; Ferrer 1999; Holt 1992; R. Scott 1985; Sheller 2000).

The ideology and discourse of liberal citizenship, however—especially in its armed Republican mode—brought with it the baggage of the patriarchal family and masculine possessive individualism, a point that Bogues quickly brushes aside in his otherwise very valuable analysis of Caribbean political thought. Feminist theorists for some time have argued that cultural formations of masculinity are the keystone of European understandings and practices of citizenship, rights, and freedoms.[1] Gender distinctions were also central to the ideological and discursive construction of freedom in colonial societies, especially following the abolition of slavery. As I discuss in chapter 5, discourses of masculinity were crucial to the construction of republican citizenship and civic militarism in nineteenth-century Haiti, leading to the exclusion of Haitian women from full citizenship and civic participation (cf. Peabody 2005; and see Sheller 2000). Maggie Montesinos Sale likewise argues that in using liberal theory, African American men "were caught in recognizing the struggle for liberty as paradigmatically masculine and largely individual. This position led them rhetorically to marginalize black women, for example, by basing their arguments for inclusion on their rights 'as men'—which included the possession of female family members." Thus, they may have "radically contested white supremacy, but also reproduced masculine individualism" (Sale 1997: 201).[2] The silencing of women's more personal or private emancipation in contrast to the public valorization of masculine armed self-liberation has been perpetuated by historians who have enshrined narratives of rebellion and of armed resistance over and above everyday forms of political action.[3]

While historians have begun to analyze how gendered discourses and exclusions shaped post-emancipation citizenship and created specifically masculine free subjects, far less attention has been paid to how alternative masculinities informed competing efforts to define and enact freedom. Recently within the Caribbean, there was a period of growing interest in contemporary modes of so-called marginalized black masculinity (e.g., Lewis 2003; Miller 1987, 1992; Reddock 2004). Such arguments often rested on assumptions about the "demoralizing" undermining of patriarchal authority and "masculine pride" under slavery (Patterson 1973 [1967]: 167–68), which were then assumed to have continued into the female-headed households seen in the late nineteenth century and twentieth century. Jenny Jemmott (2009) makes a significant contribution to this field by challenging the thesis of men's marginality in nineteenth-century Jamaica. She argues that, despite limitations in the archives, much evidence is available showing that men played an active role as husbands, fathers, and family members in the post-slavery period. I made similar points in my study of popular claim making in mid-nineteenth-century Jamaica, wherein freed men often identified themselves as heads of households, fathers of families, and husbands (Sheller 2000). Yet by re-centering black masculinity, so to speak, historians should not overlook the ways in which a heteronormative and ethnocentric black masculinity that is aligned with British patriarchal subjectivity, forms of citizenship, and political agency may at the same time marginalize alternative masculinities. Few historians have explored the *multiplicity* of "marginalised (Black) masculinities"—and, we could add, homosexual, queer, non-black, and mixed-race masculinities— in the post-emancipation Caribbean (R. Burton 1997: 11; see also Beckles 1999: 157).

Notions of masculinity informed both elite and subaltern men's and women's conceptions of individual rights, freedom, and citizenship. These masculine discourses and practices of citizenship also intersected with constructions of racial, ethnic, and class boundaries within the colonial situation. Beneath the universalizing veneer of liberal citizenship, Jamaican men acted out their particular understanding of freedom in a context of gender, ethnic, and class conflict. This produced diverse experiences of embodied freedom for differently positioned subjects. Subaltern black masculinity is often examined solely in relation to dominant white masculinity, with little indication that there might be multiple orderings of gender in relation to others who are marked as neither black nor white, such as indentured Indians or liberated Africans. Crucially, Caribbean historiography must recognize that the region is not only "black" or "Christian," or part of an Afro-Caribbean–African American nexus. It also includes non-African constituents of Asian and Indian origin, and Muslim and Hindu faiths, as well as Africans of Muslim and animist faiths. Far fewer histories exist of these other Caribbean subaltern groups, especially in regard to their gender formations and racial positioning (though see Look Lai 1993; Mehta 2004; Mohammed 1995; Schuler 1980; Shepherd 1987, 1994).

As Orlando Patterson (1991: 405) suggests, the very freedoms celebrated as citizenship often "tragically require the *them* who do not belong: the ignoble, the nonkith, the nonkin, the people we do not marry, the alien within—the Jew, the Slav, the slave, the Negro, the people who cannot vote—who demarcate what *we* are, the domestic enemy who defines whom *we* love." Thus, I want to appropriate the language of men's marginality but turn our attention against the grain toward *those men who are excluded from dominant forms of free black masculinity*. This can help us to understand how the dominant forms of modern heteromasculinity arose through processes of stigmatizing other groups of men, including those identified as sexual or ethnic minorities, which arguably has continued to fuel patterns of intracommunal violence in the contemporary Caribbean.

This chapter examines how the production and performance of post-emancipation masculinities depended on the intersectionality of a variety of different principles of inclusion and exclusion. Freedom was experienced differently by men and by women, but there were also multiple masculinities in competition with each other (Sinha 2007). By masculinities, I refer to embodied practices and discourses that serve to differentiate men from women (and boys) and that are linked to what Robert Connell (1995) calls "gender projects." Such projects serve to mark out a particular "place in gender relations," including performances of dominant or subaltern positions, different class positions, and ethnic identifications (see also Butler 1990; Mercer 1994). Rather than concentrating solely on the consolidation of whiteness against blackness, or masculinity against femininity, therefore, I explore here how Afro-Jamaican men's freedom was strategically articulated in relation to both newly arrived liberated Africans and indentured laborers from India, referred to as "Coolies." Freedom is relationally defined and provisionally practiced within a constellation of others who are more or less free, each freedom always circumscribed by relations of gender, class, ethnicity, and racialization. It is at these (marginal) points that we might pry apart the dense junctures of interlocking gender, racial, moral, and political orders that still inform (neo)liberal and postcolonial discourses of citizenship today.

Sara Ahmed (2000: 44) argues that "bodies become differentiated not only *from each other* or *the other*, but also through differentiating *between others*. . . . Difference is not simply found in the body, but is established as a relation between bodies." How did working-class black masculinity in Jamaica, Guyana, or Trinidad, for example, come to be enacted as Christian and British through an exclusion of the Coolie? How was free black Jamaican masculinity not only measured as a kind of distance from white men or a proximity to black women, but also marked as a relation of hostility toward indentured Asian and African others? My analysis of these distinctions between *particular others* will show that freedom is not an absolute condition that is generic in its effects. It is experienced and lived in specifically embodied ways, governed by—and performed within—intersecting gender orders, racial orders, moral orders, and political orders. Thus, the instituted practices of citizenship, embedded in everyday discourses and practices, inevitably produce inequalities alongside claims to political equality.

This chapter draws on government and missionary sources from the late 1830s to the mid-1860s, including the records of missionaries, governors, and other civil functionaries, but also popular petitions, records of public speeches, resolutions of public meetings, and items in newspapers, all of which have hints of the frictions within understandings of gender, race, and freedom. In them we see the effects of multiple subaltern positions within structures of dominant discourse. Through close readings of the tensions within these public texts and their official reception, I will consider how popular ideals of freedom converged around particular practices of masculinity. Tracking these subaltern (yet mainly masculine) embodied practices of citizenship through official archives, we can begin to explore the complexities of how class, gender, and racial/ethnic orders intersected in the relational constitution of subaltern freedom(s). This situated analysis of masculinities in practice can complement more general analyses of Anglo-American liberalism with a fuller account of how Jamaican freed men drew on an identity as British subjects to gain political leverage out of a certain kind of masculine identity. In chapter 5 I will conduct a similar situated analysis of Haitian discourses of masculinity in relation to ideologies of republicanism and the forging of an identity as Haitian citizen.

In identifying themselves as black, British, and Christian citizens, these freed men marked off their proximity to the white elite but also their distance from heathen foreigners (including Hindu, Muslim, and indigenous African faiths), from male indentured migrants, and from women. Indeed, their insistence on a Christian identity is a point often overlooked in most political histories of emancipation, which focus on the state-centered claims of citizens and thus miss the vehement exclusion of non-Christians. If in performing free masculinity Afro-Jamaican men were constrained by dominant racial and gender ideologies (even as they struggled against them), they nevertheless reconfigured the possibilities within colonizing ideologies and rewrote the scripts of citizenship. Like the Jamaican women considered in chapter 2, in trying to use existing political opportunities and participatory possibilities to their advantage, they challenged the existing order in some ways but nevertheless reproduced some of its heteronormative assumptions and its ethnically exclusive limitations.

Citizenship today is often understood as a set of discourses and legal rights that are enacted via scripts involving competing claimants, sometimes referred to, following Charles Tilly, as repertoires of contention. Rather than something dreamed up by political philosophers and granted by benevolent states to their population (as the rise of universal citizenship is sometimes retrospectively narrated), the making of free citizens is more like a tug-of-war in which a few inches of ground at a time are won and lost, until a sudden surge (such as slave emancipation) yanks the deadlock in one direction or another. It is a battle won not simply through armed force, although that is part of it, but, more important, through public debate that seeks to legitimate certain kinds of claims about who is a recognized participant. This chapter explores how counter-hegemonic performances of citizenship and improvisations on its repertoires expanded the idea of rights and re-created the meaning of freedom—yet nevertheless remained constrained in certain ways by gendered and racialized discourses of masculinity. Rather than reading the violence of contemporary ethnosexual politics as a dysfunctional outcome of slavery or post-slave cultures, therefore, I aim to show how in the very process of performing citizenship from below freed men gained power in ways that inadvertently consolidated other kinds of social inequality, ethnic exclusion, and erotic domination.

FAMILY AND GENDER IN LIBERAL/COLONIAL IDEOLOGY

Histories of gender and post-emancipation politics in the United States "suggest the centrality of ideologies about gender, households, and domesticity to constituting Anglo-American social orders more generally and political order in particular" (Holt 2000: 57; see, e.g., Bardaglio 1995; Edwards 1997; Gilmore 1996; Stanley 1998). Drawing on Jürgen Habermas's suggestive (but rather underdeveloped) analysis of the formation of "public man" within "the interiority of the [patriarchal] conjugal family," Thomas Holt (2000: 38) argues that classical liberalism "served colonial policymakers as an essential guide in the transition from slavery to free labor" insofar as they presumed that "stable social orders depended on the character of the citizens constituting the polity, and the stability of character depended on the efficacy of the key institutions that made the citizen"— above all, the family.[4] Colonial policymakers argued that public virtue (and well-ordered society) could only arise out of an orderly (and separate) private sphere based on idealized attributes of masculinity and femininity. Holt shows how British colonial governors, missionaries, and civil servants first tried to impose this familial model, then highlighted Afro-Caribbean deviation from the white bourgeois norm of the patriarchal family to deny full political freedom to former slaves.[5]

Studies of British colonialism have also demonstrated precisely how shifting ideological articulations of gender and racial differences structured white elite understandings of freedom and individual subjectivity (Ferguson 1992; Hall 1992, 2002; Holt 1992; McClintock 1995). In particular, the notion of masculinity was central to the construction of liberal ideologies of citizenship centered on the free white male individual, and this idea of masculinity was rooted in the bourgeois patriarchal family. Catherine Hall (2002: 125) especially has shown how the abolitionist dream of a new post-emancipation society rested on a gender order in which "black men would become like white men, not the whites of the plantations but the whites of the abolitionist movement, responsible, industrious, independent, Christian; and in which black women would become like white women, not the decadent ladies of plantation society . . . but the white women of the abolitionist imagination, occupying their small but satisfying separate sphere, married and living in regular households." When that new order arrived with the abolition of slavery in 1834, European writers like Anthony Trollope argued plainly that civilization would only proceed in the colonized world on the basis of "a clear gender order with breadwinning husband and father and domesticated wife and mother" (Hall 2002: 219). In this regard, ideologies and moralities surrounding the family, gender, and sexuality were foundational to the project of emancipation, and to the extension of citizenship to the formerly enslaved.

With the unfolding of the emancipation experiment, as some at the time saw it, the classical liberal doctrines of political freedom and citizenship that inform Anglo-American politics were gradually transformed. Throughout the years of Britain's antislavery movement, interim institution of apprenticeship (1834–38), and early decades of emancipation, British liberalism was articulated in relation to those colonial processes. In Jamaica, struggles over freedom were from the start tightly entangled with struggles over family formation and gender systems. Most studies, though, focus on the local effects of dominant formations of white patriarchal masculinity in a colonial or imperial context. While there were continuous (usually heavy-handed) efforts by missionaries and colonial governments to impose their own ideals of Christian marriage and patriarchal domesticity on the post-slavery peasantry and urban working class, black working-class Jamaicans clearly recognized the contradictions within this "civilizing project." They at times explicitly rejected it but more often adapted it to their own purposes (see, e.g., Austin-Broos 1997; Besson 2002; R. Burton 1997: 90–115; Hall 2002; Sheller 2000).

In her rich analysis of religion and moral orders in Jamaica, Diane Austin-Broos (1997: 199–200) suggests that, for those Jamaican men who identified with the church, marriage came to be "a symbol of moral elevation" and a guarantor of status. "As the plantation system declined in the period after emancipation," she argues, "the [Christian] missions' democratization of marriage had its greatest impact in the brown middle class and among those more prosperous farmers, many of whom lived in the free church villages." Here a family form emerged that mirrored a Victorian model with a sole male wage earner: "The picture which emerges is reminiscent of the respectable Victorian working class family where the husband was a sober and steady person in regular employment. The atmosphere is markedly religious and . . . patriarchal. . . . The maintenance of this type of domestic group is in part governed by the regularity of the man's employment so that there is an economic stability in the family" (Austin-Broos 1997: 200). As men moved into positions of freedom, in other words, they were also beginning to exercise certain male prerogatives of patriarchal household control. In Jamaica, the patriarchal family was underscored, for some, by Christian beliefs in the sanctity of marriage. The missionaries' concern with "re-ordering Black lower-class sexual relations," according to Austin-Broos, subsequently became "a central characteristic not only of Pentecostalism but also of Marcus Garvey's black separatism and of the Rastafarian movement. All have sought a subordination and privatization of women as an integral part of redemption" (Austin-Broos 1997: 192; cf. Chevannes 1998).

Bridget Brereton (1999: 107), in contrast, argues that "ex-slave men and women were not blindly obeying hegemonic gender ideologies nor seeking to transform freedwomen into dependent housewives confined to the home. They were pursuing rational family strategies aimed at securing the survival and welfare of their kin groups, in the face of appalling odds." Jean Besson (2002) also makes a strong case for the participation of Afro-Jamaican women in opposition, resistance, and culture building through the practices of kinship, family land, and Revivalism. Rather than seeing these as mutually exclusive understandings of Jamaican culture, it may be more fruitful to see them as opposing poles of a discursive field in which

Jamaicans themselves had to stake out gendered and racialized subject positions. The patriarchal conjugal family with a male head supported by the invisible, non-waged labor of female kin and children became one recognized basis on which freedom could be most effectively secured, especially for the "brown" middle class. But it was not the only discursive strategy available. Competing with it was the kind of oppositional culture building that Besson so doggedly tracks, and that I have traced in chapter 2. Also running alongside gender ideologies, moreover, were other kinds of languages of exclusivity and privilege, which perhaps have been overlooked.

In the struggle to become free citizens, black men narrated their own qualifications as free British subjects not only through the marking of differences between men and women, but also through explicit differentiations between the status of native and foreign, free and indentured, Christian and heathen, Negro and Coolie. They resorted to a Christian and nativist discourse of manhood to insert themselves into British political discourses that emphasized a kind of active masculine citizenship (cf. Rose 2007). In laying claim to Christian citizenship, freedom came to be constituted not only through a subordination of women, but also through an equally problematic nationalistic exclusion of foreigners and "heathens." Due to the silence of the archival sources, we can only guess at the place of homosexuality within such subject formations in the nineteenth century, but it seems plausible that the violent expulsion of men who have sex with men from the Jamaican public sphere today has its roots in these nineteenth-century formations of black Christian masculinity and its close association with heteronormative national citizenship.

BECOMING CHRISTIAN SUBJECTS

In the 1840s, a government-sponsored immigration scheme brought thousands of indentured laborers from India to Jamaican plantations. In 1845, 261 Indian workers arrived in Jamaica out of a total of 606 government-recruited migrants; in 1846, there were 1,890 Indians out of 2,441 total immigrants; and in 1847, there were 2,400 Indians out of 2,509 total immigrants. Between 1840 and 1852, 14,132 East Indians entered Jamaica, and overall up to the ending of indenture in 1916, approximately 37,000 East Indians entered Jamaica under five-year contracts that were renewable, of whom about 60 percent remained in Jamaica when their contracts expired.[6] Although there was less use of indentured labor in Jamaica than in British Guiana or Trinidad, which were experiencing growth in sugar production, this still had a significant impact on the black working class (Tinker 1993 [1974]: 81; see also Look Lai 1993; Northrup 1995; Rodney 1981; Shepherd 1994). Combined with the drop in sugar prices resulting from the Sugar Duties Act of 1846, this indentured immigration contributed to downward pressure on the wages of recently emancipated laborers and to heated political debates.

Not surprisingly, conflicts arose between those who had been enslaved on the plantations and the new arrivals who were being brought in at taxpayers' expense, a system that in effect subsidized the planter class while undercutting the autonomy of the freed laborers. This conflict initiated an ideological debate about the meaning of freedom, which had a crucial impact on the gender order and moral order of Jamaicans. Popular understandings of gender roles and the family were not simply articulated in relation to European values and Jamaican cultures of resistance; they were also set in a context in which new indentured communities offered a negative model in which "native" virtue and citizenship rights could be measured against these other others.

The planters' first initiative was to employ liberated Africans—that is, those who had been captured from slaving ships and could be signed up for contracts of indenture (Schuler 1980). The early response shows that freed people linked a critique of indenture to the question of familial autonomy and self-determination; they also seem initially to have recognized a certain kinship between themselves and the liberated Africans. Various missionary societies competed to instruct, convert, and baptize the Africans and became interested in their familial and marital status.[7] In a meeting held at Reverend Knibb's Baptist Chapel in Falmouth in February 1840, there were general complaints about the planter's "system of oppression" and specific concerns about the regulation of "captured Africans," in particular that their families should not be broken up.[8] In Falmouth, a crowd pelted police who were mistreating indentured Africans who had been arrested following an incident in which they had fled their estate.[9] A meeting of the Baptist Western Union at Oracabessa in July 1840 complained about the treatment of the Africans, who by law should have been free. The meeting resolved that "the apprenticeship to which the said Africans are subjected, is very little better in principle, and in many respects worse in practice, than that from which the labouring population of these colonies have recently been delivered; that husbands are liable to be separated from their wives."[10] In both of these cases, Baptist congregations interpreted the breaking up of families as a continuation of slavery, showing how crucial family sanctity and autonomy were to their idea of freedom.

Because the supply of captured Africans was small, however, planters next turned to the importation of indentured laborers from other parts of the British Empire. Despite the initial demonstrations of fellowship with the indentured Africans, some workers began to draw unfavorable contrasts between hardworking native Jamaican Christians and the "heathen Coolies" who began to take work on the plantations. The Baptists played a crucial part in the emerging discourse that positioned the "free man" specifically as Christian. The *Baptist Herald and Friend of Africa*, first launched in September 1839, described itself as a "cheap publication" aimed at the "labouring population" to advance the "Christian public."[11] It used a highly gendered *and* ethnonational language of English and Christian manhood in addressing the newly emancipated Jamaican peasantry as British subjects and electors. For example, in a letter to the "Electors of Jamaica" printed on 4 July 1844, the writer observed: "That which will give the man of true English spirit the highest gratification, is the circumstance of being permitted to address a body of men—holding the high position of electors, in a free country, as fellow citizens, who only a few years since, were enduring all the ignominy, and wrongs of slavery." In embracing his fellow citizens, the writer marks them as "men" and as "English," and therefore deserving. The letter continues:

> Electors of Jamaica, act a part worthy of freemen. The cause of liberty demands it of you. The cause of humanity throughout the world demands it of you. . . . If you act as Christian citizens, you have it in your power to seal the doom of slavery. You have the opportunity of demonstrating to the world, that the sons of Africa are capable of exercising the rights of citizens, even in a free, civilized community; . . . and you shall see your brethren, who are yet in bondage, before long, emerge from the degradation of slavery, and taking their position by your side in the rank of *men*, shall be animated by your example to aspire to a noble elevation among the nations of the earth.[12]

Such public discourses presented a model of Christian manhood that required action on the part of the recently freed both to demonstrate their manliness and to further the liberty of their African brethren who were still in bonds—particularly those enslaved in the United States, the presumed target of this Fourth of July address. Only those capable of exercising their rights can join the "rank of men," and only those belonging to that rank are capable of forming a "free, civilized community," one made up of "Christian citizens."

Freedom thus required men to act out their citizenship in a way that marked both gender and ethnic/religious difference, and that brought with it benefits as well as costs. The letter continues: "Let the next House of Assembly be men who, instead of wasting upwards of £111,917 in a cruel and useless scheme of immigration, will apply it to the improvement of native agriculture, the encouragement of native institutions, and the development of the native resources of the Island." The writer here makes a native-versus-immigrant dichotomy fundamental to the freed man's exercise of his rights: Not only will he take up his free manhood by voting, but he will also protect his native interests. The structure of claims to empowerment in the British colonial political context privileged a loyal, longstanding, Anglo-Jamaican subject. Just as men asserted their freedom at the expense of women, so did they claim British belonging against (and at the expense of) more recent migrants from Africa and India. As much as freedom was about being and acting manly, it was also about laying claim to being "British" and "Christian."

In a more subtle sense, acting as a free man also involved becoming "black" insofar as a black Jamaican identity was elicited both in resistance to the white elite and in opposition to African or "Coolie" migrants. Whereas Afro-Jamaican women had largely switched from plantation fieldwork into subsistence farming and marketing, as well as domestic service, indentured African and Indian women were likely to be engaged in such menial and poorly paid plantation tasks as weeding and carrying loads.[13] Thus, the arrival of indentured workers in Jamaica, living in communities with distinctive patterns of gender relations and work, was seen as undermining the new gender order on which a free society was being built (and the new gender distinctions for which women had fought, as seen in chapter 2). As early as 1847, a riot was reported "among Coolies on Bogue Estate," in which they reportedly attacked "any and all Blacks," who in turn attacked them. There were fifteen severe broken skulls and bones, and the indentured workers involved were fined between two and three pounds or imprisoned for twenty-eight to thirty days with hard labor.[14] By this time, the British market had been opened to foreign sugar (produced by slaves), sugar prices had fallen, and Jamaican plantations were beginning to fail. Many laborers were without work. Although native workers mainly directed their anger at the planters and the white-dominated colonial government, they also at times vented it on the indentured workers themselves.

A public meeting was held in December 1847 at the Brownsville Presbyterian Chapel at which planters gathered their workers together to explain the crisis. Some laborers spoke, too, about the need to stand behind the plantations and called on their fellow workers to work longer days and to do two tasks a day, if necessary, to save the failing estates. However, the majority of workers objected, including Ronald McArthur, a laborer from Retrieve Estate, who stated:

> Jamaica ruined for true, and who to blame? . . . Attorney bring Coolies to take their work and their bread—they make good house for Coolies, but anything good enough for we Black nega.—Now Coolie is the ruination of Jamaica—Coolie never can work with we; Black people can work round about them; them is the most worthlessest set a people we ever saw,—them can't work, and yet attorney give them fine house and a shilling a day for doing nothing. . . . Send back the Coolies, them robbers that are brought to this country and leave the country to us, and give us fair play and regular wages, and Jamaica will stand good again.[15]

McArthur's words indicate a competition for labor, which also hinged on access to good housing and "fair play." The planters' call for regular labor is met here with the workers' demand for regular wages, yet it is played out in a contest of worthiness between Creole and Coolie labor.

The highly significant identity of "we Black nega" in this speech is defined against the foreign Coolies through the question of who can perform better work. McArthur then called on the others to sign a petition, stating, "I am not afraid to sign this petition, because nobody can take our free from us." By naming themselves as the "emancipated labourers of this district of Jamaica," the act of petitioning became a way to assert "our free." It called on Britain not to equalize the duties on sugar, which was "conferring a boon to the [foreign] slave-holder" at the expense of those "elevated to the rank of free-born British subjects." This "elevated" British identity is in marked contrast to the debased Coolies and allows the emancipated Jamaicans to make a political claim that sets them apart from (and morally raises them above) indentured labor and foreign slave labor. If citizenship here is percolating up from below, it is doing so at the expense of others who are pushed down further.

Such debates simmered over the next decade and led the Creole and

Indian populations to distrust each other. When an "apprehended out-break" was detected in the Western parishes in the tumultuous year of 1848, some planters indicated that falling wages were a major grievance, but also that work was being given to Coolies and to Portuguese immigrants. In response, Governor Charles Edward Grey issued a public proclamation calling on the "good Subjects of Her Majesty" to "abhor and prevent the employment of violence or Threatening Language to others . . . [and to] endeavour, by soberness and steadiness of Demeanour, and by Prudence of Conduct and of Language to shew that they are worthy to sustain the character of Freemen, and to be the Fathers of Free Families."[16] Once again, a governor was closely linking civic participation and a civil society in colonial Jamaica to men's private character, based on their role in the patriarchal family. From the white elites' point of view, it remained open to debate whether black men could claim such a character, and on this hinged their claim to the rights of British citizenship. While Jemmott (2009) also identifies the extent and significance of such familial discourses among black men in this period, she does not examine the problematic exclusions inherent in being good "Fathers of Free Families." By setting themselves apart from the Coolies, native Jamaican men tried to assert their Christian character and their claim to British rights, yet they increasingly framed freedom less as a universal right of man than as a special privilege and exclusive right of British men, as good fathers of Christian families.

HEATHENS AND SAVAGES

Economic conditions were poor enough that thousands of men left Ja-maica between 1850 and 1855, recruited to work on the Panama Railroad that was being built across the isthmus by a U.S. joint-stock company. They were offered enticing wages of three shillings and two pence per day, with promises of food and medical attendance, but many died in Panama, where worker mortality was extremely high (Petras 1988: 49, 52). The colonial elite's supposed desire for stable families could hardly be sustained in such an environment. The growing lack of well-paid work for men exacerbated ethnic conflicts in the late 1850s. When a new immigration bill was proposed in 1858, many Jamaicans mobilized in opposition to it. Rev-erend J. E. Henderson, for example, prepared two memorials to the queen from his congregations in Saint James against the bill. In it he wrote that "the Immigrants it is proposed to bring are Heathens and Savages who will of course attend to their idolatrous customs in our very midst and set an example before our young people and children that must be most injurious."[17] The missionary project of building respectable Christian families, a key tenet of liberal ideologies of the deserving citizen, was framed as being undercut by heathen Indians. Building free black Christian families thus depended on the exclusion of these "Savages."

As Rebecca Scott (2000) argues in relation to the very different forms of racial marking that occurred in post-slavery Louisiana and Cuba, racial boundaries and meanings cannot be assumed, but come out of on-the-ground relations that are always contingent. The contingencies of those on-the-ground relations were fought out in a war of words in which subaltern citizens carved out claims to legitimacy in the public sphere. Marks of racial and ethnic difference were wielded to exclude Coolies from a place in British Christian civil society. The memorial went on to note that "the proposed Immigrants will not be free men and the disputes which may occur between them and their masters are to be settled on the property where they occur, and not in the public courts of the Island, thereby opening the door for a repetition of all those abuses which occurred under the old apprenticeship system." Thus, a key complaint against the indentured immigrants was that they were both un-Christian and unfree, thereby undermining the freedom that had been won by native Jamaicans. The emancipated laborers of Jamaica, however, could not simply depend on missionaries to represent them; their freedom had to be enacted through masculine citizenship. The rights and privileges of freedom also entailed duties and obligations for men: to earn a living, to support a family, to marry, and to take an active part in politics.

Distancing themselves from savagery and underlining their civility became crucial means for freed men to "act a part worthy of freemen," and the family played a central part in this framework. For example, a petition to Governor Charles Darling from the "Mechanics and Peasantries" in 1859 refers to the governor as "a husband, a father, a philanthropist, consequently a good man." The petitioners indicate a distinctive view of manhood as a foundation of a good society. They speak as "loyal British Subjects" of the injustice under which "every oppressive means must be employed to trample and reduce our aspiring to manhood" and state that they hold Emancipation Day, "the First of August as dear to us, as an English man does Magna Charter." The same group also petitioned the queen in a document with more than a thousand signatures.[18] Opening with an elaborate profession of loyalty to the queen and gratitude to the British nation, the petitioners assure that "we shall endeavour to use our positions as British subjects and strive to evince by our loyal conduct how much we prize and value our privileges as free people." Like the black insurgent protagonists described by Laurent Dubois in revolutionary Saint-Domingue and Guadeloupe, these Jamaicans also performatively "expressed themselves by speaking and acting—uninvited—in the name of the [British] nation, and in so doing they [tried to bring about] the declarations that officially made them part of that nation" (Dubois 2004a: 89).

Though clearly claiming Britishness, they nevertheless also refer to themselves in the distinctive stylization as "Your Majesty's sable subjects of Jamaica, of African descent." This is a fascinating example of what Jean Besson (2002) refers to as African Caribbean culture building, re-scripting British political language and giving new content to the ideology and symbols of British citizenship by inserting their own Jamaican subjectivity into it. A local official informed the governor that the people involved were "more a class of yeomanry than in the ordinary sense of the word a peasantry. Possessing freeholds ranging from 1, 2, 5, to 15 and 20 acres some of them, many can read and write, whose names have been used."[19] Other reports on the petitioners indicate that they had collected money to form a delegation to present the petitions and had formed a "females and juveniles Committee" to sign testimonials of attachment to the queen. This gender distinction shows a clear differentiation in the forms by which men and women could partake in politics (women, of course, could not vote or hold office), but it also indicates a capacity for women to have some public voice.

Crucially, in speaking of their "political liberty," "privileges," and "rights," these petitioners frame themselves not only as free men, but also as heads of households. They refer to the joy of "sit[ting] with all that are dear and near to us around our family hearth without fear of molestation, notwithstanding all that have been done to prevent it." Furthermore, they describe their familial aspirations in these terms: "To us it is a great deal to have something which we can call our own; something which can keep us employed and from which we may, in consequence derive our honest lively-hood for ourselves and family. All our necessities are in a manner derived from the soil; the Mechanic, or the peasant, who owns a hut and a few acres of land, feels himself contented being certain of a home and food." The petitioners emphasize the importance of a man's ability to work and to support his family as crucial aspects of their understanding of what freedom means and of how best it is to be lived. Here we see the linkage of the institution of "family land" (Besson 2002) to a particular vision of the family and domes-

ticity, in which the male breadwinner was central. It suggests an oppositional milieu of distinctive African-Jamaican culture building, yet one that
in addressing the state speaks in the language of the Christian patriarchal
family ideal.

This ideal was under threat from low wages, heavy taxation, and labor
competition, all of which were associated with the importation of indentured workers. As a stipendiary magistrate reported in 1859, the "rate of
wages still averages at one shilling per diem for a Male Adult and from nine
pence to six pence per day for a Female." He also noted that "on many
Estates they employ women to carry canes and trash, etc., work that even in
the time of Slavery was usually performed by Mules and light carts."[20]
These wage rates and gendered divisions of labor remind us of the degree
to which women were at a disadvantage in the labor market and often had
to piece together a living through a variety of formal and informal means,
combining some plantation labor with growing, processing, and marketing their own crops, taking in washing, or working in other people's
homes. Impervious to these realities and following his previous condescending and dismissive form, Governor Darling refused to see the deputa-
tion and told the Colonial Office to ignore the petitions because their
"genuineness and authenticity" were questionable and he blamed them on
"a few Agitators."

In response to the political claims of the emancipated laborers, the government stepped up its immigration schemes and increasingly excluded
"Negro" subjects from the rights and privileges of British citizenship. When
a violent incident occurred in Falmouth in August 1859, Governor Darling
described it in language clearly influenced by the reaction to the "Indian
Mutiny" of 1857. In reporting that the police shot dead three women and
wounded many others in suppressing the riot, Darling wrote:

> I deeply regret to have to acquaint Your Grace, that one of those Outbreaks
> against Law and Authority, to which the excitable and easily misguided
> Population of the West Indian Colonies are peculiarly subject has recently
> occurred in the Town of Falmouth. . . . The only explanation of the insen-
> sibility to consequences whether immediate or more remote, which these
> deluded people appear to have exhibited, must be sought for I apprehend
> in their ethnological characteristics; prominent amongst which, are an
> incapacity to exercise forethought and reflection, amounting practically to
> an utter disregard of results; and a temperament so excitable as to render it
> an easy task to arouse their passions to a perfectly uncontrollable pitch. In

these two peculiarities, highly developed as they are in the African, whether indigenous or imported from the original country, lie the foundations of nine-tenths of the serious crime and outrage which at intervals (happily not frequent) present a disgraceful contrast to the generally peaceable and loyal demeanour of the laboring classes of our Tropical Communities.[21]

Given such a discourse of African savagery and the distinctiveness of the colonies, it stands to reason that the "peaceable and loyal" laboring classes would emphasize their native British status when addressing the government. An alternative black Christian moral order placed the family at the center of its ideology of freedom, while the white elite justified the shooting of women on the basis of the "ethnological characteristics" of some of the populace of "our Tropical Communities." Civility and savagery were very much in play here, in a period when the status of laborers across the British empire was undergoing new forms of racialization (C. Hall 1992, 2002).

A few white sympathizers spoke out for the "voiceless" Coolies, many of whom did not speak English. The Jewish newspaper editor Sidney Levien (whom I will return to in chapter 4) reported of the indentured immigrants "One must see—as those who live in Montego Bay cannot close their eyes to—these wretched, hungry, houseless and outcast spectres picking up in the street a chance bone, or any putrid offal they may fall in with, to realise the suffering they hourly undergo from want of sustenance." He was unsuccessfully prosecuted for libel, as was Reverend Henry Clarke, who wrote in a newspaper in 1862 that the Coolies were "cheated, starved, flogged, and murdered." Clarke observed that "the mere fact of [an indentured laborer] having complained to me against an overseer is a complete bar on his being employed on any other estate."[22] In 1866, Thomas Harvey and William Brewin noted that "[the Coolies] have been cruelly treated, have wandered away, exposed their destitution in the western towns of the island, and have died off in numbers, so that now few remain. A faithful history of coolie immigration to Jamaica would be a sad record of human suffering and waste of life" (Harvey and Brewin 1867: 43–44).[23] The indentured workers clearly did not enjoy the same political voice and wage-bargaining power as native laborers and had few means of redress against the planters. They could not claim rights of citizenship as native Jamaicans could and had little familiarity with British political practices such as petitioning.

African migrants also remained foreign and marginal. A petition to the governor from indentured African laborers in Vere in 1865 refers to their being in the island for seventeen years, but notes that as "Foreigners" they can only beg the Governor's "pity." The petitioners refer to "great distress and poverty on account of not getting sufficient work to do so as to enable us to maintain our famil[ies]." "Our Wages on some Estate this crop is from three to four shillings per week," they explain, "which cannot maintain a man and his family for the week." And they point out that the "large quantity of Coolies located on the several Estates had caused us to go about wandering for work." The petition was submitted "on account of ourselves and family" and signed by thirty-eight men, who indicated next to their names (all standard English) whether they had wives or "housekeepers" (i.e., unmarried partners) and their number of children. Interestingly, though, the ten men with wives are listed first (with a total of thirty-four children among them), followed by sixteen men with housekeepers (with a total of thirty-three children), and a few are listed as "alone" (only one lone man is listed as having children). This ranking would seem to indicate either that marriage carried a certain amount of status or, more precisely, that those men with more status could afford church weddings to mark their standing in the community. The fact that they listed their unwed housekeepers and therefore illegitimate children in a public document reflects a stunning departure from British Christian norms of the period and shows an unfamiliarity with the normal protocols of the British petition.

They also employ a family discourse of the male provider in making claims on the government. It is possible that their wives and housekeepers were not earning wages, but it may also be the case that wage earning simply was not seen as centrally defining women's identities as family members, whereas it was crucial for the men. In any event, the governor once again treated this subaltern petition as an "untrustworthy" document "purporting to be a spontaneous emanation from the Peasantry, but in reality got up by designing persons to serve their purposes."[24] In these subaltern petitions, we see men attempting to represent the needs of their families and communities using British modes of public address that are Christian, bourgeois, and masculine in design, though also in some ways departing from the model. The petitioners lay claim to a male and Christian identity but are refused recognition. Even this meager speaking position was not available to the wives, housekeepers, and families for whom these men claimed to speak; nor was it available to the indentured laborers who were excluded from the Christian and independent masculine bases of citizenship. It is in the gaps and fissures of the historical record, as well as in the subject positions that are laid claim to, that we can see most clearly how the inscription and reproduction of gender, racial, ethnic, and sexual subjectivities took place.

GENDER, RACIAL, AND MORAL ORDERS
IN THE MAKING OF FREE CITIZENS

Contrary to government aspersions on the character of the free population, these speeches, petitions, and public interventions indicate a strong commitment to family and kin and a moral discourse founded on distinctive views of the workingman's responsibilities to his family, whether or not he was married to his partner. In a famous placard posted just prior to the Morant Bay Rebellion (quite possibly on the very silk cotton tree that appears in a photograph in chapter 4) and printed in George W. Gordon's newspaper, the people of Saint Thomas in the East were called on "to speak like honorable and free men at your meeting. . . . Remember the destitution in the midst of your families, and your forlorn condition. . . . You are no longer Slaves, but Free men. Then, as Free men, act your part at the meeting."[25] Here, reminiscent of the political discourse of the 1840s, freed men's masculinity is called on as an identity that must be performed actively. Such public acts included speaking at public meetings and signing petitions, practices that the freed men often linked to representation of the interests of their families.

The reported words of James McLaren at a public meeting held near Morant Bay in September 1865, for example, indicate his kin-based understanding of freedom. He was reported to have said: "Myself was born free, but my mother and father was slave; but now I am still a slave by working from days to days." He continued, "I cannot get money to feed my family, and I am working at Coley estate for 35 chains for 1s. [shilling], and after five days working I get 2s. [shillings] 6d [pence] for my family. Is that able to sustain a house full of family? and the people said, 'No.'"[26] This indicates how a man's wages were understood as something on which the entire family was dependent; other petitions from this period made similar complaints about low wages and the inability of freed men to support their families.[27] However, these documents also attest to a complex mapping not only of men's and women's roles, but also of evaluative comparisons of differing types of gender performances made across classes, colors, and ethnic groups. A vision of independent free manhood was often contrasted to the state of slavery, still burning in popular memory, but it was also contrasted to the dependent condition of indentured labor.

This speech was just one of many made in the spring and summer of 1865 in a series of public meetings known as the Underhill Meetings. The meetings were called in response to a letter written in January 1865 by the Baptist Minister Edward Bean Underhill to Edward Cardwell, secretary of state for the colonies, concerning starvation and poverty in Jamaica. When Governor Edward Eyre had copies of the letter printed and circulated throughout the island, requesting responses,[28] Baptist missionaries gathered dozens of pages of evidence and called for a government Commission of Inquiry into the state of the island. They reported an increasing use of indentured African and Indian laborers, as well as more use of low-paid gangs of women and children. People also complained to the missionaries about unfair taxation, laws biased toward the big planters, and lack of justice in the courts.[29] A crucial point of debate revolved around definitions of work and the extent to which Jamaican men were "idle."

Governor Eyre's report on the condition of the island in 1865 blamed the peasantry for their impoverishment. It "owes its origin in a great measure to the habits and character of the people," he wrote, "induced by the genial nature of the climate, the facility of supplying their wants in ordinary seasons at comparatively little exertion, and their natural disposition to indolence and inactivity, and to remain satisfied with what barely supplies absolute wants."[30] To this explanation he added other shortcomings, including "idleness, apathy, pride, improvidence, night-revels, gambling, social disorganization and open profligacy." By linking his explanation to a critique of working-class families and sexuality (expressed here in terms of social disorganization and open profligacy), he was also implying that black men were unable to provide the kind of moral foundation necessary for stable Christian families. In a private letter to Cardwell, Eyre observed that "the Negroes . . . live for the most part in such remote out of the way places that they are subject to few ameliorating influences. . . . The fact is they have led too isolated and too independent a life without the obligations or restraints which exist in civilised communities and in countries where the population is less scattered and detached." He wrote in another letter about the need for "educational or ministerial teaching of a daily and practical kind calculated to humanise and enlighten them," thus implying that he saw the people of Jamaica as less than human.[31]

At the Colonial Office, Henry Taylor added his own notes to Eyre's report, stating that it is "at bottom merely a question of whether the Negroe is to be industrious according to the industry of other Countries or according to the standard of industry which he has set up for himself in

Jamaica." Citing Machiavelli and Adam Smith, he added that the "Negroe Race is I think by temperament volatile and sanguine more than others and he will not exert himself to provide against rare contingencies."[32] The Colonial Office's official response to Reverend Underhill's report was that "it does not appear that [the people] are suffering from any general or continuous distress from which they would not be at once relieved by settled industry." Thus, the poverty of black Jamaicans was blamed on their attitudes toward work and their disorganized family life. As Thomas Holt points out, this view of "the Afro-Jamaicans' 'unfitness' was coupled with— indeed, was seen to be rooted in—the failure of their households and conjugal arrangements." If unable to govern their personal lives, the argument went, surely the Negroe Race was also unable to govern their own country under democratic forms of representative government (Holt 2000: 55; see Sheller 2000: chap. 3).

Especially in the aftermath of the Morant Bay Rebellion of 1865, white Jamaicans echoed this charge that the people of Jamaica were not like civilized British people. Lewis Q. Bowerbank, the custos (warden) of Kingston, for example, suggested that the British form of government did not suit the character of the Jamaican people: "I feel confident that the British Government will be convinced that if Jamaica is to continue a British colony, and as such is to be the white man's home, there must be an entire change in its constitution and form of Government, and we must retrace our steps to the time of the emancipation, and endeavour to build up a constitution suited to the wants of the people, introducing into it much more of the paternal, and less of the free, and give up the mischievous practice of introducing British statutes unsuited to a community not possessing British feelings or sentiments."[33] Here we see an explicit argument for rolling back freedom and introducing a more "paternal" mode of governance to protect the "white man's home." In the aftermath of Morant Bay, this whitening of Jamaican government was achieved by the abolition of representative institutions, replacing the three-hundred-year-old House of Assembly with the non-electoral system of Crown Colony rule in 1866.[34]

The debate about political rights and citizenship in Jamaica from the late 1830s through the 1860s was continually framed as one about the character of freed men. On one side stood the white elite's charges of idleness and unwillingness of "the Negro" to work and hence "his" failure as a free citizen (with little mention of women). On the other side was a popular discourse expressing pride in working manhood, demanding a reasonable family wage, and reinforcing the rights of former slaves to "act as free men." Both of these discourses drew on Christian family values and patriarchal notions of masculine citizenship. However, the working-class articulation of these values was far more likely to embed the free subject in the context of familial relations. The black man's freedom, as Jemmott's research also underlines, existed as a relation to family members whom he supported (including wives or unmarried household partners, children, and possibly even parents and siblings) and a wider community to which he had civic obligations.

This articulation of family values from a position of subordinated masculinity illustrates the distinctive intersectionality of gender, class, race, and ethnicity in this case. A special relation existed between conceptions of work and conceptions of masculine freedom in post-slavery public discourse. What emerges in popular speeches, petitions, and protests in the post-emancipation era is a close association between conceptions of free labor and an ideal of masculine provision for the family that are understood as the bases for British citizenship and Christian respectability. Freed men describe their work in terms of a pride in their own labor and a desire to support their families. As an ideal that was most often unachievable, the family wage became the focus of debates over free labor and fair wages in post-emancipation Jamaica. Insofar as men spoke of freedom, they spoke of it not as solitary individuals, but in connection with earning a living that would support a family and allow for familial (not personal) autonomy. A man's ability to nurture, protect, and provide for his family became key parts of the popular definition of freedom, drawn in sharp contrast to the inability to do these things under slavery and under indenture.

This examination of popular discourses of masculinity and familial duty in post-slavery Jamaica demonstrates that freedom varied depending on one's position in a racial and gender order through which the rights of citizenship were refracted. Black subaltern masculinity drew on both the liberal ideology of independence and the Christian conception of familial duty, but it also incorporated currents of working-class radicalism and Afro-Jamaican culture building. Alongside prevailing gender distinctions, however, I have shown how ethnic divisions and conflicts were used in political discourse to reinforce masculine claims to citizenship and the rights of Jamaican natives as against immigrants and foreigners. Indeed, given the importance of family and kinship in protecting the fragile liberties and rights that freed men did enjoy, it may be that a masculine identity forged through an ethnic/national identity as British subjects was preferable to one that excluded women entirely (i.e., women were crucial allies, and family subsistence and reproduction in fact depended on women's labor). Indeed, as noted in chapter 2, working-class black women were themselves significant political actors and framed their own public interventions as mothers in complementary terms. Insofar as the patriarchal marital family was actually relatively unusual in popular practice and the availability of indentured laborers presented a direct threat to freed people's livelihood and survival, freed Jamaicans—both men and women—may have strategically shifted the emphasis in the discourse of citizenship *away from* gender conflicts and toward ethnic exclusion.

If the limits of universalism in Anglo-American liberal political orders of the nineteenth century can be found at the intersection of contested and contingent gender orders, racial orders, and moral orders, there was still room to maneuver over which kinds of exclusions would prevail at any particular moment. While British colonial governments tried to erect a moral order founded on principles of bourgeois masculinity and appropriate femininity, Jamaicans used Christian discourse in a slightly different way. By imbuing themselves with the moral authority of Christian manhood and familial responsibility, Afro-Jamaican men could distance themselves from the non-Christian indentured laborers who were undermining their labor-bargaining power. Afro-Jamaican women at the same time were making claims as mothers and queens, emerging as leaders within the revival religion, and building Afro-Jamaican culture via institutions such as family land (Besson 2002). These women were not particularly confined to the private sphere (a privilege available only to white women and some "brown" women in Jamaica); however, they, too, gained access to power via "legitimate" reproductive heteronormative femininity. These counterhegemonic forms of masculinity and femininity thus came at the expense of a legitimacy gained by exclusionary and derogatory attitudes toward foreigners (and as becomes clear later, homosexuals) and a kind of popular ethnonationalism that would have lasting effects on Jamaican culture in the post-independence period.

TOWARD DOUGLA AND QUEER CITIZENSHIP

Other Caribbean countries have also faced the problem of Afro-Caribbean relations to Indo-Caribbean history, heritage, and identity, and it remains a central problem within the historiography of the region. In *The Caribbean Postcolonial*, Shalini Puri (2004: 218) explores "the political reasons for the popular and academic erasure of what we might call dougla histories," meaning histories of the intermixing or hybridization of African and Indian people, cultures, and social struggles in Trinidad and Tobago. Puri (2004: 220) argues that reclaiming the stigmatized *dougla* identity (a term originally derived from the Hindi for bastard) and elaborating what she calls an interracial "dougla poetics" through histories, literary, and visual arts "could provide a vocabulary for disallowed, deligitimized racial identities. . . . Some of the political usefulness of the term 'dougla' arises simply from its bringing into representation and public discourse a repressed reality." She sees this as a potentially progressive political project that counters both Afro-Creole nationalism and Indian mother-country fundamentalism in Trinidad, both Hindu and Muslim. It appears to offer some kind of rejoinder to the kind of ethno-national subaltern politics that I have traced here, hinting at a move beyond deeply historicized ethnocentric standoffs and toward forms of dialogue, conversation, and shared historical re-envisioning.

Puri aims to name a barred or disallowed subject position that already exists, to challenge prevailing racial and sexual norms, and to historicize and contextualize this particular form of hybridity to challenge currently existing power hierarchies and social inequalities. Clearly, a parallel project could be developed that would name the equally barred or disallowed subject position of the already existing queer Caribbean citizen (cf. Puar 1999). She draws not only on literary texts to make her argument, but also on popular texts from calypso lyrics, cultural performances such as Hosay, and hybrid musical genres such as chutney-soca, explicitly challenging existing institutional structures and racial, gender, and sexual norms. Thus, she calls into question the commonsense understanding of what the Caribbean is, and who populates it, just as one might call into question the common-sense understanding that lesbian, gay, bisexual, transgendered, and other "queer" subjects are barred from existence in places like Jamaica, or for that matter India (Gopinath 2005), when they patently are there. In chapter 9, I return to the question of queer presences within Caribbean popular culture, music, and dance. But first, I shift the terrain on which to search for citizenship from below, listening for the bass notes of another archive of the Morant Bay Rebellion and unearthing its hidden underside and erased histories.

CHAPTER FOUR

Lost Glimpses of 1865

How may the contemporary visual interpretations unfold hidden passages and textures of the past that have not come to light, and equally how may we, the scholars in gender and visuality, guard against reinforcing the selfsame stereotypes in the present by encoding other devalued meanings?

—PATRICIA MOHAMMED, "Gendering the Caribbean Picturesque"

In 2009, Princeton University Library's Graphic Arts Collection announced the acquisition of a previously unknown photograph album containing rare images of Jamaica from the period of the Morant Bay Rebellion in 1865. These images can bring an added dimension to understanding aspects of history that loom below the surface of things. They offer another kind of trace beyond the textual sources that were used in the preceding chapters, a perceptible mark not simply of what they purport to record for posterity but also of what they inadvertently capture as "witnesses in spite of themselves" (Bloch 1953: 55). These are witnesses in several regards. First there is the photographer, who literally witnessed the places where he made the photographs, leaving them as a purposeful record of that moment. Then there is the silent witness to which Bloch refers, the subtle material traces of buildings, clothing, streets, people, and plants which when skillfully cross-examined by the historian can tell us other things about the past. And third, there is also a kind of witnessing of human presence and historical trauma at a more ephemeral level, which the viewer of the photographs glimpses through what is absent in these photos, as much as what is present in the faces that look back at the camera.

This particular album is thought to have been compiled by Alexander

Dudgeon Gulland, a surgeon in the British Army, who appears in the album first in a photograph captioned "Brigadier Genl Nelson & A.D.G." and later in a labeled photograph of his military regiment in India. According to his official obituary, he was born at Falkland, Fife, and educated at Edinburgh, where he received his medical degree in 1857. He served in the 41st Foot (Welsh regiment), in the Royal Artillery, and in the 6th Foot (Warwickshire regiment), which was in Jamaica in 1865. His service also took him to the Crimea and the siege of Sevastopol (1854–56), to China during the Second Opium War (1860–62), and to the North-West Frontier of India (1868). Surgeon-General Alexander Dudgeon Gulland died at Cheltenham on 4 September 1924, age ninety-one, outlived by only one other medical officer of the Crimean War.[1]

The fifty-nine Jamaican photos are part of a larger series, which opens with views of Malta and continues to an even larger series with beautiful landscapes of Srinigar (India), stunning military prospects of the Hazara Campaign on India's North-West Frontier, and many picturesque views of Spain, Gibraltar, Guernsey, and Ireland.[2] Here I focus only on the Jamaica portion of the album, but it must be situated within this sweep of wider British military adventure in colonial lands. The Jamaica scenes are inserted as but one episode in what might be interpreted as Gulland's movement through a series of major fortified ports, sites of important military campaigns, and romantic island outposts on the far-flung fringes of empire. The overall impression of the album is of the frontiers of empire, where the landscapes and people are picturesque, where Britain's Army and Navy have brought the benefits of orderly hospitals and fine buildings, but where native uprisings had to be suppressed (sometimes with the assistance of native troops). There is a sense of the sublime in the assembled photos, both in mountain vistas and scenes of military campaigns, along with an Orientalist ethnological interest in native customs and costume and a romantic view of nature, in keeping with other typical visual representations of the British Empire (J. Ryan 1997; Sheller 2003; Thompson 2006). Yet the photos relating to the Morant Bay Rebellion seem to disrupt such conventions, pushing against the security of empire and undermining some of its visual codes.

Comparing the photographs with the known facts of the Morant Bay Rebellion, I propose a controversial argument in this chapter. Contrary to the prevailing narrative of the rebellion as a "black" uprising against a "white" colonial government—and contrary to the Jamaican nationalists' appropriation of the rebellion as a formative moment of black anticolo-

nialism—the facts of "color" as represented here, and associated alignments of identity, are far more complex. Although this deeper intricacy is
evident in some existing historical narratives of the events, it has not been
emphasized in most accounts (see, e.g., Bakan 1990; Heuman 1994; Holt
1992). Beneath the surface of the photographs lies devalued—or, at least,
de-emphasized—evidence that the people charged with sedition during the
suppression of the rebellion included black, "brown," Jewish, and white
political opponents of Jamaica's British governor and ruling elite. The
people killed by the rebels were mainly white but included non-whites too.
And the troops who put down the rebellion were not only white Britons
but also black Jamaican irregulars and, above all, the Maroons, independent self-governing communities who suppressed the rebellion by black
smallholders and were led by the white Colonel Alexander Fyfe. The whites
of Jamaica, too, were divided: English and Scottish, German and Irish,
Church of England and Baptist, Methodist and Presbyterian. Although
these may seem like minor anomalies, I want to explore the implications of
reinterpreting the intersections of race, space, and violence in new ways,
drawing on the photographs in this rediscovered album.

THE CONTEXT

The Jamaican photos can be attributed in part to Gulland himself but
also to the Paris-born, Kingston-based lithographer and photographer
Adolphe Duperly (1801–64) and his eldest son, Armand Duperly (1834–
1909).[3] Although little has been published about the history of this important family of photographers, as an artist Adolphe Duperly is perhaps best
known for his collaboration with the Jewish Jamaican artist Isaac Mendes
Belisario in producing the twelve lithographs for Belisario's *Sketches of
Character, in Illustration of the Habits, Occupation, and Costume of the
Negro Population in the Island of Jamaica* (1837–38), one of the most important graphic depictions of the Afro-Jamaican population and aspects of
popular culture in this period. Duperly also published two politically significant lithographs: one depicting a scene from the so-called Baptist War
of 1831, and one of the emancipation celebrations of 1834. His other major
work includes early daguerreotypes of Jamaica, which were lithographed
in Paris in 1844 and collected in part in *Daguerian Excursions in Jamaica*
(Duperly 1884).[4] Duperly's "excursions" included such well-known scenes
as "Market Day at Falmouth" (1840), which more than a century later,
Patricia Mohammed (2007: 25–6) writes, "continued to shape the iconog-

raphy of the region around the image of agricultural plantation and production." Duperly also ran a very successful commercial photography studio, Adolphe Duperly and Sons, from about 1840, which became Duperly
Brothers not long after the father's death on 14 February 1864.[5] Thus, the
elder Duperly's work can be said to bridge the pre-photographic era, in
which modes of representation were influenced by conventions of academic painting (including landscape, portraiture, and historical allegory),
and the emergence of photography as a new technology. The work of his
sons (and grandsons), in turn, began in the early period of photography
and continued into (and contributed to) its popularization as a new mode
of representation associated especially with studio portraiture and, later,
the tourist industry.

Although many of the photographs in the Princeton album cannot be
the work of Adolphe Duperly (because they clearly depict the aftermath of
the Morant Bay Rebellion, which occurred after his death), the portraits of
the "Victims," discussed later, may well be his, since they were most likely
taken in the studio to be used as cartes de visite, which were very popular at
the time. Newspaper advertisements indicate that the Duperly studio held
the negatives for these cartes de visite and, after the rebellion was suppressed, produced souvenir portraits of both victims and perpetrators,
priced at one shilling each: "Portraits of the late victims who fell at the
Rebellion in St. Thomas ye East. Also portraits of the Baron, Price, Walton,
Hire, Hitchens, and other victims of the Rebellion in St. Thomas ye East—
also the Arch-traitor G. W. Gordon."[6]

Thus, it seems that the landscape scenes of post-rebellion Morant Bay
and its environs were created either by Gulland himself or, perhaps, in
some cases by Armand Duperly, who was then thirty. (Armand's business
partner and younger brother, Henri, specialized in portraiture.) If Gulland
purchased the portraits that are found in his album, he is also likely to have
purchased some of the excellent landscapes, not to mention studio images,
such as "Natives of Jamaica" discussed later. Armand today is identified as
"the most important photographer of 19th century Jamaica."[7] These photographs, in turn, undoubtedly can be called the most important images of
nineteenth-century Jamaica because of their provenance, as well as their
political and social significance.

Our knowledge of the rebellion derives mainly from the Jamaica Royal
Commission, whose three members arrived from Britain about three
months after the events, took testimony from numerous witnesses, and
published a report with extensive documentation in 1866. The events of the

Morant Bay Rebellion, in brief, involved an uprising in which several hundred black smallholders attacked a meeting of the local government of Saint Thomas in the East, killing and injuring many officials and volunteer militiamen, and then swept through nearby plantation districts killing specific people with whom they had grievances, mainly but not exclusively whites. The rebellion followed on the heels of a period of public meetings known as the Underhill Meetings, involving peaceful expression of grievances through petitions (Sheller 2000). Thus, we know that popular complaints included a series of economic issues related to wages, land tenure, access to markets, and labor rights; political issues related to unfair taxation, no justice in the courts, and elite-biased government policies; and civil issues that included voting rights and access to health care, education, and land. In that sense, the unrest was not an uprising so much as a social movement associated with some leaders of the political opposition, a movement firmly rejected by Governor Edward John Eyre and by higher officials in the Colonial Office. At some point, a disgruntled group at a small hamlet called Stony Gut, led by a Native Baptist deacon named Paul Bogle, began to plan a more violent attack, which apparently arose out of disputes against local officials with whom they were embroiled in several political and court battles (Heuman 1994).

More immediately, the violence began during a trial for assault held in the Morant Bay Courthouse on 7 October 1865, during which James Geoghagan disrupted proceedings by shouting that the convicted defendant should not have to pay any costs, as described in chapter 2. He was ordered to leave the court. When he did not go quietly, the judge ordered his arrest. His sister Isabella then challenged the police, and when they got outside, a "mob" that included Bogle and some of his followers rescued Geoghagan. Several days later, the police went up to Stony Gut with warrants to arrest those involved, but the policemen instead were captured and made to swear an oath to "cleave to the black." The next day, 11 October—the day of a local vestry meeting—several hundred people marched into the town of Morant Bay, pillaged the police station of its weapons, and then confronted the few volunteer militia who were protecting the meeting. According to Gad Heuman (1994: xiii), "Fighting erupted between the militia and the crowd and, by the end of the day, the crowd had killed eighteen people and wounded thirty-one others. Seven members of the crowd died. In the days which followed, bands of people in different parts of the parish killed two planters and threatened the lives of many others."

On 12 October, a British warship was already heading toward Morant

Grave of eighty Rebels near Morant Bay. Jamaica

1. "Grave of eighty rebels near Morant Bay, Jamaica."

Bay. Martial law was declared from 13 October until 13 November. During this period of massive repression, nearly one thousand prisoners were brought to Morant Bay; just under two hundred were executed, including seven women, and another two hundred were flogged, some having suffered torture to extract confessions (Heuman 1994: 137). But many others were killed during the suppression, in which British troops and Jamaican auxiliaries were greatly assisted by the Maroons, who had expertise in mountain warfare, tracking, and hidden ambush. They terrorized the local people, burning entire villages to the ground, shooting people on sight, and gathering up others for arrest and punishment. The leaders of this suppression appear photographed in the album for the first time in history, and I return to their story later.[8]

One page in the album, in one of the few indications of the extent of the violence unleashed in suppressing the rebellion, contains a photo captioned "Grave of eighty rebels near Morant Bay, Jamaica" (figure 1). At a sharp-angled crossroads, the grave apparently lies beneath a simple mound in front of a large tree; if the roads' configuration is still geographically identifiable, archaeologists could possibly locate the bones. Standing nearby are two men, a boy, and a donkey cart, with what appears to be a thatched hut behind the fence. The mound is sprinkled with a white substance—perhaps lime to suppress the odor of rotting bodies. In the *Colonial Standard* of 27 October 1865, a "blue jacket" soldier reported that the dead were being "packed like sardines" in gravel-filled graves.[9] Witnesses before the Royal Commission gave evidence that prisoners at Morant Bay were forced to bury the executed, presumably in mass graves much like this one.[10] Yet none of these burial sites has been identified, marked, or commemorated, in part because the British government had a strong interest in keeping them hidden. How can we understand the appearance of this unmarked and forgotten mass grave, this faint trace of a violent and contested history of citizenship from below?

THE PHOTOGRAPHS

But this is the end of the story. Let us go back to the beginning. The Jamaican portion of the album opens with six pages of views, mainly of Port Royal. These are remarkable records of a substantial nineteenth-century city and military garrison that is no longer standing, having been destroyed in part by the great earthquake of 1907 and finished off by Hurricane Charlie in 1951. The photos show architecturally significant buildings, including a large church, military barracks, officers' and surgeons' quarters, substantial military and naval hospitals, and a very extensive dockyard area of post-and-beam buildings with wood-shingled roofs, flanked by a long, elegant three-story edifice with a tall clock tower.[11] These photos of Port Royal speak of a Jamaica of British colonial wealth and seaborne military power; one shot offers a glimpse of "Her Majesty's Ship 'Duncan' in the distance," an intimidating triple-masted warship.[12] In a kind of double haunting, the old ruins of an even earlier Port Royal exist from the 1692 earthquake, submerged in shallow water near the existing town.[13] Like the submerged ruins, the photo album offers ghostly images of a lost city, appearing in the present as if surfacing from beneath a shallow sea, with fleeting images of those who peopled it.

The album moves next into a series of views of officers' houses and soldiers' barracks on the steep ridges of Newcastle, high up in the hills above Kingston, where the air was considered healthier. As if moving higher up in the hills could replicate the bracing northern cheer of Newcastle, England, its name must have provided comfort to feverish soldiers. Views of Up Park Camp follow, showing an open prospect across a grassy area toward several long, two-story buildings with louvered verandahs. But the quiet should not deceive, for this was a major military camp where troops were quartered and soldiers exercised. After the outbreak of the rebellion, two hundred people who were arrested in and around Kingston were taken there, some of whom were transported to Morant Bay to be tried by court-martial. Given the few signs of activity, these photos were likely taken either before the events of October 1865 by the Duperly studio, which had been producing scenes of Jamaica for some time, or afterward by Gulland, who clearly had access to and interest in military sites. On the next page, Up Park Camp again appears, with cows placidly grazing, but now surrounded by three portraits, and here begins the record of the rebellion as assembled by Gulland.

In the upper left corner is a portrait of George William Gordon, captioned "G. W. Gordon Hung at Morant Bay 23rd October 1865." Gordon was a member of the wealthy brown elite who owned plantations, published newspapers, and served in the House of Assembly. But he was also closely connected both politically and religiously with the people in Saint Thomas in the East who were involved in the rebellion (especially Paul Bogle). He had led a number of public meetings involving some of them and was embroiled in political disputes and court proceedings with those whom they attacked. He was arrested in Kingston immediately after the uprising on the orders of Governor Eyre, taken to Up Park Camp, then transported to Morant Bay, where he was tried by court-martial and quickly executed. The portrait has been reproduced ever since Gordon was declared a Jamaican national hero in 1965, and this photo of him has been used to produce numerous commemorative images. Yet the placement of the portrait here, right next to the view of Up Park Camp, does raise a hint of the controversy surrounding the legality of his arrest and rendition to Morant Bay.

In November 1865, as conflicting opinions roiled in London, Secretary of State for the Colonies Edward Cardwell questioned Governor Eyre:

> I wish to know whether your approval of Gordon's execution rested on evidence of his participation in the insurrection itself, or the actual resistance of authority out of which it arose, or, as your letter to Major-General O'Connor might give occasion to suppose, on evidence of the lesser offence of using seditious and inflammatory language, calculated

indeed to produce resistance to authority and rebellion, but without proof of any deliberate design of producing that result.

It is a matter of obvious remark that Gordon was arrested in Kingston, to which martial law did not extend, and taken to Morant Bay for trial, under martial law. Her Majesty's Government await with much anxiety your explanation on the subject.[14]

Controversy swirled around Gordon's execution and eventually led to Eyre's recall to England, where he was tried and acquitted. Accounts of Gordon's role and the political consequences of his execution can be found in several published histories, so I will not dwell on that here (see Heuman 1994; Sheller 2000). Suffice it to say that Britain's reputation for upholding the rule of law was at stake here, and it was severely tested.[15]

In another dispatch, Cardwell enclosed a newspaper extract and asked whether the events it described were true. A Captain Ford in charge of the irregular troops in Saint Thomas in the East reported that the soldiers had taken Gordon's black coat, vest, and spectacles "as a prize"; were each day killing one of the cattle from his nearby estate; and were "quartering on the enemy" as much as possible. The black troops, Ford claimed, "shot about 160 people on their march from Port Antonio to Manchioneal. . . . This is a picture of martial law; the soldiers enjoy it, the inhabitants have to dread it; if they run on their approach, they are shot for running away."[16] Even if most white elites considered Gordon an "Arch-traitor," as the Duperlys described him when advertising their souvenir portraits, many poor Jamaicans and those in opposition to Governor Eyre were shocked by his treatment. One of the most startling pieces of evidence to appear among the documents collected by the Royal Commission is an anonymous letter delivered to the custos (warden) of Kingston. Written in everyday language, it gives a poignant sense of poorer people's reactions to the suppression of the rebellion:

> We tell you of what happen in St. Thomas-in-the-East; that the Governor sent to shot every man and woman, old and young, and to burn down every house. That it is a damn shame to see this, but God will save them from the second death the innocent ones them, Lord save them.
>
> This Governor send men to shot without law, not to seek for the rebels alone and the riotors. We let you know this, and to believe this as St. Thomas-in-the-East burn down where we get the best of yam produce. What is the use we live again, for we will starve to death almost, and our best black men are going to shot. Well, Sir, it is but one death, as Mr. G. W.

Gordon is gone, the poor man's friend, for in the House not a man remember the poor man. Well, we will burn down the town down to the ground, and kill you and kill ourselves if you don't bring back every man you take away from Kingston. We don't care of our lives or your lives or property. Not all the soldiers or men-of-war ships can do good. We will bring judgment to Jamaica at once, at once. . . .

We, as black and brown, and poor whites so we don't care for burn lose lives, so bring them back and let them go. You will laugh at my writing, but I don't care at that. Death, death for all, and [breaks off].[17]

It is significant that the self-attribution of this anonymous letter to "black and brown, and poor whites" indicates a cross-racial political alliance based on class more than color. Although color was significant to the rebels in regard to their famous oaths, "Colour for Colour" and "Cleave to the Black," it is also notable that not all of the victims were white, that much of the violent suppression was carried out by black irregular troops and Maroons, and that some of the defenders of the people were "brown" or Jewish. The photographs begin to reveal some of this more complicated story.

Brigadier-General Abercrombie Nelson attempted to uphold the rule of law and objected to the courts-martial of several others who were detained at Up Park Camp. Thanks to his refusal, they instead faced civil courts and ultimately escaped execution. Indeed, the portrait of one of those men appears on the same page with Gordon's, in the upper right-hand corner. It is a faint, indistinct image, the man's face nearly disappearing into the background; he has a concerned expression, mouth slightly open, with gray whiskers. He looks almost grandfatherly. The handwritten caption beneath reads, "Mr. Levine,—Tried by Civil Power and Convicted" (figure 2). Sidney Levien (as he spelled it) was a member of Jamaica's small Jewish minority and editor of the *County Union* newspaper of Montego Bay.[18] In numerous editorials throughout the 1860s, he stood up for the poor, the emancipated, and the indentured and championed their cause. He was a strong critic of Governor Eyre and his Executive Council, even in the immediate aftermath of the Morant Bay Rebellion. In an editorial on 17 October, he blamed the governor for the uprising: "But when the Governor and his advisers take upon themselves to make their will the law of the land, and that law is cruelly obnoxious to the people—when the Governor and his advisers run riot in their abandonment of practice and propriety— the lower classes become equally callous on their part and riotous in their way. A Government that sows the wind must expect to reap the whirlwind."[19]

According to his own testimony before the Jamaica Royal Commission, Levien was arrested on 1 November by about thirty marines who came to his home in Montego Bay, marched him out under gunpoint, and refused to allow him to see his family. He was transferred by ship to Morant Bay and kept a prisoner there from 2 November until 7 December, with no means of communication and even though martial law ended on 13 November.[20] Brigadier-General Nelson objected to Levien's trial by martial law, and no charges were made against him.[21] Governor Eyre had to accede to this determination, and Levien was released on bail under a writ of habeas corpus, whereupon the governor instituted civil legal proceedings against him, charging him with seditious libel and with conspiring with Gordon, Paul Bogle, and others to foment rebellion. He was acquitted of conspiracy but found guilty of seditious libel on the basis of the editorial of 17 October and sentenced to prison for twelve months.

Levien, too, should be a Jamaican national hero, but he is not, probably because, as a Jew, he did not fit the needs of a postcolonial, independent Jamaica, which built its identity around Creole nationalism and then what Deborah Thomas (2004) calls "Modern Blackness." His life represents the radicalism of a certain strain of Jewish identity in the Americas that has resisted easy incorporation into the elite mercantile class with which it is mainly associated. His writings and this photographic trace of his image hint at a yet-to-be written history of a radical Jewish Atlantic, allied with antislavery and labor movements, civil-rights advocacy, antiracism, and social democracy.

It seems as though the page with the portraits of Gordon and Levien ought to be completed with the well-known tintype portrait of Paul Bogle, the leader of the rebellion, which is also attributed to Adolphe Duperly and Sons but does not appear in the album. Apart from Gordon and Levien, none of the alleged instigators of the rebellion—or the actual perpetrators, or the hundreds of people who fell victim to government repression—appears in the named photographs. In their absence, a series of images captures other aspects of the aftermath of the repression, around which hover traces and evidence of these lives, and even fleeting images.

The next page has several views of Morant Bay, clearly made after the rebellion because they feature the burned-out ruins of the courthouse, where many of the white victims were killed and many of the political prisoners were subsequently flogged and executed. The town looks much

2. "Mr. Levine" (Sidney Levien).

Execution of Rebels at the ruins of the Court House, Morant Bay.

3. "Execution of Rebels at the ruins of the Court House, Morant Bay."

shabbier and poorer than Port Royal. In the view captioned "Morant Bay from the Harbour," we catch a glimpse of figures standing near buildings at the end of a wooden wharf: five men and seven women wearing white dresses and head wraps. Two other men are seated at a building in the foreground, and the ruins of the courthouse can be seen jutting up to the left. Alongside the views of Morant Bay is a photograph of a sketch captioned "Execution of Rebels at the ruins of the Court House, Morant Bay" (figure 3). It depicts eighteen people hanged from a long wooden scaffold, three more in the upper archway of the ruined building, and one under the stairway, making twenty-two executions in total. It seems likely that the men on the scaffold are the most significant leaders of the rebellion: Paul Bogle, his brother Moses, James Bowie, James McLaren, and the fourteen others who were hanged with them (Heuman 1994: 139).[22] The other bodies are probably those executed earlier and put on display to intimidate the population. A military vessel can be seen in the harbor. Groups of sailors stand to each side, with armed soldiers on each corner, guarding a group of bystanders that includes at least three women in full skirts and some men in top hats. We know that people under arrest at Morant Bay were forced to watch the executions, and this group of bystanders under military guard may be prisoners who themselves would be tried and flogged, and in some cases executed, over the coming days.

Although the political leadership of the rebellion is generally attributed to Bogle and the men he organized and armed, the movement also had interesting communitywide elements. The crowd that marched on Morant Bay on 11 October was led by Letitia Geoghagan, the mother of James, Isabella, and Charles, who were all involved in the initial fracas at the courthouse on 7 October. As a "brown" member of the volunteer militia later testified, "She first fired a stone, and several other women followed her, and then the men rushed right in."[23] She and one of her sons were executed, along with dozens of other rebels, following the imposition of martial law. These very public executions in front of other prisoners, as depicted here, were meant to serve as a warning to the entire population. The burned-out courthouse, its ruins seen in the photographs looming over the small town, was left standing as a reminder of the suppression and executions that took place there under martial law.

Thousands of people were also flogged, some by the Maroons as they drove through nearby districts burning the villages and provision grounds, and others by order of Gordon Ramsey, the dictatorial and erratic provost-marshal at Morant Bay. One Baptist, Reverend James H. Crole, was reportedly "ordered to get two dozen, but his body presented such a milk-white appearance that the provost-marshal's cheek was suffused with a blush of shame, so that he recalled the order."[24] Approximation to whiteness did, then, protect some from flogging and execution, but not from suspicion of sedition. Ramsey's blush of shame at Crole's milk-white skin also hints at a kind of queer erotics, as it was usually accounts of the bared flesh of women that were used by abolitionists to elicit such a response. The shame associated with homosexual desire is here sublimated beneath a kind of racial shame at the punishment of a white body. The assertion and shoring up of the power of white masculinity is best carried out on black bodies, and the illegal suppression carried out after the Morant Bay Rebellion is justifiable only if it is cast as white colonial rule being exercised over unruly black natives. Yet for those who attempted to assert citizenship from below, the truth of "race" was never so straight cut.

THE VICTIMS

In the roll call of "Victims" (figure 4), we can see a certain version of Victorian white masculinity, suited and bewhiskered, often accompanied by walking stick, hat, and watch chain, all accoutrements of the responsible British Christian patriarch. In one image, a married couple stands, identified as "Captain Hitchens & Wife." She is wearing full white skirts, a perfect picture of Victorian propriety. The caption ends, "murdered." The murder of women carried a particular significance in British colonial culture, following closely on the lurid accounts of the "Indian Mutiny" of 1857 (which was frequently invoked by those who survived the Jamaica rebellion), during which white women were killed and victimized. As Mohammed (2007: 16) argues in relation to the racial portrayal of women in visual culture of the colonial Caribbean: "The white woman is never displayed toiling in the garden or hot sun, and if she is in charge of any work, . . . then she is generally well clothed, hatted and shod for the occasion. In many settings she is displayed not as a dislocated unattached single female but always under the watchful eyes of her family[;] her beauty must be maintained and nurtured for her role in life, [being a] wife and [dedicated to] motherhood."

Children appear in two of the photographs, suggesting the reproduction of the white colonists in Jamaica. In one atypical image, the nervous-looking Colonel Thomas Hobbs is shown holding a baby, but the caption reads, "died mad."[25] In another, the wife of Reverend Victor Herschell, dressed in dour dark clothes with head demurely covered, holds her baby; to the left of her photograph is one of her murdered husband, comfortably seated with crossed legs in the center of the page. According to the account of the rebellion by a former member of Eyre's Executive Committee, published in 1866, "It is not generally known, except in Jamaica, that much of the ill-blood which resulted so fatally in St. Thomas-in-the-East was caused by the illegal permission to the late Rev. V. Herschell to rebuild the chapel at Bath in that district. . . . There is every reason to believe that serious illegalities had been allowed to exist in St. Thomas-in-the-East by the local authorities, and this was one of them" (Price 1866: 130). In fact, many of the victims shown on this page were at the center of popular grievances and charges of corruption for which no redress had been found through the courts. They were specifically targeted during the uprising, in contrast to the restraint shown by the rebels in protecting other people and property, according to some of the evidence of the Royal Commission.

There is an embodied and material character to citizenship in these pho-

4. "Victims of the Jamaica Rebellion of 1865."

tos. Masculine character, respectability, and a certain gravitas and public presence were crucial to the production of citizens in nineteenth-century Jamaica. The photos are staged in a studio, but the use of architectural balustrades, finely made chairs, and formal clothing all hint at the spatiality of citizenship as a mode of being in the world. Such spatial forms were explicitly contrasted with the thatched huts and crowded yards of the poor black peasantry and the squalid living conditions of the urban black population. They also continue to shape representational practices in terms of how poverty and citizenship are visually presented. These photos represent a culture of respectability and a symbolic performance of citizenship from which most of Jamaica's people were excluded. They exude gendered codes of respectability based on the middle-class patriarchal Christian family, as well as expectations of heteronormative "whiteness."

Significantly, we also find on this page a finely dressed black man, "Mr. Price, Murdered." Charles Price, a builder, was one of the small elite of successful black men in Jamaica who embodied respectability, owned property, voted, and served in the local government. He was also one of the few blacks marked out for death by the rebels at Morant Bay. Those who cornered him reportedly taunted him: "'Price, don't you know that you are a black nigger and married to a nigger?' They said, 'Don't you know, because you got into the Vestry, you don't count yourself a nigger.' He said, 'Yes, I am a nigger.' They said, 'Take a looking glass and look on your black face.' And Price said, 'Yes, I am a nigger.'"[26] This is a complex moment of literal self-reflection on racial embodiment, adumbrating issues taken up by postcolonial theorists such as Frantz Fanon (1994 [1967]). It tells us something about race and class as socially constructed performances that run up against embodiment, skin, and other people who force Price to surface as "a nigger."

In contrast to the respectable victims, the grouped portraits on an earlier page, labeled "Natives of Jamaica," show people dressed in ragged clothing, with bare feet and evidence of laboring bodies (figure 5). An older man with a graying beard, tiredly seated, has one foot wrapped in some kind of homemade boot and the other bare foot centered in the foreground. Even the patch in his bedraggled trousers is ripped. His furrowed brow and the bags under his eyes speak volumes of a hard life, yet he seems to carry a kind of embodied wisdom. In another photograph a ragamuffin girl catches the viewer dead on with a hard stare of incredible self-presence; anchored to the ground on solid, large feet, she might be mistaken for a boy, but the clothing and head wrap suggest not, even if the bare legs would startle the Victorian viewer. Is there a sexual provocation in her bared thigh? Certainly, later studio portraits of washerwomen would play on such titillation, but this image is more problematic in its stark capturing of real poverty, perhaps representing the first efforts of Henri Duperly in a genre he would later dulcify.

The group of four children also features a small boy in the center who gazes fiercely at the camera. Another boy's bare feet jut forward into the lower ground of the photo; these eloquent feet speak of hard work, long walks on bad roads, the history of everyday life of the poor. Finally, another man poses with a large basket on his head, his torn shirt knotted onto his shoulder. His face is worn and sad, but his neck, arms, and shoulders appear young and strong. Each portrait reminds us of the total absence of bare feet in elite portraiture, where men appear in polished shoes or boots

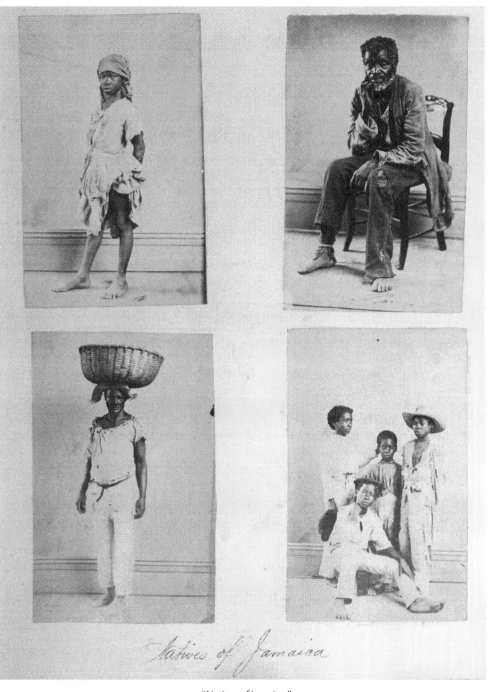

5. "Natives of Jamaica."

and ladies have their shoes covered by long skirts. These images bring humanity back down to earth, grounded, solid, emblems of the hardworking bodies that have kept these people alive through drought, disease, and the hunger of hard times.

Although they foreshadow later studio portraits of actors posing as "picturesque" poor laborers, which became popular as tourist postcards from the 1880s onward, there is something more hard-edged and disturbing here.[27] Mohammed (2007: 23) has written about the Duperly grandsons' book *Picturesque Jamaica* (1905), with sixty-three photographs, including staged scenes of cane cutters, banana carriers, market women, and women being led off to jail: "Why does the Jamaica-born Duperly select these compositions as picturesque? They obviously represented work roles undertaken by black women in Jamaica, but for whom are these constituted as picturesque, surely not the women and men in the photos? We have no names of the women, no clue as to their identities, they are in fact largely silent in the historical and anthropological text." These later photographs recuperate the Jamaican working class into safe poses of productivity and law and order, which had been so severely fractured in 1865. A male overseer among the cane cutters and a black constable reinforce the colonial order in which these women labor, yet they also re-center orderly black masculinity.

If a few black men like Charles Price, or brown men like Gordon, or Jews like Sidney Levien were accepted, however reluctantly, as citizens, what about the other "natives" of Jamaica? Crucial to the practice of citizenship is the "scrutiny and regulation of actual or potential citizens," according to Barry Hindess (1993: 32–33), in which the "idea of the citizen as a free and independent person can also serve to justify the paternal regulation of significant sections of the population." Saidiya Hartman (1997: 127) has also explored the fashioning of a kind of indebted servitude in the post-emancipation United States, which pivoted on the transformation of former slaves into "a rational, docile, and productive working class—that is, fully normalized in accordance with standards of productivity, sobriety, rationality, prudence, cleanliness, responsibility, and so on." This is exactly the kind of discourse we hear in the response of Governor Eyre to the petitions of emancipated Jamaicans who were demanding greater democratization in the 1850s and 1860s. He dismissed their poverty and suffering, attributing it to "idleness, apathy, pride, improvidence, night-revels, gambling, social disorganization and open profligacy."[28]

The swirling political debates that instigated the Morant Bay Rebellion concerned precisely the scrutiny and regulation of the formerly enslaved as potential citizens, and we can imagine how the people in these "native" photos might have been scrutinized by the elite. While often positively embraced as part of a discourse of equality and inclusion, citizenship is always also about inequality, subordination, and exclusion of some categories of people. The Jamaican colonial government and elites consistently rejected the capacity of the emancipated peasantry and urban poor to be "independent persons" capable of self-governance, and they often used the charge of sexual profligacy and moral failings to demonstrate the need for guidance by respectable whites, by missionaries (and their wives), and by a paternalistic state. Thus, the contrast between the portraits of the "victims" and the "natives" serves to distinguish different categories of imperial citizen and colonized subject.

THE MAROONS

The Maroons are often romanticized as the epitome of subaltern resistance against oppression, having successfully re-created their own Afro-Caribbean culture in the interior mountain strongholds of Jamaica (and Suriname). But they also raise thorny questions through their alliance with the colonial state against other black Jamaicans. They had a special claim to alliance with the colonial state's political regime, in which they exercised self-governance and special autonomy based on terms granted in a 1739 truce (Bilby 2005). Paul Bogle failed to enlist them in his cause, and perhaps they turned on their neighbors involved in the rebellion with particular zeal and brutality because it was a key way to put into practice their independence and to express the "warrior" qualities that they valued most, according to Kenneth Bilby, which were "physical strength, courage, toughness, determination, resourcefulness, indomitability, and, at times, ruthlessness" (Bilby 2011: 579). In the album, the white Colonel Fyfe is identified as the subject of a photograph, which is in fact an extremely rare portrait of a group of Maroons, presumably posed in a studio (perhaps the Duperlys') shortly after they put down the Morant Bay Rebellion (figure 6).

Critical studies of colonial visual cultures of representation suggest how historical forms of racialization and sexualization continue to inform contemporary racial and sexual geographies (Collins 2004; Golden 1994; Mohanram 1999; Roberts 1997), but seldom do such studies call into question the unity or inherent obviousness of "blackness" as a category. By considering the relation of the Maroons to the Morant Bay rebels, whose slogan was "colour for colour," and to the white-governed colonial state, we find the limits of "blackness" within colonial nationalist discourses. As Bilby points out, the suppression of the Morant Bay Rebellion was a definitive moment for the Moore Town Maroons, and they preserved a living memory of it in their songs and oral tradition. Some of those songs underline their own distinctive color identification as what they called "true blue" (Bilby 2011: 575). Colonel Fyfe, furthermore, while identified as white, also understood his own positioning as Scottish. Bilby (2011: 582) argues that Fyfe requested that Governor Eyre's commission of him as commanding officer of the Maroons should style him as not only "Colonel" but also "Chief," "as I wish to consider them Jamaican Highlanders." Thus, concludes Bilby, he "evidently saw himself as no less than a latter-day Scottish clan chief leading his adopted African clansmen into battle."

Although they are difficult to see, six Maroons are actually present in this photo, dressed in jungle camouflage and wielding rifles, with four crouched down miming positions of hidden attack. It is a fearsome show of military might, with the white colonel seated in a pose of relaxed power, while two Maroon leaders stand in proud strength behind him. Colonel Fyfe had led the Maroons in suppressing the slave rebellion of 1831–32 and was a "highly respected figure among them. In addition, he was a stipendiary magistrate, the custos of Portland, and a member of the Legislative Council."[29] Governor Eyre called on Fyfe in this new crisis, and the two of them met about two hundred Maroons at Port Antonio on 15 October. The HMS *Wolverine* returned four days later with weapons and ammunition to arm them, a story that individual Maroons could still recount to Bilby more than a century later, as he tape recorded in 1978 (Bilby 2011: 576; and see Bilby 2005: 345–49).

One of the unnamed Maroons in the photograph is likely to be Captain Joseph Briscoe, standing in the center behind Colonel Fyfe and appearing seated in the center of a second photograph, although no one knows for sure. Briscoe was a key leader who, "occupied the position of highest authority among the Maroon fighters and who played a very prominent role in the events of 1865" (Bilby 2011: 583). According to testimony gathered by the Royal Commission, he shot many people on sight and attacked others indiscriminately. The Maroons reportedly killed even the old and the sick and flogged hundreds of people in Bath, many of whom were indentured Africans who worked on nearby estates (Heuman 1994: 134–36). The Maroons used their militarized power and legitimate access to coercive violence to set themselves apart from other black British subjects. In

6. "Colonel Fyfe" (and six Maroons).

line with other studies of "different manifestations of political masculinity" reviewed by Mrinalini Sinha (2007: 265), here "masculinity clearly operates as much through differences *between* men as through differences between men and women. . . . This emphasis on the social differences *between* men serves ultimately to pry apart any automatic connection between the gendered discourses of masculinity, on the one hand, and bodily men, on the other." It also pries apart the unity of the category "black" in Jamaica in 1865, displaying internal fault lines, just as was found in chapter 3.

Thus, the album lends further evidence to the argument that the rebellion was not simply a matter of black versus white, as it has so often been portrayed, nor was it a "black" anticolonial uprising in any simple way. Although Paul Bogle and his allies had sought to create a color-for-color alliance, it had splintered on the shoals of political allegiances, class differences, and fiercely embodied forms of masculinity through which people performed distinctive roles of citizenship. It is also relevant that at the trials in February 1866 of those arrested in Kingston on sedition charges, including Sidney Levien and two Baptist ministers (Reverend Edwin Palmer and Reverend John Hewitt Crole), the juries were described as majority black, followed by brown, and a minority of white jurors.[30] Many blacks rallied in support of Governor Eyre after the rebellion, including the Maroons of Charles Town, who wrote a petition in his support in February 1866.[31] And Colonel Fyfe, meanwhile, appears to have identified deeply with the Maroons whom he led. Thus, while the rebellion is commemorated and remembered as a "black" uprising against "whites," the photographs remind us that these are politically defined identities—fractured, complex, and unstable.

In chapter 3, I noted similar fault lines in the identities of "Her Majesty's Sable Subjects" and the liberated Africans who were brought to Jamaica as indentured laborers after the abolition of slavery. When we look beneath post-independence nationalist historiography, we can see other fault lines running through the political formations that cross-cut presumed racial categories with complex patterns of ethnic identification, landholding, family formation, and class identity. These subtle inter-embodiments are crucial to unearthing the silences of history, including the unmarked grave of the dozens of rebels killed by the fierce, proud Maroons. The Maroons in the photo bear a resemblance to other armed men whom I consider in the next chapter: the sword-bearing citizens of revolutionary and post-independence Haiti and their much later progeny, the Tonton Macoutes. These armed men serve as reminders of the two-edged nature of the sword of state power, whether of police, militaries, paramilitaries, or even "peace-keepers," which is so often turned back on the people. Nationalist histories tend to silence such irreconcilables, preferring to celebrate the unity of the nation and the political representation of the masses. But as we know, the state may turn against the nation (Trouillot 1990), and this is one of the key barriers to post-slavery citizenship. We need to better understand the legacies of armed masculinity, both black and white, and the mutual homo-sociality of armed terror that led these Maroons to pose for a studio portrait with Colonel Fyfe.

THE SACRED TREE

Another striking photo in the Gulland album is not of a person or a building but of a great silk cotton tree (figure 7). The "portraiture" of trees was a common genre in this period, as seen in the Jamaican work of the British artist Joseph Kidd and in other tree portraits made by the Duperlys. Trees later became a popular subject of tourist photography and part of the tropical picturesque tradition. Tom Cringle's Cotton Tree in Saint Catherine, for example, was a much photographed Jamaican tourist site.[32]

The huge, gnarled tree possesses as much character as a human face. Its trunk is about fifteen feet wide at the base, tapering toward a point at the crown. Its battered-looking, ancient roots stand half on land and half in water, which seems to lap at the base of the tree, forming a junction not only of crossroads but also between water and land, and thus between the spirit world and the material world, the world of the living and the world of the dead. From the "God Tree" of the Asante, the sacred Kindah tree of the Accompong Maroons in Jamaica (Besson 1997: 214), and the famous *mapou* tree of Bwa Kayman in Haiti to the great silk cotton trees venerated as places of the spirits, whether by the Maya or in Trinidad, particular trees have special symbolic meanings and social functions within indigenous Caribbean, African Caribbean, and Indo-Caribbean cultures (see chapter 7). Their colossal boughs offer the greatest amount of shade (and often grow above underground aquifers), so they make good community gathering spots, markers of major crossroads (like Half-Way Tree in Kingston), and places to post public notices. The Guiana Maroons, for example, had a prohibition against cutting silk cotton trees, while Dutch slave catchers punished runaways by nailing them to cottonwoods. This kind of reverence for and political struggle over trees leads the historian Geri Augusto (2009: lxii) to refer to them as part of a "liberation flora," knowledge of

The Cotton Tree at the Cross Roads near Morant Bay, where the rebels assembled immediately before the attack on the Court House.

7. "The Cotton Tree at the Cross Roads near Morant Bay."

which was tied to plant-based "militant medicines." This is a powerful site by any reckoning, a repository of ancestors and sacred spirits.

Unlike a tourist photo of a famous big tree, this image comes to us unusually embedded in a specific political context. The caption reads, "The Cotton Tree at the Cross Roads near Morant Bay where the rebels assembled immediately before the attack on the Court House." It is extremely important that the Morant Bay rebels are reported to have gathered at a tree such as this. It is known that they were Native Baptists, with a blended Christian and Afro-Caribbean belief system, and that they made their allies swear on a Bible and take oaths by drinking rum and gunpowder. But here, for the first time, we can see a specific location where they gathered their forces, and it has self-evident sacred meaning within Afro-Jamaican belief systems. Before the rebellion, similar sites were used for public meetings, and public notices were posted on the trunks of trees, including a controversial handbill written by George W. Gordon on the "State of the Island," which was reported to have been "posted up on a cotton tree in the main road at Morant Bay."[33] Perhaps Native Baptists, like the deacon Paul Bogle and his people from Stony Gut, also carried out more ceremonial rituals at this crossroads under the shade of a sacred tree. It reminds us again that we must look for subaltern histories below the surface of the image, tangled in the roots of trees, close to the ground, submerged in the water.

What is the meaning of a tree partly submerged in water? Why is a segment of a wagon wheel sticking out from the base of the tree, just behind the seated man? Could it have some ritual purpose? (In the rebel's call to war of 17 October 1865, Bogle wrote, "It is time for us to help ourselves. Skin for skin, the iron bars is now broken in this parish, the white people send a proclamation to the governor to make war against us, which we all must put our shoulders to the wheels, and pull together."[34]) The leaves and branches of the tree have moved, blurring the image and lending the tree a dynamic, living spirit. Can it speak to us across the centuries of its long life? Was this tree also venerated by the Maroons, who refused to help Bogle on that day and who captured him six days later and delivered him to his executioners? What happened when the tree died? No archive holds this information, although local oral histories might. Only the tree holds the stories of "the forgotten ones them," as Jamaicans say, and perhaps also their spirits.

The photo album is also a kind of marker of a crossroads where the past meets the present, the material meets the representational, and the tracks of history meet the reinterpretations of each viewer. It challenges us to "unfold hidden passages and textures of the past that have not come to light," as Mohammed (2007: 1) says, and to decode "other devalued meanings." For example, a man named Marcus Garvey attended an Underhill Meeting in Saint Ann's Bay in July 1865, chaired by Gordon. He probably saw or even helped distribute the placards that were printed at Gordon's newspaper office and posted around Saint Ann and Saint Thomas in the East in August 1865, with the words, "Remember that he only is free whom the truth makes free—You are no longer slaves; but free men."[35] Maybe he told this story to his son, Marcus Mosiah Garvey, famed founder of the Universal Negro Improvement Association, who gave a speech in Canada in 1937 in which he declared, "We are going to emancipate ourselves from mental slavery because whilst others might free the body, none but ourselves can free the mind." The speech was printed in Garvey's magazine, *The Black Man*, a complete edition of which was edited and published in 1975 by Robert A. Hill, who happened to give a copy to Bob Marley in 1976. Soon thereafter, Marley wrote "Redemption Song," an anthem that has inspired millions around the world with the lyrics "Emancipate yourselves from mental slavery;/None but ourselves can free our minds" (quoted in Hill 2010). Only as I read Hill's article about this connection did it come back to me that it was the words of the song, echoing in my head, that had made the words in the archival document of 1865 jump out at me, catching my attention.

And so the wheels of history turn: Gordon's words transmitted to Pa Garvey, then to Marcus Mosiah, then to Bob Marley via Robert Hill, and then to a Jewish American student reading documents in the British National Archives, tracking the connections across time. Some of history's hidden textures, I have argued, are the sheer complexity of meanings and experiences of race and color in colonial Jamaica as they coordinated with class, gender, religion, and practices of citizenship. As I noted in *Democracy after Slavery* (Sheller 2000: 238–39), according to Amy Jacques Garvey, her father-in-law Pa Garvey was a learned man known as "the village lawyer," with a house full of books and newspaper. He was descended from the Maroons and brooded all his life over their betrayal of Paul Bogle and earlier slave rebellions (Clarke and Garvey 1974: 29–30). With this direct line from 1865 to today, the tangled roots of Jamaica's racial history come alive, enhanced by the subtle textures of the past that come to light in a photo album. My aim is not to deny the significance of black or white, African or British identity in Jamaica, but to show how both were dynamically forged out of complex coordinates, relations, and political processes, cross-cut with shades of gray and formations of masculinity. Rather than the photographs giving us a self-evident "factual" record of "race," then, these photographs open up the fluidity of racial categories, their changing meanings over time, and their contested historical interpretation.

CHAPTER FIVE

Sword-Bearing Citizens

From the slave uprising of 1791 to the declaration of independence in 1804, the Haitian Revolution shook the slaveowning European powers to their core. Throughout the Atlantic world, the young Republic of Haiti became a powerful symbol of black liberation and racial equality, a harbinger of African emancipation, and a beacon of hope for the anti-slavery movement. Revolutionary self-emancipation, however, also carried with it a burden of self-defense from the embittered slaveholders whose navies circled Haiti's shores and controlled regional trade routes. Facing a continuous threat of invasion over many decades, an ongoing civil war, and the refusal by the slaveholding regimes in France, Britain, and the United States to recognize Haitian independence, the Haitian Republic had to remain on a military footing long after the revolution ended. In these difficult circumstances of state formation, a martial image of the male citizen took on special salience; indeed, building black masculinity became a central task in the construction of Haitian national identity. In seizing the reins of power and constructing a militarized and masculine model of citizenship, the victors of this slave revolution created a political paradox that still plagues Haiti: The egalitarian and democratic values of republicanism were constantly undercut by the hierarchical and elitist values of militarism. The paramount sign of this fundamental contradiction was the exclusion of women from the wholly masculine realms of state politics and citizenship; even as the Haitian Revolution destroyed some forms of domination, the process of social change that occurred in the post-independence period replicated others.

Through an analysis of the language of citizenship in official documents, newspapers, and intellectual writings (including perceptions of Haiti by European contemporaries), I argue that the exclusion of women from full citizenship aided in the construction of an elitist, coercive, and autocratic state in Haiti, to the detriment of the ideals of freedom and equality that underpinned the revolution and that continued to resurface in episodic peasant resistance against the state. After briefly reviewing the historiographical background for a gendered political history of Haiti, I trace the masculine rhetoric of Haitian citizenship to three sources: (1) the revolutionary republican tradition of armed egalitarianism, transposed into the heroic figure of the rebel slave and the black general; (2) the postindependence institution of men's rights to land based on participation in armed defense of the nation; and (3) the influential political network of Freemasonry, with its homosocial brotherhood and constitutive exclusion of women.

The republican veneration of arms-bearing men in a brotherhood of manly civic duty—along with a devaluation of women's work and social contributions—helped to create an authoritarian and statist political system that privileged military elites and significantly undermined the radical democratic premises of the Haitian Revolution. A political discourse of male-centered familial relationships served to uphold non-democratic state structures, with damaging long-term consequences for the freedom the Haitian people had won. Despite a somewhat democratic constitution, elites within the Republic of Haiti embraced military republican ideals, which legitimated the empowerment of a small elite, with long-lasting impact on Haitian political culture. The relationships between family rhetoric, militarism, and masculine identities after slavery, I suggest, are crucial not only to understanding the authoritarian path of political development taken in nineteenth-century Haiti, but also to critically evaluating why the "masculinization" of power was historically—and remains—incompatible with the egalitarian values that inspired the Haitian Revolution. There were, however, alternative cultural currents of subaltern masculinity and women's empowerment, which I will turn to in chapter 6.

FOUNDATIONS FOR A GENDERED POLITICAL HISTORY OF HAITI

Rods, swords, scepters, staffs, sharpened sticks, flags: These are the symbols of power identified by Richard Burton as central to nineteenth-century "Afro-Creole" cultures of opposition. Burton (1997: 12–15) perceptively argues that "the rod in its multiple manifestations becomes the symbol of both power and popular opposition to power in the Caribbean." It is these phallic symbols that are wielded both in the playful spirit of opposition and in the hard play of political power. As Burton hastens to point out, though, this is a "male-dominated culture of reputation and play" from which women historically have been absent; moreover, this oppositional culture has the quality of a "double-edged sword" that can be turned back on its wielder, since it both "challenges and reinforces the status quo." It is precisely this double-edged nature of Afro-Creole masculine cultures of opposition that I seek to point out in the formation of the Haitian Republic. How did the military struggles of revolution, war of independence, civil war, and national defense become institutionalized in ways that inadvertently turned armed force back on the Haitian people, thus replicating a colonial culture of domination?

My analysis of gender and power in Haiti draws on two streams of recent theorizing on the subject. On one hand, feminist historiography has shown how symbols of gender and actual structures of sexual differentiation inform systems of power at the level of the nation-state. As Joan W. Scott argued more than twenty years ago, gender is "a primary way of signifying relationships of power." Whether in authoritarian or democratic regimes, she suggests,

> power relations among nations and the status of colonial subjects have been made comprehensible (and thus legitimate) in terms of relations between male and female. The legitimizing of war—of expending young lives to protect the state—has variously taken the forms of explicit appeals to manhood (to the need to defend otherwise vulnerable women and children), of implicit reliance on belief in the duty of sons to serve their leaders or their (father the) king, and of associations between masculinity and national strength. High politics itself is a gendered concept, for it establishes its crucial importance and public power, the reasons for and the facts of its highest authority, precisely in its exclusion of women from its work. (Scott 1988: 44, 48)

Building on feminist political theory (Brown 1988; Fraser 1992; Riley 1995) and historiography of the exclusion of women from the bourgeois public sphere (Landes 1988; Ryan 1990), a wide range of work has now emerged on gendered representations of the state and citizenship, on various political cultures of masculinity, and on the rhetoric of masculine citizenship (Clark 1995; Dudink et al. 2004; Dudink et al. 2007; Gardiner 2002; Hall

2002; Nelson 1998). Much of this historiography of masculinity, however, has focused on "modern Western culture," with some significant exceptions of work on European colonies such as India (Sinha 1995, 1999).

Despite growing interest in how symbolic struggles over race, class, and gender constitute the politics of national identity and inform popular oppositional cultures in the Caribbean, there has been little research into the gendered symbolism of citizenship and state power within Haiti (although see Francis 2003 for one relevant contribution that also draws on a comparison with Jamaica). This is especially surprising given its significance as the first independent "black republic," carefully watched by surrounding colonial powers and seen as a litmus test of black self-government by many abolitionists. Indeed, some recent studies of rhetorics of masculinity gesture toward the Haitian Revolution as a key moment that "gave the concept of modern citizenship in revolutionary France its famous universalist content" (Sinha 2007: 267), as if that included black women. Another line of historical research has focused on the "feminization" of the Antilles and of the black race in the writing of Europeans during the colonial period, yet there has been little analysis of gender discourses within Haiti.[1] More thorough analysis of the construction of gendered citizenship in Haitian political discourse is surely overdue. What can an analysis of Haitian rhetoric of masculinity draw from and contribute to this wider historiography? Feminist arguments concerning the masculine rhetoric of military republicanism in revolutionary France and in the early United States are especially relevant, since Haitians drew on the same philosophical sources in constructing their republicanism and used similar rhetorical strategies and exclusions, as I show later.

At the same time, I also draw on the recent interest in the construction of masculinity in labor history and of black masculinity in particular. As Robin D. G. Kelley points out, the school of social history "from below" epitomized by the work of E. P. Thompson was not only very Eurocentric but also "very manly." Citing scholars such as W. E. B. Du Bois and C. L. R. James, as well as recent work by Paul Willis, David Roediger, and others on white working-class masculinity, Kelley (1994: 112–14, 23–24, 31–32) explores, among other things, the valorization of "manliness" and a "language of masculinity" in American working-class culture.[2] African American labor history now increasingly acknowledges the centrality of male gender identities to the formation of a black working class, and these insights might fruitfully be extended to the Caribbean, where far more research has focused on class, color, and female gender identities (Barrow

1998b; Martinez-Alier 1989; Momsen 1993; Shepherd et al. 1995; Yelvington 1995). From a somewhat different perspective, scholars of African American religion have explored the discourse of manliness that developed around the idea of "Christian manhood" in the post-emancipation period, which served to valorize and validate freed men's leadership of their communities (Raboteau 1997).[3] This historical research points to the importance of concepts of masculinity during the transition out of slavery in the United States; might we find similar themes in the Caribbean context? Is there something specific about the post-slavery condition that produced a revaluation of masculinity and elicited celebrations of manhood?

These strands of scholarship are very suggestive for interpreting the meaning of masculinity in nineteenth-century Haiti, but there are few previous studies in this area (even in the fifteen years since this research was originally published). Concern with gender has been more prevalent in the ethnographic study of contemporary Haitian culture (Brown 1991; Charles 2003; Herskovits 1964 [1937]; Mintz 1993), but micro-level studies of local practices or family structures generally have not been connected to the macro-construction of power relations at the level of the state. One line of approach might be to follow those who have identified a macho "caudillo" culture in post-independence Haiti. In a sweeping analysis of sugar island slavery across the Caribbean, for example, Arthur Stinchcombe (1996: 300–305) groups post-independence Haiti with the Dominican Republic, Cuba, and Puerto Rico as " 'big man' cultures," where "manliness" was a central virtue of leaders.[4] However, much differentiates Haiti from other caudillo states, not least its thoroughly Afro-Creole culture, which, as Burton (1997) recognizes, links it to places such as Trinidad and Jamaica more than to Mexico or South America. Unlike its Latin American neighbors, Haiti also has a long history of fieldwork by women and of women's predominance in market trading. Any study of masculinity in Haiti, then, must grapple with the specificity of its sexual division of labor, as well as its Afro-Creole culture of opposition and its intellectual linkages to military republican rhetoric in both France and the United States.

Did Haitian leaders employ appeals to manhood, elicit the obedience of sons, or associate national strength with masculinity, and, if so, what effect did such rhetoric have on the construction of citizenship and the nation in the post-slavery period? Were women excluded from high politics, and if so, how did their exclusion distort the meaning of freedom and citizenship? Wigmoore Francis (2003: 123) offers a rare reading of the early-nineteenth-century writings of Pompée Valentin, Baron de Vastey, the "mulatto son of a Frenchman" who fought with the armies of Toussaint Louverture and Jean-Jacques Dessalines and became secretary and chancellor to King Henri Christophe and field marshal of the Haitian Army. She argues that his writings on women "betrayed a masculinist orientation rooted in European patriarchal assumptions" (Francis 2003: 129). Perhaps other Haitian historians have avoided such questions because there are few primary sources to guide one in answering them; women were indeed marginalized from the public sphere and are thus largely absent from the archives, which were written by men, for men, and mostly about men. In consequence, macro-historical approaches have usually focused on women only to the extent that they constitute a distinct portion of the labor force; diplomatic histories or studies of "high politics" often ignore gender altogether, since women seldom appear as major actors in the historical record, and even histories more attuned to broader political culture pay far more attention to constructs of race and class than to those pertaining to gender.[5]

A major problem facing the historian of gender (or for that matter, sexuality) in Haiti is the meager range of primary sources available for the nineteenth century. Many of the original archives of the Haitian state have been destroyed over the years.[6] Thus, there is great dependence on the writings of a few Haitian historians, such as Thomas Madiou and Beaubrun Ardouin, a smattering of newspapers that have survived, and the records kept by hostile foreign consulates and the (often racist) publications of European visitors. Moreover, since the bulk of the population was illiterate and largely excluded from everyday political participation, any understanding of power relations drawing on *written* sources is unavoidably filtered through the prism of a few elite men's perceptions. Nevertheless, this should not deflect us from pursuing these questions, as the sources are rich in their way and demand further interrogation. Above all, rather than searching for rare accounts of women and their political actions—proverbial but always precious needles in the haystack—why not also turn to the wealth of material on the symbolic construction of masculinity? How was masculinity envisioned and invoked in post-independence Haiti? What kinds of male heroes and actors were celebrated? Do sex, gender, and familial relationships find their way into the historical record in unexpected places?

I focus on three aspects of gender analysis identified by Joan Wallach Scott (1988: 43): (1) "culturally available symbols that evoke multiple (and often contradictory) representations"; (2) "normative concepts that set forth interpretations of the meanings of the symbols, that attempt to limit and contain their metaphoric possibilities"; and (3) "social institutions and organizations" such as kinship, the labor market, and education. To explore these areas, I draw on four kinds of pertinent sources: Haitian official documents, including laws, codes, and government proclamations; publications by Haitian intellectuals, including historians, newspaper contributors, and publicists; European official documents, including consular papers and other foreign-office correspondence; and publications by European and American observers, visitors, or commentators.[7] Since the symbolic and normative dimensions of gender and sexuality have been neglected in Haitian historiography, I turn to them now with an important caveat: The written record is far removed from the lives, ideas, language, and practices of the bulk of the Haitian population. While I seek some of these tracks of history in chapter 6, additional tools and contributors will be needed to unearth what James Scott (1990) calls "hidden transcripts."

The first generation of Haitians who abolished slavery and threw off European domination were infused with a strong sense of civic duty and military patriotism, leading them to symbolize the citizen as soldier and the soldier as citizen. The first constitution of 1805 institutionalized these republican military traditions in its vision of a fraternal brotherhood-in-arms of all men of African descent. Armies of self-emancipated slaves (and even older bands of independent Maroons) stood for African self-determination, black independence, and Haitian national autonomy. To its wary slaveholding neighbors, Haiti was "a symbol that meant export of revolution . . . [and] a racial symbol of powerful and rich blacks, black rulers, black generals winning wars" (Stinchcombe 1996: 247). Thus, a fundamental aspect of the Haitian nation-building project was the elevation of the black man out of the depths of slavery into his rightful place as father, leader, and protector of his own people. Familial imagery was closely allied with a masculine call to arms and a depiction of women as grateful recipients of men's protection, as we shall see in the rhetoric of each of the early consolidators of state power.

MAKING HAITIAN CITIZENS: MILITARISM AND MASCULINITY

Popular figures of African masculinity and military prowess served a significant function in materially achieving and symbolically marking the transition from slavery to freedom in many parts of the Americas. Violence anointed manhood in many post-slavery contexts but especially in Haiti, where freedom was won by force of arms. At least since the days of François Makandal and Boukman Dutty—leaders who are thought to have drawn on African martial arts and Vodou ritual to give rebel slaves mystical powers in warfare—the male warrior has been venerated in Haiti. Women also celebrated these war heroes. Thomas Madiou (1985–91 [1847–48]: 3:102–3; my translation) reports that on 1 January 1804, during independence celebrations, "Women and young girls, richly attired, were mixed among the warriors whom they exalted with their patriot songs." The celebration of this tradition in popular culture and in national symbols has helped instill pride and self-respect for many generations. To begin to interrogate the ways in which various governments have used these popular images should in no way be seen as a criticism of the men who fought for freedom or as a judgment on this mode of emancipation. Nevertheless, I will argue that the rhetorical construction of gender identities in Haitian nationalist discourse was cynically manipulated by ruling elites to contain the currents of democratization that were surging through the Atlantic world in this period.

Throughout its first decades, the Haitian state suffered diplomatic isolation, ongoing external threats, and civil war up until 1820, necessitating military government and a strong executive commander of the armed forces.[8] From the very beginning, plantation workers did not necessarily benefit from the "freedom" they had won; even Toussaint Louverture, the great hero of the revolution, created a system of military enforcement of agricultural production that some suggest was not much different from slavery (Trouillot 1990: 43–45). Facing a hostile world, governing regimes used familial imagery to bind competing regions, classes, and colors together. In the first constitution of General Jean-Jacques Dessalines, for example, the nation was envisioned as a family, the emperor as its father, and all the people as of one color: "All distinctions of color among the children of one and the same family, of which the Head of State is the father, necessarily ceasing, the Haitians will henceforth be known only by the generic denomination of blacks [*noirs*]."[9] The comparison of citizens to children and the one-father, one-color ideology defused tensions between the mostly mulatto *anciens libres* and the black *nouveaux libres* by making all citizens equal. Paternalism enforced the authority of the chief of state as father of this new nation, while republican fraternalism reinforced unity and military solidarity.

Although they proclaimed the egalitarian values of revolutionary republicanism, early Haitian leaders also seem to have valued hierarchical power structures modeled on the patriarchal family and on military discipline. Ever since the revolution, most Haitian leaders have been military men. As Michel Laguerre (1993: 26) argues, "The existence of the indigenous army preceded that of the nation and, in effect, made possible the state and the first government of the republic. After independence in 1804, the military, in addition to providing internal security and defense against foreign aggressors, was also the government." Indeed, Article 9 of the first constitution stated, "No one is worthy of being a Haitian if he is not a good father, a good son, a good husband, *and above all a good soldier*" (emphasis added), foreshadowing the militarization of the state, the marginalization of women, and the depiction of citizens as male protectors of family and nation. The consequences of this, Laguerre continues, were "the lack or weakness of civilian institutions on which democracy could flourish, the militarization of civilian institutions, military paternalism, the institutionalization of corruption, and the transformation of the role of the military as the permanent government of the land."

As a result, armed force was used against the civilian population and against political oppositions. Popular military ideals were easily transposed into the state-making projects of post-independence elites, who drew on military symbolism to generate national unity but also to suppress any dissent or opposition. The national symbol, appearing on the flag and on coins, was a palm tree, symbol of liberty throughout the Caribbean, topped with a republican liberty cap and surrounded with a bristling array of spear-tipped banners, cannon, bayonets, and military drums.[10] This coat of arms also "appears alongside images of the spirits in temple wall paintings [and] the *vévé* for Ogou Feray is an abstraction of the Haitian coat of arms" (Brown 1997: 441–42; R. Burton 1997: 249).[11] The warrior, in fact, became the consummate symbol of the state, and the founders of Haiti seem to have drawn on the powers of Ogou to lend the state popular legitimacy. Even today, red-scarfed Dessalines is "served" as an ancestral *lwa* embodying the indomitable warrior essence alongside other warriors represented by the various manifestations of Ogou, *mystères* descended from ancient Dahomean gods of warfare. Burton (1997: 250) points out that "the various Ogous symbolize in the first instance the spirit of bellicose resistance. . . . More specifically, Ogou Feray is said to represent Toussaint, Christophe, and Dessalines in their struggle against the French, and to this extent any ceremony in honor of the warrior [lwa] becomes 'an archetypal ritual, a reenactment of the beginnings of the nation,'" as Leslie

Desmangles (1992: 152) put it—although, as Joan Dayan (1995: 28, 139) cautions, "The religious rituals associated with [Ogou Desalin] keep the ambiguities of power intact."[12]

Ogou Feray is syncretically represented by the classic Catholic chromo-lithograph of Saint James the Greater, the vanquisher of the Moors, always depicted on the attack, his sword drawn, on a white horse. As Laennec Hurbon (1995: 75) observes, "When his servants are possessed by him, they put on red neckerchiefs, carry swords and flail energetically, even brutally," in a possession performance of military masculinity. A French print of Toussaint Louverture from 1802 (figure 8) depicts him as "leader of the Black Rebels of Saint Domingue," and like Ogou Feray, he is mounted on horseback, looking back with his sword drawn high overhead. He wears a French military uniform, with a blue jacket, sumptuous gold braid and epaulets, a red sash, white cockaded tri-corner hat, white breeches, and polished black boots trimmed in gold. Along with Dessalines, who succeeded him and declared the independence of the Republic of Haiti, the dance steps and songs commemorating these members of the Ogou family of deities ritually enact through culturally patterned bodily practices the forging of iron, the stoking of fires, and the wielding of weapons. As Candice Goucher (2010: 1) points out, "Iron in the Atlantic world both enslaved and liberated Africans"—from the making of the shackles that bound slaves to the weapons with which they liberated themselves and the tools with which they survived. Iron technology is an ambivalent "two-edged sword," just as the meanings of masculinity embodied by Ogou Feray represent contradictory impulses toward both liberation and oppression.

These military figures carry a two-edged sword that can be turned back on the Haitian people themselves. Karen McCarthy Brown (1997: 441) similarly observes of the warrior cult that "militant imagery is the perfect vehicle to handle the complex social negotiation which is the work of Ogou. Soldiers are given powers beyond those of the ordinary citizen. Ideally [but not always] they use them to defend the group. . . . The anger of Ogou vacillates. It is directed outward toward the enemy, but can quickly turn toward his own people when they fail him. . . . Time and again the Haitians have experienced their leaders turning on them. . . . Ogou's anger comes full circle and ultimately is directed against himself." Brown has put her finger on the duality of militarism as both an emancipatory force and a self-destructive force; it is this paradox of power that double-crosses any simple interpretation of Haitian history, or of citizenship from below more generally. Expanding on this point, Burton (1997: 243) argues that the

8. Toussaint Louverture, "Chef des Noirs Insurgés de Saint Domingue" (1802).
Courtesy of the New York Public Library.

culture of opposition in Afro-Creole societies simultaneously undermines *and* reinforces patterns of colonial and postcolonial domination. As he puts it, "The 'weapons of the weak' can all too often be turned against them not by the powerful from whom, symbolically or in fact, they seized them, but by those of their own 'kind' whom they have placed (or who have placed themselves) above them."[13]

If the good *Haïtien* was a soldier, what of good *Haïtiennes*? The constitution made no mention of mothers, daughters, wives, or female workers, farmers, or traders—except for purposes of taxation. Civic worthiness was a matter of manliness, and arms meant freedom. In fact, freedom had always had different connotations and pathways for men and for women coming out of enslavement (Bush 1990; Higman 1984; Morrissey 1989). Throughout the Americas, there was a strong link between men's emancipation and military service; male slaves were manumitted in return for risking their lives by almost every colonial power during most outbreaks of major warfare in the Americas, including the freeing of slave soldiers during the Haitian Revolution, the U.S. Civil War, and the Cuban Ten Years' War. In contrast, the majority of women who were manumitted (or gained higher-status occupations during slavery) often did so via sexual relations with white men or through familial relations as their offspring. Within the power structure of slave societies, freed *men*'s armed service connoted respectability, citizenship, and public service; *women*'s freedom, on the other hand, often came at the price of sexual vulnerability, non-citizenship, and dependence on private relationships. Freed men and freed women thus experienced very different paths to freedom and different kinds of insertion into the public political process once free.[14]

For Haitian men, citizenship first took the form of military service, and the army became one of the main avenues of men's political participation, as well as a route to landownership. No sooner had the French landowners and British and Spanish occupying forces been driven out of the island than military leaders seized the land of the former plantations; landholding generals quickly dominated government both in the Kingdom of Haiti, which formed in the north, and in the Republic of Haiti in the south.[15] Christophe maintained the big northern estates intact, under the control of a few successful generals who formed a new aristocracy; his courtly entourage reinforced the masculine ideal of the noble warrior. When the French tried to negotiate a Haitian protectorate in the post-Napoleonic period, he responded in the language of a proud military tradition: "How dare you speak to us of masters and slaves? To us, a free and independent people; to warriors covered in noble scars won on the battlefields of honor. . . . How dare you propose to men free for twenty-five years, who still hold weapons in their hands, to depose themselves and return to the chains of ignominy and barbarous slavery!"[16] Taking up arms and carrying the scars of warfare entitled this proud nation to its freedom. When he became king, the experienced general congratulated his subjects that the "military art which defends the country is brought to perfection. The social virtues which form good fathers of families, good sons, and chaste spouses, are practiced."[17]

To legitimize military power, the kingdom celebrated familial ideals. Free Haitian manhood was built on protecting the family and the nation, with women and children depicted as grateful dependents. When the birthday of Madame Christophe was celebrated in 1807 with "great pomp," public addresses were made praising her role as "virtuous wife" and "mother of the unhappy, consoler of the afflicted, protector of widows and orphans . . . who fears not to face the miasma of hospitals in order to spread a healthy balm on the wounds of the defenders of the fatherland" (Madiou 1985–91 [1847–48]: 4:32–33). Yet the king's title was declared "hereditary in the male and legitimate descendants of his family in a direct line, by elder birthright, *to the exclusion of females.*"[18] The queen's role, as she herself put it, was to "delight in being a tender mother" to the Haitian people, and "the sacred tie of marriage was respected, that tender union which binds man to woman, creates virtuous companions, and attaches the citizen to his country, the great family of the state, by the image of his own and of domestic happiness; as the greatest encouragement to which, the supreme head furnishes, himself, a touching example of the conjugal virtues."[19] Encouragement of family life was not only rhetorical; it also found its way into law and social institutions. The Code Henri bound proprietors to "treat their respective laborers with true paternal solicitude," outlawed "female licentiousness," and encouraged childbirth by exempting pregnant women and nursing mothers from field labor, just as in the British colonies during the "amelioration" period in the 1820s.[20] Thus the monarchical state manipulated gender relations in the service of state power: good families made good subjects.

In the Republic of Haiti in the south, during Alexandre Pétion's presidency women were constitutionally disfranchised along with "criminals, idiots, and menials" (Leyburn 1980 [1966]: 243). General Jean-Pierre Boyer, Pétion's successor, quickly won control not only over the northern kingdom, in 1820, but also over the former Spanish colony of Santo Domingo in 1822. Now anyone born in any part of the island could become a Haitian citizen, as could anyone of African or Amerindian descent who chose to emigrate to Haiti. Only whites were barred from owning property or exercising the rights of Haitian citizenship. However, the law did not apply equally to all Haitians; the Civil Code of 1825 specified that a Haitian woman who married a foreigner forfeited her citizenship. This was a way to prevent foreign white men from owning property in Haiti through marriage, but it underlines the constitutional marginalization of women from the republic (Ardouin 1860: 9:319). It also led to confusing status problems; when a Haïtienne married a "*blanc*" (the term used for any foreigner), she lost her citizenship rights, yet her children were nevertheless eligible to claim citizenship on the basis of their partial African ancestry.

With the ongoing threat of French invasion through the early to mid-nineteenth century, the military remained the most significant branch of the executive, while the elected Chamber of Deputies had little power. British Consul Charles Mackenzie described the situation in 1827: "The government that is now established professes to be purely republican . . . but in practice it may be said to be essentially military. The whole of the island is divided into departments, arrondissements, and communes. These are all under the command of military men, subject only to the control of the president; and to them is entrusted exclusively the execution of the laws, whether affecting police, agriculture or finance. There is not, as far as I can learn, a single civilian charged with an extensive authority."[21] By 1840, there were approximately 25,000 men in the army and 40,000 more in the National Guard, equaling more than one-tenth of the entire population and perhaps close to one-fifth of the adult male population.[22] Women were excluded from military service, from voting, and from holding political office. Beyond their normal military duties, the army also essentially functioned as the local government, with each commune under the authority of soldiers. A military spirit pervaded the state and irrevocably molded the meaning of citizenship. This "republican monarchy sustained by the bayonet," as Jonathan Brown (1972 [1837]: 2:259) described it, is "a nation of soldiers [in which] every man is required to be a soldier and to consider himself more amenable to the commands of his military chief than to the civil institutions of the government." Brown (1972 [1837]: 2:266–67) refers to "a sort of African janizaries, half citizen and half soldier. . . . The civil is everywhere subservient to the military power." As Boyer himself put it in one of his proclamations to the army and the

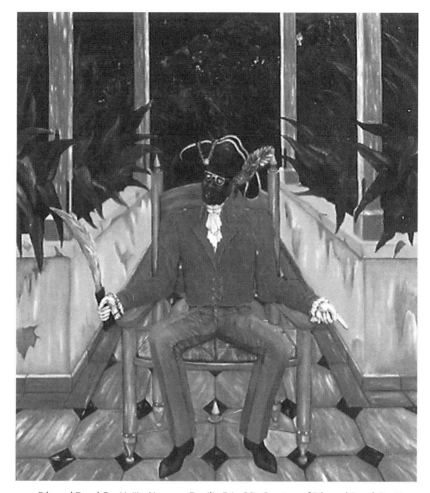

9. Edouard Duval-Carrié, "Le Nouveau Familier" (1986). Courtesy of Edouard Duval-Carrié.

people: "Arms and land, these are our strengths. . . . Imitate the people of antiquity, and let us be warriors and cultivators at the same time" (quoted in Linstant 1851: 3:42–44). Military spending, not surprisingly, was the largest portion of public expenditures in Boyer's budgets, although ordinary soldiers were poorly paid.[23]

When the Wesleyan Methodist missionary James Hartwell arrived in Port-au-Prince in 1840, he was immediately met by a "ragged" soldier who took him to the local commandant to get his papers, and he later described a rural soldier as "a man called Captain, no regimental number, no shoes or stockings, with a spur girt on his naked ankle, a sword tied round his waist with a piece of tailor's list, and an old straw hat."[24] The Haitian expression for someone who has gained authority, according to Jean Comhaire, is that he "*fè zépero*," or grew spurs, just like this captain. Comhaire also observes that before the U.S. invasion of 1915, rural commandants, or "chefs de section," were appointed by the army general in charge of each arrondissement and often came from wealthy peasant families; they have "always been the official link between the two culture worlds of Haiti"— that of the French-speaking governing elite and that of the rural peasantry (Comhaire 1955: 620–23; Laguerre 1993: 49). It is precisely these sword-carrying, spurred figures of masculine empowerment who emerge out of the Afro-Creole culture of opposition yet risk reinventing a culture of domination perpetrated by an elite-run state hierarchy. These soldiers can give us pause before romanticizing what I have called citizenship from below; the armed subaltern citizen also poses many dangers, especially to women and children, and in many states (including contemporary Haiti), the demobilized, underpaid, and underfed soldier has proved particularly lethal, as have other embodiments of armed masculinity (including policemen, escaped convicts, gangsters, and even, sadly, UN peacekeepers).

The twentieth-century painting *Le Nouveau Familier*, by Edouard Duval-Carrié, depicts Jean-Jacques Dessalines in the tricorner hat of historical soldiers, holding a saw-bladed machete drawn like a sword and wearing the red and blue dress of Ogou Feray (see figure 9). However, the addition of sunglasses and a throne-like seat associate him with the limitless coercive power of the Tonton Macoutes, henchmen of the dictator François Duvalier's state terror squads. Yet his frilly collar and cuffs, gold detailing, and pointed shoes also hint at the flashy "bling" culture of masculinity in the dancehall, a topic to which I return later via the artwork of the Jamaican artist Ebony Patterson.

THE USE OF FAMILY SYMBOLISM IN THE CONSOLIDATION OF STATE POWER

Despite the death or expulsion of much of the white population of Saint-Domingue during the revolution and wars of independence, Haiti built on the cultural legacies of Europe, as well as those of Africa. Haitian republicanism was in fact even more adamantly virile than French republicanism, which, as Lynn Hunt (1992) argues, symbolized revolution as the sons' overthrow of the king as father, and, as Joan Landes (1988) argues, substituted a masculinist language of fraternity and civic brotherhood in rejecting the effeminacy of ancien régime salons. The gendered symbolism of Haitian politics swung between discourses of republican fraternalism and patriarchal presidentialism, much as Richard Burton finds in Martinique and Guadeloupe, which shared similar French political traditions: "the brothers systematically excluded their sisters, mothers, wives, and mistresses from active participation in the wholly masculine procedures, electoral and other, of the Republican confraternity. And before that, of course, the 'brothers' had repeatedly quarreled fratricidally amongst themselves, provoking the regular return of patriarchal figures committed to the restoration of order at all costs" (Burton 1993: 71). Whatever the value of military fraternalism may have been in the revolutionary period and in the self-emancipation from slavery, its institutionalization after independence undermined the complementary revolutionary ideals of liberty and equality. Military republicanism, which initially served the necessary purpose of building a new state and new citizens from scratch, soon became the only raison d'être for a state in which there were few civil institutions to balance an overwhelmingly military power. This section will explore how the discursive construction of the male citizen was used to consolidate state power and resist European domination.

In addition to civic republicanism, the Haitian statist model of democratic citizenship also borrowed blueprints from one of the most important elite associations in France and her colonies, the Order of Freemasons. While proud of their independence and freedom, Haitian elites were nonetheless engaged in a "civilizing process" of moral education and self-improvement, with an eye to themselves as an example to the world. Freemasonry was crucial to this process and became a significant feature of nineteenth-century Haitian politics. In the lodges, men became "citizens" insofar as they wrote constitutions, elected leaders, and ruled themselves through means that simulated democratic governance. The lodge was a "school of civic sociability" and self-cultivation for the bourgeois man, and it laid the foundations for modern civil society. Yet in creating a new secular citizen, Freemasonry promoted patriarchy and presumed that only literate and educated men "could be entrusted to act ethically and to think disinterestedly in the interests of society, government, and improvement" (Jacob 1991: 21, 123; see also Habermas 1989 [1962]; Koselleck 1988; Landes 1988). The same class and gender exclusions were replicated in Haiti, despite its national origins in slave revolution.

Early accounts of Haitian Freemasonry stress the importance of these elitist but meritocratic societies in the development of democracy. A newspaper from 1836 describes the importance of Freemasonry to the emergence of free men from slavery and reveals the qualities that were valued in a man in this period:

> An institution which taught one to lead an active and productive life, to love one's neighbor, to conduct oneself honorably, in order to merit the esteem and confidence of all; which brought one to instruct oneself with the aim of instructing in turn one's brothers, to acquire the gravity and the tact necessary for directing gently and affably and obeying with dignity; which left to each one his individual liberty, modified only on rare occasions and for the good of all; an institution which recognized no other superiorities than those of knowledge, of capacity and of virtue, where the young man could figure by his merit amongst his elders and learn to respect and to venerate them: an equal expression of democracy would not fail to attract the attention of those pushed by a beloved enthusiasm to walk down the road of progress.[25]

Haitian Freemasonry promoted an ideology of progress based on learning to both direct and obey one's brothers and to advance on the basis of merit and virtue; however, as seen here, it also insisted more paternalistically that young men show due respect and veneration for their elders. The author noted the multitude of lodges throughout the republic in 1836 and reminded his reader to "never forget that it is above all in Masonic Societies that our fathers formed themselves." This symbolic genealogy of citizenship, passed from father to son—as well as the outright exclusion of women from participation in all-male Masonic lodges—left Haitian women politically invisible and in many cases publicly silenced (though not fully).

Masonic practices permeated Haitian political culture of the early to mid-nineteenth-century. Victor Schoelcher (1843: 217n; my translation) wrote that there were twenty-three Masonic lodges in Haiti, and "one in derision calls the senate the twenty-fourth, because one of the first statutes of the freemasons is never to talk politics in their meetings." The Haitian historian Beaubrun Ardouin (1860: 9:77n1, 11:5n1; my translation) noted that President Boyer was "the Grand-Protector of the Masonic Order in Haiti, and the president of the Chamber [was] almost always a Freemason like him." The English missionary Mark Bird (1869: 186) also reported that many government personnel were members of the Order of Freemasons and that "this institution is so widely extended in Hayti that it has become a distinct feature in Haytian society." Bird believed that there were about one thousand Freemasons in Port-au-Prince alone and numbers in due proportion to population in second-tier and third-tier towns of the country.

Haitian citizenship, therefore—forged in revolution and consolidated through the ties of Freemasonry—was from the beginning based on a republican fraternity of brothers-in-arms with a streak of loyal filial obedience. Perhaps because these features seem so ordinary, so typical of the nineteenth century, they have seldom been researched or commented on; of course this was a military society, women were excluded from politics, and "universal" suffrage meant adult male suffrage. Yet the outcome was not so straightforward; nor was the rhetoric unopposed. The vast social changes wrought by revolutionary emancipation also set in motion an undercurrent of popular culture that was not so easily shaped to the ends of an elitist military state. It is this other, oppositional "Afro-Creole" world that swirled below the surface of power, raising doubts among the powerful and giving hope to the powerless. But before turning to these contradictory forces, let us see how these symbolic representations of gender were normatively invoked.

Haitian intellectuals echoed the masculinist discourse of military republicanism and the paternalistic discourse of Freemasonry in their writings on nationhood, in which they exhorted their compatriots to be obedient sons and live up to the example of their fathers. Baron S. Linstant, a Haitian writer well known in abolitionist circles, published a series in a Jamaican newspaper in 1842 describing the civic duties of Haitians in terms of father–son relations:

> We, therefore, the sons of the conquerors of our independence must by our energy, in the new fields of science, and by our determined rejection of every selfish feeling, help our fathers to complete the object of all their struggles. These are sentiments shared by the whole Haytian people; already a generation of young men begin to seek instruction of every kind abroad, and at home they are anxiously pursuing every means of improvement. . . . Rich in the experience of their fathers, as well as in the sciences of Europe, they are training themselves to follow worthily the traces of the heroic founders of the Haytian Republic.[26]

The sense of both an obligation to the past and a vision of the future placed a burden on the shoulders of this generation of young men to join together in brotherhood and vindicate their fathers' legacy. As a petition of 1843 expressed this sense of historical mission, "Citizens! Dessalines and Pétion call out to you from the depths of their graves; Grégoire [eighteenth-century French abolitionist Abbé Henri Gregoire (see Sepinwall 2005)] watches you from the heights of heaven, Isambert [French abolitionist François-André Isambert] speaks to you: save Haiti, your communal mother; stop her from perishing. . . . Save her. . . . The abolitionists will rejoice in it and applaud you; the people will bless you and posterity will engrave your names in marble and bronze" (Madiou 1985–91 [1847–48]: 7:507; my translation).

Women had no place in this construction of the nation and its moral destiny, except as mothers of warriors and symbols of the nation itself, which was envisaged as the great "mother" of the people whom male citizens must venerate and protect. An imagery of the manly duties of citizenship infused the language of Haitian nationhood, and young and old generations of men were called on as fighters to protect the mother nation, sometimes inverting the traditional image of France as the mother nation. Toussaint Louverture was said to have challenged Napoleon's expeditionary force in 1803 by saying, "A son owes submission to his mother, but if she unnaturally aims to destroy her offspring, nothing remains but to entrust vengeance to God" (C.M.B. 1850: 83). Updating the imagery, Dumai Lespinasse, a newspaper editor and political leader, called Haiti "the mother of African liberty," subtly echoing the French republican symbolism of "Marianne," the bare-breasted (white) female personification of liberation from bondage: "Perhaps the days are not very far away when the Republic of Haiti, this mother of African liberty, surmounting the clouds which encircle her, will throw herself beautiful and radiant in the midst of the nations—then, sirs, you will remind yourselves with joy and enthusiasm of having extended your hand in the bad days, to this beautiful country, destined, I venture to say, to become the refuge and the rally-point of all Africans who are truly free and independent."[27] This African Marianne, like the figure in France (Agulhon 1981) and in other French Caribbean territories (Burton 1993), elicits the helping hand of honorable male citizens, men whose freedom she guarantees in her very embodiment of the radiant Black Republic (on the gendering of British and American abolitionist symbolism, see Sheller 2011a).

Likewise, the Manifeste de Praslin, a key defining text of the liberal revolution of 1843, called forth "all the fathers of families who care for the future of their children" to join the revolution. It referred to the country as "our first mother" and, with a touch of melodrama, demanded that the reader "see miserable Haiti, suffering, dressed in rags, nearly a slave, trembling under the weight of injustice and arbitrary power, degraded under this regime of immorality!" (Madiou 1985–91 [1847–48]: 7:415–16; my translation). The only direct reference to actual women in the entire revolutionary manifesto is as family members, and even there the reference is addressed to men, urging them on as paternal protectors: "See your children deprived of instruction, nourishment of civilized man, last sacrament of the republican; see them menaced with soon becoming victims of tyranny. Plunge your regards into this fearful future for them, if you do not shelter them with your paternal wings. Hear the plaints, laments, reproaches, the just reproaches of your wives, your mothers, your daughters, your sisters, who accuse you of cowardice, pusillanimity, torpor" (Madiou 1985–91 [1847–48]: 7:415). Haitian women were part of this symbolic construction of the nation only in the roles of wife, mother, and sister—never as citizens in their own right.

The symbolic nuclear family played a crucial ideological role as the incubator of good Haitian citizens. In a cross-national analysis of the social construction of democracy, George Andrews and Herrick Chapman argue that variations in paths to democratization lead to different kinds of legitimizing discourses. In cases influenced by what they call an "organic statist" ideology, limitations on democratic participation were often justified by a particular rhetoric of familial relations: "The effect—and . . . purpose—of such rhetoric was to undercut the liberal ideal of broad-based political participation, or, failing that, to channel such participation in ways acceptable to ruling elites. Nowhere was this clearer than in the political discourse on gender and the family. . . . The consequence of such rhetoric was to bar the majority of the population from direct political participation and to confine it to a secondary role in the 'private' sphere" (Andrews and Chapman 1995: 21). In Haiti, the private family was sometimes seen as a "nursery" for citizens. For example, Félix Darfour, editor of *L'Éclaireur Haytien ou le Parfait Patriote*, argued that the family was a school for citizenship, for there "the citizen, the public man, the magistrate is nothing more than a man. . . . His house, temple of virtues is a perpetual school of good examples and wise maxims, of good deeds and obedience, of tenderness and respect." One can only assume that women were the teachers in this school but serving a conservative function: "Private life becomes therefore, also a perpetual lesson for public life: it transforms the obedience of children into that of subjects, the union of brothers into that of citizens, the love for the family into that for the fatherland, the attachment to domestic peace into that for public repose, the particular interest into the general interest. Presided over by values, private life is already in consequence a domestic government, which prepares one for submission to civil government."[28] Another liberal-republican newspaper, *Le Manifeste*, argued in its opening editorial that the "periodical press is also a mother, happy and fecund. The greatest statesmen, the most able ministers, the most adroit diplomats, the most savvy publicists have come from her womb."[29] Here the republican institution of a free press becomes the metaphoric mother of active male citizens, while women themselves are excluded from public expression.

Family rhetoric served a conservative function not only in excluding women, but also in avoiding participatory democracy. As in other "organic statist" democracies, conservative elites in Haiti also "portrayed the nation-state as a harmonious, integrated community in which competing class interests could be reconciled and smoothed away by enlightened elders ruling with the best interests of the society at heart" (Andrews and Chapman 1995: 20). In Haiti, this took the form of comparing the people to children to justify "enlightened" leadership by their wise elders; mulatto elites denied any conflict of interest between classes or colors, even as they argued that the people were not "ready" to govern themselves (cf. Nicholls 1996). In 1842, for example, Beaubrun Ardouin published a newspaper, *Le Temps*, in which it was suggested that "the boy passes through adolescence before arriving at virility. . . . A young people . . . must not make haste more than it should. . . . It does not suffice for such a people, having adopted certain institutions that old nations could procure for themselves only over the succession of centuries, to then believe that they are in a state to put them into practice right away."[30]

This produced an angry retort from Telismon Bouchereau's more liberal *Le Patriote*: "One compares the Haitian Nation to an infant, barely out of diapers; one recommends that he defend himself from the presumption and illusions of adolescence; 'do not make haste more than you should.' And when, then, will we leave this infancy? What! Do you not see that the child has become a man? . . . Do you not think, to the contrary, that he should regret his youth, passed in inaction? . . . The hour of his manhood has sounded."[31] It was precisely this cry of "manhood" that was expressed in the liberal revolution of 1843 that soon followed this exchange of views on the readiness of the Haitian people to participate in their own government. A generation of young men challenged their "fathers" to live up to the ideals of the republic and succeeded in deposing President Boyer. Boyer himself turned family imagery against the liberal revolution, calling it "perverse" for "arming citizen against citizen, brothers against brothers, sons against their fathers!" (quoted in Madiou 1985–91 [1847–48]: 7:447; my translation). Opposition was seen as a corruption of the sanctity of the civic family, an oedipal drama on the national stage.

The use of the imagery of childhood to depict political immaturity was prevalent in racist discourse of the nineteenth century, which compared non-white people, slaves, women, and servants to children to justify their civil and political subordination. In Haiti, Charles Mackenzie, the representative of the British Foreign Office (and himself a man of color), described the Haitians as "young Barbarians."[32] Likewise, the French Ministry of Foreign Affairs gave its representatives, who were in Haiti to negotiate a treaty of recognition, these instructions: "It is a case of showing the superiority of the civilized white over the half-savage negro; one must consider the Haitians as big children, pardon them their stupid blunders, and always show them a kind, indulgent face."[33] In this patronizing setting where Africans and their descendants in the New World were denied "full manhood rights," as they were known at the time, it is not surprising that Haitian independence became a matter of proving their manhood; the relationship between men and women in Haiti thus became implicated in defending the masculinity of the Haitian man. All eyes were on the Haitian man; even advocates of slavery abolition such as James Redpath in the United States promoted Haiti as a destination for African American emigration precisely because it was the "one country in the Western World where the Black and the man of color are undisputed lords; . . . where the people whom America degrades and drives from her are rulers, judges, and generals; men of extended commercial relations, authors, artists, and legislators" (Redpath 1970 [1861]: 9).

In 1882, Haitians were still defending themselves against charges of immaturity, now cloaked in scientific racism. An attack published by Léo Quesnel in the French *Révue politique et littéraire* so outraged a group of Haitians studying in Paris at the time that they published a series of responses. One despaired, "Quesnel has no fear in denying the quality of adults, of men properly speaking, not only to all negroes in general, but to Haitians in particular, and presents them as forming a race of children or of *minus habentes*, incapable of raising themselves to virility, and condemned to an irremediable inferiority" (quoted in Auguste et al. 1882: 151; my translation). Quesnel's social Darwinism reinvigorated earlier beliefs in Africans' lack of manhood, with the same outcome as for previous generations: Young Haitian men had to prove their manhood in European and

American public spheres in order to prove their capacity, and capability, for self-government. This external "gaze" on Haitian culture—along with actual military threats and power over the Haitian state—thus insidiously shaped Haitian self-presentation, distorted the gender order, and demanded a virile model of citizenship.

CHAPTER SIX

"You Signed My Name,
but Not My Feet"

In seeking to get further beneath the history of citizenship, we can turn the soil and dig deeper into the nineteenth century. Haiti is an unusual case in the comparative study of post-emancipation societies because its revolutionary war of 1791–1803 stands alone as the only successful case of simultaneous armed self-liberation and declaration of independence from colonial rule. Unlike in other colonial territories in which slaves were emancipated, the economic and state apparatus were also prised from French control. Following independence in 1804, however, a strong class and color divide remained between the elite freedmen (*anciens libres*) who had been planters and slaveowners prior to the revolution and the majority of the population of former plantation slaves, some of whom rose up through the ranks of the revolutionary army to become generals and landowners in their own right. This chapter will consider the specificity of ongoing forms of control and resistance in this unusual context, in contrast to other post-slavery societies where white planters and former slaveowners remained in control. Given the ongoing social inequalities and political struggles in Haiti's post-independence period, what forms could control from above and citizenship from below take? In a situation of successful revolutionary emancipation, how would embodied freedom be exercised?[1]

Peasants in post-independence Haiti had an expression: "Vous signé *nom* moi, mais vous pas signé *pieds* moi (You signed my name, but you haven't signed my feet)" (Ardouin 1860: 10:23n1). This notion of embodied action (freedom of movement) outweighing a formal contract signed on paper is exemplary of what we might call subaltern tactics of resistance. It shows a knowing agent who goes along with the formalities of signing a contract (perhaps insofar as it will serve purposes of getting a wage and not being arrested for vagrancy), but who then asserts the freedom to leave when the time comes. Moreover, it is phrased as a direct address to a holder of power who is trying to enforce the contractual obligation; it is a public moment for the "hidden transcript" (J. Scott 1990). Resistance is precisely being able to work with and against the system at the same time, to defy power even while appearing to serve it. In this case, it is also a continuation of the Haitian tradition of *petit marronage*, escaping the plantation system of control as and when necessary. The success of this strategy is evident in the collapse of Haiti's plantation economy in the early nineteenth century, as I discuss later. It is indicative of the power of embodied freedom within vernacular culture.

The folk saying has further resonance, however, as a commentary on the discrepancy between historical materiality (the earthy feet as "lived experience") and the written record of history (the signature tracks left as remnants in the archives). When we write in the name of the Haitian peasantry, how much has escaped us? When does the peasant walk off the pages of the historian's archive and leave only an absence in the historical text? Marc Bloch (1953) once wrote that the task of the historian is to seek out the "traces" left in the historical record by tracking more subtle "sources in spite of themselves." Michel-Rolph Trouillot, however, challenges us further by calling into question any will to better historical knowledge, given the "silencing of the past" and, in particular, the silencing of the Haitian Revolution. However ardently the historian seeks the traces of lost facticity, Trouillot (1995: 29) reminds us, "Facts are not created equal: the production of traces is always also the creation of silences." Efforts to turn up facts belie the existence of the "unthinkable," that which "one cannot conceive of within the range of possible alternatives, that which perverts all answers because it defies the terms under which the questions were phrased" (Trouillot 1995: 82).

In terms of Western thought, Trouillot argues, the Haitian Revolution was unthinkable in its time and remains largely marginal to the main historiographical narratives of modernity, which have focused on the American and French revolutions as the measuring rods of the "Age of Democracy." A corollary to this is the way in which Haiti's history after the revolution has been warped and forgotten. When remembered, it is either turned into a travesty of despotic barbarism, political incompetence, and economic decline (within Euro-American historiography) or celebrated as the unquestioned consolidation of a heroic anticolonial independence (within Haitian and wider Caribbean historiography). The erasure of the historical figure Sans Souci, a very successful general who led the African faction within the revolution, was carried out not only by white European writers, but also by King Henri Christophe, who killed him and then built an elaborate palace nearby that bears the name Sans Souci. Trouillot (1995) reads this as an elite silencing of the subaltern war within the war, with the victors controlling the story that is recorded for posterity. Against such silencing, I want to bring back into focus the relation between the decline of planter control and the emergence of peasant agency in nineteenth-century Haiti. If we think of freedom as a continuous variable, it is clear that slave emancipation everywhere led to struggles over the liberties that planters would lose and that the formerly enslaved would gain (Sheller 2000: chap. 2). Even in Haiti—or, perhaps, *especially* in Haiti—the problem of implementing freedom remained the core social and political question.

Yet the apparent lack of any political agency, any sign of resistance, among the Haitian peasantry has produced a gaping silence in Haitian history. In his introduction to James Leyburn's *The Haitian People* (1980 [1966]), for example, Sidney Mintz verged on dismissing altogether the possibility of peasant political agency in Haiti. Although admitting that Haitian peasants occasionally played a political role, Mintz argued that this was exceptional; in general, the peasants had been "unable to break out of a stagnation that is economic as well as cultural," making them wholly "apathetic." He lamented: "Seemingly mute and invisible, apparently powerless, the peasantry of Haiti remind one of Marx's famous dictum that peasants possess organization only in the sense that the potatoes in a sack of potatoes are organized" (Mintz 1989: 270, 297). The Haitian peasantry, it would seem, is not a good candidate for exemplifying a post-slavery revolutionary (or even resistant) subaltern ideology. What happened to C. L. R. James's Black Jacobins (James 1963)? What can explain this apparent political apathy? Or is it a mistaken appraisal of Haitian political culture? How much do we really know about past instances of peasants' political activism and resistance, especially in a field where both sources and primary research are thin on the ground? Can history ever sign these feet, or do our very modes of asking questions make this history unthinkable?

Much of the perspective of slaves, indentured laborers, and other workers—in particular, women—is missing from the historical record and can never be directly discovered, however hard one tries. The strategy here instead would be to identify the gaps in the historical record, the human losses, and the resistances of which there will never be a record. Yet Bloch's notion of "witnesses in spite of themselves" may still be of some use here. Even colonial archival records may provide clues, especially in the shape of what is missing from them—the blanks or breaks in the record. Studies of the Haitian Revolution, in particular, have followed up on Trouillot's (1995) analysis of the event as "unthinkable history." Susan Buck-Morss (2000) and Sibylle Fischer (2004) have examined the sleight of hand in Hegel's pivotal chapter in *Phenomenology of Spirit* (1807), on lordship and bondage, asking how it could have been written as if Haiti and its revolution did not exist. Fischer further shows how studies of the American and French revolutions elided the question of slavery by absenting the Haitian Revolution altogether and explores the deep silence around the revolutions in Cuba, in the Dominican Republic, and even in Haiti itself. She demonstrates how "the disavowal of radical antislavery became constitutive [both] for emerging national cultures in the Caribbean and [for] metropolitan political discourse" (Fischer 2004: 274).

Mainstream contemporary historiography of the Haitian Revolution has thus been compelled to grapple with fictional echoes, drawing not only on archival sources, but also on fictional works such as Alejo Carpentier's *The Kingdom of This World* (1967) or Derek Walcott's plays on Toussaint Louverture; the history of Guadeloupe likewise takes inspiration from Carpentier's *Explosion in a Cathedral* (1963) and Daniel Maximin's *Lone Sun* (1989). As Laurent Dubois (2004b: 13) observes, "These novels are part of a corpus of Caribbean literature that has sought to recover and evoke the histories of these islands and has played a crucial role in drawing attention to the region's past." Using an imagery of multiple terrains and subterranean sedimentations, Maximin excavates a reimagined subaltern history. "By combining fragments of existing historical sources with invented ones and placing them as historical documents within his novel," argues Dubois (2004b: 13–14), "Maximin confronts the silences of the archives by creating an archive containing histories that, if they are impossible to recover, are necessary to remember. Maximin's work, like that of the Martinican writers Edouard Glissant and Patrick Chamoiseau, raises the question of whether the stories of slaves can in fact ever be recovered through archival documents recorded by the masters and institutions who held them in bondage." Nevertheless, in his own work Dubois goes on to use these archival sources to great effect. He shows especially how legal documentation leaves an archival track and how former slaves used the right to documentation to legitimize their free status, their familial relationships, and their bequests of property through inheritance. In this chapter, therefore, I continue with the perilous yet precious effort to track the Haitian peasantry's walk toward freedom.

STATE CONTROL AND THE
BAREFOOT TRACKS OF RESISTANCE

What was the reality of freedom for Haiti's post-revolutionary plantation laborers and "reconstituted peasants," and what evidence do we turn to in trying to reconstruct that historical reality?[2] Although the Haitian Revolution succeeded in ending slavery and achieving national independence far before many other slave societies, it is generally argued that the real winners of the revolution were not the mass of freed slaves but the old *mulâtre* landowning elite (the anciens libres) and the new *noir* generals (the nouveaux libres) who seized the state (Nicholls 1996; Trouillot 1990).[3] Thus, it is crucial first to recognize that the political process of revolutionary self-emancipation entailed the continuation of certain forms of control, even in Haiti. In the early decades of state consolidation, social and political control actually passed not to the self-liberated slaves who had achieved the unthinkable revolution but to a small elite that protected its own interests and suppressed much of the potential radicalism of the revolution. As Trouillot (1992: 149) argues in an important essay on the "inconvenience of freedom," the privileged group of *gens de couleur* were at first "reluctant to admit the fact that the end of slavery signalled the slow replacement of the plantation system by a peasant-based society." They instead "tried to overcome the obstacle that the growing peasantry represented to their pursuit of wealth and prestige by resorting to politics and, to a lesser degree, to commerce."

Civil war from 1805 to 1820 divided the former French colony into a Republic of Haiti in the south and a Kingdom of Haiti in the north, keeping both governments on a constant military footing. These initial decades of state formation tended toward what one foreign observer paradoxically described as "republican monarchy sustained by the bayonet" (Brown 1972 [1837]: 2:259). Military control was reinforced by Haiti's precarious position in a world controlled by the major slaveholding nations, all of which refused to recognize Haitian independence and some of which were plotting Haiti's recapture.[4] The early decades of the nineteenth century were a period of major realignment of colonial power in the Americas. The Haitian Revolution sparked French territorial retreat not only in the Caribbean, but also in North America, where large territories were turned over to the British and the United States. Iberian colonial control in large parts of the Americas was also being dismantled from 1810 to 1824, and a realignment of external links toward British economic agents and interests was increasingly taking place (Stern 1993 [1988]: 56). These shifts in power were associated with expansions of "Creole" power and the emergence of new American centers of gravity, as local elites redeployed colonial apparatuses of control and profit taking toward their own interests. In Haiti, too, the profits of the plantation economy were momentarily tilted back into local coffers.

As soon as the French landowners and foreign occupying forces had been driven off the island, Haitian generals seized the land of the former plantations and the reins of state power. In the northern Kingdom of Haiti, King Henri Christophe maintained the big estates intact and under the control of military men who formed a new aristocracy. In the south, the republican military traditions of the revolution were institutionalized by the constitution put into place by Dessalines in 1805, and President Alexandre Pétion thereafter distributed land to the veterans of the wars of independence. A decree in 1809 gave full title to property taken from former sugar plantations according to military rank: 25 carreaux for colonels, 15 carreaux for battalion chiefs, 10 carreaux for captains to second lieutenants, and 5 carreaux to noncommisioned officers and soldiers (Lacerte 1975: 81).[5] In 1814, Pétion carried out another extensive distribution of land taken from coffee estates to officers in active service. He granted 35 carreaux to battalion or squadron chiefs, 30 carreaux to captains, 25 carreaux to lieutenants, and 20 carreaux to second lieutenants; land was also distributed in smaller grants to government employees, hospital employees, and members of the judicial administration as a way to pay salaries (Lacerte 1975: 82–83). As one contemporary put it, Pétion had "republicanized the soil" (Lepelletier de Saint-Remy, quoted in Lacerte 1975: 83–84). His land distribution achieved what Caroline Fick (1988: 269) calls "a stabilizing compromise between the hegemonic mulatto elite and the economically dispossessed masses," although as noted in chapter 5 it still excluded women.

But revolution, war, and the flight of former slaves from the plantations (despite government efforts to enforce labor) all contributed to a rapid collapse in sugar exports, which plummeted from more than 141 million pounds on the eve of the French Revolution in 1789 to a meager 2.5 million pounds in 1820. At the same time, annual coffee production fell from a high of almost 77 million pounds in 1789 (when coffee exports matched white-sugar exports in value) to a low of 24 million in 1822.[6] A British businessman who visited Haiti in the early 1820s described how various methods of keeping the big estates cultivated had failed since the abolition of slavery. First, sharecropping was tried on government-owned land, with the cultivators given one-third or one-fourth of the crop. This had to be abandoned, and the next experiment was "to purchase canes from the cultivator, who was put in possession of the land, the Government, or Owner, retaining the Mill, Boiling house, etc. in his possession, and grinding the canes purchased from the cultivator." This also failed, because the central factories could not obtain enough canes and because the cultivators continually disputed the prices being offered. Finally, the little sugar being produced had to be paid for by wages, with men offered $3 per week and women and boys $1.50.[7] As the unsympathetic (and pro-slavery) British Consul Charles Mackenzie reported in 1828, the plantations had been broken up, and labor could not be enforced: "The very little field labour effected is generally performed by elderly people, principally old Guinea negroes. No measure of the government can induce the young creoles to labour, or depart from their habitual licentiousness and vagrancy."[8]

Control over agricultural production and export revenues became the main task of the state, providing its sole access to hard currency with which to pay off the 150 million franc indemnity that had been agreed with France in exchange for recognizing Haiti's independence in 1825. Like the earlier rural code of Toussaint Louverture, President Boyer's Code Rural of 1826 provided for the "protection and encouragement of agriculture" through a strict regime of rural police surveillance and regulation of work contracts and trade. Proclaiming agriculture to be the "principal source of the prosperity of the state," the code ordered that all citizens who were not state employees (civil or military) and were not licensed to engage in particular professions "must cultivate the land." As the Haitian constitutional historian Louis Joseph Janvier noted, Boyer's code was equivalent to "slavery without the whip" (Janvier 1886; cf. Dayan 1995: 14). Most important, it declared that agricultural workers were not allowed to leave the countryside and go to the towns or cities without authorization from a justice of the peace; nor could their children be apprenticed in the towns. Mobility was tightly restricted by a pass system, and cooperative ownership of land was outlawed. The longest section of the code pertained to the duties of the Rural Police, charged with arresting vagabonds, maintaining order in fieldwork, maintaining discipline of work gangs, and overseeing road building. The code also specifically outlawed collective ownership of farms and worker self-management in "sociétés."[9]

Rather than an apathetic peasantry, these codes indicate a fluid and mobile population that was trying its best to abandon the sugar and coffee plantations. At the local level, however, resistance remained difficult. With up to 40,000 men in the army, the National Guard, and the Rural Police, armed power not only fostered social climbing through patronage and political pacts, but also served as a brake on resistance. The soldiers and other government employees who received land grants helped to exercise control over the more numerous landless laborers, the former slaves who were now called "cultivators." Local "big men" also siphoned off taxes and license fees from the small traders, mostly women, who made up the backbone of the local economy. We can also guess that men exercised control over the labor of their own family members, especially women and children. So even as the Haitian state and its co-opted agents resisted the foreign powers who controlled the colonial world system (and exercised some degree of control over foreign merchants), they were also largely engaged in controlling Haiti's own population and thwarting efforts at resistance.

Variations in post-slavery peasant autonomy in the Caribbean are generally attributed to a combination of economic, geographic, and political factors that together determine the *availability of land for peasant settlement* (Besson 1995; Higman 1995a; Mintz 1989; Stinchcombe 1996). It is through independent landholding that former slaves gained a modicum of self-determination. Post-slavery peasantries "gained a more secure foothold in the larger and more mountainous territories [such as Haiti and Jamaica and] were more attenuated or constrained in smaller or flatter islands" (Besson 1995: 73). The French colony of Saint-Domingue already had one of the best-developed "proto-peasantries" in the Caribbean because of its combination of early, intensive sugar plantation, large size, and mountainous landscape. Its rugged interior had helped to foster both Maroon autonomy and long-established traditions of landholding kin groups (Besson 1995: 77; Mintz 1989: 241). Peasant landholding as an alternative to sugar monoculture thus became the key terrain for wresting power and some degree of self-determination from the post-slavery planters and the states they controlled throughout the Caribbean (Besson 1979; Bolland 1981; Fick 1990; Mintz 1989; Rodney 1981). Unlike other post-emancipation peasantries, however, Haitians faced not an entrenched white planter class backed by a distant colonial state but new local elites who claimed to share their interests and identity.

Mobility is a key component of freedom, enabling escape from personalistic relations of domination, yet Haitian plantation workers, or cultivators, had few freedoms in the early days of the republic. The "Law concerning the policing of estates and the reciprocal obligations between proprietors, farmers, and cultivators" of 1807 stipulated that all cultivators had to sign work contracts and, once contracted, could not leave the property. Disputes were to be settled in front of a justice of the peace (invariably a landowner), and any cultivator who provoked a "movement" of any kind, by word or deed, would be tried for "disturbing public order." Written permission was needed from plantation managers to travel within a parish (checked by military patrols), and passports were needed for travel between communes.[10] The existence of such laws implies that a certain number of people were breaking their contracts, moving from place to place in search of better work or living conditions, and that some were even joining together in some kind of movement, labor protest, or perhaps even strike.

Peasant landownership is one of the most significant measures of peasants' civil rights and personal liberties in former slave societies, for with landownership came control over everyday family decision making, as well as some degree of economic autonomy (Sheller 2000). Although landholding generals dominated government, they nevertheless struggled to maintain control over their plantation workforces. The most significant change in agricultural production after independence was a shift to small-scale coffee export. "Just as the less prosperous among the whites and the freedmen of Saint Domingue had found an economic alternative in coffee," observes Trouillot (1990: 60), "so a growing number of the post-revolutionary peasants and small landowners had turned to that crop for similar reasons. It required little start-up capital, its cultivation and processing required much less labor than did sugar cane, and it sold well on the export market." Annual coffee exports stabilized at 35–40 million pounds from the late 1820s to the 1840s, indicating viable production. By 1859, Haiti was the fourth largest coffee producer in the world (after Brazil, Java, and Ceylon), and coffee constituted 70 percent of its exports (Dupuy 1989: 95).[11]

In shifting into coffee cultivation, Haitian rural people appear to have built on the foundations of existing autonomous slave traditions established in what Mintz (1989: 146) called the "interstices" of plantation society, little cracks in which embodied freedom could bubble up from below. Contrary to his image of an unorganized mass of scattered peasants, however, the rural working class and small *habitants* of Haiti in fact practiced their own genres of association and cooperation. Gerard Barthélémy (1989) argues that Haitian peasants developed a self-regulating culture based on egalitarianism and inter-individual reciprocity "outside" of state structures—or, we might say, beneath the state. Collective work groups, which can be traced back to the nineteenth century (such as Sociétés de Travail, Combites, Escouades, and Avanjou), shared labor outside the monetary system, worked land collectively, served as friendly societies, and in some cases elected leaders (Barthélémy 1989; Courlander 1960). Workers' associations—rooted in the plantation work gangs but looking forward to new forms of collective work based on equality, reciprocity, and use of the electoral process—contained the seeds of popular political participation. Even the conservative historian Beaubrun Ardouin remarked on "the introduction of the principle of election of all the offices necessary in a rural farm, by the cultivators themselves forming associations" (quoted in Barthélémy 1989: 93–94). Thus, a form of direct democracy at the local level was founded on the republican egalitarianism of the revolutionary period and survived throughout the postcolonial period as a major form of rural self-organization.

THE ECONOMIC AND SOCIAL POSITION OF WOMEN

To understand the position of women in post-revolutionary Haiti, one must begin with some understanding of the sexual division of labor under colonial slavery. Historians of slavery have shown that status divisions within slave societies tended to give enslaved men more opportunities than their female counterparts to achieve positions of some independence and material reward; emancipation, likewise, was experienced in different ways by each sex, with women facing new forms of subordination (Jones 1985; Morrissey 1989; Reddock 1985; Shepherd et al. 1995). At the height of the Haitian sugar boom of the 1770s and 1780s, according to David Geggus, enslaved "men were eight times as likely as women to escape from the drudgery of fieldwork into a post offering some independence and status." This occurred because "females had much less access than their male counterparts to positions of independence, skill, and prestige. The number of specialist positions open to women was extremely small, and they offered only limited rewards" (Geggus 1996: 262; Reddock 1985). Barred from becoming sugar boilers, sailors, blacksmiths, coopers, and carpenters, both enslaved and freed women were left with less prestigious jobs in domestic service and precarious petty marketing as some of the few occupations outside fieldwork. Thus, from the start, non-white women in slave societies occupied the lowest economic and social rungs in the plantation system.

During Saint-Domingue's colonial period, however, free women of color took advantage of the more open opportunities of thriving urban ports such as Cap Français and Port-au-Prince to engage in various kinds of business, ranging from property speculation (in real estate and slaves) to small retail trading, innkeeping, and prostitution. "The majority of free women of color," writes Susan Socolow (1996: 292–93), "certainly led precarious economic lives, but notary transactions suggest that many played important roles in the local economy, acting independently, unlike white women, who were rarely visible acting on their own." Despite their prominent economic role, free women of color were often caricatured in European writing of the period as creatures of sexuality, luxury, and sensuality. Their public, urban, independent roles were linked to images of decadence, disorder, and sin in the colonial imagination, particularly in the case of the "*mulâtresse*," who was envisioned as the illicit progeny of the debauched union of white male and black female slave (Mohammed 2000). The very existence of free urban women of color was seen to threaten the Christian moral foundations of European colonial society.

Women's participation in trade in the Republic of Haiti thus built on patterns established during the colonial period and carried with it the heavy baggage of colonial racial and sexual inequality. Nevertheless, commerce was preferable to fieldwork. In addition to the sheer backbreaking nature of work in the canefields and coffee hills and the rigorous time discipline imposed by overseers, a motivating force for women to prefer marketing activities over fieldwork must have been the low wages offered to freed women compared with men. James Franklin reported in 1826 that "the wages are from 2½ to 3 dollars a week . . . for an able-bodied cultivator. Women who work in the fields get the same wages as boys about 14 years of age, which is about 1½ dollars."[12] Thus, women were receiving half the wages of men for similar work. Franklin also reported that on the small properties, "Picking and preparing the coffee is the work of the females, except pulping which is performed by the males in a rude wooden machine to serve the purpose of a pestle and mortar." Work with machinery, however rustic, was usually a higher-status occupation. Article 57 of the Rural Code of 1826 specified that in the case of sharecropping, which was fairly common, all first-class workers, male and female, were to receive the same share; however, social "safeguards" may well have kept women out of the first class category, relegating them to second class (receiving two-thirds of the full share) or third class (receiving one-half of the full share).[13]

Thus, many women found better opportunities as small traders. Marketing by women was extended in the postcolonial period and legally codified by the Rural Code of 1826. A letter from Consul-General Mackenzie shows that marketing by women was already well established in Haiti by 1826. Complaining to the Foreign Office about the limitations on retail trade by foreign merchants, he described the "*marchandes*" this way: "The purchasers from the foreigner cannot under such regulations be the great body of consumers. An intermediate class is thus created, chiefly if not exclusively composed of women, called 'marchandes,' who employ a number of hucksters that traverse the country, attend the markets, and give an account of their transactions to their employers, either every evening, once a week, or once a month, according to their characters."[14] The code stated that "no stores, wholesale or retail, shall be established, nor shall any commerce in foodstuffs be done in the countryside, under any pretext whatsoever."[15] Only licensed peddlers could sell goods, and the code provided for a special class of ambulatory peddlers to circulate through rural districts but to reside in the towns. This group consisted almost entirely of women and came to be known as "Madan Sara." The women literally used their feet to get by, much like their counterparts the higglers of Jamaica.

Many European observers of Haitian society in the mid-nineteenth century lambasted the economic role of Haïtiennes, which conflicted with their own ideologies of "public man" and "domestic woman."[16] The reaction of Jonathan Brown, an American who visited Haiti in 1837, is typical, equating labor by women with barbarism and lamenting the lack of a work ethic among men: "As is the case with all barbarous nations, the females are compelled to perform most of the labor. Those of the country employ themselves in cultivating the soil, while the men spend their time in traversing the country on horseback, in drinking, smoking, and other habits equally unprofitable" (Brown 1972 [1837]: 281). Mintz quotes this account of a marchande in 1854, depicting the extent of women's financial independence:

> Elsiné—I name her first because she was the head of the house—was a wide-awake, intelligent, amiable and well-conditioned black woman, about forty years of age; Emilien, her faithful consort, was not near as intelligent, nor quite as fat, nor quite as tall, nor quite as dignified as Elsiné. . . . She is the capitalist of the concern, and does all the business. He has no more to do with the direction of affairs, in or out of the house, than

if he were her child. She is worth from fifteen to twenty thousand dollars, all of which she has made as a dealer in provisions. Elsiné began her commercial career in the market without any money; by gradual accumulations she got some capital ahead, and now buys from the commission merchants in large quantities, and sells on credit to retail dealers—mostly to girls whom she has trained, and upon whose business she keeps a careful eye. . . . Besides this house she owns all the other houses on the block, and is building all the time.[17]

Elsiné's success shows a marchande operating not only as a debtor but also as a creditor to other women and, beyond that, as a real-estate developer and landlord. As Mintz (1993: 239) observes, the European writer found this "a strange inversion of the ordinary relations of husband and wife" and notes that "Emilien appeared perfectly conscious of his inferiority, and as contented with the narrow sphere of connubial duty assigned him, as a prince-consort to the mightiest Queen in Christendom." The bemused comments of this white Victorian man belie a certain discomfort with domestic and sexual dominance by women (reminiscent of European views of "Quasheba" in chapter 2), with the husband reduced to a childlike role that undermines his masculinity.

Although marchandes exercised a certain degree of financial independence, many were at the mercy of foreign creditors and of men, who could take advantage of their access to credit. Even successful marchandes fell into debt because of their subordination to men, and seemingly independent women could be "kept" by men: "Many of the marchandes are high in credit, and fulfill their engagements with the most scrupulous integrity; though too many of them have been made the scape-goats for their husbands or keepers, who, after having consumed all that they could obtain on credit from the foreigner, leave them to their fate. Those, however, who maintain their reputation, generally pay the merchants once a fortnight, or even at shorter periods."[18] As this shows, market women were indebted to the foreign mercantile houses that advanced them credit to buy both the local agricultural produce and the foreign imported goods that they sold. However wealthy individual women might become, they were still subject to the requirements of an unequal world economy that rested on the commodities produced by slavery.

A crucial outcome of this legal codification of women's marketing was the creation of a segmented economy in which the more profitable export crops (*haut commerce*) such as cotton, coffee, and mahogany were channeled through foreign mercantile houses that were allowed to operate out of eleven open ports, while the less profitable regional internal markets for local food produce (*petit commerce*) were left to Haitian women—and even there, they operated on credit extended by foreign merchants, mainly against the coffee crop.[19] "In the Haitian rural organization," argues Georges Anglade (1982: 69; my translation), "one sees a predominant role for women in the least lucrative circuit, that of perishable products (*vivres*), while men dominate in the circuit of commodities (*denrées*). From incomplete observations was founded the myth of the woman as the 'principal economic agent of the rural world,' when these women, massively present in the markets, in fact shared in activities limited to the movement of only perishable products." Anglade's perceptive analysis is equally applicable today, when Haitian women can be seen engaged in vast amounts of small-scale, almost minuscule trade (often that which can be carried on their heads) that appears to keep the local economy afloat. Yet Haitian women's economic independence was (and is) circumscribed by the inequalities of both the world economy and the local structure of gender relations. Most traders were trapped in a circuit of small trade, which required intense work, returned tiny profits, and left them vulnerable to debt. With a faltering economy and heavy state taxation, women's marketing in the nineteenth century was a labor-intensive, high-risk, and low-return activity (much as it remains today). Despite high levels of participation in agricultural labor and marketing, Haitian women generally have owned less land than men, had less capital to invest, earned lower wages, and enjoyed less autonomy (Larose 1975).

On the other hand, Haitian women had access to credit to a degree quite unusual for the time, and unthinkable in Europe, where women were largely excluded from commercial credit. A revision of Haitian civil law in 1840 granted special legal rights to women because of their de facto independent financial status, and Article 201 for the first time ensured financial independence for *married* women: "The wife may, without the authorization of her husband, receive both mobile and immobile capital, take on debts, stand security, acquire and alienate by free title or title subject to certain payments, even stand in judgment, and generally make all species of legal acts and contracts" (Ardouin 1860: 11:119). Ardouin conceded that this legal emancipation of married women was an unavoidable outcome of their existing financial independence, but he hypothesized that it would disappear as Haiti "advanced in civilization." Haitian civil law not only allowed married women independent incomes; it also allowed women's inheritance with none of the restrictions of male primogeniture—land and other goods were apportioned equally among all siblings, male and female alike, including those born out of wedlock. Modernizing elites complained about this situation, and the Manifeste de Praslin of 1843, harbinger of the liberal revolution, actually bemoaned the "bizarre civil law," which "eroded marital authority and paternal power." Following Jean Besson (2002), we might instead interpret it as another form of Caribbean culture building, re-adapting European legal institutions for new circumstances by formalizing women's economic autonomy—an autonomy that had emerged from below.

POPULAR REBELLIONS, EMBODIED FREEDOM, AND SPIRITUALITY

Gender distinctions were deeply embedded in the entwined networks of republican militarism and liberal Freemasonry that shaped the upper echelons of Haitian political society in the first half of the nineteenth century, as I argued in the previous chapter. An inescapable contradiction was also created by the prominent role of women in the economy. Because women played a significant economic role in Haiti's labor force and markets, they at times became key political protagonists. Contrary to the rhetoric of masculine citizenship, women in Haiti did in fact exercise a number of public roles. Despite their political exclusion and the militarization of the state, they found ways to seize citizenship from below, especially during the political crises of 1843–44.

The fact that Haitian women were central protagonists in several important political events during the liberal revolution of 1843, for example, stands in stark contrast to the rhetorical version of Mother Haiti protected by her brave sons but unable to defend herself. The English missionary Mark Bird (1869: 88) admitted that "in some cases even the women have been engaged in some of the great struggles for national independence" but lamented that this reflected the "deeply-rooted military character" of the country. The historian Thomas Madiou observed that women in Les Cayes composed "a powerful propaganda in favor of the revolution" (Madiou 1985–91 [1847–48]: 7:455; my translation), and contemporary newspapers reported that old people, women, and children came out to cheer the popular army who gathered in Les Cayes.[20] Even more important, women actually took part in the fighting. The women of Léogâne, "while singing, dragged two large cannon from fort Ça-Ira into the town, and placed them in a battery facing the plain of Dampuce"; two shots from these cannon killed thirty soldiers, one of the highest death tolls in a single event during the largely nonviolent revolution of 1843 (Madiou 1985–91 [1847–48]: 7:468; my translation).

Several sources report that after suffering military desertions and defeats, President Boyer's final defeat came with the intervention of the women of Port-au-Prince. When the president ordered a battalion of *grenadiers* (National Guard) to join the battle on foot, "The battalion began to march, but as soon as it arrived at Morne-à-Tuf, it was stopped by an innumerable multitude of women. . . . [Boyer] was assailed by a new disturbance of women, who followed him and cursed him, abusing him in the most scathing manner." Like some of the Jamaican women described in chapter 2, this group of women took to the streets, used apparently vulgar language, and intervened on the public political stage. According to another version, it was the wives, mothers, and sisters of the National Guard who blocked the route and insisted "that they would not let go the soldiers unless [Boyer] put himself at their head," thus challenging his masculinity and bravery (Madiou 1985–91 [1847–48]: 7:468; cf. Bird 1869: 226).[21] Here, too, as in the Jamaican case, we see ties of kinship forming a significant basis for women's political solidarity and mobilization. That evening, Boyer reportedly "lost hope" and embarked on a British ship to Jamaica. Without the support of the women of Port-au-Prince, who not only were significant economic actors as marchandes but also apparently exercised influence over the soldiers, he had no social base to oppose the revolution.

The active role of women in revolutionary mobilizations is not the only indication of a more complex reality behind the gendered rhetoric of both liberal and conservative elites. We have few direct sources from peasant actors in the nineteenth century, since most were illiterate and few government records were preserved from this period. However, the evidence we do have suggests that there were alternative visions of race, class, and gender, as well as a different vision of Haitian nationhood submerged in a subaltern consciousness. The peasant movement known as the Piquets, led by Louis-Jean-Jacques Acaau, publicly articulated trenchant criticisms of the elite view of Haitian citizenship. Their name refers to the sharpened sticks carried by the "army of sufferers," as they called themselves, and certainly resonates with Burton's analysis of Afro-Creole oppositional culture. The Piquet Rebellion of 1844 followed closely on the heels of an important episode of liberal opening and closure in Haiti, the liberal revolution of 1843. This episode of peasant resistance offers evidence of the structure of political opportunities for peasants to openly contest elite control of the post-slavery state.

Acaau, a former member of the rural police, led the revolt of the "army of sufferers" in 1844, affirming "respect for the Constitution, Rights, Equality, Liberty."[22] As Leslie Manigat argues (and David Nicholls agrees), the Piquet movement "was the fruit of the conjunction of interests between big and medium black proprietors and small peasant *parçellaires* (landholders), equally black" (cited in Nicholls 1996: 276n68). I have argued elsewhere (Sheller 2000) that the movement went beyond questions of a "war of color," as it has often been portrayed, insofar as it articulated a class-conscious democratic ideology. However limited the success of this moment of political uprising, it is nevertheless a crucial clue to the unthinkable: an indicator of the freedom that might have been. This flickering ember of the democratic aspirations of the post-slavery peasantry was perhaps even a harbinger of the European movements of 1848, as some contemporaries noticed. Without romanticizing it, we can nevertheless read it as a dense knot in the grain of narratives of democratization, which usually move from Europe and North America out to the colonies. What if we thought the unthinkable and followed the footsteps of peasants in their path to freedom? And what if we found female protagonists along the way?

To begin with, Acaau explicitly denied that the Haitian "family" were all one color, thus challenging the elite's paternalistic familial imagery. To the contrary, he recognized divisions of color, class, and status, summarized in the famous saying of the Piquet Rebellion: "Nègue riche qui connait li et écri, cila mulâte; mulâte pauvre qui connait pas li et écri, cila nègue (The rich black who can read and write is a mulatto; the poor mulatto who cannot read or write is black)" (d'Alaux 1851: 112; my translation). Acaau and his lieutenants were also famous for donning the rough white clothing, sandals, and straw hat of the peasant (along with machete and pistols), as noted by Madiou (1985–91 [1847–48]: 8:149), initiating a style of leadership that was surely a rejection of the militaristic uniforms of Ogou-like leaders. Perhaps this was an assertion of the peasant values of the lwa Cousin Azaka, a trickster figure who also dresses in peasant costume; it was certainly associated with the use of sacred rites. Finally, it is thought that the Piquet movement included women in roles of leadership, and seems to have rejected the domestic ideology that confined women to the private sphere. According to one Haitian historian (although the evidence for this is not given), a woman named Louise Nicolas "is credited with organizing the [Piquet] movement in 1844" (Bellegarde-Smith 1990: 70).

British Consul Thomas Neville Ussher observed that Acaau "is a man of some instruction for a negro, has great influence over his followers which he has acquired by Obeah [*sic*, he uses the Jamaican term] practices, and affects the dress of a labourer."[23] Many Haitian leaders, from the Jamaican born *houngan* Boukman Dutty (who led the ceremony at Bwa Kayiman in August 1791 that initiated the Haitian Revolution) to President François Duvalier (who often presented himself as Baron Samedi while in office from 1957 until his death in 1971), are said to have used the powers of Vodou in leading the masses, but the question is what kind of symbols a leader draws on, and for what purpose. French Consul Maxime Reybaud, who went by the *nom de plume* Gustave d'Alaux, described Acaau's manner of communicating with the people: "the bandit Acaau came barefoot to the wayside cross of the parish, dressed in a species of canvas packing-sheet and wearing a little straw hat, and there publicly vowed not to change his clothing until the orders of 'divine Providence' were executed. Then, turning towards the negro peasants convened by the sound of the *lambi*, Acaau explained that 'divine Providence' ordered the poor people, first to chase out the mulattos, second to divide up the mulatto properties" (d'Alaux 1851: 111). Standing at the crossroads of history, in his bare feet, Acaau successfully mobilized the peasantry of the South. A Methodist missionary described their rough and ready army as "a great many men armed with sticks of different sorts of wood; they sharpened the edge, and applied poisonous gum to it, so that any wound which might not be dangerous, would through the poison become so. The sticks were from 8 to 10 feet long."[24] But what were they fighting for?

The Piquet movement had more aims than simply the seizure of mulattos' property or the imposition of black rule. Reybaud compared their ideology, in retrospect, to that of the European movements of 1848, calling it "negro communism":

"Unhappy innocence" plays, for example, the same role in the proclamations of Acaau as "the exploitation of man by man" in certain other proclamations. "The eventuality of national education," this other chord of Acaau's humanitarian lyre, corresponds visibly to "free and obligatory instruction," and insofar as he reclaims in the name of the cultivators, who are the *workers* down there, "reduction in the price of foreign merchandise and augmentation in the value of their crops," the black socialist has certainly found the clearest and most comprehensible formula for this problem of the white Acaaus: reduction of work and increase of salaries. (d'Alaux 1851: 115)

Reybaud consoled himself that "black communism would run aground like white communism on the extreme morcellation of property." It is clear that the Haitian peasants identified their enemies in class as well as color terms. Theirs were the hybrid peasant/proletarian aims of other post-emancipation social movements in the Caribbean (Sheller 2000). Their grievances were not simply against mulatto power but against abuses of martial law, violations of the constitution, and the subversion of democracy by President Boyer and his armed agents of control. Yet they also drew on vernacular religious practices to mobilize the people.

Tracking the bare footprints of peasant democracy across the few primary documents that remain in the archives suggest that the Piquets attempted to use democratic means of political address, publicizing and justifying their claims in proclamations and in newspapers and claiming to uphold the democratic constitution of 1843. They mobilized supporters through public gatherings, with religious leaders and some spiritual content to the message. Their leaders symbolically used the dress and Creole language of the peasantry to show in actions the kind of equality and participation that they were speaking about in words. The timing, form, and stated grievances and demands of the Piquets all suggest a class-conscious *and* color-conscious movement, with democratic aims and a clear critique of landowner-merchant domination and unmitigated control of the state. The possible role of women in the movement also hints at a more egalitarian collective ideology and a more inclusive practice of citizenship from below. A slightly later populist movement, related to the Piquets, was known to have included the so-called Amazons of Salnave, the female mobs who supported the popular nationalist President Sylvain Salnave (1867–69): "veritable furies of the civil war, arms bared, skirts tucked up, armed with large cutlasses . . . making the bourgeoisie tremble" (quoted in Desquiron 1993: 61; my translation). We are reminded that women, too, can be mounted by the warrior lwa Ogou.

Like freed slaves elsewhere, the self-liberated people of Haiti had to negotiate the terms and conditions of their freedom—not with white planters backed by a colonial state, as in Jamaica, but with landowning generals backed by force and legitimized by a continuing foreign threat to Haiti's independence. Defensive militarization of a weak state undermined the development of potentially democratic civil institutions in Haiti. The control of the state and its armed forces by a small elite had a strong negative impact on democratization. The army became one of the main avenues of political inclusion, as well as a route to landownership. Military republicanism, which initially served the necessary purpose of building a new state and citizens, became the raison d'être for a state in which there were few civil institutions to balance an overwhelmingly military power. The majority of the population had little influence over the government and little protection from its exercise of control, whether through taxation or through armed force. Efforts to resist the state via mobility and physical escape in the end contributed to further social exclusion and political silencing of the peasantry and of women.

Steve Stern (1993 [1988]): 58) points out that throughout Latin America there were "repeating cycles of effort to establish a 'popular' version of social identity and right that laid claim on 'national' politics, identities and rights of citizenship." These efforts, seen in the notable "cycles of liberal opening and closure, inclusionary social mobilization followed by exclusionary repression and retreat," are also evident in Haiti (Sheller 2000). Unlike those in the Latin American republics, however, the rulers of Haiti had a special claim to representing the interests of former slaves, the "sons of Africa," and the "black" people of the world. Thus in their struggles over inclusion and exclusion the identity, *noir* became a key nexus for debates over legitimacy. As Trouillot (1992: 165) puts it, the peasantry was "pushed to the background, [and] remained politically marginal, while *noiriste* leaders loudly claimed power in its name by virtue of sharing the same complexion." As in Jamaica, political mobilizations around "black" or "noir" identities enabled some claims on popular citizenship while simultaneously constraining how and by whom such claims could be made.

Thus, Haitian peasants became the "*mounn andéyo*," the outside people (Trouillot 1990; cf. Nicholls 1996: 245–46), or what Barthélémy (1989) calls "*le pays en dehors*," the nation outside. It is these outside people who were displaced from their land and poured into Port-au-Prince in the period of neoliberal opening of the rural economy in the 1980s and 1990s, filling the capital with homes incapable of withstanding an earthquake. The peasantry condensed their experience into another pithy saying, which seems to bear some relation to the first: "Constitusyon sé papié, bayonet sé fer (Constutions are paper, bayonets are iron)." While the state appears to work through paper and signatures, it is clear to the people that what really matters is the bayonet, which cuts straight through the niceties of citizenship written on flimsy paper and through the bodies of those who would assert their rights as citizens. If the state's weapon of choice is the bayonet, the people's resistance is in the feet. Moving beyond the reach of the state is one of the few means of resistance in situations in which freedom is seemingly won, yet self-determination remains elusive; it is the art of not being governed (J. Scott 2009).

Looked at on a larger stage, though, the saying tells us something else: The revolutionary Haitian republic succeeded in escaping the colonial powers and writing a democratic constitution, yet the bayonets of France, Britain, and Spain and, later, the gunboats of the United States remained turned on the renegade upstarts. It is this international community that imposed its will on the Haitian government and exercised control through demands for debt repayments and, when necessary, military occupation. Like the Maroons of Jamaica, the legacies of winning self-determination are still entangled with colonial power and military force. Today, Haitians still must pay homage to the bayonet (or now the weapons of the United Nations peace-keeping forces known as MINUSTAH) even as they seek to hold their leaders and other power holders to their word. While this is a national history in some respects, it is also an international story about the limits of self-determination and autonomy in a world in which the meanings of "blackness," and the legitimacy of black citizenship, are still overdetermined by forms of structural violence that transcend the postcolonial state. Citizenship from below is today also to be found in the camps of the internally displaced, who since the earthquake of January 2010 have had to make claims for justice, democracy, and dignity aimed not just at the Haitian state, but also toward the international organizations that act as a de facto unelected government.

CHAPTER SEVEN

Arboreal Landscapes of
Power and Resistance

Plants are deceptive. You see them there
looking as if once rooted they know
their places; not like animals, like us
always running around, leaving traces.
—OLIVE SENIOR, "Plants," *Gardening in the Tropics*

Land and its uses have been one of the key sites of social struggle in post-slavery societies, as well as sites for the reproduction of national belonging, family, and culture on a wider material terrain. Social relations of power, resistance, and oppositional culture building are inscribed into living landscapes of farming, dwelling, and cultivation. Claims to power (both elite and subaltern) are marked out by landscape features such as plazas, roads, pathways, vantage points, and significant trees, all of which proclaim use rights over, ownership of, or the sacrality of particular places. Trees especially have been used to identify, symbolize, demarcate, and sustain various Caribbean places, meanings, and state institutions. The historian Geri Augusto (2009: lxii) even refers to trees such as the silk cotton as part of a "liberation flora," knowledge of which was tied to plant-based "militant medicines" developed by African, indigenous American, and Maroon cultures of the Caribbean. The study of trees (and other plants) and their place in systems of knowledge and practice can inform another dimension of history from below, which moves beyond the written archive to encompass alternative modalities for the performance of citizenship, national belonging, and embodied freedom.

Plants, though rooted, leave other kinds of traces. Insofar as "new meanings and uses of woods and forests have often accompanied patterns of colonial conquest" (Macnaghten and Urry 2000: 167), such transformations of arboreal landscapes are very evident throughout the Caribbean region. Tropical woodland was one of the primary objects of European colonial acquisition, and the twin processes of deforestation and forest conservation shaped the earliest efforts at Caribbean colonization (Grove 1995) and continue to mark tensions over capitalist development versus environmental conservation. European colonizers furthermore marked out their ownership and power with martial avenues of trees along major military grounds such as the Champs de Mars in Basse-Terre, Guadeloupe, and the Parade in Kingston, Jamaica. Major sugar plantations were noted for their stands of trees, their regal royal palms, and the majestic trees that shaded the planters' houses. In the post-emancipation period, trees would come to be central features of romantic adventure travel and touristic scenery (Sheller 2003). Yet all the while, local knowledges of "liberation flora" were pressing up from below, inspired by the generative power of the plants themselves. Olive Senior (2005: 63) describes the reproductive energy of plants as invasive, colonizing, and prolific:

> Yet from the way they breed (excuse me!)
> and twine, from their exhibitionist
> and rather prolific nature, we must infer
> a sinister not to say imperialistic
>
> grand design. Perhaps you've regarded,
> as beneath your notice, armies of mangrove
> on the march, roots in the air, clinging
> tendrils anchoring themselves everywhere?
>
> The world is full of shoots bent on conquest,
> invasive seedlings seeking wide open spaces,
> matériel gathered for explosive dispersal
> in capsules and seed cases.

Thus, she suggests, plants contain a kind of natural militancy, conquering territory with explosive growth. But the powers of plants might also be propagated and harnessed by those who know the secret powers of root, bark, leaf, and flower, whether physiological or spiritual, as found in the practices of Jamaican Maroons, Obeahmen and bush doctors, or Haitian Piquets, houngans, and mambo.

Trees and woodland play a significant part in the mythology, symbolism, ritual and folk traditions of many cultures throughout the world—and, hence, in national landscape iconographies and identities (Arnold and Guha 1995; Darby 2000; Matless 1998; Rival 1998; Schama 1995). But it is not only power holders who stake out their claims with trees. The enslaved, the freed, and the indentured workers of the Caribbean planted, claimed, owned, tended, respected and bequeathed trees of their own. As noted in chapter 4, many kinds of trees are revered in Caribbean societies: "For the slaves and their descendants trees had a spiritual dimension and, like the eternal land, symbolized the continuity of kinship groups and communities" (Besson 1995: 93). From the sacred Kindah tree of the Accompong Maroons in Jamaica (Besson 1997: 214) to the famous *mapou* tree of Bwa Kayiman in Haiti and the great silk cotton trees venerated as places of the spirits in Trinidad, particular trees have special symbolic meanings and social functions within African Caribbean and Indo-Caribbean cultures. Family burial grounds were often placed under a tree, such as a calabash tree (Olwig 1997: 143), at the back of a family yard. As the repository of the ancestors' spirits, such trees become symbolic of the "family tree" (Maurer 1997) and were used for the burial of the placenta after a child was born (Augusto 2009). For those coming to the Caribbean from South Asian religious and cultural origins, trees have also been "seen as places of dwelling where 'humans and nature' were indissolubly linked" (Macnaghten and Urry 2000; Shiva 1989). All trees have a temporality and a seasonality, which can be used to mark rhythms of human birth, life, and death, as well as forms of acquisition, property, and power.[1]

This arboreal vitality, however, can take on quite widely differing symbolic meanings, can support highly varied social performances, and can become the material grounds for opposed "productions of space" (Lefebvre 1991: 90). As David Arnold and Ramachandra Guha (1995: 15–16) argue in relation to South Asia, the natural environment, including woodland and trees, "needs to be understood, too, as a contested space, a site of conflict and confrontation—but also a space of flight and evasion—between competing economic activities and between the social groups dependent upon them." Nature is not only socially constructed; it is also always fraught with competing practices of using, ordering, and imaging; natures are plural and contested (Macnaghten and Urry 1998), especially in colonial contexts. Although Barry Higman argues that different material forms of spatial organization reflect deep cultural contestation, his ordering of categories is overly fixed and typological:

> In the Jamaica of the eighteenth and nineteenth centuries, there were two competing attitudes to space and its organization. One, derived from the European frame of mind, sought to create a rigidly ordered, geometric landscape. The other, with its roots in Africa, placed a greater value on fluid, natural lines. The slave plantation system, a product of the European model, sought to impose a total imperial design on man and the land. . . . Within the plantation system, however, slaves were sometimes able to pattern small areas according to their own conceptions of spatial order. (Higman 1988: 291)

Higman detects these competing spatial orders in plantation maps and surveys from the period, as well as in commentaries by missionaries, officials, and other chroniclers of daily life. However, it seems overly reductionist to assume that there is a single "European" or "African" "frame of mind"; that only the European is orderly and only the African places value on fluid, natural lines.[2] We can nevertheless agree different organizing principles and traces of lived experience are evident in the remnant patterned landscapes of plantation societies, which reflect the varying interests of export-oriented investors of capital for large-scale commodity production, versus the people who lived and worked in and around such enterprises, engaging in various forms of productive and reproductive labor that left different kinds of traces on the land.

We might go further and propose not only that these spatial orders represent "competing attitudes" but that they are material evidence of the bitter struggle for resources, land, and livelihood that accompanied the abolition of slavery (as well as survival under slavery). Sylvia Wynter (1971) has referred to this underlying tension in Caribbean history in terms of "plot and plantation," meaning the tensions between the structures of the plantation and the autochthonous structures of the plot system which grew up in and around them. Several historians have traced the development of the small plot and the slave provision ground within the interstices of the plantation in ways that were "simultaneously dependent and antagonistic" (Tomich 1993: 222; and see Marshall 1993; Mintz 1979). Actions such as squatting, "capturing" land, and refusing to move off of land were essential to the escape from slavery and its legacies of durable inequality and injustice, and at times such land struggles triggered major political struggles such as the Morant Bay Rebellion in Jamaica in 1865 (Sheller 2000). Each little plot, each grove of trees, each small garden represents a kind of triumph of the enslaved and the emancipated, even while contributing to the maintenance of the overall plantation economy. Even after slavery ended, the colonial government struggled to control the landscape. The *Report by the Central Board of Health, of Jamaica* (1852: 257), for example, concluded, among other things, that "no trees, excepting cocoa-nuts, should be allowed in villages, and no bushes, excepting useful plants, such as pepper plants. The desire of privacy in dwellings is peculiar to the natives of Asia as well as to the Africans, and it is most easily secured by trees and shrubs."

Other historians have compared family land to a kind of "commons" that emerged and persisted in disparate Caribbean territories, even though it was an "informal and extra-legal institution outside the bounds of colonial, statutory law" (Maurer 1997; Olwig 1997: 138). Beneath the surveys, the plans, the maps, the law, and the command structure of the colonial plantation was an underside of customary, informal, extralegal, and local practices, which produced other forms of space and place. Jean Besson (1979, 1984, 1992, 1995, 2002) especially has shown how both land and trees were customarily owned and transmitted among slaves and their descendants. "In the post-slavery era," she writes, "trees, like land, also symbolized the fruits of freedom" and were known to be transmitted to descendants in parts of Martinique, Haiti, Jamaica, and Barbuda (Besson 1995: 93). This appropriation and humanization of the landscape is the sine qua non of being human, and free. As the Barbadian novelist George Lamming puts it, "The way we see, the way we hear, our nurtured sense of touch and smell, the whole complex of feelings which we call sensibility, is influenced by the particular features of the landscape, which has been humanized by our work."[3] Thus, humans shape, or cultivate, the landscape, while it in turn shapes, or cultures, us. With that family land, argues Besson (2002), came an entirely original system of unrestricted cognatic descent, by which extensive kin networks could ground their freedom in a place of ancestral belonging.

Following the theorist of space Henri Lefebvre (1991: 86), we can note not only that such lived space is socially "produced" from the raw material of nature, but also that *"social spaces interpenetrate one another and/or superimpose themselves upon one another."* In other words, despite the existence of dominant social orderings of space and legal systems to uphold that ordering, in practice other social productions of space nevertheless emerge alongside or are directly superimposed on hegemonic space. Higman (1988: 291) points out very clearly how this might occur: "Planters were generally reluctant to interfere in the organization of existing plantation villages and seem not to have attempted to rearrange their spatial structure. In this the planters showed an unwilling recognition that what they liked to describe as spatial disorder was in fact fundamental to the fabric and coherence of the plantation community, and hence to the maintenance of their labour force." The spatial practices of the enslaved community, in other words, were not hidden so much as tolerated; plantations' spatial order was dependent on a certain amount of "spatial disorder." Interpenetrating or superimposed social spaces, we might generalize, are often necessary to and constitutive of each other; but this does not make them harmonious. Besson goes even further in suggesting that family land was an appropriation and overturning of the colonial order of property and kinship, a creative cultural invention that rejected the planters' moral and legal order. In a larger sense, the competing colonial empires and the later patchwork of post-independence nation-states were only one spatial order imposed on the lands of the Caribbean yet always interpenetrated with alternative spatialities, whether of the indigenous inhabitants or those rerouted and rerooted from Africa, India, or elsewhere. Their everyday practices of production and reproduction (re)shaped the landscape, including the human sensibilities that perceived its meaning and form and the forms of personhood, family, and belonging that were made possible by its living vitalities.

Forest and trees also populate the Caribbean literary imagination, where they play an important symbolic role in struggles over history, memory, and self-determination. The Jamaican writer Michelle Cliff (1996 [1987]: 1), for example, writes about the process of "ruination" as a kind of decultivation of the colonized land. As discussed by Jocelyn Stitt (2007: 70), "*Ruinate*, the adjective, and *ruination*, the noun, are Jamaican inventions. Each word signifies the reclamation of land, the disruption of cultivation, civilization, by the uncontrolled, uncontrollable forest. When a landscape becomes ruinate, carefully designed aisles of cane are envined, strangled, the order of empire is replaced by the chaotic forest. The word *ruination* (especially) signifies this immediately; it contains both the word *ruin*, and *nation*. A landscape in ruination means one in which the imposed nation is overcome by the naturalness of ruin." Here ruination is described as an active process of decolonization assisted by nature, in which chaotic wildness helps to uproot the imposed civilization of the colonial order. Yet Stitt (2007: 70–71) points out, the guerrillas in Cliff's novel *No Telephone to Heaven* establish a new nation by first clearing the ruinate land of the main character Clare's grandmother: "They found, in the process of clearing the land, things that had been planted long before—before even the grand-mother—which had managed to survive the density of the wild forest. Cassava. Afu. Fufu. Plantain." These survivor species are notably Caribbean (cassava, or manioc) and African in origin and name (Fufu), suggesting the provision grounds, language, and cultivation practices of the enslaved connecting to the ancestral and indigenous and taking mangrove-like root beneath and throughout the protective foliage of the dense forest. While there is a tendency toward a kind of Romantic nationalism in such imagery (just as in essentialist imagery of the mother as bearer of the nation), according to Stitt, Cliff's work arguably moves toward a non-essentialist paradigm of national identity (and citizenship) in which connections to place, land, and family are nonlinear and destabilized, interstitial and rhizomatic, precarious achievements.

These wild forests as ciphers of subaltern historicity also appear in Edouard Glissant's conceptualization of the "submarine roots" of Caribbean regional history, "floating free, not fixed in one position in some primordial spot, but extending in all directions in our world through its networks and branches" (Glissant 1989: 67, quoted in DeLoughrey 2007: 17). Through the homonym of routes and roots, Elizabeth DeLoughrey highlights the dynamic mobility of Caribbean identity, which is about not the replacement of the nation as site of belonging with the scattered seeds of diaspora but, rather, the destabilization of the linearity and boundedness of the nation itself. Nana Wilson-Tagoe (1998: 33) also points out that Caribbean writers such as Wilson Harris have "consistently called for the deconstruction of [a] monolithic and linear history and argued for a perspective and methodology that would reconstitute the region's history to include larger spaces and forces: other landscapes, other pasts and mythologies which though seemingly 'lifeless' may yet yield . . . the kind of erosion necessary for the deconstruction of imperial history." These larger spaces and forces, like the plants in Olive Senior's poem "Plants" (2005: 63), have an erotic force that transcends the scale of human lives and disrupts the ordering projects of states. Plants are protean, imperialistic, bent on reproduction by exercising a kind of agency from below that is both generative and destructive.

Through a study of trees and their relation to humans, I suggest, we can track the competing ordering, reordering, and *dis*ordering of the Caribbean landscape and the social struggles that came to be materialized in that landscape—a kind of citizenship from below the ground itself. Drawing on historical archives, literary sources, and visual imagery mainly from the

Anglophone and Francophone Caribbean, this chapter builds on emerging cultural approaches in the geography, sociology, ecology, and political economy of land in the Caribbean (and wider colonial worlds). It offers another version of embodied freedom—embodied not only in human subjectivities, but also in the interactions (both material and spiritual) of humans with the living plants that make up the lived landscapes and sensibilities of the Caribbean. It first traces the importance of trees in the development of plantation economies and discourses of empire—from mahogany, lignum vitae, and fustic and other dyewoods through palms, fruit trees, and botanical collections. It then turns to the contestation of these arboreal landscapes by Afro-Caribbean agents who claimed particular trees for their own projects of survival and meaning making—sacred ancestral trees, liberty trees, family land trees, gathering-place trees. The concluding reflections on multi-method approaches to tracing social struggles over arboreal landscapes of power and resistance suggest that what is taking place is not merely local culture building, important though this is, but also transnational processes of culture building that cross boundaries and borders, generating a larger kinship from the ground beneath our feet.

LANDSCAPES OF POWER

Trees have long been crucial to the projects of empire building, colonization, and discovery of "new worlds." Christopher Columbus wrote frequently about the beauty of the forests he encountered in the Antilles and of their potential economic uses. Palm trees in particular deeply informed initial European impressions of the region's unusual flora (although many palms now found there are not indigenous to the region), and the palm has become a key symbolic icon representing the entire Caribbean. The earliest manuscripts giving European impressions of the New World focus on unusual plants to be found in these new climes and their novel uses. The Drake Manuscript, or *Histoire naturelle des Indes: Les arbres, plantes, fruits, animaux, coquillages, reptiles, insectes, oiseaux, etc, qui se trouvent dans les Indes*, of the late sixteenth century (Kraemer and Klinkenborg 1996), for example, was written by an anonymous member of Francis Drake's party, who painted close to two hundred naïve watercolor images of West Indian plants and animals and scenes of the lives of Indian, European, and African inhabitants of the Spanish territories in the New World. A palm tree is conspicuously depicted, along with a description of how the indigenous people made a palm wine that tasted like sherry.

The palm was especially crucial in the early period of colonization because of its multiple uses, and descriptions of this one, from a seventeenth-
century account of the Buccaneers, remain striking for their sheer sense of
novelty and wonder:

> There are an abundance of Palm Trees found here, some of which are two
> hundred foot high, having no branches but what are upon the very top;
> every month one of these branches falleth off, and at the same time an-
> other sprouteth out; the leaves of this tree are seven or eight foot in length,
> and three or four in breadth, with which they cover their houses instead of
> Tyles: Also they make buckets of them to carry their Water in. The body of
> the Tree is so big, that two men can scarcely grasp it in the middle; yet the
> heart of it is so soft, that if two or three inches be pared off its outside, the
> rest may be sliced like new Cheese. The Inhabitants have a way of extract-
> ing an excellent Drink from this Tree; for gouging it a little above the Root,
> they [fr]om thence distill a sort of Liquour which in short time by fermen-
> tation becometh as strong as the richest Wine. (Exquemelin 1684 [1678]:
> 178–79)

Not only is the size of the tree staggering in terms of height, breadth, and
gigantic foliage, but it also serves diverse needs of the people found on this
island, which the Europeans called Hispaniola. Europeans adapted technology of plant use from the indigenous peoples of the region, as well as
assisted in the importing of plants, people, and technology from Africa. Yet
they seldom knew the *meanings* of these plants.

Early modern science was very much directed toward botanical discovery and utilitarian application, as well as observation, imitation, and
appropriation. Early colonizing expeditions often noted the "advantages"
to be had from the forests of islands such as Trinidad, "issuing very rich
Gumms, from others Rich Oyles, Balsoms, and Odoriferous Rossins, abun-
dance of Woods, Proper for Dyes. The very Mountains Covered with Large
Cedars, White wood and Excellent Timber for Building" (quoted in Wahab
2004: 90). Tropical hardwoods and dyewoods were highly valued, including the West Indian cedar (*Cedrela mexicana*) used for building and furni-
ture making; the locust (*Hymenaea courbaril*) for large beams; the extremely hard ironwood (*Bunchosia nitida*) for fencing and mill rollers; and
the dyewoods fustic (*Chlorophora tinctoria*) and lignum vitae (*Guaiacum
officinale*) (Watts 1990: 155). Lignum vitae was not only initially believed to
cure syphilis (in conjunction with treatment with mercury) but also contained essential oils that preserved the wood from drying out and made it

ideal for making marine navigational instruments. Clocks made from lignum vitae by John Harrison in the eighteenth century allowed the first measurement of longitude, which had revolutionary effects on European seafaring. Thus, the "discovery" of this tree (already used by native informants) transformed navigational practices and enabled colonization itself to proceed.

Finding new plants and their uses was not only a primary concern in exploration of the New World; it also underwrote an entirely new attitude toward the natural world, in which it was demystified, classified, and secularized (Sheller 2003: 43). An acquisitive and utilitarian attitude toward natural entities prevailed in the eighteenth century in a cornucopia of botanical plenipotency:

> The natural produce of Jamaica, besides sugar, cacao, and ginger, are principally pimento, or, as it is called, allspice, or Jamaica pepper. . . . Besides this they have the wild cinnamon tree, whose bark is so serviceable in medicine; the manchineel, a most beautiful tree to the eye, with the fairest apple in the world, and when cut down affording a very fine ornamental wood for the joiners. . . . Here is the mahogany, in such general use with our cabinet makers; the cabbage tree, a tall plant famous for a substance, looking and tasting like cabbage, growing on the very top, and no less remarkable for the extreme hardness of its wood, which when dry is incorruptible, and hardly yields to any tool; the palma, from which is drawn a great deal of oil, much esteemed by the negroes both in food and medicine; the white wood, which never breeds the worm in ships; the soap tree, whose berries answer all purposes of washing; the mangrove and olive bark, useful to tanners; the fustic and redwood to the dyers, and lately the logwood; and their forests supply the apothecary with guaiacum, sarsaparilla, china, caffia, and tamarinds; they have aloes too. (Charlevoix 1766: 1:309–10)

Charlevoix's report suggests a combined interest in spices, medicine, food, ornamental wood, and various useful plant products, reflecting the diverse ends of European exploitation of tropical forests. The West Indies provided a wide range of materials that were incorporated into European material culture both in the tropics and at home, enabling the creation of innumerable new commercial and domestic products from a very early date. As in other colonial enterprises, West Indian forests were mined for all that was useful, displacing indigenous rights, needs, and forms of knowledge (Arnold and Guha 1995; Shiva 1989). As early as the seventeenth century, deforestation was already evident on some Caribbean islands (Grove 1995), and the West Indian colonists' "voracious consumption" of wood for buildings, ships, fuel, and barrels made them dependent on New England forests by the late seventeenth century (Cronon 1983: 111–12). Wood was thus essential to state building and colonial power.

Lists such as these were themselves part of a new genre of imperialism. Laura Brown identifies such extensive lists of "natural products" in travel narratives of the early eighteenth century with the "rhetoric of acquisition," in which "the mere act of proliferative listing . . . and the sense of an incalculable quantity express the period's fascination with imperialist acquisition" (Brown 1993: 43). While this rhetoric made its appearance in the early modern period, it continued to play an important part throughout the period of colonial expansion, right up through the U.S. imperial projects of the late nineteenth century. A guide published in 1898 for prospective North American entrepreneurs who might wish to exploit the "resources and opportunities" of Cuba, for example, lists the areas of forestry in which Cuba excelled:

> The forests of Cuba abound in numberless hard, rare, and dye woods of the finest grain and colors, both somber and brilliant, suitable for practical and ornamental purposes, including mahogany, sabicu, rosewood, redwood, logwood, fustic, majagua, bamboo, and ebony. There is an abundance of lignum-vitae, so much sought after in the manufacture of block-sheaves, and of heavy balls used in bowling alleys, and of lancewood—exported for carriage shafts, surveyors' instruments and the like. Cedar, used for the inside of drawers and wardrobes, and for cigar boxes, and the tamarind, whose wood, bark, leaves, and flowers have an economic value, abound. (Hyatt and Hyatt 1898: 74)

Revamping Charlevoix's eighteenth-century rhetoric of acquisition, the island is described as an economic opportunity for investors, with many new uses for tropical hardwoods. Written by the U.S. consul and vice-consul during the U.S. military occupation of the island, this appeal to American investors, manufacturers, and merchants spells out the natural-resource base of state power and economic imperium.

Alongside economic acquisition, however, there was a second genre of colonial production of space, which depended not on the extraction of resources but on the elaboration of scenery and landscape as a form of mastery. Here nature served more as an allegorical vision of man's taming of the wilderness and an expression of his power to control and shape land

and nature (which was very much a male pursuit linked to ideas of masculinity). Landscapes of power had a long provenance within Europe well before the transfer of landscaping practices to colonial realms. In Britain, for example, from the medieval period woodland was "almost invariably the private property of the manorial lord" or the crown, and although villagers had some rights to collect firewood or materials for house building, "These rights were usually quite stringently limited" (Williamson and Bellamy 1987: 79). Enclosure was applied not only to arable areas, but also to "common waste" and "represented the triumph of individual ownership over the rights of the rest of the community" (Williamson and Bellamy 1987: 94). "It would not have been possible for a landowner to develop an elaborate 'status landscape' without having first eradicated the rights of other people to the land. There would have been no point in planting an avenue or an ornamental clump of trees if the cattle of the peasantry were free to browse the carefully sited saplings. Moreover, a landlord's pleasure in the prospect of his park might have been considerably diminished if he were constantly faced with the sight of local villagers wandering across it" (Williamson and Bellamy 1987: 136–37).

One of the reasons that non-landed entrepreneurs entered the West Indies trade was precisely so that they could enjoy such "status landscapes," whether by building grand plantation prospects in the West Indies or by using the profits extracted to acquire or build such properties back in England. In the Caribbean, too, trees were enrolled in elite projects of spatially inscribing property, immortality, and perpetuity, in prospects that became the stuff of landscape painting and travel writing. This is not to say that the landscape was an entirely European imposition. The tropical environment had its own, powerful affects on those who entered it, while the agency of the enslaved, the indentured, and the emancipated also refashioned nature's uses, meanings, and contexts. The close inter-positioning of the West Indian sugar estate and the English country estate is indicative not of a linear genealogy from one to the other but also of the two-way traffic of "transculturation" transforming both the colonial landscape and the home landscape (Gikandi 1994; Pratt 1992; Wahab 2004).

English landscape gardening was greatly influenced by Italian art, and the similarity between art and parkland "lies in the scope of the landscape, in the wide prospects and in the relationship between the foreground and more distant objects" (Williamson and Bellamy 1987: 146). As Amar Wahab

(2004) shows in his study of Trinidadian landscape painting, a similar sense of "prospect" was imported into Caribbean landscapes such as those of nineteenth-century Trinidad, which continues to inform the landscape design of Caribbean hotels and tourism developments. In their efforts to open up extensive vistas to their grand homes, or from their homes to the sea, West Indian planters exercised some of the same autocracy of landed elites in England, who enclosed land, redirected roads and footpaths, and flattened sections of villages or removed entire communities if they offended the view. But they also faced some of the same social tensions and struggles over land use and the unwelcome mobility of people and livestock across their "private" property, just as social struggles take place today over rights of access to beaches and scenic coastlines that have been appropriated by private developers to the detriment of local citizens.[4]

There was an underlying threat of chaos and a profusion of the disorderly Caribbean landscape, with its threats of ruination. As Nancy Leys Stepan (2001) argues, "To even the most enthusiastic tropicalist of the nineteenth century, it seems, tropical nature was too much—too disorderly, chaotic, large—and too different from the remembered landscape at home" (Stepan 2001: 54). By midcentury, a "dismay at tropical excess" was linked to notions of tropical decay, tropical disease, and death (Stepan 2001: 48). Tropical profusion and decay were held up against European systematic enclosure, cultivation, and scientific agricultural management and found wanting. Such contrasting valuations of nature often carried over into valuations of the racialized populations of differing regions of the world. Trees became shorthand for such ideologies, with meanings that could carry over the centuries, as, for example, in a photo caption from Patrick Leigh Fermor's celebrated book *The Traveller's Tree* (1955 [1950]: n.p.): "This photograph illustrates not only the great distinction of the Haitian bone-structure, but the extreme pallor and beauty of many of the mulatto elite in Petionville. She is the palest of mamelouques or sangmélées, as Moreau de Saint Méry would have said; paler far than a Neapolitan or a Sicilian. In every way—intellectually, linguistically and sartorially—her background is French, and the lime and chestnut trees of Paris would be a far more appropriate background for her than these breadfruit leaves." Here, the superiority of a lighter racial type is seen to lift the photograph's subject out of the local landscape and place her in a European bio-region among the limes and chestnuts. The breadfruit leaves are too large, too crass, and too tropical to frame her pale skin. In such embodied encounters of tourism, which I explore further in the next chapter, not only is acquisition of tropical lands closely associated with sexual negotiation, but sexual agents offer up their own fetishized, racialized bodies as so many pieces of mahogany, bamboo, or more subtly tempered cocoa and coffee with cream.

Finally, a third genre of descriptive writing employs a romantic discourse of "Tropical Nature," which has come to deeply inform modern tourism in the region. I have described elsewhere how Charles Kingsley's work popularized this genre (Sheller 2003). Here the palm tree begins to evoke beauty and relaxation rather than power and property. E. A. Hastings Jay (1900: 34–35), for example, wrote of his "Four Months Cruising in the West Indies" in 1900 in terms of the scenery's relation to earlier literary representations of the tropics: "Here, for the first time, was the tropical beach! How often, from childhood, I had tried to picture it from Kingsley's vivid descriptions or the histories of the early explorers. There were the cocoa-nut palms, with clusters of green cocoa-nuts growing all along the sea-line out of the soft white sand, with beautiful rainbow colours in the water as it moved lazily backwards and forwards, glittering in the brilliant sunlight." Turning away from the plantations and their post-slavery labor problems, the tourist instead gazes on what was understood to be "untouched" nature—the jungles, the forested hills, the beaches, the "lazily" moving sea. By the mid-nineteenth century, the palm has become a symbol of exotic and romantic places, corralled into Victorian "palm-houses" and domesticated as a garden feature. From nineteenth-century romantic prints to twentieth-century tourist brochures, the ubiquitous image of the palm sums up the Caribbean tropics so effectively that it has been turned into a brand icon and marketing logo, a symbol of leisure, relaxation, and carefree living.

Can we recover the "underside" of the Caribbean landscape, in Glissant's sense (see Wahab 2004), and reclaim the subaltern historics that course beneath the landscapes of capitalist development? Glissant (1989) himself writes about the metaphorical opposition between the European oak tree, with its deep roots, singular thick trunk, and strong symbolic autonomy, versus the Caribbean mangrove, with its multiple, entangled root systems, living in water and in soil, on the margins between sea and land, part of an open, fluid space. As Isabel Hoving (2002: 126–27) argues, for Glissant the mangroves serve as a model for a fluid, relational Creole identity (*identité-relation*), in contrast to the root identity (*identité-racine*) represented by the European oak. Nations, cities, and landscapes, in this view, "are the complex points of convergence of many cross-cultural and transnational relations," in which plants have been transplanted and shaped into new landscapes through "complex, layered, violent histories of ripping away and abduction" (Hoving 2002: 127, 131). If we follow the logic of citizenship from below down into the ground beneath our feet, are alternative identities and subjectivities pressing up through the soil, identities related to place and nation in different ways? What can social and political struggles over trees tell us about competing claims to belonging, self-determination, and collective identity? In the remainder of this chapter, I turn to these alternative landscapes of Caribbean citizenship, in search of other means of accessing the subaltern histories of freedom that lie in the land beneath the well-turned earth, in the roots of the trees, reaching their vast shady boughs, or like the mangrove their upturned roots, toward the heavens.

LANDSCAPES OF RESISTANCE

Trees have long been at the center of social and political struggles in the Caribbean. In Bwa Kayiman, Haiti, a great mapou tree stands where the ceremony was held in 1791 inaugurating the slave uprising that sparked off the Haitian Revolution. The mapou, or silk cotton, is a sacred tree inhabited by spirits, and throughout Haiti ceremonies continue to be conducted and offerings made by *serviteurs* of the lwa under trees such as those photographed in the *lakou* (or household compound) of Nan Souvenance at Easter (Hurbon 1995: 66–67, 100). When the floods come following heavy tropical storms and hurricanes, these have been some of the few trees left standing in which people could take shelter from the deluge. "Although wounded by the drought and under persistent attack from the Protestants," who were praying for the demise of the ancient "voodoo" tree in the run up to the bicentenary, "the enormous, ancient tree [at Bwa Kayiman] hung on."[5] In the eyes of some, the mapou at Bwa Kayiman remains a powerful symbol of the resistance of the Haitian people to foreign domination, slavery, and exploitation, marking the continuity of African traditions and ancestral spirits.

However, it was another tree that was chosen (probably by educated elite statesmen) as the symbol of the Haitian state: the palm tree in the guise of a Liberty Tree surmounted with the liberty cap of the French Revolution. Both the cap and the tree of liberty have a long transatlantic symbolic history, having played a part in revolutionary political upheavals in Italy, the Netherlands, England, colonial America, France, and, finally, the Caribbean. The Caribbean version of the Liberty Tree picks up on the classical tradition of its association with slave emancipation in ancient Rome (e.g., the Phrygian bonnet) as interpreted via the French Revolution. Historians of the revolution such as Ernst Gombrich and Mona Ozouf link the revolutionary Liberty Tree to the popular folkloric traditions of the maypole in France, but in Haiti it may tap into a much older cultural equivalent—the *potomitan*, a wooden column around which the dances of Vodou ceremonies take place. The potomitan stands in the middle of the peristyle and is symbolic of a path linking "the heavenly and the earthly worlds"; encircled by two snakes symbolizing Dambala and Ayida Wedo, it "resembles the tree of life," and offerings are placed at its base (Gombrich 1979: 199; Hurbon 1995; Ozouf 1988: 240). Some images commemorating emancipation show the chains of slavery being buried at the base of a liberty palm on which an emancipation proclamation is pinned.

The straight, narrow royal palm tree certainly resembles the potomitan; thus, like other symbolic references, it may have a dual meaning in Haiti— on the surface European, republican and secular, but underneath African, communal, and spiritual. There may be even more specific synchronies or dual meanings of the palm. According to the ethnologist Alfred Métraux (1972: 362), the palm is sacred to the lwa Aizan, who in Haiti "is represented as an old woman, and who, as Legba's wife, protects markets, public places, doors and barriers. She is said to be the oldest of all the divinities and is therefore entitled to the first offerings." As an old woman, Aizan reminds us of the vernacular respect for women's power and their significant role in markets and public places, as noted in earlier chapters. In its Dahomean origin, "Aizan is the name given to spirits older than the mythical founders of the tribes. In fact they watch over the latter, as also, over houses and markets" and are represented by "fringes of palm leaves" (Métraux 1972: 362). Perhaps, then, for the Haitian peasantry the palm was embraced as a national symbol of founding liberty not because it echoed European Liberty Trees, but because it very effectively represented the sacred origins of their nation and suggested Aizan's spiritual protection of their markets, public places, and borders.

The Haitian adaptation of this symbol is also linked to republican traditions of the American Revolution. Various groups in the United States still plant Liberty Trees, and the symbol continues to have contemporary resonance in the Caribbean. In the colonial Americas, the Liberty Tree took on major significance in the form of ancient oak or elm trees that were designated public gathering places in village or town squares and that became flashpoints for protest against British rule. In 1775, Thomas Paine published his poem "Liberty Tree" in *Pennsylvania Magazine*, which made reference to British tyrannical powers gathering to cut down the Liberty Tree.[6] The Haitian revolutionary leader Toussaint Louverture is said to have stated: "In overthrowing me, they have uprooted the trunk of the liberty tree. It will grow back because its roots are many and deep." When he was deposed from power and went into exile in the Central African Republic, Haitian president Jean-Bertrand Aristide quoted Toussaint and "likened himself to a tree of peace," which would also grow back "because its roots are L'Ouverturian," seemingly conflating the Liberty Tree with the more religious symbol of the Tree of Peace.[7] Perhaps Glissant's multi-rooted mangrove would have been a better symbol for both liberty and peace, to which many rather than a singular figurehead leader would contribute; washed by tides, inhabiting the margins between the land and the spirits of the ocean, the mangrove alludes to a wider ancestral and transnational kind of human freedom.

Tales of uprooted Liberty Trees come to us from other parts of the Caribbean, as well. In their celebrations of Emancipation Day (1 August) in Jamaica, church congregations planted coconut palms as symbols of liberty and held annual festivals in which the trees were watered.[8] In at least one case, though, a missionary reported that his congregation "planted a cocoanut tree, the emblem of liberty—this had been pulled up since, by some of the gentlemen in the neighbourhood, we have replanted it, and as one of the people remarked, 'they pull up we tree, but them can't take away we August.'"[9] Here, too, the Liberty Trees were lightning rods for symbolic political battles. Perhaps because these slender palm trees were so vulnerable to attack (and represented a limited European notion of political liberty [Bogues 2009]), freed people turned back to their thick-trunked mapou, or silk cotton, trees for symbolic and real shelter under which Caribbean freedom could be achieved. Like the Morant Bay silk cotton tree discussed in chapter 4, the behemoth boughs of the silk cotton offered the greatest amount of shade, often growing above underground aquifers and thus making good community gathering spots, places to post public notices, and markers of major crossroads (like Half-Way Tree in Kingston). It is also worth noting that in southern India, "Different trees symbolize different forms of continuity: while the large banyan tree represents the village community as a whole, the coconut palm symbolizes the life cycle of individuals" (Giambelli 1998; Macnaghten and Urry 2000: 167). While the palm may have served as a transatlantic symbol of liberty for a time in the Caribbean, the embracing buttressed trunks and generously shading boughs of the giant silk cotton trees usurped its place in popular practice. Such trees attest to the consanguinity of spiritual and political action, linking together the retrospective veneration of the ancestors and the prospective enacting of freedom. Thus, they are also an important meeting point of political agency and what I broadly define as erotic agency, a crossroads of the creative, sexual, and divine life force.

Besides these spiritually and politically charged trees, though, I also want to call attention to more mundane trees, the fruit trees and edible plants found around kitchen gardens and on small plots of family land. While some trees stand out from the forest, so to speak, others blend into it and present more subtle forms of cultural (and cultivational) opposition. Augusto (2009: lxiii) notes that the well-hidden Maroon communities in the interior of Guyana (and Jamaica) "with their neat gardens were a testament to the reclaiming of symbolic power and the creation of new space for knowledge practices and living, liberated zones," where "liberation flora" could be cultivated. In these hidden regions, powerful *obia* (related to the Jamaican term "Obeah") could be cultivated in traditional balm yards, and knowledge of plants with unique medicinal and magical properties could be maintained and passed on through the generations. Africana studies has begun to explore a wide range of geographies of these plant-based knowledge systems, in which the enslaved are now understood as skilled botanical practitioners whose knowledge of plants was crucial in shaping landscapes and agricultural systems throughout the Americas.[10]

Likewise, as "proto-peasantries" grew up in the "interstices" of the plantation, as Sidney Mintz (1979) argued, those interstices were very much botanical and temporal. That is to say, peasant culture building took place where slave cultivation did not compete with plantation commercial crops in terms of either the spaces it occupied or the time it occupied in cultivation. Arrowroot, for example, was "a botanically hardy plant, it could be grown under a variety of soil and topographical conditions and could be cultivated on marginal lands. It required little care during the year, thus being consonant with the limited time slaves had to work on their own plots (as well as releasing them for other activities). The plant did not, by and large, compete with plantation commercial crops, thus posing little economic threat to plantations" (Handler 1971: 84). Coffee trees played a similar role of enabling small-scale production to take hold following the abolition of slavery (Trouillot 1993). As Douglas Hall (1959: 188) suggests, coffee estates that were abandoned as unprofitable in the post-emancipation pe-

riod were sold off in small parcels to peasants, which could be made productive by employing family labor and inter-cropping and thereby stopping soil erosion: "There could be standing trees, which, if thoroughly
pruned, would continue to yield. . . . Because the pruned tree would take
about three years to give another full crop, the peasant often planted provisions between the coffee, thus raising cash-crops and at the same time
binding the soil against further deterioration." These small plots with their
trees thus offer us material evidence of an alternative spatial order, or what
Lefebvre (1991: 164) calls "superimposed spaces," that grew up in the interstices of the plantation, interpenetrating its spaces and eventually becoming
central to post-emancipation social and cultural formations. Travelers such
as Philip Gosse, for example, noted that Jamaican plantation workers'
houses in the 1840s were usually found in "some secluded nook, approach-
able through a narrow winding path" to protect their privacy and noted the
"variety and grandeur of the various trees" surrounding them (quoted in
Higman 1988, 243).

The idea of superimposed spaces might apply to provision grounds
tucked away in the hilly backlands of sugar estates, the kitchen gardens
crowded around the dwellings of the enslaved or the freed workers, or even
the alternative uses made of time while using plantation spaces. Woodville
Marshall (1993: 203) argues that slaves' success in the Windward Islands
"in creating and defending corners of independent existence fostered the
growth of attitudes toward both plantation labor and independent activities that affected labor relations in the postslavery period." Dale Tomich
(1993: 222) likewise argues for Martinique that "such activity offered an
opportunity for slave initiative and self-assertion. . . . These practices both
shaped and were shaped by Afro-Caribbean cultural forms, through which
the definitions of social reality of slavery and the plantation were at once
mediated and contested. Slaves themselves created and controlled a secondary economic network which originated within the social and spatial
boundaries of the plantation but which allowed for the construction of an
alternative way of life that went beyond it." Within these spatial boundaries, then, more than one system of cultural ordering, meaning making,
and practical usage was at work. The same cultivated tracts and majestic
trees that constituted planters' claims to power and made picturesque scenery for European travel writers might have rather different resonances for
those who lived and worked among them. Europeans' and North Americans' interest in trees, whether as economic resources, figures in a landscape prospect, or elements of the tourist picturesque, are fundamentally at

odds with Afro-Caribbean (and Indo-Caribbean) investment in trees as spiritual repositories—as a crucial part of family land and, hence, markers of kin relations, community, and ancestry, and as living interlocutors in a lived space of political and social relations.

Trees are part of "material cultures" through which memories are "activated" and narrated. As Divya Tolia-Kelly (2004: 314) has shown for the British Asian diaspora, the "prismatic qualities of material cultures ensure that these cultures become nodes of connection in a network of people, places, and narration of past stories, history and traditions. Solid materials are charged with memories that activate common connections to premigratory landscapes and environments." Trees can be considered one such node in a network of connections between people and places and the stories they tell. As she argues for the postcolonial migratory context, acts of "rememory" and "memory-history" encoded in material cultures and embedded in everyday life can challenge bounded and static nationalistic landscapes. Thus, the seeding of trees into African Caribbean and Indian diasporic networks of landholding, kinship, spirituality, and historical memory activates a different "context of living" and in some cases creates "syncretized textures of remembered ecologies and landscapes" that may signify a particular "identity, history and heritage"; thus, other "lives, lands and homes are made part of this one" (Tolia-Kelly 2004: 315–16). In reading Caribbean landscapes in this way, we can re-imbue them with the more complex cultural activities and multiple activations that actually underlay their production, cultivation, mobility and meaningfulness (cf. Tolia-Kelly 2006).

Not only were subaltern "superimposed" landscapes culturally rich and materially productive, but they also had effects back on the landscape of power. A thousand hands working in small ways to shape the land to their own needs, a thousand feet trudging up into the remote hills, could easily outweigh the overweening gestures of the planter's prospect, the impotent laws of the colonial administrator, or the imperious gaze of the traveler. Above all, though, these trees also carry a spiritual meaning that was beyond the ken of the ruling elites. Anthropological studies from many parts of the Caribbean point to the far-ranging significance of many different trees. In his study of Vodou in Haiti, for example, Métraux (1972: 92) notes that "the *loa* [lwa] are also present in the sacred trees which grow round the *humfo* [temple] and the country dwellings. Each *loa* has his favourite variety of tree: the *medicinier-béni* (*Tatropha cureas*) is sacred to

Legba, the palm tree to Ayizan and the Twins (*marassa*), the avocado to Zaka, the mango to Ogu and the bougainvillea to Damballah etc. A tree which is a 'resting place' may be recognized by the candles burning at the foot of it and the offerings left in its roots or hung in its branches." Thus, the trees, seemingly bereft of symbolic or spiritual significance for Europeans, were in fact full of multiple meanings to various communities of indigenous, African, and East Indian origin and were drawn into a complex web of religious practices and material interactions, including Vodou in Haiti, Obeah in Jamaica, Candomblé in Brazil, and Santería in Cuba. Bottles were sometimes hung in their branches; umbilical cords were sometimes buried under them; and burial grounds were marked by specific trees.[11]

In addition to their spiritual significance, trees were planted around slave huts and on provision grounds for practical reasons—to provide shade, building material, medicine, and foodstuff—while not requiring a great deal of labor input once the land was cleared and planted. We know that trees played a significant part in enslaved and emancipated communities' efforts to carve out space for themselves in plantation societies, marking landholding claims that provided some degree of economic autonomy, as well as a kind of spatial hold on a familial terrain. Fruit trees in particular were central to the creation of subaltern property and informal tenures, which were often recognized in common practice and became fundamental to systems of kinship and inheritance. Laurent Dubois (2004a: 30) observes the ways in which trees represented an alternative social cartography in Guadeloupe. "In the 1830s, the abolitionist Victor Schoelcher visited a plantation in Martinique where a huge mango tree stood in the middle of a cane field, stunting the cane that grew in its shade. The planter would have cut down the tree, but it was owned by an enslaved man, who had already promised to pass it on to his descendants. According to Schoelcher, there were similar cases involving fruit trees owned by slaves on other plantations." For Dubois, such trees were part of the alternative landscape of gardens and informal markets through which the enslaved "cultivated networks that crisscrossed, and therefore undermined, the highly structured world of the plantations"; even official maps sometimes identified these "other patterns and practices that emerged within and against this order . . . a world formed by the interaction of colonial policy and daily practice" (Dubois 2004a: 31). In bequeathing trees to "some yet unborn" descendants, as Schoelcher put it (quoted in Tomich 1993: 235), slaves were not only establishing competing claims to space, to land, and to productive property in trees; they were also creating new systems of kinship, descent, and inheritance, with durable temporalities.

In her study of the town of Martha Brae in Jamaica, Besson further shows how trees planted in the period of emancipation maintained familial significance to descendants of the emancipated over generations. Appropriated landscapes created in the interstices of the plantation spatial order during the era of slavery carried over into the post-emancipation period. They became historical markers of the descent group's claim to particular plots of land. In one case, for instance, "Morgan stressed the ancient postslavery origins of the house and the fruit trees growing in the yard. . . . 'These fruit trees out there: no-one around here [in Martha Brae] can tell you how long they is here. Nobody in the district can tell you when them plant here.' Similar sentiments were expressed about the ancestral trees in the house yard of the Thompson Old Family. The idea that trees and land are symbols of the continuity of kin groups and communities is widely spread among Jamaican and other Caribbean peasantries, and derives from the protopeasant past" (Besson 2002: 166). Because burial practices at one time took place in families' yards, and trees often marked such gravesites, these familial plots also represented a continuation of the kin group through a physical connection with the spirits of dead ancestors. In another case, an informant remarked on the genealogy of particular trees, which had been transplanted by his grandfather, a former slave from a specific plantation:

> Like Morgan McIntosh of the Minto Old Family, William remarked on the ancient postslavery history of the fruit trees on the one-acre plot of the Thompson family estate. He knew the origin of each tree brought as a sapling by his ex-slave grandfather, from the protopeasant adaptation on Irving Tower Plantation to this land in Martha Brae: "*This* nasberry tree— according to what my mother told me—this nasberry tree and that one there; the star-apple tree here; and these three nasberry tree along the road there; all of them came from Irving Tower. From the slave days they came out there. My grandfather bring it and plant here, and they catch [grow]. So there was quite a few tree here that really came from Irving Tower during the slave days. So we know of it." (Besson 2002: 176)

Rather than an erasure of the plantation past, then, the story of the trees marks the movement of an ancestor and his trees from the plantation to the family land and instantiates the justice of an ongoing claim to the fruit of the old plantation. So these fruit trees represent both continuity with the plantation past and symbols of the will of people to survive, and transcend, the limits of the plantation through what Besson calls proto-peasant adaptation and Caribbean culture building.

What Besson's work opens our eyes to is the extent to which this proto-peasant past might be found in the living landscapes and "archi-textures," to use Lefebvre's term, of Jamaica's rural countryside, villages, and small towns. The very settlement patterns, plots, and provision grounds that remain in the twenty-first century—and especially their long-lived and precious trees—offer clues to the social production of space and the politics of landscape in the nineteenth century. The differing textures of landscape in different regions or even particular hamlets of, say, Jamaica, Trinidad, Cuba, or Guadeloupe may have a great deal to tell us about the forms of social contestation in the slavery and post-emancipation period, about the differing interpenetrations between plantation and plot in the production of space, and, hence, about the different textures of freedom as lived in these places. Continuities and discontinuities in spatial orders, represented in part by the planting, transplanting, and uprooting of particular species and botanical individuals and the stories people tell about those plants, can tell us a great deal about social histories and social memories. And the planting of new gardens, such as those described by the Antiguan writer Jamaica Kincaid, continues to be "an occasion for action, pragmatic planning and performance," a "lived space" rather than an exercise in control, order, or visual pleasure (discussed in Hoving 2002: 132). In her making of (and writing about) gardens and of home as a place "of maneuvering through the world in an ethical way," Hoving argues that Kincaid shows that these "uneasy" places of dwelling are sites "where the erotics and the politics are explicitly present in their intertwining" (Hoving 2002: 137–38). Such an erotics and politics of gardening as performative place making is a crucial, if neglected, dimension of citizenship from below.

CHAPTER EIGHT

Returning the Tourist Gaze

Tourist, don't take my picture
Don't take my picture, tourist
I'm too ugly
Too dirty
Too skinny
Don't take my picture, white
man

—FÉLIX MORISSEAU-LEROY, "Tourist"

Tourism is a crucial aspect of the "sustained contact and exchange among the peoples of the Atlantic world" (Roach 1996: 29) and of the world history of "bodies in contact" (Ballantyne and Burton 2005). Caribbean peoples have long dealt with the arrival, departure, and visits of travelers and tourists. And tourists have long enjoyed privileges of moving through the Caribbean both by land and by sea, gaining a kind of overview that allowed them to construct local people as rooted to the place and natural scenery as an unchanging tropical backdrop (Sheller 2004). Tourism can be understood as a form of embodied encounter between foreign travelers and local people that involves corporeal relations of unequal power. By referring to embodied encounters I mean simply that the physical materiality of the bodies brought into proximity in such moments of encounter matters in particular ways. The space of the beach, for example, can be a place of leisure for the tourist and a place of work for the local person, and work must be managed in a way that does not intrude on leisure. One way that this is achieved is by clearing beaches entirely of local bodies or restricting them to certain marginal areas while extending the social relations of the all-inclusive resort to entire islands (see Titley 2005). Another way is for local bodies to be enlisted in the pleasure experience— getting closer to the tourist's body, for example, by braiding hair or massaging tired muscles. The way tourists and local people face each other, look at each other, hear each other, smell each other, or touch each other are all part of the power relations by which forms of gender and racial inequality are brought into being along with national boundaries of belonging and exclusion (see Ahmed 2000).

Aaron Kamugisha (2007: 28) argues that tourism directly "configures Caribbean citizenship" in a number of ways, including how "landscapes are rigorously reconfigured to present a vision that the tourist might enjoy, the enclosure of desirable spaces along the shoreline and the rehabilitation of capital cities and towns to more closely approximate models to be found in the urban north Atlantic." Thus, building on the analysis of spatiality in the previous chapter, here I consider how the spaces of citizenship and nationalism are interpenetrated by tourist practices, and how those engaged in citizenship from below struggle to re-appropriate the tourist space in which they have been subordinated. "Tourists occupy a space which we might term 'extra-territorial citizenship,'" argues Kamugisha (2007: 29), appropriating space and comforts while making Caribbean citizens feel alien in their own land. The unequal relations found in the prevailing forms of sex tourism throughout the Caribbean are most indicative of this self-alienation (Brennan 2004; Kempadoo 1999). Thus, Kamugisha (2007: 30) succinctly argues that "gender and sexuality are crucial factors in any critique of the coloniality of citizenship," and it is here that we must try to apprehend "some of the most pervasive and crude denials of citizenship in the Caribbean postcolony" if we are ever to explain "the crises of citizenship within the contemporary Caribbean state."

The recognition and *signification* of bodily differences is one of the key ways in which racial categories are socially constructed (Hall 2000: 20; Higginbotham 1992), and colonial travel writers were crucially positioned to be able to do this work of signification. Yet as Frederick Cooper and Ann Laura Stoler (1997: 3–4, 7) argue, "The otherness of colonized persons was neither inherent nor stable; his or her difference had to be defined and maintained. . . . [To this extent,] a grammar of difference was continuously and vigilantly crafted as people in colonies refashioned and contested European claims to superiority." In this chapter, I argue that these grammars of difference are elaborated through relations of looking, which are fundamental to tourism and travel writing. We can understand tourism as a kind of (post)colonial contact zone (Pratt 1992) in which the grammars of racial difference are crafted, through embodied encounters and the construction of what John Urry (1991) calls the tourist gaze. While not discounting the other bodily senses, Urry draws on Georg Simmel (1997: 111), who argued that the eye effects the connection and interaction of individuals; it is the "most direct and purest interaction that exists." People cannot avoid taking through the eye without at the same time giving. The eye produces "the most complete reciprocity; of person to person, face to face" (Simmel 1997: 112). In colonial contact zones, of course, such reciprocity of the gaze is highly skewed, since looking or gazing always enacts unequal power relations. Just as film studies recognizes the effects of the dominant masculine gaze within cinema to determine unequal "relations of looking" between men and women (Kaplan 1983; Kuhn 1982), so, too, does tourism (and the travel writing that describes the touristic encounter) rest on a dominant gaze that determines unequal relations of looking between tourists and those they define as locals or natives of the place they are touring.

Yet gazing on another requires a certain degree of proximity, which puts the gazer at risk: Embodied encounters leave a space for contesting the gaze, deflecting the gaze, returning the gaze, appropriating the gaze, and destabilizing the power of the gaze. As Félix Morisseau-Leroy's poem "Tourist" suggests, the encounter with the tourist gaze is fraught with tension, threat, and counter-gaze (Morisseau-Leroy 1999: n.p.):

> Don't take my picture, white man
> Mr. Eastman won't be happy
> I'm too ugly
> Your camera will break
> I'm too dirty
> Too black
> Whites like you won't be content
> I'm too ugly
> I'm gonna crack your kodak
> Don't take my picture, tourist
> Leave me be, white man

Every embodied encounter is a moment of improvisation, role-playing, and interaction in which a re-scripting of power is always risked, including the breaking of cameras. The poem seems to give voice to the kinds of photographic subjects seen in chapter 4, the ragged and barefoot "picturesque" natives of Jamaica.

The embodied encounters of tourist photography are a patterned performance of gestures, memories, and "restored behaviors" (Roach 1996). In his profound reading of forms of "circum-Atlantic performance," Joseph Roach (1996: 25–26) argues that "genealogies of performance attend not only to 'the body,' as Foucault suggests, but also to bodies—to the reciprocal reflections they make on one another's surfaces as they foreground their capacities for interaction. Genealogies of performance also attend to 'counter-memories,' or the disparities between history as it is discursively transmitted and memory as it is publicly enacted by the bodies that bear its consequences." I suggest that the touristic encounter is just such a performance, in which the "kinesthetic imagination" is put into play in an orchestration of behavior and expressive movements that serve as what Roach (1996: 26), drawing on the work of dance historians and critical performance studies, calls "mnemonic reserves"—that is, "patterned movements made and remembered by bodies." These patterned movements include both the racial etiquettes of enacting deference and servility or superiority and ease and the counter-memories of resistance by which people enact their own dignity and agency in public spaces through gestures, postures, and performances that refuse to cooperate in their own subordination.

Here we find what Roach calls the "pedestrian speech acts" (quoting de Certeau 1984: 98) of walking in the city (or along the beach), the oral and corporeal "environments of memory," and the forms of kinesthetic imagination and memory transmitted and transformed through movement and dance (Roach 1996: 26). If a corporeal politics is central to mobilizing, imagining, and transmitting practices of black citizenship and memorializing crucial "places of memory," then its histories are sedimented both in spaces (especially architectural cityscapes) and in the "behavioral vortices" of bodies (especially styles of dance and performance) (Roach 1996: 26–28). Crucial to the U.S. Civil Rights Movement, for example, were the small-scale battles over black bodies occupying "white" public spaces—on streetcars, at lunch counters, on street corners and sidewalks, and more widely in the racialized institutional spaces of segregation. Collective spaces of public display, congregation, and mobility can be read alongside more explicit forms of political mobilization, such as the parades, civic ceremonies, festivities, public holidays, outdoor electoral campaigning, and riots that

Mary Ryan (1997) associates with the raucous democracy of major American cities such as New York, San Francisco, and New Orleans in the post–Civil War era. When politics takes to the streets, crowds, noise, festivity, and riot all play their part, but the street may also become a site for politics by other means: the politics of embodied interactions, counter-gazes, and discomfort.

Consider figure 10, an illustration by Bill Ballantine for an article on Haiti that appeared in *Holiday* magazine in March 1950. It depicts a photographic studio in Port-au-Prince; in the foreground, a well-dressed Haitian family appears—a man, a woman, and four children—waiting for their portrait to be taken, with other black-and-white images hanging on the nearby wall. Behind them, two white, presumably U.S. American, sailors are having their photograph taken by a black photographer. A portrait of Toussaint Louverture hangs on the wall to the left, and on the right appears an unfinished painting of what appears to be the classic image of Louverture on horseback, with sword drawn, discussed in chapter 5. The image is a complex layering of various practices of visual representation, from the oil paintings to the photographic family portrait, the sailor's souvenir snapshot, the gaze of the illustrator, the magazine illustration, the gaze of the *Holiday* reader, and the gaze of the reader of this intertextual archive. Only one gaze faces directly back at the viewer: that of the Haitian mother holding her child. This raises the hint of a question: What does she see, and what does she want us to see? We might also begin to wonder what varied forms of masculinity are being portrayed here, including the honorable soldier-father of the nation, the black bourgeois father of a family, the photographer as artist, and the intimately touching white sailors.

This chapter offers a history of the embodied encounters of tourism through a reading of representations of Caribbean people looking back at white travelers and tourists in travel writing of the late nineteenth century and early twentieth century, as well as some Caribbean reflections on the appearance of the tourist. Having considered earlier how citizenship was seized, extended, and reinvented by popular publics in the nineteenth century, my focus here shifts to the ongoing embodied interactions that continued to construct relations of gender, racial, and sexual hierarchy in the late nineteenth century to the early twentieth century. I have argued that several challenges to methods of historical research arise from the responses of historians both to anticolonial movements and to postcolonial theory, including the incorporation of literature and poetry as evidence and inspiration and the practice of alternative ways to read litera-

A RINGING BELL replaces the birdie to fix attention of camera portrait sitters. Reflectors once were saucepans.

tough nut of West Indian politics, dictator of Haiti's neighbor, the Dominican Republic). Spain never seriously settled the west of the island. There never was much gold in Hispaniola. Mexico and Peru blossomed as treasure houses, luring the venturesome. When, in 1697,

France and Spain concluded a continental tussle with the Treaty of Ryswick, France achieved title to the western third of Hispaniola. France planted sugar. And imported slaves.

DRAWINGS BY BILL BALLANTINE

Negroes of all the diverse tribes of Africa's west coast—Iboa and Foules, fat Aradas and lean-lipped Mandingos, Bambaras and Franc-Congos—were hauled in packed slave ships; and in less than a hundred years, black slaves outnumbered white Frenchmen by pretty

102   HOLIDAY/MARCH

10. Bill Ballantine, "Photo Studio," illustration, *Holiday* magazine, March 1950.

ture, visual culture, and material culture as methodological contributions to historiography. In chapter 7, I explored the methodological contributions of studies of material culture and historical geography to tracing otherwise silenced subaltern histories. In this chapter, I explore another such methodological departure through a reading of colonial travel writing not for what it says or describes but for what it does not say and fails to describe. In both cases, these alternative methods are crucial to extrapolating modes of citizenship from below that escape the formal politics of the nation-state. The subaltern subjects of each chapter instead address the modes of movement of Europeans into and out of Caribbean space and stake their own claim on that space as both local and transnational.

Travel writing is one of the key sites for the production of racialized and gendered subjects in colonial contact zones (Ballantyne and Burton 2005; Duncan and Gregory 1999; Gikandi 1996; Pratt 1992; Spurr 1993). Postcolonial theorists, however, have shown that there are always instabilities and ambivalences within colonial discourse through which one can read the agency of the subaltern. Not only can we read those texts in which the "empire writes back" in answer to the colonizer (Ashcroft et al. 2002; Gikandi 1996); we can also search out the fault lines in imperial texts such as nineteenth-century travel writing to reveal what Edouard Glissant (1989) calls the "underside." In particular, I argue that by paying attention to moments of gazing and self-consciousness about being looked at within travel writing, we can begin to pursue a genealogy of performance of the oppositional disruption and everyday deconstruction of the tourist gaze. Rather than focusing on the power of colonial travel narratives to demarcate racial and gender boundaries, therefore, the approach here draws on postcolonial discourse analysis to identify points of instability, anxiety, disruption, and opposition to the colonial gaze found in the public "vortices of behavior" of the circum-Atlantic world (Roach 1996).

In previous work (Sheller 2003), I considered the ways in which a form of West Indian Orientalism informed Anglo-American travel and writing about the Caribbean. Here I revisit this argument by addressing how we might read travel writing in ways that tease out disturbances within systems of racial discourse that upheld the colonial power to name and define the colonized. In reading for the fissures and submerged fault lines in the discourse of imperial power—the signs of the repressed colonized other with and through whom the imperial self is consolidated and narrated—we can begin to recognize the actions of the colonized through the resistances and frictions that disrupt the imperial gaze (see Wahab 2004). As Simon Gikandi (1996: 19–20) argues, "If power still resides in the metropolitan center, even after empire, what is the meaning of a reversed gaze at the culture of Englishness? . . . Colonial and postcolonial theorists have spent a lot of time analyzing how Europe constitutes itself as a subject gazing at the other, but rarely have they examined how the other gazes at Europe. . . . Colonial culture is as much about the figuration of the metropolis in the imagination of the colonized themselves as it is about the representation of the colonized in the dominant discourses of the imperial centre." Here Gikandi contrasts "the representation of the colonized in the dominant discourses of the imperial centre" with "the figuration of the metropolis in the imagination of the colonized." However, I suggest that it is not so easy to separate these two figurations into purely opposed categories, especially when the dominant discourse tends to choke off any counter-discourses; rather, submerged within the dominant discourse we can at times hear the reverberations of an oppositional voice or feel the effects of someone gazing back, someone refiguring the metropolis.

Stuart Hall has noted a counter-strategy within the politics of representation that works "*within* the complexities of representation itself, and tries to *contest it from within*." As Hall (1999: 13) explains, "Since black people have so often been fixed, stereotypically, by the racialised gaze, it may have been tempting to refuse the complex emotions associated with 'looking'. However, this strategy makes elaborate play with 'looking', hoping by its very attention, to 'make it strange'—that is to de-familiarise it, and so make explicit what is often hidden." By working with representational practices —not just looking back, but making looking strange or, in some sense, queering the gaze—black artists have been able to lay bare the politics of looking. Divya Tolia-Kelly and Andy Morris (2004) have connected this strategic looking to the work of contemporary artists such as Kobena Mercer, Yinka Shonibare, Chris Ofili, and Kara Walker. We could also add black filmmakers such as Isaac Julien, who have explored the gaze especially on the black male body. In their work, there is an elaborate play with looking (Golden 1994). In these "imaginary movements" we can locate the "displaced transmissions" by which historic practices are adapted to changing conditions in ways that allow not simply for reproduction or repetition, but for improvisation, revision, detours, and deflections— hence "transformations of experience through the displacement of its cultural forms" (Roach 1996: 28–29).

In revisiting the archive of Caribbean representations, I also want to make it strange, in Hall's sense. Is it possible to use a turning of the gaze as a historical method? Can we look back at colonial representational practices in a way that makes them strange or recognizes the estrangements that disturb the tourist's gaze? Can we discover Caribbean agents working within the representational practices of the tourist picturesque to undo its power? I will draw on an archive of popular travel writing that emerged with the development of organized tourism in the Caribbean in the late nineteenth century, facilitated by faster passenger steamship services and the building of tourism infrastructure such as docks, roads, and hotels (Anim-Adoo 2011). Guidebooks and travel narratives from this period can be found not only in major colonial depositories, but also in the urban public libraries of any major port city. With titles such as *Down the Islands*, *Cruising in the Caribbees*, or *A Touch of the Tropics*, they are generally unoriginal and often poorly written, patronizing, and extremely offensive. The racist material I quote is indicative of the mundane embodied encounters of what might be called everyday imperialism.

However, this type of travel writing can be read not simply as an instance of the power to define racial categories and impose them on colonized others, but also for more subtle traces of bodily encounters with places and with others—encounters that leave their queer mark on the author and on the text. The white imperial subjects who emerge from these texts are not simply self-authored and authorized; they are also the unstable products of their disturbing encounters with the Caribbean and its subjects. Krista Thompson has pursued similar subjects in *An Eye for the Tropics*, her fascinating study of visual representations in Jamaica and the Bahamas. As she suggests, "In the early twentieth century, black working classes and emergent black middle classes (or 'brown' in the case of Jamaica) at times contested tropicalized images, precisely because these representations typically imaged blacks as rural, exotic, primitive, and unmodern, despite their modernizing efforts" (Thompson 2006: 13). In the final sections of this chapter, I examine instances in which Caribbean people are shown to be intervening in the production of photographs, challenging the white touristic viewer. This raises the question once again of the significance of absences in the archive, and I conclude by considering where we might find alternative visions of the Caribbean of the nineteenth century and the early twentieth century from a Caribbean perspective.

INSTABILITIES WITHIN IMPERIAL TEXTS

James Duncan (1999: 157) argues that in imperial travel writing, "Occasionally the native is summoned to appear before the reader. But the native is certainly not summoned in order to speak . . . but rather to be seen, to stand in for the Orient [or, in our case, the Caribbean], which is to say to add to the picturesqueness of the scene." In this construction of scenery, he argues, the picturesque "is not simply a way of seeing, it is simultaneously a way of doing, a way of world-making" (Duncan 1999: 153). In 1932, for example, John van Dyke wrote sketches of the people and landscape of

Jamaica that enact precisely this kind of politics of the picturesque: "Seen along the Jamaica roads, under the broken sunlight filtered through palm and bamboo, the black is decidedly picturesque. He has the fine line and movement of an animal, the dark skin born of a tropical sun, and the female of the species comes in to help out the picture with the glow of bright clothing. Male and female after their kind they belong to the landscape as much as the waving palm or the flowering bougainvillea or the gay hibiscus. They are exotic, tropical, indigenous, and fit in the picture perfectly, keeping their place without the slightest note of discord" (Van Dyke 1932: 23–24). Dark skin and colorful clothing, sunlight and shadow, exotic peoples and tropical landscapes are depicted here as a harmonious whole. In picturing plantation workers, market women, washerwomen, and other people at work through the frame of the picturesque (often taking pictures of them), tourists enacted the common-sense imperial understanding of "the black" as a tropical type, a racial type, or, here, a different "species" or "kind" belonging to this different landscape.

But local people subjected to the tourist gaze were not unaware of these modes of vision, and there were a variety of ways in which they might manage this encounter. These might range from reactive strategies such as avoiding the gaze, challenging the gaze, or playing out the expected role as scenery, or it might include more proactive strategies such as stage-managing in advance when and where tourists might be allowed to gaze at local life, channeling tourists into particular zones, or manipulating tourists' expectations for increased monetary gain. If the positioning of self and other in the colonial text is always an inter-positioning, then we should be able to identify moments of anxiety, instability, and disruption even in the most banal travel writing. How can we read such moments of subaltern agency, in which the tourist's gaze is returned, deflected, managed, or appropriated? Beyond the power of the tourist gaze, there are also traces of what I call returning the tourist gaze—that is, modes of resisting the power of the gaze to define one's being. Here I will first identify three possibilities for finding evidence of such interactions in a typical example of colonial travel writing.

My text is Edward Agnew Paton's *Down the Islands: A Voyage in the Caribbees*, published in 1888. First, we might read for the unstated negative —a troubling undercurrent that a positive statement seeks to conceal. Paton describes his trip by steamer from New York on a winter cruise through the Lesser Antilles. Arriving in Antigua, he comments, "At intervals along the road we passed darkies of every age, of both sexes, on their way to or from town, carrying baskets of fruits and vegetables; we heard some of them singing, but as we approached they stepped aside to make way for us, and watched us in silence, always ready and delighted to return our greetings" (Paton 1888: 66). His terminology reflects the everyday racism of the northern United States, while his idea of going "down the islands" and viewing the friendly "darkies" suggests a sense of proprietorship and being at home as he moves through this landscape. The tourist's condescending and intrusive gaze turns local life into part of the scenery, in which the locals are expected to remain silent except when called on to return a greeting or offer a service. Nevertheless, the very possibility of their *not* stepping aside and *not* remaining silent suggests a certain power dynamic at play: Is it possible that in some instances the locals do not step aside and are not delighted to return white men's greetings? Perhaps such things have happened to the author in the United States. And what of the fact that the people stopped singing? They step aside and watch in silence— but is it really a friendly and accommodating silence? Their watchfulness enters the text and inseminates it with these little questions, these pregnant pauses.

Tourists like Paton viewed Caribbean people as silent and passive objects to be gazed on or, here, "ready and delighted" to meet a white man and return his greeting. In other instances, he pursues a woman through the streets to be able "to inspect, with approving criticism, the object of my admiration from tip to toe, and from every point of view." Having sized the woman up, and later sketched her, he sighs to his reader, "Alas! I must confess it, this Aryan kinswoman of mine was as brown as any Hindu cooly girl in Georgetown, and all of her East Indian sisters are as dusky as richest rosewood, as brown and dark as rarest mahogany" (Paton 1888: 177–78). Gikandi (1996: 106) argues that "a certain epistemology of blackness generates the imperial aesthetic. Simply put, blacks can be processed and controlled when they are turned into ethnoerotic objects. They are visualized as objects that are simultaneously attractive and repulsive, different from established cultural norms but at the same time belonging to the human family." There is certainly an ethnoeroticism at work here, as Paton claims the figure as his "Aryan kinswoman" but then uses her objectified skin color to make her strange and re-establish racial distance. Attraction and repulsion are two sides of the same coin.

As I have argued elsewhere, tourists in the Caribbean used comparisons between Africans and Coolies to mark the African body as especially repulsive and developmentally "below" the "Aryan" (Sheller 2003). As Sara Ahmed (2004: 89) notes: "The spatial distinction of 'above' from 'below' functions metaphorically to separate one body from another, as well as to differentiate between higher and lower bodies, or more and less advanced bodies. As a result, disgust at 'that which is below' functions to maintain the power relations between above and below, *through which 'aboveness' and 'belowness' become properties of particular bodies, objects, and spaces.* Given the fact that the one who is disgusted is the one who feels disgust, then the position of 'aboveness' is maintained only at the cost of a certain vulnerability . . . as an openness to being affected by those who are felt to be below." Thus, as a second strategy, in reading for the disturbing effects of what Gikandi calls the "repulsive," we can see the ways in which disgust registers the vulnerabilities of the white body. In these texts, then, the "in-between" body of the East Asian woman and the "hybrid" body of the mulatta stand for the potential transgression of racial boundaries (Young 1995) and the sexual vulnerability of the white man to those who are "below" him. This historically has given Caribbean women room to manipulate and play off the tourist gaze.

Third, we can be on the lookout for the tourist gaze being countered by Caribbean people who return the gaze. The 1880s were a period of economic depression in the Caribbean, in which the sugar industry was in decline but banana plantations were growing and giving increased economic autonomy to small landholders. But unemployment levels were high, and many men had few alternatives except migration in search of paid work, while women had to higgle and hustle to get by.[1] This is the context in which Paton mentions in passing that in Saint Lucia, "Along the beach there were crowds of negroes, but few of them were engaged in any work. They lolled about on the sand, squatting in the shade in picturesque groups, chatting, laughing, meantime slyly watching us, wondering, no doubt, what we outlandish people could find that was quaint or extraordinary in their appearance" (Paton 1888: 263). Reflecting the anxiety of the white ruling class, Paton tries to contain this scene under the label "picturesque." But their "sly watching" undermines his gaze and forces him to become reflexive about his own outlandish appearance. He is made to wonder how they see him, and thus his own surveillance and power to name and define is called into question. He expresses "no doubt" about what they are wondering about him, but the doubt already infiltrates this encounter in which the tourist feels his gaze being mirrored.

GRAMMARS OF DIFFERENCE AND
WHITE FEMALE TOURISTS

Nineteenth-century tourists constructed their own cultural modernity, civility, and whiteness against a background of Caribbean tourist sites and proximity to racialized others (Sheller 2003). Nineteenth-century travel books, such as *Travels in Santo Domingo*, depict on the contents page a "brown woman" or "mulatta" as a fantasy of racial difference in the hybrid Caribbean. She offers up many different things to the reader/viewer: the contents of the book (inscribed on her basket); the fruit of her country, including the pineapple, a symbol of welcome; and her own body both through her labor in marketing and in the implication of possible sexual availability. Barefoot and kneeling, her figure also represents the entire Dominican nation and, in a sense, what the Hispanic Caribbean as a whole has to offer. The allure of the Caribbean as a place of sexual transgression and racial hybridization, embodied in its beautiful brown women, elicited colonial efforts to stabilize racial boundaries. Efforts to classify all of the racial permutations in the Caribbean led to arcane typologies such as that by Médéric-Louis-Élie Moreau de Saint-Méry, with its 172-odd categories, and debates over the supposed sterility of certain human "crossbreeds." It was the very impossibility of such systems of ordering that drove many Europeans to insist on the fundamental difference of races and to attempt to reinforce and shore up racial boundaries through systems of inequality, discrimination, and segregation. In addition to efforts to locate and identify pure racial types, fantasies of transgressing racial boundaries were central to processes of drawing those boundaries in the first place.[2]

Collecting images and being able to make such racial comparisons authoritatively became the central purposes of Anglo-American travel through the West Indies. Sady Brassey, an Englishwoman who toured the Caribbean in 1885 (accompanied by her two black poodles) happily observed "a little Madrasee boy, bearing on his shoulder a huge bundle of sugar-canes . . . his little naked figure standing out in strong relief against the sunset sky, formed quite a pretty picture" (Brassey 1885: 134). What makes an exotic working child into a pretty picture? As the notion of a grammar of difference suggests, gazing on a variety of racialized others allowed white travelers to make comparisons between different racial groups and thus position themselves via a kind of triangulation. White female tourists especially shored up their own femininity and imperial subjectivity via comparisons between "Coolies" and "Negroes." Brassey said of Trinidad that "the coolie traders, with their dark-brown skins, fine smooth black hair, and lithe figures swathed in bright-coloured shawls, their arms and legs heavy with jewelry, the produce of their spouses' wealth, were quiet and graceful in voice and action; and presented a striking contrast to the buxom black negresses, with their thick lips, gay turbans, merry laughter, and somewhat aggressive curiosity" (Brassey 1885: 120).[3] Such descriptions combine elements of racialization and gendering, blurring physiological traits (skins, hair, lips) with cultural adornments (shawls, jewelry, turbans) and practices (grace, laughter), all of which are aligned from the unmarked position of the privileged white woman. Yet the "somewhat aggressive curiosity" of the black women whom she encounters hints at a certain discomfort in the face of the subaltern's returned gaze, her audibility, or perhaps even her unwelcome touch. When does curiosity become aggressive? What are the women curious about? And why is Brassey's own touristic curiosity not seen as being aggressive?

In the account of a white U.S. American tourist, Susan de Forest Day, we also find signs of anxiety over racial boundaries and the marking of difference as she encounters a racialized space of embodied looking. Stopping in St. Thomas on her cruise in 1899, Day finds that the "streets are thronged with black people of every varying shade. . . . The absence of white faces is very strange. . . . We amuse ourselves by watching the crowd, and by being stared at by them in turn, but we are always greeted with a courteous bow, and sometimes with a few kind words, which quite counteract the stare" (Day 1899: 34). The staring makes Day aware of the absence of white faces and, hence, of the strangeness of her own whiteness. Day also manages her racial discomfort by making comparisons between the African Caribbean and Indo-Caribbean people who stare back at her, noting, for example, "an old Indian coolie, whose aristocratic features and delicate skin are a joy after the retreating forehead and flat noses of the dusky African" (Day 1899: 148). Skin, hair, noses, lips, foreheads, hands, and feet all appear in these texts as the signs of racial superiority or inferiority, an implicit contrast being made with the features of the white authoress. Yet a kind of insubordination lurks not far beneath the surface of these narratives of the touristic encounter, as does an unstated question about how these white women's bodies also serve as standard-bearers for a system of racial differentiation and purification. It takes "kind words" and "a courteous bow" to return Day to her position of superiority as she is subjected to the other's gaze.

Hinted at in these embodied encounters is the question of black and Indo-Caribbean working-class culture, and especially the intrusion of working-class women into public space and the bodily, urban, national, and imperial politics that surrounded efforts to control these women (see Alexander 1994; Austin-Broos 1997; Edmondson 2003; Thomas 2004; chapter 2 in this volume). Black and brown women have long occupied public spaces in many Caribbean port cities because of their role in markets and service work (domestic service, laundry and hotel service), as well as in prostitution. But in those roles, they have also used their public presence to seize the political stage and make claims for their rights and freedoms, as I argued in chapter 2. Touristic descriptions of black women, and their contrast with Indo-Caribbean women, become a way to mark race, gender, and class through practices of objectification, differentiation, classification, and distancing. But they also point toward the alternative movements that M. Jacqui Alexander (2000 [1994]: 375) calls "the decolonization of the body" through the work of countering these ideological "dismemberments" of Caribbean bodies.

Within colonial travel writing, then, we can uncover a submerged history of forms of bodily proximity and encounter that begin with the power dynamics of the master–slave relation and extend to contemporary forms of tourism and service work. In 1895, for example, Charles Augustus Stoddard enjoyed watching women unloading coal from a British steamer in Saint Thomas. Balancing hundred-pound baskets of coal on their heads as they walked up and down a plank to the ship, the women are described as "black, rough, course in face and feature beyond description, they seemed like huge human beasts of burden. With long arms, great prehensile hands and fingers, large, misshapen, and unshod feet, with dirty turbans on their heads, bare breasts, and rags half-concealing their nakedness, they marched up and down the planks for hours, a weird and disgusting spectacle" (Stoddard 1895: 30–31). The women coaling the ships are dismembered into fingers, hands, feet, and bare breasts; they are dehumanized and animalized, as are the market women in Guadeloupe whom Stoddard describes as "chattering and chaffering, screaming and gesticulating like monkeys, over little piles of fruit and vegetables" (Stoddard 1895: 101–2). These kinds of descriptions distance the writer from degraded black labor and naturalize whiteness as a kind of bodily superiority. Yet the very weirdness of this "disgusting spectacle" suggests that it troubles the viewer: Can he be unaware that his sleek, fast, modern steamer operates only on the basis of this degraded female labor? Is not the very condition of possibility for his tourism the exploitation of these workers?

The body is a key site in the exercise of gender and racial domination and resistance, such that representations of Caribbean peoples' bodies revolve around deeply contested power relations. The body itself was, of course, the central terrain in the exercise of domination and resistance under regimes of slavery. As Alexander (2000 [1994]: 365) argues, "Colonial rule simultaneously involved racializing and sexualizing the population, which also meant naturalizing whiteness. . . . Here too, identities were collapsed into bodies. Black bodies, the economic pivot of slave-plantation economy, were sexualized." Colonial socialization into British norms of respectability disciplined black middle-class and working-class subjects through the institutions of the nuclear family, the church, and the law, and later through projects of economic development that included the tourism sector as the route to national salvation. But just as the enslaved, and later the emancipated, found forms of agency by which to challenge these institutional structures that controlled their intimate lives, so, too, did those conscripted into the tourism economy find ways to deal with the embodied encounters demanded by tourism (see e.g., Brennan 2002; Gmelch 2003). It was in these tense encounters that people forged another kind of citizenship from below.

DISRUPTING THE SPECTACLE

People are not simply scenery, and the questions we must continue to ask are: In what ways can the Caribbean subject not merely resist being objectified and animalized but turn the counter-gaze into a form of corporeal power? Is there any evidence within the tourist accounts of a Caribbean agency (re)shaping these embodied encounters? Sexual economies were a central aspect of early touristic encounters, and Caribbean women certainly exercised a certain degree of agency in setting the terms for such sexual-economic transactions. The early tourism industry in the Caribbean made few distinctions between hotels, inns, and brothels, while the "services" available to tourists often included sex. For example, Charles William Day's *Five Years' Residence in the West Indies* served as a kind of guide to brothels. He writes about visiting "the great mulatto lioness of Barbadoes, Miss Betsy Austin, of the Clarence Hotel, the lady so celebrated by Captain Hall and divers other amusing writers on the Antilles" (Day 1852: 12). He also refers to her sister Miss Caroline Lee, who runs another establishment, the Freemason's Hall, "which to the initiated means much more than meets the eye. The lady is the Venus of the Antilles, and is at present understood to be under the protection of a Mr. B—, who has almost deserted a charming wife and family for this dingy Cyprian god-dess" (Day 1852: 13). He then goes on to note that the "drollest part of the matter is that, most likely from ignorance, respectable passengers by the steamers take their wives and daughters to a locale that one would suppose to be sufficiently notorious, as no one in Barbadoes pretends to be ignorant of the nature of the establishment" (Day 1852: 13). He describes other boardinghouses kept by "mulatto" and "white ladies" (Day 1852: 62). Thus, we see a blurring of brothels, boardinghouses, and inns and a general acceptance of the existence of interracial prostitution, concubinage, and other sexual-economic transactions. Day even notes one such type of ser-vice transaction involving laundering: "There is a way of getting one's linen kept in good order, but it is not palatable to all persons: it is to maintain friendly relations with a mulatto lady, who then prides herself on your being a credit to the community" (Day 1852: 24).

In an interesting passage from *At Last: A Christmas in the West Indies*,[4] Charles Kingsley (1873: 88) writes about Port-of-Spain, Trinidad:

> I fear that a stranger would feel a shock—and that not a slight one—at the first sight of the average Negro woman of Port of Spain, especially the younger. Their masculine figures, their ungainly gestures, their loud and sudden laughter, even when walking alone, and their general coarseness, shocks and must shock. It must be remembered that this is a seaport town; and one in which the license usual in such places on both sides of the Atlantic is aggravated by the superabundant animal vigour and the perfect independence of the younger women. It is a painful subject and I shall touch it in these pages as seldom and as lightly as I can.

The slippage in Kingsley's text from "shock" at the young women's "coarse-ness" to an evident erotic charge to the encounter is replicated by the pornographic tone of the text ("touch[ing]" the subject "lightly," yet tit-illating the reader nevertheless). This exemplifies the attraction of the repulsive, the pull of disgust, and the sexual aspect of the racialized en-counter, all of which imply an embodied negotiation of power. The de-scription of the "loud and sudden laughter" of a woman walking alone suggests that she has seen the white tourist, registered his gaze, and chosen to deflect it with discomfiting laughter. These descriptions echo earlier representations of the independent figure Quasheba, as discussed in chap-ter 2, and lower-class black women's subversive occupation of public space.

Certainly, the enjoyment of a holiday in the Caribbean was often marked by tense encounters with local people. In a guide for British tourists published in 1889, one author noted: "Let me add one warning. Remember the negro is a man and a brother, that in the West Indies there is no distinction of colour, and that rude remarks or unconcealed laughter may involve you in much-to-be-regretted unpleasantness" (Bukeley 1889: 23). Turning the abolitionist slogan "Am I Not a Man and a Brother?" into a cynical charade, his words clearly mark out the tensions of tourism in British colonial societies. As in Paton's comment about the men laughing and slyly watching him, or Brassey's comment about the merry laughter of the market women, which she linked to their aggressive curiosity, laughter here is also a marker of a social rift that makes one group a source of amusement for another, and a source of discomfort. But contrary to expectations of colonial domination as a one-way process, it is the market women who can make comments and laugh out loud at the white tourist, while the white tourist is instructed to conceal his own laughter and keep his remarks to himself. Laughter, then, may be one sign of a negotiation of agency between differentially empowered groups.

At times, a kind of subtext of fear and annoyance creeps into these travel texts, disturbing the comfort and complacency of the colonial viewer. E. A. Hastings Jay, visiting Barbados in 1900 at a time when eleven passenger steamships made regular stops at the island (Gmelch 2003: 3), describes boatmen "swarm[ing] round the steamer like flies round a horse's head," presenting a threat to the imperial subject who, like the powerful horse, is unable to swat away the swarming flies (Hastings Jay 1900: 26–29). Throughout his travels around the Caribbean Hastings Jay is perturbed by the people who return his gaze (although he had no shame about staring at and photographing them). On several occasions, he describes his discomfort at being observed. In Barbados, he says,

> We sat down to eat our lunch in a shady place, whereupon a dozen negroes of various ages and sizes made a little group, three yards off, and proceeded to contemplate us as if we were there for the purpose. If we had been waxworks, or statues in a museum, they could not have stared at us with more utter indifference to our feelings. When a white man does stare he generally looks a little shame-faced about it, but the Barbadian negro is entirely devoid of any feeling of the kind. He merely thinks there is something to amuse him, and will come and deliberately take his stand just in front of you, and gaze at you until his curiosity is satisfied. (Hastings Jay 1900: 52–53)

Much like Paton, Hastings Jay is forced to become the object of the gaze and does not like it one bit. His exploration of the difference between the white man's gaze and the Barbadian gaze is suggestive of the dynamics of colonial power, for his very discomfort at being an object of amusement and curiosity precisely describes the forms of objectification of blacks found in texts by white writers, including his own. He even employs the optical metaphor of the "glimpse" in titling his own work.

On arriving in Kingston, Jamaica, Hastings Jay (1900: 204) writes: "We were nearly deafened by the yelling and screeching of a score of shabby-looking negroes, all of whom wanted to carry one's bag at the same time." As with cases of loud laughter, audibility and volume are as important as relations of looking (if not more so) in exercising control over a public space. After finding peace at last at the Rio Cobre Hotel, he complains,

> Even in this beautiful spot we were found out and shadowed by a growing squadron of little black boys, who at length drove us back to the hotel. They stared at our faces, clothes, and boots, and more than ever at R.B.'s camera, which he had brought out in search of subjects. We differed somewhat as to the attitude which should be adopted. I was in favour of strong measures, being at the time not a little influenced by the attentions of sundry mosquitoes and sand-flies. R.B., on the other hand . . . regarded little nigger boys as beneath his notice. (Hastings Jay 1900: 211–12, 216)

The tourist tries to regain the upper hand by reducing the boys to insects, but such encounters nevertheless disrupt his viewing pleasure. The tourists search out subjects who will become objects, passively posing before the camera, yet they find themselves uncomfortably to be the objects of local interest. Why is this gaze so discomfiting? Being looked at, a seemingly harmless form of contact, thoroughly disrupts the power relation of imperium in these texts.

Many instances also have been recorded of Caribbean people intervening to stop photographs from being taken. Thompson gives this example from the Bahamas in a text written by Amelia Defries in 1917, during the Afro-Bahamian masquerade of John Canoe, "an event that brought black revelers from over the hill into the white business district of the city, [and] provides a snapshot of local inhabitants' responses to the camera." As Defries takes out her camera, a black woman stops her and says "Ma'ma—put your photograph thing away; dey doesn't want to be took. . . . Dere was a fellar takin dose last year—and a man got wild, and bit his ear. . . . Dey don't want no one carrying away der faces dressed up dis way" (Defries 1917: 78, quoted in Thompson 2006: 113–14). Thompson (2006: 115) interprets the threat as protecting the taboo against photographing masquerades, which carry spiritual power, and as testament to the fact that the masqueraders "operated beyond the boundaries of the colonial state's control," invading the city center on one day of the year in a way that was "untamed, hostile, and threatening." Stopping photographs from being taken is also an interesting intervention in the construction of souvenirs, documents, and, thus, archives; it is a strategy that leaves a gap or silence in the visual record, making what is *not* photographed as significant as what is photographed. The textual records of such altercations around photography effectively frame these absences, as in the challenge to the tourist photographer in the poem with which this chapter began, thus bringing them to our attention. Here are several other examples.

While visiting Haiti in the 1920s, during the period of the U.S. occupation (1915–34), the U.S. American travel writer Blair Niles offered this fascinating account of a tense encounter with a Haitian in a chapter titled "A Monkey on a Postcard":

> Perched on the edge of the narrow sidewalk a small negro boy read aloud to himself. . . . He was a tiny black boy, with a battered straw hat several sizes too small, and blue overalls many sizes too big. He could not possibly have seen more than seven rainy seasons fall upon the thirsty streets of Cape Haitian. Yet these were the words he read in his breathless rhythm: Ca-lam-I-té // Mo-ral-I-té // Ti-mid-I-té // Sé-gur-i-té. Enchanted by this little person who, squatting on the ledge of sidewalk, oblivious of passers-by, read to himself such serious words, I cried out to the photographer that I must have him. . . . The infant reader was charmed to pose, and the picture was just about to be snapped, when there broke through the gathering an elderly mulatto man. . . . This little mourning mulatto vehemently proclaimed that the photograph should not be.
>
> "I . . . I oppose myself!" he exclaimed.
>
> "But why?"
>
> "Because I will not have it!" And a storm possessed the saffron body in the dingy garments. "I will not have the child put on a post card and labelled a 'monkey'! That is why you want the picture. And I will not have it!" . . .
>
> [B]ut he would allow the boy to accept some sweets. . . . [N]ow an ivory smile added itself to the eyes which rolled in the black little face. (Niles 1926: 9–10)

Even as he tries to ridicule the Haitian who stopped his photographer, Niles enacts the very objectification and racist discourse that the man sought pre-emptively to oppose—his racist descriptions of the ivory smile, the black little face, the saffron body, and so on. The boy is presented in words, if not in pictures, as a monkey on a postcard for the amusement of armchair tourists at home. Nevertheless, Niles's narration of this event records the agency of a Haitian man who boldly opposes the photographic representational practices of a white tourist (the creation of postcards) and links that opposition to a critique of the evolutionist paradigms of social Darwinism (blacks as monkeys).

By slipping into a dialogic discursive mode, this text hints at a postcolonial subjectivity within the independent Republic of Haiti during the sensitive period of U.S. occupation, which imposed blatant forms of U.S. racism and segregation in a society with a more subtle color continuum. The exclamation, "I . . . I oppose myself!," appears in the form of a stuttering subject, an apparent translation from French (*Je m'oppose* [I object]) or Creole into English, with both the stutter and the faulty translation key signs of postcolonial positionality (Gunew 2003). But even from this position, the interloper is able to interject into the text the definitive statement: "That is why you want the picture. And I will not have it!" Although Niles controls the writing of this text, the force of the Haitian man's intervention, proclaiming what "you want," seems to call into question Niles's resolution of the situation and (despite his framing efforts) undermines his racial subjectivity as superior to "mulatto" and "black" others. This intervention can be read in relation to the long history, even by the 1920s, of the use of photographs in projects of racial classification. Stepan's analysis of Louis Agassiz's use of photographs to record Brazilian "racial hybrids," for example, shows "the photograph's artificiality as a representational device, as well as the artificiality of the very racial truths the photograph was supposed to denote" (Stepan 2001: 88). Here we see a Caribbean agent intervening in the making of such photographs, with full awareness of their racial implications.

This text comes in the wake of a long history of racist depiction of Haiti, dating especially to James Anthony Froude's *The English in the West Indies; or, The Bow of Ulysses* (1888), which Gikandi explores in his analysis of Englishness and the culture of travel. However, we can also find Caribbean responses to Froude, which call into question his authority to define the Caribbean. Gikandi explores how J. J. Thomas, an obscure black schoolmaster, published *Froudacity* in 1889. He suggests that the "counter-discursive strategies contra Froude" in Thomas's text "has to be considered as an example of the ways in which the colonized subject fashioned itself by both questioning and appropriating the civilizational authority of English-ness" (Gikandi 1996: xiv, 113). What he calls the "slippage inherent in what would appear to be the totalized apparatus of imperial discourse" (Gikandi 1996: 113) disrupts its claims to expertise, objectivity, and disinterested universalism by reversing the gaze and speaking back (Davis 1888: 36–38). I have so far considered two kinds of evidence of the disruption of the gaze: the making of the white tourist into a spectacle for the black gazer and the direct intervention by Caribbean agents in photographic and textual repre-sentations of Caribbean people. If these can be characterized as forms of (re)turning the gaze, we can also go further and consider other ways to disrupt or destabilize relations of gazing by working from within represen-tational practices, as Stuart Hall put it.

By the mid-twentieth century, advice was being given to tourists on how to be more self-conscious about their relations with local people. Thomp-son gives the example of Orford St. John, whose essay "How to Behave in the Tropics," published in 1949, counseled:

> You will be looking through the glass at a strange new world. But there will be others outside the glass looking in.
>
> So do not view the figures that people the landscape as though they were clowns and acrobats in a circus. They are not in the least picturesque. They are human beings like you. When you are tempted to regard them as quaint, remember that they too are watching you. Their way of life is different from yours and yours also is "different." The behaviour of tourists also, may sometimes recall the circus. And when it comes to staring, the Jamaican will probably win. (Quoted in Thompson 2006: 240–41)

Here Thompson argues that St. John flips the script and calls attention to Jamaicans as viewing subjects and, moreover, as human beings with their own viewpoint and interests. He introduces the notion of a self-reflexive tourist who is more aware of his or her own presence, and strangeness, in the local scene.

This takes us to another image by Ballantine, which appeared in *Holiday* magazine in an article entitled "Voodoo Village" about Jacmel, Haiti, which is described as "a pleasant town where black magic is a homely part of community life." In figure 11, we see Ballantine's depiction of a street scene in Jacmel whose caption reads: "The American painter offered *Maman* Celie, all pearly teeth and beehive bosom, fifteen dollars to sit for him. She lifted her voice angrily, threw a plantain at him and drove him away." The scene is full of market women carrying trays of goods on their heads or

11. Bill Ballantine, "Maman Celie," illustration, *Holiday* magazine, November 1951.

spread out on blankets on the ground; several mothers and many small children; a policeman eating a banana; and the tourist/painter dressed casually in tropical shorts and shirt, carrying his equipment, with a camera hanging around his neck, face to face with the enormous-busted woman flourishing a plantain, mouth open like an opera singer. The italicized honorific "*Maman* (Mother)" echoes the local respect for this big market woman. However, we learn in the final paragraph of the article that Maman Celie's objection was not simply to being painted. The American painter "wandered into the market and was fascinated by the wonderful bulk of *Maman* Celie. He asked in his very good French, if she'd sit for him for a fortnight. He offered her fifteen dollars, as much as she could hope to earn in a month at the market." What she was angry about, she told the author later, was " 'fifteen dollars, . . . to live with a man for two weeks. It's too little!' She paused and reflected. 'Or much too much,' she added." In other words, she had taken the phrase not to mean sitting for a painting, but to mean some kind of two-week sexual-economic transaction. This tells us something about the prevalence of sex tourism in this postwar period, as well as this Haitian woman's capability to negotiate her own worth by physically intimidating and "driving away" an overly intimate *blanc* in the public space of the market. Yet it is also reminiscent of the old stereotypes of Quasheba, discussed in chapter 2, as the forward and loud market woman whose femininity is placed in question.

In the face of such racist depictions as "Voodoo Village" it is significant that Jacmel has become one of Haiti's most important centers for visual arts. The artists of Jacmel, which is now depicted as a "city of artists," have worked hard to produce their own self-representations and to create institutions for the advancement of art, from the Fosaj Art School to the Cine Institute, whose young filmmakers started making documentaries in the immediate aftermath of the earthquake in January 2010.[5] Even with their gallery and studios partially destroyed by "*goudougoudou* (the earthquake)," the artists of Jacmel have once again picked up their paint brushes (see figure 12). Yet far more work still needs to be done on the ways in which Haitian painting and other self-representations circulate as art market commodities.

THE COUNTER-GAZE

In reading the optics of imperial power in white travel writing of the nineteenth century, then, we can suggest several ways to read for the underside of colonial histories and to locate subaltern agency, which can be understood as the bodily basis for citizenship from below. First there are the instabilities and fissures within the texts themselves—hinting at anxieties, reversals, and disruptions of the imperial "will to power." (On this strategy in the reading of landscape painting, see Wahab 2004.) Second, we can read these moments as textual evidence of subaltern agency that might

12. Artists at work in Jacmel (2010). Photograph by the author.

be generalized as examples of what James Scott (1990) calls the revelation of the hidden transcript—moments in which resistance surfaces in everyday practices of touristic encounter and is recorded in the imperial narrative effort to contain that resistance, such as forms of staring, "aggressive curiosity," laughter, following, propositioning, or interrupting the touristic encounter on the part of the supposedly colonized. Finally, we can find examples of recorded conversation or entire written texts that respond to the colonial text, answering back and appropriating its authority, making counter-claims from a self-consciously Caribbean or West Indian standpoint (Ashcroft et al. 2002; Gikandi 1996), thereby articulating and elaborating a local or "creole gaze" (Wahab 2004). Many of these themes have been explored especially in the visual arts of the Caribbean and the Caribbean diaspora, including painting, performance art, and film.

Here we might also consider the ways in which Caribbean agents have not just returned the gaze but have also deflected, directed, manipulated, and parodied it, both by shielding some things from view and by performing certain acts to attract tourists for economic gain. The tourist economy can be beneficial in some respects, and Caribbean nations often have competed to attract tourists and to profit from tourism. In his study of workers in the Barbados tourist industry, for example, George Gmelch refers to the kinds of resistance practiced by those who have to deal with tourists despite overwhelming rude, racist, or ignorant behavior or comments, because "the customer is always right." He includes parody, gossip, ridicule, and unflattering stereotyping of tourists, as well as occasional "displays of rudeness," "altercations," and "obstruction" to show that workers are not "defenceless," despite the asymmetries of the host–guest relation (Gmelch 2003: 193). My reading of his oral histories suggests further strategies, including challenging the above–below hierarchy by asserting a sense of equality or inverting this hierarchy; exercising a kind of benevolent or charitable attitude toward tourists, which can be a form of empowerment; and using work in tourism to increase one's social and cultural (as well as economic) capital.

In conclusion, this postcolonial reading of the grammar of difference within colonial travel writing suggests that there is what Amar Wahab (2004: 15–16), building on Mary Louise Pratt, calls a "dynamic economy of gestures at inter-positioning between colonizer and colonized that does not always preserve the dialectical power relations between both subjects." Through processes of asymmetrical exchange, "inter-positioning," and "inter-framing," there are evident struggles over racial representation. We find white gendered subjects trying to negotiate complex fields of racial looking, in which their own gazing and their narratives of that gaze are anxiously undermined by counter-gazes and embodied encounters that throw into relief their otherwise invisible whiteness. Postcolonial discourse analysis indicates that it is precisely such disruptions that lead to the anxiety of repetition of racist grammars of difference: black bodies are stabilized again and again within racist texts precisely because they always exceed, challenge, and escape efforts at racial classification. Yet because whiteness is never self-evident and can be made visible only by proximate encounters with black, brown, and bronze bodies, it can also be destabilized within such encounters. Efforts to return the tourist gaze thus begin the crucial work of denaturalizing ideas of race by conjugating its grammar in new ways that shift the subject, the object, the verb, and the gaze itself in these embodied relations of looking. In reading the underside of texts for signs of this counter-discourse, we can expand the historiographical toolkit to include literary methodologies and visual-cultural approaches influenced by postcolonial theory. Beyond the literalness of the text and illusion of authorial power, Caribbean subjects co-created these embodied encounters and effectively co-wrote the texts of colonial travel through their corporeal assertions of personhood.

One contemporary example can help illustrate this process. Gina Athena Ulysse offers an astute example of the affect of the body surface in her auto-ethnographic account of working with informal commercial importers in Jamaica. She describes the exacting techniques and practices of color, class, and gender differentiation that she must negotiate with her body to carry out her fieldwork. The gaze of her ethnographic subjects work on her as she works on them—pressing her to get her hair processed, to wear makeup and polished nails, to make her clothing more respectable or feminine—so that she might more successfully navigate the public and private spaces of this field. On the streets of Kingston, "a female loses claim to her body, as it becomes the property of men who occupy this space. The female body became their text, if you will, a map onto which the boundaries of the class dimensions of the spatial order can be demarcated" (Ulysse 2002: 18). Thus, the ethnographer's short-haired, dark-skinned, but class-privileged, boundary-crossing North American body must be redone, with the help and insistence of an "informant" who "rescues" her by correcting her inappropriate embodiment.[6] This is an account not only of multiple (gendered, classed, nationally located) blacknesses and their inter-positioning, but also of how a body surfaces in a particular way and "takes certain shapes over others, and in relation to others" (Ahmed 2000: 43). Like the other examples considered in this chapter, Ulysse rewrites grammars of difference and calls into question embodied performances of racialized differences and their inscription into urban landscapes.

Furthermore, Ulysse challenges when, where, and how history is done, and for what audiences or publics. She has decided not only to publish her academic research but also to perform her poetry about her Haitian identity and perspective at academic conferences and to publish it in academic journals to open up disciplinary norms to alternative modalities of performance, expression, and theory:

> Spokenword became her chosen medium. She deploys it to both explore and push the blurred border zones between ethnography and performance. She considers these works "alter(ed)native" forms of ethnography constructed out of what she calls "recycled ethnographic collectibles" (raw bits and pieces that seem too personal or trivial) through which she engages with the visceral that is embedded, yet too often absent, in structural

analyses. Her ultimate aim with such works is to access/face and recreate a full and integrated subject without leaving the body behind. An inter-disciplinary scholar-artist, Ulysse weaves history, statistics, personal narra-tive, theory, with Vodou chants to dramatize and address issues of social (in)justice, intersectional identities, spirituality and the dehumanization of Haitians and other marked bodies.[7]

Faye Harrison explains that this kind of "ethnoperformance," as she dubs it, "involves modes of creative expression that assume varied forms: spoken word, dance, and other kinds of creative productions." Harrison (2005: 23) advocates "developing anthropologically informed performative practices as one among many strategies for reaching wider audiences and raising critical consciousness. Multigenre forms of artistic/cultural production are evocative of meanings, perceptions, and experiences difficult to express through the conventions of normal social science. These may be dimen-sions of knowing that resonate with potential audiences." Crucial here is Ulysse's praxis of reclaiming "the visceral that is embedded, yet too often absent, in structural analyses." In re-creating through spoken-word perfor-mance "a full and integrated subject without leaving the body behind," she is able to counter what she calls dehumanization through actions that I describe further in chapter 9 as the creative and artistic element of "erotic agency." We can think of this as another way to return or counter the (anthropological) gaze. Ulysse also engages in social activism and advocacy for women and for Haitians in the interdisciplinary nexus that connects academic and nonacademic praxis.

Do we still need authoritative textual histories, and if we do, for whom and for what purpose? What would such a history look like or sound like? Who else might take part in it and, in that taking part, transform the history that is produced or performed? This return of the gaze brings us back up against questions of citizenship by reminding us of the audiences for whom history, or anthropology, or literature are written. Authoritative academic texts about nation and citizenship not only engage with national public spheres; they also serve to constitute their inclusions and exclu-sions. Anthropological texts are framed as either studying elsewhere or self-reflexively turned on "ourselves." And literary texts become canonized into national or regional literatures and read in relation to a specific na-tional context. Diasporic and transnational writing is significant precisely because of its inter-positionings and its performative agency in represent-ing the underside of more conventional categories of belonging. It tunnels below the surface of the nation to bring into play passageways of interconnection to other places, other landscapes, and other temporalities. But the anti-representational strategies of resisting and returning the tourist gaze and the anthropological gaze are equally important in asserting the right to claim locality, place, and spatial agency. Erotic agency can consist of a performance of sexual citizenship as the right of refusal rather than always being a performance of sexualized embodiment. And it may be found in the insistence on self-imagination and self-representation beyond the terms of the nation-state and the "good" citizen-subject.

CHAPTER NINE

Erotic Agency and a Queer
Caribbean Freedom

Three young girls, black, kinky-headed, barefooted, with bandanas tight
around their hips, were dancing and singing in strong husky voices, at the
top of their lungs. . . .

The bandanas [of the dancers] were kept pulled down across the buttocks,
the knot just above the vulva. Several times I saw a girl take the knot in her
hand and make it flop and thrust like a penis. This was the girl who danced
more vigorously than any of the others.

The men did no singing; some whistled the melody and danced rather
spasmodically toward each other or in pairs. I wondered at the time if there
was anything of homosexuality in their relation, and later, when I questioned
Polines, he said, "They is bad girl, fuck each other with dey finger."

—ALAN LOMAX, "A Tour of Street Music—The Mascaron," 26

Histories of sexual citizenship have shown how state policies, welfare
systems, and legal systems have all served to constitute a heteronormative national citizenship that excludes those with same-sex and other
non-normative sexual orientations from the rights and protections of citizenship (see Berlant 1997; Canaday 2003; Cossman 2007; Richardson 1998,
2000). Many Caribbean feminists have also pointed out the pressure to
perform reproductive heterosexuality as a form of national citizenship,
with the state (and the church) in many cases violently policing same-sex
intimate relations (Alexander 2005; Wekker 2006). Thus, the language of
the family and its interpersonal intimacies can be read in primary texts as
evidence of larger biopolitical processes. Elizabeth Povinelli (2006: 10)
analyzes love, intimacy, and sexuality, for example, not in terms of "desire,
pleasure, or sex per se," but as being "about things like geography, history,

culpability, and obligation; the extraction of wealth and the distribution of life and death; hope and despair; and the seemingly self-evident fact and value of freedom." The formation of heterosexual families has been particularly pertinent to such national politics of intimacy, as I have shown for both Jamaica and Haiti. Some historians have argued that where "the heterosexual family played such a central role in the nation's public imaginings that motherhood could be viewed as a national service, female nonreproductive sexuality and female-female eroticism were constrained, as a consequence, to operate within the domestic (or at least the private) domain" (Parker et al. 1992: 7). Beneath the stories of heterosexual family formation that so strongly emerge in the transition out of slavery, what else lies hidden in the bottom of the archive? Fragments such as the quote from the music collector Alan Lomax's *Haitian Diary* hint at more going on beneath the surface.

Modern ideas of freedom revolve around the intimate sphere: its morality and management and its relation to the public sphere. In the case of the post-emancipation co-constructions of black masculine subjectivity and black feminine respectability, however, the valorization of motherhood for the nation was constantly destabilized by the racist discourse of black promiscuity and hypersexuality linked to middle-class worries about an over-reproductive sexuality (i.e., the racist fear of unconstrained, animalistic sexual excess and too many black—and "mixed-race"—babies being born out of wedlock). The drive to constrain women's eroticism thus concerns both eradicating nonreproductive queer sexualities *and* constraining the over-reproductive heterosexualities of the working class, especially the racialized lowest tier of workers. As bell hooks (1994: 127) points out, "The black body has always received attention within the framework of white supremacy, as racist/sexist iconography has been deployed to perpetuate notions of innate biological inferiority." Thus, movements for black liberation have always had to address emancipation at the level of sexual politics, including the channeling of black sexuality into hypernormative modes of respectability (Collins 2004). Caribbean popular sexualities, then, are always political acts operating in a politicized context.

In a very helpful commentary on the political forms of citizenship in the contemporary Anglophone Caribbean, Aaron Kamugisha (2007: 22–23) attributes the continuing "coloniality of Caribbean citizenship" to three elements, which he summarizes as elite domination, the tourism industry, and the "*gendered and heteronormative gaze* of the Caribbean state." He draws on Percy Hintzen's critique of the emergence of Afro-Creole nationalism among the post-independence middle classes in the Anglophone Caribbean, which effectively supplanted anticolonial mobilization and its more radical projects of egalitarian citizenship (Hintzen 2001). This ideology maintained the persistent inequality of the masses and hid from view the "racialized allocation of power and privilege" (Kamugisha 2007: 26, quoting Hintzen 2002: 493). Afro-Creole nationalism also institutionalized a second-class citizenship for women in the Commonwealth Caribbean, according to Tracy Robinson (2000, 2003, as discussed in Kamugisha 2007: 32), through a system of constitutional law and jurisprudence that was premised on the patriarchal division of the public and private sphere and women's access to rights only via men, who continue to be the paragons of citizenship. Finally, it made foundational the criminalization of homosexuality, as M. Jacqui Alexander's groundbreaking work has shown. Thus, Kamugisha (2007: 35) concludes, citizenship "has been constructed not merely on the denial of the experiences of the black and Indian masses but also on the denial of the experiences of women and homosexuals—in short, everyone who did not fit the template of 'white bourgeois heterosexual man' in its now brown/black male Caribbean configuration." This recognition opens up a whole new aspect for social and political histories of freedom and emancipation, citizenship and the state, while calling into question the silences in entire generations of historiographical writing.

Normative performances of both masculinity and femininity effectively delimited freedom to particular embodied forms and shaped sexualities in relation to race, ethnicity, class, and gender in ways that continue to resonate today. In all of these instances, the commonality is the recognition that because racial and ethnic politics is played out sexually, and sex is played out through a racial and ethnic politics, a politics of the body and of sexual citizenship must be central to any liberation movement and to any theory of freedom. Most troubling in this long view of the sedimented histories of sexuality is the need to understand why some working-class black communities (e.g., in modern Jamaica especially [cf. Skelton 1995]) so vehemently disavow same-sex eroticism and expel outlawed "deviant" subjects from the public realm, often leaving them open to violent assault without protection of the law (Smith 2007).[1] Despite the criminalization of homosexuality in many Caribbean states, queer Caribbean activism, literature, and arts nevertheless are thriving and increasingly draw on diasporic networks and virtual (online) publics to promote social and legal reform. Gay, lesbian, and queer diasporic writers and academics have laid the foundations for a critique of the sexual governmentalities of the neoliberal/

neocolonial Caribbean state and have dared to imagine dissenting subject positions that challenge both Caribbean homophobia and First World homonormativity (see, e.g., Glave 2005, 2008; Wekker 1997, 2000, 2006). Whether in the fields of literature, literary studies, legal studies, sociology, or cultural studies, a spate of new work has appeared on sexual citizenship in the Caribbean, and new attention is being paid to queer sexualities and same-sex eroticism.[2]

Following the arguments made about gender, race, and ethnicity throughout this book, sexuality does not simply emanate from within an already formed subject. Rather, it is interactively elicited through encounters between bodies and sexual geographies, which include spaces of belonging and safety, ethnosexual borders and frontiers, and modes of normalizing, policing, and surveilling sexualized bodies and places.[3] Sexuality is rooted in place, politics, relations of power, and access to or exclusion from the rights of citizenship. Claims to citizenship are rooted in and enacted through sexual relations, including relations of domination through which those subjects with access to the legal protections and rights of citizenship can use their position to exploit non-citizens, as well as disciplinary state relations in which non-normative sexualities are criminalized. Sexual citizenship is about the relationships between sexuality and politics; between bodies and governments; and between forms of embodied power and national and transnational biopolitics. To think sex and citizenship together is to assert the insistently embodied corpo*reality* of citizenship in everyday *practice*, as against the disembodied, abstracted, juridical citizens of constitutional law who in fact are semantically and symbolically coded as white, male, propertied, and heterosexual.[4]

This raises the question of whether there is a domain that we might call a queer Caribbean, or even a theoretical effort to queer the Caribbean. According to Alexander, a Caribbean feminist theorist who explicitly identifies herself as lesbian, the laws around indecency, obscenity, and perversion are crucial to the control of the public sphere and the definition of national citizenship in many Caribbean societies. "Policing the sexual" by "stigmatizing and outlawing several kinds of non-procreative sex, particularly lesbian and gay sex and prostitution," functions, according to Alexander (2000 [1994]: 360), as a "technology of control, and much like other technologies of control becomes an important site for the production and reproduction of state power." Rather than speaking for any particular subaltern group, her approach is to lay bare the political mechanisms by which law comes to be written in patriarchal and heteronormative ways that exclude some people from citizenship. Thus, she argues, when heterosex-uality is naturalized as law, as in Trinidad and Tobago and the Bahamas, "Not just (any) *body* can be a citizen any more, for *some* bodies have been marked by the state as non-procreative, in pursuit of sex only for pleasure, a sex that is non-productive of babies and of no economic gain" (Alexander 2000 [1994]: 360). Only prescribed forms of heterosexual conjugal sex are legal, alongside the commodified and hence economically productive het-erosexuality sold on the tourism market (see also Alexander 1997).

By historicizing contemporary legislation, Alexander writes into history the invisible gay, lesbian, and other queer subjects within the Caribbean. Many young gay, lesbian, and transgender Caribbean nationals are pursuing academic training outside their home countries, allowing them a greater degree of freedom by forsaking national citizenship. Alexander's work raises the question of where history is produced not simply in terms of the pro-duction of nativist national history but, rather, in terms of the complex dis-placements that only allow partial histories to be written in any place or time. Some histories can only be written from another place. Here we might think of Audre Lorde's important critique of the U.S. invasion of Grenada in 1981, which she wrote as an American with Grenadian ancestry who visited the island just weeks later to see the effects (Lorde 1984). One's geographical positioning may make different issues and questions salient; provide differ-ent kinds of contexts, means, and opportunities for working; and enable or disallow certain kinds of projects.[5] Of course, this still leaves open the ques-tion of Alexander's own positioning as a diaspora intellectual in relation to feminists working within the Caribbean, who do not necessarily embrace her work, as Faith Smith (2007) points out. Yet the dialogue across these arenas (and with the work of non-Caribbean theorists with a deep and abid-ing interest in the region) is the best possible grounding for building a trans-national, intersectional feminist/queer project of citizenship from below.

THEORIZING EROTIC AGENCY

A postcolonial politics of sexual citizenship must pay attention not only to the intimate inter-bodily relations that are the fundamental basis for human dignity and freedom, but also to the collective processes, public spaces, aesthetic forms, and material cultures that are mobilized in the struggles between erotic subjugation and erotic knowledge. The notion of erotic power appears in the work of several Caribbean and African Ameri-can feminist theorists and derives from the practices of embodied freedom that emerged out of the African diaspora experience of enslavement. In "Uses of the Erotic: The Erotic as Power," one of her most influential political essays (originally a talk delivered in 1978), Audre Lorde, the daughter of Grenadian immigrants to the United States, declared: "There are many kinds of power, used and unused, acknowledged and otherwise. The erotic is a resource within each of us that lies in a deeply female and spiritual plane, firmly rooted in the power of our unexpressed or unrecognized feeling. In order to perpetuate itself, every oppression must corrupt or distort those various sources of power within the culture of the oppressed that can provide energy for change. For women, this has meant suppression of the erotic as a considered source of power and information within our lives" (Lorde 1984: 53). In contrast to many discussions of sexual citizenship, Lorde's understanding of the erotic moves beyond the sexual as a purely physical relationship to encompass a wider realm of feeling and the sensual. Lorde recognizes the erotic powers of the body as a source not merely of pleasure but also of power and information. The erotic is a kind of pervasive energy that can be a source for social and political change.

Notably, Lorde situates the erotic as a spiritual energy, not simply a physical one, and it is a source not only of power but also of "information," which is to say that it rejects the division between body and knowledge, matter and mind. She continues: "The very word erotic comes from the Greek word eros, the personification of love in all its aspects, born of Chaos, and personifying creative power and harmony. When I speak of the erotic, then, I speak of it as an assertion of the life force of women; of that creative energy empowered, the knowledge and use of which we are now reclaiming in our language, our history, our dancing, our loving, our work, our lives" (Lorde 1984: 55). The erotic, then, is clearly more than the sexual, though it may encompass the sexual. It includes the power of love, knowledge, creativity, and life force itself. And it appears not only in the context of sexual relations, but also in the context of other forms of creativity. "The erotic is the nurturer and the nursemaid of all our deepest knowledge" (Lorde 1984: 56).

The erotic is also, for Lorde, crucially connected not only to personal empowerment but also to social change: "In touch with the erotic, I become less willing to accept powerlessness, or those other supplied states of being which are not native to me, such as resignation, despair, self-effacement, depression, self-denial. . . . Recognizing the power of the erotic within our lives can give us the energy to pursue genuine change within our world, rather than merely settling for a shift of characters in the same weary drama" (Lorde 1984: 58–59). Erotic agency, in sum, is the antithesis of enslavement. It appears not only in the context of sexual relations, but also in the context of other forms of creativity, including all kinds of work. It is also, crucially, connected not only to personal empowerment but also to social change. It is an empowerment of the "I" but also a turning toward the "world" and, moreover, toward the divine. Erotic knowledge, according to Lorde, is the bridge between the spiritual and the political.

Lyndon Gill (2010: 304–5) in particular has built on her work in elaborating his key concept of erotic subjectivity: "Stretching the erotic so that it might include the sensual alongside the political and the spiritual allows it to approach the deeper resonance—not altogether foreclosed by essentialist slippages—that Lorde brings into view. Both a way of *reading* and a way of *being* in the world, erotic subjectivity lays claim to a broadened notion of the erotic—encouraged by Lorde's imaginative proposition—in order to propose an interpretive perspective that is at once a mode of consciousness." So Gill, too, calls on us to perceive the sensual, the spiritual, and the political as entwined modes of consciousness within trans-Caribbean cultures, ranging from the Carnival and calypso music traditions of Trinidad and Tobago to contemporary forms of gay activism.

Alexander also explores the work of the erotic as a sacred act as well as a political undertaking. She significantly adds to the lexicography of "work" as economic and sexual, as discussed later, a third spiritual dimension: "The focus on spiritual work necessitates a different existential positioning in which to know the body is to know it as a medium for the Divine, living a purpose that exceeds the imperatives of these plantations. Put differently, it is to understand spiritual work as a type of bodily praxis, as a form of embodiment" (Alexander 2005: 297). The struggle for bodily empowerment, therefore, is not simply a matter of sexual agency and sexual citizenship. It is more significantly also a matter of a sacred praxis of the body. Alexander calls for the knitting together of mind, body, and spirit as experienced in what we call spirit possession and for a bodily praxis that would become a "meeting ground of the erotic, the imaginative and the creative" (Alexander 2005: 320, 322).

In chapter 2 I presented evidence of women's efforts to stake out a kind of embodied freedom that challenged British colonial emancipation policies and practices. These efforts can be understood as the beginnings of sexual citizenship because freed women used their subject positions as mothers and community leaders, and their bodily presence in the public spaces of the street and market, to make visible a kind of corporeal power that could erode the racial, gender, and class exclusions of liberal bourgeois citizenship and middle-class missionary Christianity—or, at least, make apparent their contradictions and fault lines. In hindsight and in view of Lorde's argument, we can read back into these movements a kind of erotic knowledge generated from women's struggle for freedom and for familial self-determination. Embodied freedom can then be understood as a continuum that ranges from the negative liberties of freedom from constraint to the more positive liberties of participatory action and agency, recognizing the fundamental matrix of the body as the basis for any exercise of freedom. Citizenship is not only embedded in local contexts of action. It shapes bodies to those contexts of interaction as a condition for entering public discourse.

In highlighting the embodied politics of freedom, the limits of citizenship repertoires were also exposed as positioning political actors in various normative guises that legitimated their claims on the state. In chapters 3, 4, and 5 I showed how questions of sexual citizenship especially informed the performance of racialized masculine freedom and protonational subjectivity. Heteronormative discourses of familial reproduction underpinned both Haitian nationalism and Jamaican black British subjectivity in the nineteenth century, reproducing nationalist forms of masculine embodiment as a basis for citizenship. These genealogies of specific forms of sexual citizenship suggest that claims to reproductive empowerment and racial or ethnic kinship are foundational to entrance into national public spheres and to the border-maintenance projects that exclude those non-citizens who are seen as unfit to reproduce the nation. This is not due to a failure or limitation in state capacity. Rather, it is fundamental to the operation of citizenship regimes.

Nevertheless, the social organization of black popular publics in the post-slavery Caribbean were a crucial antecedent to contemporary efforts to bring the body into public political discourse and to make visible a bodily erotic politics of race, class, ethnicity, gender, sexuality, and spirituality. Crucial to such bodily negotiations of freedom is the ability to drag them into the public sphere, in effect *to make public the pubic* (cf. Berlant and Warner 2002). Against the privatization of violence, abuse, and terror within the household, the workplace, or the closed community, diverse forms of sexual agency in contemporary Caribbean and African American popular cultural forms—and feminist readings of these forms—engage *in public* with these intimate inter-embodiments, revealing the body as a locus of national and transnational relays of power. Beyond explicit claim making, chapters 7 and 8 also turned to more subtle, nonverbal ways in which spatial practices are also shaped by competing embodied practices and inter-bodily relations of spatiality and the gaze. Beneath the dominant discursive regimes, there are subaltern projects of counter-claim, counter-gaze, and counter-performance, including the performance of alternative moral orders, alternative masculinities, alternative sexualities, alternative spiritualities, alternative spatialities of everyday life, and alternative identifications beyond and beneath the nation, tunneling under its borders and escaping its governance.

Caribbean national projects of subject-citizen formation, furthermore, have always had certain transnational elements, including the awareness of an international antislavery public sphere in post-emancipation Jamaica or the awareness of a pan-African identity in post-independence Haiti. National identities and forms of citizenship in the Caribbean have always been in dialogue with more transnational forms of identification throughout the twentieth century, as well, especially because Caribbean workers, political leaders, and intellectuals traveled throughout the Caribbean, around the Atlantic world, and beyond. In moving beyond the national historiographies of freedom and citizenship that I sketched for nineteenth-century Jamaica and Haiti, this concluding chapter examines how embodied freedom has come to be located and performed in public spaces that are no longer oriented only toward a national public sphere. This chapter examines two periods of transnational mobility that are associated with anxieties over sexuality, generating state efforts of biopolitical control and popular efforts of resistance via erotic self-determination. Both involve the mobilization of sexualities, but in very different ways.

In the first section, I trace the implications of sexual citizenship for Caribbean women in relation to the racialization of fertility, birth control, and eugenics as forms of biopower applied within the colonial Caribbean and in black diasporic communities from the early twentieth century until today. Here, with the protesting mothers and yearning fathers of the post-emancipation Jamaican plantation in mind, I aim to show how state intervention in regulating sexual reproduction and heteronormative models of patriarchal control have placed Caribbean women's bodies at the center of national and transnational regimes of state power. In the second section, I further pursue the genealogy of sexual citizenship through a reading of the debates surrounding sexuality, homophobia, and working-class agency in the genre of Jamaican (and transnational) popular performance culture known as dancehall. Here, too, the deployment of Caribbean men's and women's bodies and sexualities remain a focus of state concern and legal intervention. The transnational approach taken here begins to undermine the notion of citizenship as a solely national status, showing how local practices of sexual citizenship coalesce into larger transnational understandings and practices of embodied freedom. Moving from birthing to dancing, from transnational birth-control programs to transnational boycotts of Jamaican music, my aim is to show the politics of the erotic that lies at the core of postcolonial citizenship.[6]

While acknowledging the limitations of post-slavery embodied practices of freedom that have been recuperated into heteronormative nationalist racial projects, my analysis nevertheless leads into a concluding reflection on the power of the erotic as a potential for freedom as theorized by Caribbean feminists and queer theorists. This is in no way meant to undermine or displace the need for collective projects of political mobilization in the more formal public sphere, but it is an expansion of our understanding of the impetus for political subjectivity and the matrix in which political agency can arise. I not only draw on queer and feminist theorizations of sexual citizenship—especially those that have been formulated in dialogue with African American history and black feminist theory—but also treat them as a kind of primary text, evidence of a public arena of contemporary sexual/racial politics. In discussing the work of M. Jacqui Alexander, Patricia Hill Collins, Carolyn Cooper, Kamala Kempadoo, Denise Noble, Patricia Saunders, Sonjah Stanley-Niaah, and others (some of whom have engaged with each other in contentious critical debate), I will extend my historical analysis of post-emancipation citizenship toward the horizon they have opened for thinking through sexual citizenship as a crucial aspect of freedom in the contemporary Caribbean and circum-Atlantic world. Although the arena of debate surrounding Caribbean sexual politics remains highly contentious, with much disagreement among the contributors on whom I have drawn, taken together they constitute an emergent space for a more hopeful politics of the erotic that engages a positive praxis of embodied freedom in critical transnational arenas.

RACIALIZED BIOPOWER

In *The History of Sexuality*, Michel Foucault posits the idea of "biopower" to describe the state's management of the population, its calculated interventions in biological processes, and the "explosion of numerous and diverse techniques for achieving the subjugation of bodies and the control of populations" (Foucault 1990 [1978]: 140). In the nineteenth century, he argues, a "bio-politics of the population" emerged that "focused on the species body, the body imbued with the mechanisms of life and serving as the basis of the biological processes: propagation, births and mortality, the level of health, life expectancy and longevity, with all the conditions that can cause these to vary" (Foucault 1990 [1978]: 139). Through this lens, the control over sexuality and procreation can be understood as central to the exercise of state power, and struggles against it.

Alongside capitalism, colonialism was, of course, crucial to the emerging focus on the species body—more particularly, the racial body, which was closely linked via tropical medicine and governance to the emerging "problems of birthrate, longevity, public health, housing, and migration" (Foucault 1990 [1978]: 140). In analyzing the located practices of citizenship in the post-emancipation Caribbean, it is crucial to begin from these bio-political "mechanisms of life": sex, pregnancy, births, longevity, health. Nancy Stepan's work reminds us how the tropical natural world came to be understood and represented as physically and morally threatening to the health and wealth of imperial powers, whose men might succumb not only to a plethora of horrific tropical diseases but also to racial degeneration through sexual (and intimate cultural) relations with native or enslaved women (McClintock 1995; Stoler 1995).[7]

Foucault's approach can inform our understanding of historical evidence concerning slave breeding and prostitution of enslaved women by slaveowners, as well as nineteenth-century theories of miscegenation in which sexual intercourse across racialized groups was posited as promoting civility through gradual "whitening" of the population (Kempadoo 2004; Mohammed 2000). Biological reproduction was closely linked with the reproduction of race and nation, and it was controlled and constrained within the categories of heteronormative and racially normative governance. Black women's association with ungoverned sexuality was in part due to the threat their reproductive capacities posed to the maintenance of organized racial boundaries, and the maintenance of whiteness in particular, with all of the political and property rights it could convey. As in other, comparable colonial situations, various legal constraints and customary practices of copulation, coupling, and legitimacy of offspring shaped the racial, color, and class structure of Caribbean societies (see, e.g., Beckles 1999; Findlay 1999; Martinez-Alier 1989; McClintock 1995; Sinha 1995; Stoler 1995). Middle-class "reformers," churches, and paternalistic colonial governments sought to "uplift" the poor classes by condemning their familial forms and sexual practices. In Jamaica, national leaders, reform organizations, and government commissions all blamed sexual promiscuity, the rarity of marriage, and the absence of male household heads as the causes of poverty, which was seen as a kind of moral failing (Austin-Broos 1997: 30–32). Thus, sexuality became a focus of national projects of constituting a "moral order," and black lower-class women were often the targets of moralizing interventions.

Despite the seeming centrality of sexuality to transitions from slavery to freedom, it has been something of an absent presence in Caribbean studies. In an extremely helpful overview of the subject, Kamala Kempadoo (2004: 15–25) has shown how an extensive body of research exists on the supposed "deviancy," "disorganization," and general pathology of Caribbean sexuality (including sociological and anthropological studies of the family, kinship, and childbearing practices in many different Caribbean societies); yet there is very little that addresses women's sexual agency, even within Caribbean feminist research. Against the prevailing negative literature on Caribbean sexual practices, Kempadoo (2004: 3–4, 11) proposes a "bottom-up" approach in which "sexualized Caribbean bodies come forward in this study as self-actualizing and transformative—as sexual agents that shape and are shaped by larger political and economic forces, social structures and institutions, and relations of gender, ethnicity, and race." This has important implications for how historians might approach sources that have not yet been plumbed for their evidence of sexual agency rather than of exploitation or deviancy.[8]

Kempadoo (2004: 2) asks a crucial set of questions that can serve as a guide for future studies of Caribbean sexuality:

> To what extent, I ask here, can we read the "excesses" or "vulgarity" of Caribbean sexuality not simply as European inventions that refract upon Europeanness and that negate or demean the history and agency of the Other, but also as sedimented, corporeally inculcated dispositions that are lived and practiced every day? Can we speak about embodied sexual practices, identities, knowledges, and strategies of resistance of the colonized and postcolonial subject without lapsing into notions of an essential native sexuality? Is it possible to explore the knowledge that is produced through Caribbean sexual praxis, and to ask whether sexual resistances offer a potential for a politics of decolonization or narratives of liberation?

Through her research on prostitution and other forms of "transactional sex,"[9] Kempadoo explores the "sexual economy" not only in terms of exploitation and oppression, but also in terms of the interplay of structural inequalities with possibilities for agency, autonomy, and potentially transformational praxis. From the era of slavery up to the contemporary global economy, she shows how forms of labor engaging "sexual energies and parts of the body" are integral to Caribbean economies and have been crucial to national and transnational capitalism. Thus, her important work enables us to connect the histories of Caribbean sexuality with questions of national citizenship, transnational mobility, embodied freedom, and agency as lived through the sexed and raced body today.

Bodily contacts of various sorts in the colonial "contact zone" were fraught with meanings and implications that went beyond the individual bodies in question to encompass wider skeins of race, nation, culture, and civilization. Black women's bodies had come to be associated with sexually transmitted diseases by the late nineteenth century (Gilman 1985: 231), and the regulation of sexual relations was fundamental to the production of racial, class, and national boundaries. As John Comaroff and Jean Comaroff (1992: 215) observe, the rise of biomedicine was an integral aspect of changes in the project of colonization from the eighteenth century to the twentieth century so that, as "philanthropic dreams hardened into colonial realities, the black body became ever more specifically associated with degradation, pollution and disease." Not only was infection understood as "emanat[ing] from the black female body" in British South Africa in the late nineteenth century, but there was growing medical concern over the intimate relation of white families with black nurses and domestic care workers: "The gateway to infection had become the innocent and vulnerable European infant, whose care, increasingly in the hands of African women, brought blacks into the most private reaches of colonial life" (Comaroff and Comaroff 1992: 229).[10]

Following from an understanding of sexual citizenship and embodied freedom grounded in an appreciation of the legacies of slavery and the insights of black critical theory, we can trace the significance of a politics of eroticism via Lauren Berlant's reading of Harriet Jacobs's narrative, *Incidents in the Life of a Slave Girl* (1861). Jacobs's story shows not only "how central sexuality was in regulating the life of the slave" but also "a variety of other ways her body was erotically dominated in slavery—control over movement and sexuality, over time and space, over information and capital, and over the details of personal history that govern familial history—and links these scandals to a powerful critique of America, of the promises for democracy and personal mastery it offers to and withholds from the powerless" (Berlant 1997: 233). Here Berlant hints at a wider field of erotic domination that includes not only sexuality but also other dimensions of bodily integrity and freedom and that was crucial to slavery and its modes of wresting away not only another person's labor but the broader control over movement, time, space, information, capital, and kinship through which human self-definition and agency are elaborated. Here I focus on the arena of childbearing or "reproductive" politics as one of the key elements of erotic subjugation of women.

The history of reproductive freedom in the Americas is inevitably grounded in the ongoing salience of the limited recognition of the slave's humanity and the formal legal recognition and protection of the rights of the property owner in the flesh of the slave. As Saidiya Hartman (1997: 98) argues, under the legal systems of slave regimes such as those in the United States and the British colonies, "The issue of motherhood concerned the law only in regard to the disposition and conveyance of property and the determination and reproduction of subordinate status. The concept of 'injury' did not encompass the [slave's] loss of children, natal alienation, and enforced kinlessness. The law's concern with mothering exclusively involved questions of property." The slave was considered a subject before the law only as "criminal(ized), wounded body, or mortified flesh," argues Hartman (1997: 94). "Paradoxically, this designation of subjectivity utterly negated the possibility of a nonpunitive, inviolate, or pleasurable embodiment, and instead the black captive vanished in the chasm between object, criminal, pained body, and mortified flesh." As legal systems were modified to abolish slavery, to enfranchise the freed, and eventually to protect their civil rights, they did not necessarily undo the underlying principles of individual property that governed constraint and freedom. The questions of violations of the body, sexual rights, reproductive rights, and the protection of the child remained embroiled in institutionally embedded practices of racial subordination, white supremacy, and patriarchal power.

In a prescient article, Hortense Spillers articulated a powerful theory of the body in slavery and in post-slavery societies well before the sociology of the body had become fashionable. Spillers (1987: 67) posits that the sociopolitical order of the New World, "with its human sequence written in blood, *represents* for its African and indigenous peoples a scene of *actual* mutilation, dismemberment and exile. First of all, their New World diasporic plight marked a *theft of the body*—a willful and violent (and unimaginable from this distance) severing of the captive body from its motive will, its active desire." The abstract asexual body of the universal free human existed, conceptually, only in opposition to the sexualized, racialized, captive body of the powerless slave. Although sexual citizenship has only recently been theorized (e.g., Bell and Binnie 2000; Berlant and Warner 2002; Cossman 2007; Evans 1993), it has its unspoken roots in these inter-bodily relations of enslavement, resistance, and emancipation.

One of the key outcomes of this theft of the body is the loss of gender distinctions between male and female bodies, which as chattel property are placed outside the social systems of gender and kinship practices. As a result, Spillers (1987: 67) argues, "The captive body becomes the source of an irresistible, destructive sensuality; . . . at the same time—in stunning contradiction—the captive body reduces to a thing, becoming *being for* the captor." This translates into what she calls "pornotroping," a sheer "power-lessness" that resonates through social systems and cultural meanings. This physical expression of abject disempowerment can be understood in oppo-sitional relation to ideas of citizenship that were emerging at the same time in European political thought, as a set of practices governing competent membership in society (Turner 1993).

Spillers draws a crucial distinction between the body and the flesh, which she argues is the central distinction "between captive and liberated subject-positions." Referring to the archival litany of "altered human tis-sue" in its horrific "laboratory prose" of "anatomical specifications of rupture"—the brutal laceration, rupturing, wounding, scarring, and punc-turing of the flesh by iron, whips, chains, knives, canine patrols, bul-lets, and branding irons—she suggests that the "undecipherable markings on the captive body render a kind of hieroglyphics of the flesh whose se-vere disjunctures come to be hidden to the cultural seeing by skin color" (Spillers 1987: 67).

Such violence is also closely linked to the development of birth-control technology via experimentation on Caribbean and African American women (Roberts 1997). Collins (2004: 101–2) points out that the origins of modern gynecology itself lie in surgical experiments performed on slave women by Marion Sims in his backyard hospital in Montgomery, Ala-bama, between 1845 and 1849. Medical research was carried out using the bodies of the enslaved, such that "the procedures adopted for the captive flesh demarcate a total objectification, as the entire captive community becomes a living laboratory" (Spillers 1987: 68). Spillers's delineation of the entanglements of living flesh and blood with gender and racial orders, kinship systems, and legal systems shows precisely how intimacies of desire and sexuality are produced (and entrapped) within a transnational world economy in which human flesh was bought and sold, a national state system in which slavery was legally codified and enforced, and regional practices in which slavery was normalized and made domestically intimate. It is important that "contemporary post-colonial critics have attempted to recuperate this battered black body and, increasingly, to utilize it as the source of empowerment and agency rather than continuing to represent it as the site of pain and victimhood" (Narain 1998: 256). The concept of erotic agency is one way to express this recuperation.

BIRTH CONTROL AND EROTIC EMPOWERMENT

In the post-slavery Americas (including Latin America, the Caribbean, and North America), the history of birth control as a form of reproductive freedom is fatefully entangled with the eugenics movement of the early twentieth century and the belief that overpopulation of "inferior races" was a major cause of poverty (Briggs 2002). The development of birth-control methods remains tainted by experimental research on poor women in the Caribbean, lack of adequate provision of appropriate birth-control methods, and lack of proper follow-up care. Medical consumers in much wealthier countries such as the United States have benefited from medical research carried out on poor women (Davis 2003 [1981]). The liberal feminist movement for reproductive choice supports women's embodied autonomy and self-determination; however, it is complicated by the racialized and gendered politics of colonial legacies, liberal individualism, and histories of state-sanctioned violence against black and Third World women. It is also entangled with the powerful "reproductive futurism" that Lee Edelman (2004: 2) argues makes "the image of the Child as we know it" central to the naturalization of the heterosexual and patriarchal social order, while excluding the black child from the national ideal image in many nations across the post-plantation Americas.

According to Angela Davis (2003 [1981]: 359), the crusade for birth control by the white reformer Margaret Sanger had its roots in her working-class origins, her membership in the Socialist Party, and her commitment to "the interests of working women" before the First World War. However, the rise of neo-Malthusian and eugenic ideas in the early twentieth century made the birth-control campaign "more susceptible . . . to the anti-Black and anti-immigrant propaganda of the times. . . . The fatal influence of the eugenics movement would soon destroy the progressive potential of the birth control campaign" (Davis 2003 [1981]: 360). Davis follows the historian Linda Gordon in suggesting that in the 1920s and 1930s, Sanger gave public approval to compulsory sterilization laws for the "unfit." In 1939, the Birth Control Federation of America planned a Negro Project, about which it was argued: "The mass of Negroes, particularly in the South, still breed carelessly and disastrously, with the result that the increase among Negroes, even more than among whites, is from that portion of the population least fit, and least able to rear children properly" (Davis 2003 [1981]: 361). As Nicola Beisel and Tamara Kay (2004: 511) demonstrate, the language of race and republican motherhood has even deeper historical roots in the mid-nineteenth century antiabortion campaigns by physicians and in the feminist campaigns of Susan B. Anthony and Elizabeth Cady Stanton, who argued that "abortion threatened the social hegemony of Anglo-Saxons."

The articulation of a woman's right to bodily autonomy, self-determination, and control over her fertility and children imported arguments from the abolition movement (Beisel and Kay 2004: 513) but turned them toward white nativist claims for Anglo-Saxon women's liberation from male exploitation and private patriarchy. Later, when the language of birth control transmuted into a language of population control, argues Davis (2003 [1981]: 361), the birth-control campaign was "called upon to serve in an essential capacity in the execution of the U.S. government's imperialist and racist population policy." Black feminists have reframed the entire liberal discourse of choice, suggesting that white feminists in the 1970s should have been more aware of the history of sterilization abuse when they began their campaign for abortion rights. Collins (1999: 119) observes, "Ideas about idealized and stigmatized motherhood within family rhetoric contribute to the links among family, race and nation. As a result, the issue of who will control women's mothering experiences lies at the heart of state family planning decisions. When attached to state policy in a racialized nation-state like the United States, this question of controlling the fertility of women within different race, class and citizenship groups becomes politicized (Davis [2003] 1981). Eugenics movements illustrate the thinking underlying population policies designed to control the motherhood of different groups of women for reasons of nationality and/or race." Afro-Caribbean women's practices of motherhood have long been stigmatized by elites, by the church, and by state agencies that sought to promote marriage and "respectability," even as we have seen that some Jamaican and Haitian women struggled in the nineteenth century to articulate their own right to motherhood and familial self-determination. This racialized politics of reproduction and biopower became entangled with transnational forms of sexual subjugation through practices of birth control as population control.

Experimentation with population control and birth-control methods in the United States is deeply rooted in the Caribbean, especially Puerto Rico and Haiti. In a study of race, sex, and U.S. imperialism in Puerto Rico, for example, Laura Briggs describes debates about prostitution, birth control, overpopulation, and sterilization that were played out on Puerto Rican women's bodies. Following Ann Laura Stoler's analysis of "discourses of sexuality as a tool of empire" (Briggs 2002: 21), Briggs argues, "Overpopulation, eugenics, and birth control programs intervened in debates about whether the island was entitled to independence, and whether the 'race' of the island's inhabitants was 'black' or 'Spanish.' The notion that through overpopulation poor women were responsible for the economic ills of the island simultaneously served to mask U.S. capitalist extraction and to provide an occasion for further U.S. involvement" (Briggs 2002: 108). An entire social science of the "deviant" Puerto Rican family arose ranging from texts such as Oscar Lewis's *La Vida: A Puerto Rican Family in the Culture of Poverty—San Juan and New York* (1965) (discussed in Briggs 2002: 184–85) to Daniel Patrick Moynihan's *The Negro Family: The Case for National Action* of 1965 (known as the Moynihan Report). Postwar population-control measures, Briggs (2002: 108) argues, "made certain kinds of reproductive autonomy impossible for many Puerto Rican women" and were "fundamental to the establishment of a pattern of using the island as a laboratory for [birth-control] research: Puerto Rico would go on to become the test site for Depo Provera, IUDs and the pill." Interventions by mainland liberal feminists to help Puerto Rican women ironically served to erase Puerto Rican women's long struggle for autonomy, agency, and sexual citizenship, reiterating discriminatory racial projects and patriarchal power.

We might also consider Carolle Charles's study of poor and working-class Haitian women's discourses on the use of their own bodies. As in Kempadoo's analysis of transactional sex, here, too, exchange of sex for money is recognized as the founding condition of sexual praxis under conditions that arose under slavery but continue to inform post-slavery struggles for economic survival. Charles begins by noting the powerful social and political forces that are at play in "the regulation and control of women's bodies" and that are "reproduced and reinforced through patterns of behavior, forms of representation, and cultural practices" (Charles 2003: 169–70). Her analysis of "body politics" calls for attention to "practices and dynamics of sexual politics and of sexuality as they relate to kinship relations and to racial and class practices inherited from slavery and transformed with the postcolonial state. It is also important to look at the impact of poverty in defining the relationship of sexuality to struggle for economic survival and strategies of social mobility" (Charles 2003: 170). In paying close attention to poor and working-class Haitian women's own accounts of their bodies and sexualities, she offers insight into an alternative discourse that gives new meaning to bodies as they are deployed within sexual relations, childbearing, and kin-making practices. When such women describe their bodies as "my piece of land," as a "resource, an asset, a form of capital that can reap profits if well invested" (Charles 2003: 170), Charles argues, they are contesting hegemonic ideas and beliefs, redefining sexuality, and creating possibilities for the negotiation of space and some room for self-expression and empowerment. At the very least, this transactional view of sexuality, as in Kempadoo's analysis of contemporary sex workers, is "an expression of consciousness of the existing relations of gender oppression and inequality" (Charles 2003: 170).

In Haiti, too, the issue of birth control continues to be fraught with the power dynamics of transnational relations, as I have noted in previous work on problems with the testing of the contraceptive Norplant in the mid-1980s (Sheller 2003: 172–73).[11] Collins (1999: 126) notes that even while black women "often welcome these temporary sterilization 'choices', this exercise of choice must be viewed in the context of the limited nature of choices that working-class black women have in areas of sexuality and fertility." In June 1996, I visited Haiti with the London-based Haiti Support Group, and we interviewed Rose-Anne Auguste, the Coordinator of Klinik Sante Fenm Kafou Fey in Port-au-Prince (Arthur and Dash 1999: 133–34). With some public funding and further funding from the nongovernmental organizations (NGOs) Partners in Health and Family Planning and International Assistance, the clinic was providing maternal and infant health programs, health education, and family planning. I draw on this as just one small example of the degree to which limitations on political citizenship take the form of lack of sexual self-determination, loss of control over one's own fertility, and adverse health outcomes for poor Haitian women.

Auguste pointed out the problems that poor women had in negotiating with male partners over birth control, their lack of access to education and other basic resources such as housing, and hence their "loss of control over their fertility." She pointed out the root of the problems in the failures of the state:

The greatest frustration of this work is that it is like just putting a small bandage on a very deep wound. The underlying problems are unemployment, poor conditions in the slum areas, inadequate housing, lack of clean water, etc. The health clinic cannot change these conditions—that is the responsibility of the state. Yet the state is dealing neither with the underlying causes of these terrible conditions nor with the resulting poor health of the people. Thus the clinic is only the minimum intervention—ideally the state must take up the real problems. We are not like some NGOs who replace the state by providing private services. We are engaged in a struggle to have people's rights to life and health recognized. Nor are we like some NGOs who carry out experiments using Haitian women. We believe in helping women and respecting the dignity of Haitian women.[12]

Here we can see the grounding for a discourse of women's health as a right of citizenship, which the state has an obligation to provide to all citizens. We can compare this to political philosopher Martha Nussbaum's "capabilities approach" (2007: 4), which envisages certain basic entitlements that should be protected by constitutional law. These begin with life, bodily health, and bodily integrity, including reproductive health and security from sexual assault and domestic violence (Nussbaum 2006, 2007). International aid agencies and NGOs, however, often have failed to situate health care—and, in particular, reproductive health—in the context of a discourse of citizenship. Instead, it is imposed as a form of charitable intervention frequently based in ideologies of population control (and barely veiled eugenics) rather than citizens' empowerment and "people's rights to life and health."

In the 1990s feminist organizations within the Caribbean, such as Development Alternatives with Women for a New Era (DAWN), mobilized against the testing of Depo-Provera and the introduction of the contraceptive device Norplant "without the knowledge or consent of women, enabling and reinforcing the metropolitan ideology of backward Third-World women as silent, yet willing receptacles of the technologies of development and modernity" (Alexander 1997: 72). They argued that,

> multilateral agencies and national governments continue to treat women in an instrumental manner with respect to population programmes. For example, there is little understanding among policy makers of the mixed responses to family planning programmes by Third World women themselves. While there can be little doubt of the considerable unmet need for birth control among women, the methods actually available are all highly

unsatisfactory. Many international pharmaceutical companies treat Third World Women as guinea pigs for new methods; chemicals such as Depo Provera (which is banned in most advanced industrial countries as dangerous to health) are widely dispensed to Third World women, often with the knowledge and participation of international agencies (Sen and Grown 1987: 47–48).

As in the case of Puerto Rico, there are still recent instances of forcible use of fertility control. At the same time that USAID was promoting Norplant in Haiti, Haitian refugees were being intercepted by the U.S. Coast Guard and interred at the U.S. military base at Guantánamo Bay in Cuba, where some detainees who were HIV-positive reported that Depo-Provera, a long-acting progesterone-like contraceptive, was forcibly injected without knowledge or consent of the Haitian women subjected to medical "treatment" there (Farmer 2005: 62–63).[13]

Today, when Haiti has lost up to three hundred thousand people in the earthquake of January 12, 2010, and more than half a million remain homeless, some in the United States still express the idea that Haiti's population of 9 million is too large for the island to sustain and in part blame this "overpopulation" for the loss of life in the earthquake. Just as in the past, while those like Auguste are trying to promote sexual self-determination for women—and when the rape of women and children remains a grave, ongoing human-rights crisis—the international aid community's discourse of "protection" of women and children fails to recognize the deeply structural violence that denies women sexual agency and more extensively negates their erotic subjectivity. The horrific vulnerability of women and children to sexual attack in the tent camps; the impunity of rapists; and the seeming incapacity of the government, the police, the United Nations, and the NGOs to address this situation attest to the need for fundamental rights of bodily integrity and sexual self-determination as a basis for citizenship.[14] Beyond these basic human capabilities, Nussbaum (2006, 2007) also calls for the protection of sense, imagination, and thought; emotional development; practical reason; and play, among other things. These are all wider aspects of what Caribbean theorists call erotic agency and such human capabilities are indicative of the freedoms that those who survived enslavement struggled for, yet which still remain to be achieved. The bodily integrity of women and children is not a side issue. It is at the core of creating a state that can guarantee the life, safety, and freedom of its citizens.

WORKING THE BODY

In their essay "Queer Nationality," Lauren Berlant and Elizabeth Freeman (1997: 149) note that "crucial to a sexually radical movement for social change is the transgression of categorical distinctions between sexuality and politics, with their typically embedded divisions between public, private, and personal concerns. The multiplicity of social spaces, places where power and desire are enacted and transferred, need to be disaggregated and specified." To conjoin a politics of sex and citizenship is to insist not only on the primacy of inter-bodily relations as the basis for human dignity and freedom, but also on the importance of those aesthetic forms—whether poetry, music, dance, fashion, style—that, as Davis (1998a: 179) puts it, "encourage awareness of the political character of sexuality" and offer "the possibility of understanding the social contradictions [people] embodied and enacted in their lives." Reproductive sexuality was one arena in a struggle for erotic knowledge and self-determination. Here I turn to another arena that has been equally important: the Caribbean transnational popular cultures of music, dance, and performance, many of which have some grounding in a sacred practice.

"Exploiting the limits of the permissible, creating transient zones of freedom, and reelaborating innocent amusements" were the means that the enslaved developed to wage a practice of "politics without a proper locus," according to Hartman (1997: 50–52); such practices of "transforming need into politics and cultivating pleasure as a limited response to need and a desperately insufficient form of redress" continue to inform citizenship from below today. Yet we need to resituate this idea of pleasure in a sacred praxis of erotic agency in which the body is a vehicle for the spirit. Growing out of the popular cultures of the post-emancipation era, Caribbean counter-publics in many shapes and forms continue to work on the body, work with the body, and work the body as conduit to a collective project of liberation. Nevertheless, sexual agency has long been a two-edge sword, both implicating the sexual subject in relations of domination and subordination and offering a route out of such relations, which may be seized as an enabling possibility. The mere exercise of sexual agency within personal relations does not in itself overturn broader social structures of inequality, including unequal access to the rights and protections afforded by recognition as a citizen; however, as an aspect of a wider field of erotic agency, sexual performances may enable some forms of maneuver, negotiation, and exchange.

In the era of Caribbean decolonization of the late twentieth century, a period arose of diverse mobilities across transnational black communities accompanied by the circulation of cultural commodities, including music; fashion; and performances of spoken language, song, and dance. In these transnational spaces of black vernacular popular culture, Denise Noble (2008: 114) identifies "an apparent correspondence between the absorption and reinforcement of an erotic secularization of the body and black identity within black popular culture, and a particular late modern mode of freedom invested in a sexualized, commodified, and hyper-individualized self." As she further explains:

> Despite the freedoms that decolonization has brought for many Black people—especially in Black Atlantic regions of the African Diaspora, it seems to me that freedom remains a constant and daily preoccupation within Black vernacular discourses and cultural practices: its fulfillment, its adequate signs and its contested meanings. These struggles for, negotiations over, and diverse conceptions of freedom increasingly take place outside the terms of party politics and political nationalist movements that characterized earlier anti-colonial and civil rights politics. Instead they are increasingly being traced out on the intimate contours of the body and the self; in strategies of self-development, self-fashioning and personal freedom, expressed increasingly through the *articulation* of neo-liberal conceptions of freedom with racialized discourses of ethnicity, sexuality and gender. (Noble 2008: 110)

Noble's thoughts on the salience of personal freedom, and its vernacular-secular forms of bodily self-fashioning, point toward the significance of sites such as Jamaican dancehall culture as a public arena for working on forms of embodied freedom while also being cognizant of their problematic relation to neoliberal conceptions of freedom. While racial-sexual economies are not simply sites of oppression in which bodies are marked and marketed as raced, gendered, sexualized commodities, but are also arenas for self-definition, self-empowerment, and alternative performances of the self, this does not absolve them from the contradictions of neoliberal subjectivity. In this section, I explore the expansion of embodied freedom that is implicit within the transnational vernacular culture of dancehall alongside the debates over its intensely hypermasculine homophobia and misogyny. As in my earlier explorations of post-emancipation sexual citizenship, here, too, we can see how histories of racialized discourses of ethnicity, sexuality, and gender create dilemmas surrounding the practice of personal freedom yet also may open up new realms of possibility for imagining the work of embodied freedom and erotic agency beyond the constrictions of the individual subject of a national citizenship regime, or of the free market.

What happens when embodied citizens use erotic performances and sexual lyrics to make public expressions of subordinate sexualities into a political intervention? Creating public spaces and esthetic forms for reclaiming and speaking one's own body and sexuality are crucial elements of cultures of freedom in the post-slavery black Atlantic and trans-Caribbean (cf. Brooks 2006, 2011; Collins 2004; Golden 1994; Henke and Magister 2007). In his study of culture, politics, and the black working class in the United States, for example, Robin D. G. Kelley (1996: 8–9) calls for a "history from below" that "emphasizes the infrapolitics of the black working class," which includes "issues of economic well-being, safety, pleasure, cultural expression, sexuality, freedom of mobility, and other facets of daily life." Beyond the formal institutions of daylight community organization such as churches or mutual benefit societies, he argues, we must also attend to what is hidden in the dark of "the night—the dancehalls and juke joints, the barbershops and bars, the rich expressive cultures of the secular 'forms of congregation' that enabled African Americans to take back their bodies for their own pleasure rather than another's profit" (Kelley 1996: 44–45). Kelley explores the forms of masculinity that this struggle elicited, which have something in common with those I have identified in post-independence Haiti and post-emancipation Jamaica. Sexual politics are lowdown and dirty by definition, yet this is precisely what makes it important to bring them into the light of day—or, rather, this is what makes it important to bring political theory into the dark of the night.

If we turn to dancehall as a site of "corporeally inculcated dispositions that are lived and practiced every day," as Kempadoo (2004: 2) puts it, we can find here forms of kinesthetic imagination and memory transmitted, politicized, and transformed into movement and dance (Cresswell 2006; Roach 1996: 26). Tim Cresswell draws on the dance scholar Norman Bryson's understanding of "social kinetics" as the ways in which dance forms are "symptomatic of wider changes in a sense of movement" (Cresswell 2006: 10). He relates a dance such as the can-can, for example, to mass-production in factories and new forms of mechanical transport so that understandings of dance open out to "larger social processes that turn on redesigning and stylization of action and gesture" (Bryson 1997: 71). Performance studies offer ways to recognize and read across time the "spectacular performances" of "bodies in dissent" so beautifully delineated by Daphne Brooks (2006, 2011), from the age of minstrelsy right up to the "sonic black feminism" of Mamie Smith, Big Mama Thornton, Nina Simone, Aretha Franklin, Grace Jones, and, in our time, Beyoncé Knowles, Lauryn Hill, and Janelle Monae. We could add to Brooks's list Jamaican dancehall performers like Lady Saw (see Cooper 2004) or Ce'cile.

In dancehall's styles of bodily performance we can see Caribbean sexual praxis precisely in the forms that Kempadoo (2004: 2) refers to as "embodied sexual practices, identities, knowledges, and strategies of resistance of the colonized and postcolonial subject." To analyze this sexual praxis would require going beyond a scribal literary reading of lyrics; it requires a reading of the entire embodied performance, including the glittery sequined clothes and gyrations of the male performers as much as of the female performers. It would require recognition of the erotic power of performance itself and the open-ended seductions that are performed even as deviant sexualities are lyrically disavowed. Perhaps we might find in these assertive public sexualities what Berlant (1993: 177) calls the "strategies of corporeal parody" in camp, youth, sexual and ethnic subcultures that "recast and resist the public denigration of the nonhegemonic 'other' body." Even more important, we can begin to think about the "dancing mobiles" and "kinetic" cultures that Gill (2010) has beautifully explicated in the work of the Trinidadian mas creator Peter Minshall, which also combine the sensual, the spiritual, and the political in a living, moving, erotic subject.

I return to these corporeal performances later but first trace some of the transnational historical context for a vernacular culture of the black Atlantic that deals explicitly with women's sexual autonomy. Davis (1998a: 4) argues that sexuality "was one of the most tangible domains in which emancipation was acted on and through which its meanings were expressed. Sovereignty in sexual matters marked an important divide between life during slavery and life after emancipation." The focus on issues of love and sex in the blues repertoire was linked "inextricably with possibilities of social freedom in the economic and political realms"; thus, "the personal and sexual dimensions of freedom acquired an expansive importance, especially since the economic and political components of freedom were largely denied to black people in the aftermath of slavery" (Davis 1998a: 10). In her reading of the corpus of work of Gertrude "Ma" Rainey, Bessie Smith, and Billie Holiday, Davis (1998a: 24) argues that "these blues women had no qualms about announcing female desire. Their songs express women's intention to 'get their loving.' Such affirmations of sexual autonomy and open expressions of female sexual desire give historical voice to possibilities of equality not articulated elsewhere. Women's blues and the cultural politics lived out in the careers of the blues queens put these new possibilities on the historical agenda." Davis (1998a: 29–30) further argues that women's blues also thematize men's violence against women in ways that "suggest emergent feminist insurgency in that they unabashedly name the problem of male violence and so usher it out of the shadows of domestic life where society had kept it hidden and beyond public or political scrutiny." This can be dated back to the public politics of abolition, wherein slave narratives such as Jacobs's *Incidents in the Life of a Slave Girl* and eyewitness accounts such as James Williams's *A Narrative of Events, since the First of August, 1834, by James Williams, an Apprenticed Labourer in Jamaica* (Paton 2001) named and spoke openly of the sexual abuse of women under slavery and even after emancipation.

Hazel Carby (1986: 12) likewise argues that the classic women's blues of the 1920s and early '30s "is a discourse that articulates a cultural and political struggle over sexual relations: a struggle that is directed against the objectification of female sexuality within a patriarchal order but which also tries to reclaim women's bodies as the sexual and sensuous objects of song." Beyond themes of heterosexuality, some songs in this genre name female-to-female sexual relations and "engage directly in defining issues of sexual preference as a contradictory struggle of social relations" (Carby 1986: 18; Davis 1998a: 40). According to Collins, it was through a blues culture that working-class black women rejected both archetypal respectability and the stereotypes of the debased jezebel and instead "defined their sexual selves in terms much closer to erotic sensibilities about Black female expressiveness, sensuality, and sexuality." Urbanization of the southern rural African American population moreover allowed free women to escape "the sexual exploitation of slavery as well as the demands of having thirteen babies in insular Southern rural families" while at the same time fostering "the increased visibility of lesbian, gay, and bisexual (LGB) African Americans" in urban spaces such as Harlem (Collins 2004: 72–73). All of these readings alert us to the importance of musical venues as sites for the negotiation of sexual autonomy and what might more widely be understood as erotic agency. These arenas of contested vernacular culture, then, are central to sexual citizenship and embodied freedom. It is precisely this milieu of mobile urban dance culture of the 1930s that sent Alan Lomax on his quest to research vernacular musics of the U.S. South and the Caribbean. On his trip to Haiti in 1936–37, accompanied at some points by the writer Zora

Neale Hurston (who was working on *Tell My Horse*, her book about Southern black and Caribbean folk beliefs and spiritualism), he stumbled on the scene that opened this chapter, of women who reportedly not only had sex with women but danced openly in public, expressing their erotic agency to the hilt, alongside some gay men.[15]

I want especially to consider debates surrounding sexuality and sexual expression within Caribbean music, because this has been one of the key sites for the most extensive contemporary discussions of Caribbean sexual agency. Crucial to the bodily negotiations of emancipation and embodied freedom was the ability to drag sexual issues into the public sphere, in effect *to make public the pubic* (or to reveal the already pubic nature of the masculine public sphere—the words "pubic" and "public" not coincidentally both deriving from *pubes* [young men]). Against the privatization of violence, abuse, and terror within the household, the workplace, or the closed community, diverse forms of sexual agency in contemporary Caribbean and African American popular cultural forms—and feminist readings of these forms—engage *in public* with the violences of intimate interembodiments, revealing the body as a locus of national and transnational relays of power. Thus, any analysis of the bodily politics of dancehall must engage with the negotiations of its meaning as it leaves the semiprivate realm of particular dancehalls to enter the wider public spheres of national radio, international music marketing, Internet blogs, and international academic debate. In Jamaica, recent assessments of the "unfinished business" of emancipation address the crisis of persistent gender inequality and especially unprosecuted sexual crimes such as incest, spousal rape, and rape of women, girls, and boys (Narcisse and Wedderburn 2009). Can dancehall culture be a site for public acknowledgment and debate around such issues? And what about violence in male or female same-sex relations? Why, we might add, do Narcisse and Wedderburn in an essay explicitly addressing "ignored voices" choose to remain silent on issues of sexual citizenship, homosexual human rights, and state violence and criminalization of queer citizens? In what ways do musical and performative cultures simply reproduce taken-for-granted forms of social violence and marginalization?

To begin to answer these questions, it is important first to recognize the collective and public character of Caribbean musical forms. The embodied corporeal performances associated with Caribbean music not only potentially support personal agency and sexual subjectivity, but they also have been described as constructing autonomous counter-spaces and collectively shared counter-ideologies of freedom. In a study of revolutionary ideology in Caribbean culture, Joy Mahabir (2003: 129–30) argues that rhythm, antiphony, and asymmetry in black musical forms support "subversive effects" in which "urban and rural working classes use music as part of a soundscape of resistance." From the "overamplified sound systems that emerged in the slums of West Kingston and spread throughout the Caribbean, U.S. and Britain, [to] the music trucks seen in every Caribbean parade, [and] the maxi-taxis that blast music daily for their passengers," these musical forms "create a free, communal sound system whose entire configuration—appropriated public space, working class crowds and amplified music—would embody a protest against 'Babylon.'" As these systems evolved into Jamaican dancehall and African American hip-hop, their "spatio-political affront against the ruling classes" also encompassed a sexual affront against respectability and a fashion affront against good taste, as the "culture associated with the music must be made to seem overly defined by everything that is unacceptable and shocking to the bourgeoisie" (Mahabir 2003: 130, 134). Thus, we can reread the histories of popular forms of sexuality, dance, and outdoor loudness as cultures of protest and corporeal re-positioning, constituting what Kelley (1996) identifies as a Gramscian ad hoc war of position.

Such an approach has been further advanced by Julian Henriques, who argues that in addition to the "bass culture" expressed within the loud, low auditory registers of Jamaican sound systems, there is another dimension of baseness:

> Jamaican sonic sensibilities can [also] be described as a *base* culture, drawing attention to the social grounding of the culture. . . . The baseness of the culture is literally the ground of the earth, soil, dirt or "dutty," as it is called in the lingo. With their flat-footed stamp the dancer emphasizes their earthly connection, as a distinct contrast to the pirouettes and leaps of the European classical tradition, which aspire to have as little contact with the ground for as long as possible. Furthermore, the dancing is literally bottom-up with its signature "bumper-grinding" sexually explicit choreography, where the bass note is struck by the body itself—displaying its fecundity and celebrating its fertility. (Henriques 2008: 227)

This represents a clear politics of dance—or more widely, what Cresswell calls a politics of mobility and Bryson calls a social kinetics. Movements that the dance theorist Jane Desmond (1997) has described for West African dance in which "pelvic articulation features prominently along with polyrhythmic relationships between stepping patterns in the feet and concurrent arm gestures" are precisely the kinds of socially encoded movement that were regulated out of "polished" forms of white high culture such as ballroom dancing (quoted in Cresswell 2006: 127). Stanley-Niaah (2008: 344) also analyzes such moves in terms of a wider "performance geography" that spans "Black performance practices from the Middle passage slave ship dance Limbo, to ghettoes where the Blues, Kingston's Dancehall, and South African Kwaito emerged . . . and challenged the very contexts that militate against their emergence." The limbo, of course, involves passing *below the bar* and re-emerging on the other side, this passage below being symbolic of a passage between earthly and sacred realms, life and death. The stylization of this dance form, in other words, like the earthy feet of the Haitian peasantry in chapter 6, is a form of black diasporic politics and embodied consciousness that can be interpreted in relation to the forms of (trans)national citizenship from below that I have examined in earlier chapters.

For the wider black diaspora, Paul Gilroy (1991: 199) has also noted how both soul and reggae music address "issues of gender conflict, sexuality and eroticism" and "the autonomous field of political action which they map out." The body is crucial here: "In these cultural traditions, work is sharply counterposed not merely to leisure in general but to a glorification of autonomous desire which is presented as inherent in sexual activity. The black body is reclaimed from the world of work and, in Marcuse's . . . phrase, celebrated as an 'instrument of pleasure rather than labour'. Sexuality stands therefore not only as an area of conflict in its own right, but as a symbol of freedom from the constraints of the discipline of the wage" (Gilroy 1991: 202). Thus, in the African American vernacular speech, "The word work can mean dancing, labour, sexual activity or any nuanced combination of all three" (Gilroy 1991: 203). Noble (2000: 157) similarly argues that the "inversion of work to signify sexual activity can be seen as a valorization and assertion of the playfulness and recreational possibilities of Black bodies in defiance of [the] alienated corporeality" associated with enslavement. Gilroy (1991: 203, 210) links this polysemy of work to a carnivalized space of the party, in which the bodily "residues of work" are "transposed into a source of collective pleasure"; parties challenge the chronotopes of capitalist wage labor as the "period allocated for recovery and reproduction is assertively and provocatively occupied instead by the pursuit of leisure and pleasure." Kempadoo's analysis of sexual economies offers a more sanguine view of the ways in which transactional sex (linking sexual work with work for pay) historically served as a resource "for women to secure emancipation and economic security or to obtain freedom from violent and oppressive racial systems of labor" and more recently has enabled women to "autonomously improve their economic positions and survival chances" (Kempadoo 2004: 54–55).

Gilroy's analysis of black cultural forms emphasizes the convergence of music and dance, the dialogic or interlocutory relation between performer and audience, and the attempt to blur distinctions between art and life in cathartic "collective processes" that may create an "alternative public sphere" (Gilroy 1991: 214–15). Similarly, for Mahabir, Carnival is a transformative "democratic space" that offers "a communal space of creation, leisure, and pleasure that is anti-elitist and anti-capitalist. It is a space appropriated by grassroots culture, a counter-space that threatens capitalist relations by unifying masses and allowing them to predominate. The reproduction of this space is self-consciously acknowledged in the Carnival through the rehearsals of revolutionary history manifested in its form" (Mahabir 2003: 142). Mahabir's Althusserian analysis, however, reduces the political complexity of cultural performance to a class ideology that is intrinsically anti-capitalist and revolutionary. Joseph Roach (1996: 252) offers a more complex reading of the unstable relation between Carnival and the law in New Orleans, suggesting that they "conspire together to craft a contingent margin of behavior that remains easily within the laws' reach, if need be, but hovers provisionally outside their reach" in a liminal and ludic space. Or, as Hartman (1997: 50) puts it, paraphrasing Michel de Certeau, the "tactics that comprise the everyday practices of the dominated have neither the means to secure a territory outside the space of domination nor the power to keep or maintain what is won in fleeting, surreptitious, and necessarily incomplete victories."

Nevertheless, Hartman's exploration of "performing blackness" as an entanglement of "dominant and subordinate enunciations of blackness" is very suggestive of the ways in which "particular patterns of movements, zones of erotic investment, forms of expression, and notions of pleasure" can coalesce into "a counter-investment in the body and the identification of a particular locus of pleasure, as in dances like the snake hips, the buzzard lope, and the funky butt. This counter-investment in all likelihood entails a protest or rejection of the anatamo-politics that produces the black body as aberrant" (Hartman 1997: 57–59). Insofar as the reappropriation of captured sexualities in the post-slavery cultures of music, dance, and celebration constitute a form of citizenship from below via counter-investment in the pleasures of the body, their political import remains subject to heated debate. In the next section, I read some of the debates within black Caribbean and African diaspora feminist readings of dancehall culture as primary texts of a sexual counter-public. While vernacular cultures of performance certainly challenge the legal and juridical practices governing racialized sexuality in the post-slavery trans-Caribbean, the jury remains out on whether they offer a liberatory space of erotic agency or instead reproduce hegemonic forms of masculinity and heteronormativity that marginalize minority sexualities. Various musical genres can of course be deployed within many different kinds of political contexts, with different meanings and complex relations to both powerholders and the disempowered, the hunter and the prey (Averill 1997).

One fascinating exploration of these issues can be found in the work of the Jamaican artist Ebony Patterson. Her recent body of mixed media collages, *Gangstas for Life* (2008–), explores the shifting and contradictory notions of masculinity in dancehall culture. The series of installations consists of "ornate portrait-like images of young Jamaican males that are glamorized with glitter, paper doilies, and elaborately patterned wallpapers, fabrics, and wall stencils, and combined with gilded toy soldiers and brightly colored toy guns that ironically refer to the trivialization of gun violence in contemporary Jamaican culture." Patterson's work "probes the contradictory interplay between the hardcore masculine posturing of the 'gangsta' and the feminized personal aesthetic that is now the norm among males in the dancehall culture and exemplified by such practices as skin bleaching, eyebrow shaping, and the wearing of flamboyant clothing and 'bling' jewelry and accessories."[16] What is especially fascinating about this work was her realization that it intersected with the iconography of the Haitian sequined flags, or *drapo*, used to represent the lwa:

> This formal relationship, the boundary-crossing gender dynamics in Haitian Vodou culture in which practitioners are frequently possessed by [lwa] of the opposite gender, and the similarities and connections between the gang cultures of Jamaica and Haiti became the point of departure for her entry into the 2009 Ghetto Biennale in Haiti. For this project, Patterson recontextualized photographic images of young black males within the iconography of Haitian Vodou, referencing the [lwa] Erzili Danto, Erzili Freda, Ren Kongo, Ayida Wedo and the Marasas (sacred twins)—all except for the latter female. . . . The installation captured the splendor of the sacred arts of Haitian Vodou and the bling aesthetic of contemporary

gangsta culture and provocatively merged and interrogated the spiritual and the material, the male and female, the traditional and the contemporary, and the Haitian and the Jamaican.[17]

In perfect refrain to the arguments in this book, her work repositions the "tuff" Jamaican gangsta in relation to the gender-bending embodiments of Haitian Vodou spirituality, interrogating the complex relation between performances of masculinity and femininity. Does the Jamaican artist Vybz Kartel's bleaching of his skin have anything in common with the fair-skinned beauty of Erzili Freda, the Haitian lwa of love and romance, who manifests herself on men's bodies as much as women's? Certainly, both are invested in performances of class privilege and material success. Dancehall participants who dress in flamboyant materials, colors, and jewelry while asserting super-masculinity and spouting homophobic lyrics also demand our attention. They problematize power, concentrating its sources into a kind of *pwen* (point, or concentration of forces) that animates the political tensions of sexual citizenship. This is not to claim agreement with their politics but to recognize that, just as in the performances of the Voduisant mounted by the lwa, there is an erotic politics at stake that is fundamental to contemporary citizenship from below.[18] If it is promulgating forms of masculinity that endorse sexual violence, then we need to ask why, and we need to examine the structures of citizenship that produce these specific embodiments.

EROTIC AGENCY AND CARIBBEAN FREEDOM

Just as the blues did in the early twentieth century, Jamaican popular music in the late twentieth century provided one of the prime contemporary sources for an ongoing dialogue about sexuality and freedom within a transnational black counter-public. In contrast to Gilroy's (1991, 1995) reading of the sexist and homophobic lyrics within dancehall as politically conservative, Carolyn Cooper suggests that DJs' slackness "can be seen to represent in part a radical, underground confrontation with the patriarchal gender ideology and the pious morality of fundamentalist Jamaican society." With sensitivity to the stylistics of slackness in Jamaica, she suggests that "in its invariant coupling with Culture, Slackness is potentially a politics of subversion. For Slackness is not mere sexual looseness—though it certainly is that. Slackness is a metaphorical revolt against law and order; an undermining of consensual standards of decency. It is the antithesis of

Culture" (Cooper 1993: 141). Are the vivid sexual displays and bodily gestures of slackness a "corporeal parody" of the reigning moral order of
culture? Can "raw" language, lyrics, and sexual expression be served up as
counter-discourses to national sexuality, or do they merely feed into pre-
existing pornotropes of national and transnational racial and sexual subordination?[19] And how do feminists address the apparently misogynistic
and homophobic lyrics of some genres of dancehall, ragga, gangsta rap, and
hip hop?

To answer these questions, I want to trace a series of debates within the
black/Caribbean/diaspora feminist and queer analysis of the vernacular
cultures of Caribbean sexual citizenship from the nineteenth century onward. These debates serve as a kind of primary source in and of themselves
for the emergence of an alternative public discourse concerned with articulating, analyzing, and advocating for black women's and men's non-
normative sexualities and embodied freedoms. Thus, I read a wide range of
these academic texts in close detail, treating them as public texts and
following them across transnational locations that revolve around the Caribbean but involve audiences, theorists, and publications that are Caribbean, U.S. American, British, and Canadian. Here I am especially interested in how these Caribbean-identified theorists are entering the terrains
of citizenship studies, area studies, and cultural studies via an engagement
with vernacular cultures of sexual expressivity that are usually considered
"below" polite conversation or legitimate politics.

The debate begins in the nineteenth century. In her analysis of the
contrasting public spectacles of middle-class women's respectability and
working-class dancehall vulgarity in the Caribbean, Belinda Edmondson (2003: 5) argues that the policing of women's public image has been
closely linked to various forms of nationalism since the nineteenth century: "English perceptions of the pathological masculinity of black Caribbean women, highlighted against other racialized femininities such as
those of white and Asian women, were—and arguably still are—the basis
for black (and later, Indo-Caribbean) nationalists to police the public
images of their women, and this policing meant scrutinizing their public
behavior." Among those who were scrutinized and found wanting were the
Trinidadian Jamettes, disreputable urban "black women associated with
the barracks yards, gangs, and the streets," who were "also active as 'chan-
terelles,' or calypso singers, and their 'carisos,' songs, were habitually casti-
gated as being lewd and erotic, and for allegedly instigating obscene dancing" (Edmondson 2003: 5). Edmondson argues that nationalist concerns

with social progress and proving their modernity/civility (within a racist international system that questioned blacks' capacity for self-rule) led to anxieties about black women's performances in the public sphere that required "decorous spectacles" of black womanhood such as beauty pageants "as its antidote" (Edmondson 2003: 5). She traces the emergence of an "eroticized yet decorous" performance of displays of beauty by middle-class black and brown women (Edmondson 2003: 15), which rendered their visibility in the public sphere more acceptable within national and global culture.

Debates over public displays of sexuality permeate the performance of class, color, and national distinctions in the Caribbean. Deborah Thomas (2004: 114), for example, in her study of a community on the outskirts of Kingston, Jamaica, shows how "popular culture provides a space within which people perform, debate, and, to an extent, contest ideas about gender and sexuality"; middle-class residents distanced themselves from the "noise" and "slackness" associated with the dancehall sessions of the "poorer set." She links middle-class respectability to the legacies of "creole multiracial nationalism" by which the brown middle class positioned itself as a leader of the nation into independence by making a "respectable state" and legitimized their leadership by "reproducing the colonial value system" (Thomas 2004: 57). Thus, Thomas shows how contemporary popular discourses of sexuality and efforts to control the exercise of variant sexualities are closely tied to both colonial legacies and postcolonial nation-building efforts. The public emergence of what she calls ghetto feminism among "scantily clad and sexually explicit female" DJs such as Tanya Stephens, Lady Saw, and Ce'cile challenged "two primary aspects of the creole nationalist project—the pursuit of respectability and the acceptance of a paternalistic patriarchy" (Thomas 2004: 252). Through "its public affirmation of female agency, especially as this is related to sexual desire and fulfillment," such ghetto feminism "created a space for a new *public* advocacy . . . by women for women" (Thomas 2004: 253, 256). Nevertheless, Thomas notes, black feminists especially in the United States "have been wary of condoning the use of erotic power as a means of battling sexism expressly because of the historical legacies enfolding black female sexuality" (Thomas 2004: 256) and, perhaps, because of their own struggles for national citizenship via respectability.

Noble also wrestles with the ambivalent response of black female audiences (especially in the diaspora) to the "often outrageously sexy, rude and unashamed enjoyment of Black female sexuality" in ragga music, using it as an opportunity "to raise questions about eroticism and sexuality in Black life" (Noble 2000: 149). "The celebration of the Black female body is a particularly strong theme within Ragga music," she argues, although the "racist history of European ideas of sexuality complicates any attempt by Black women to assert their sexual selves in the public domain" (Noble 2000: 154–55). "The shame and discomfort that many Black women feel about the ways in which we are celebrated in Ragga centre [a]round its apparent demand for our complicity with a racist sexual iconography of the Black female body" (Noble 2000: 155). Nevertheless, much like Davis and Carby in regard to the twentieth-century U.S. context, Noble contends that "the claiming of bodily integrity and autonomy through the celebration of uses of the body in pursuits of leisure and pleasure—song, dance, sport and sex; and the creation and claiming of public spaces of Black autonomy" (Noble 2000: 157) can be understood as the foundations of sexual citizenship and erotic autonomy.

Ragga lyrics, Noble argues, "typically emphasize Black women's sexual agency and advocate a libertarian individualism where women have autonomy from patriarchal marital domesticity and the cult of motherhood" (Noble 2000: 159–60). Challenging bell hooks's (1990) critique of "what is vulgarly called 'pussy power,' " as used in the Spike Lee film *She's Gotta Have It*, she observes:

> Ragga women engage in exhibitionism which is crude, vulgar, shocking, sexy and powerful. . . . [I]n dances which simulate clitoral masturbation and women in controlling and dominant sexual positions, and clothes that imprint the vagina on the observing gaze, the Ragga Queens construct a sexual subjectivity which is centred on the vagina as the locus of female sexual agency and generative power which does not tie it inevitably to reproduction, that is open and inclusive to a wide continuum of desire: autoeroticism, lesbian desire and an active powerful heterosexual eroticism. Through the elaboration of a gynocentric mode of signification, Ragga women create a gender symbolism that hints at what remains largely unspoken and unacknowledged in the vast majority of Ragga lyrics—that is, the possibility of a Black lesbian or bisexual presence in the dancehall and in Black identity. (Noble 2000: 162)

Against the argument that black popular cultures are simply in the service of capitalist commodity culture, the male gaze, and heterosexism, Noble instead reads the ragga queen's garish and loud appearance as a kind of kitsch drag in which "erotic style [is used] to play with the sexist gullibility of the male gaze." "Her style presents us with a highly processed, commodified appearance," she suggests, "reveling in a kind of consumer fetishism in which women's consumption of style can signify personal economic agency, social power and sexual agency over the consumerism (sexual and material) of men" (Noble 2000: 158). Thus, a diasporic dancer such as Afua Hall performs as "Afreeka," a stereotypical Jamaican dancehall queen, precisely because she understands dancehall as what she calls a "place of freedom" and "community."[20]

In a later reconsideration of this argument, however, Noble (2008) explicitly distances herself from this analysis, specifically in the context of seeing her daughter and her friends perform Jamaican-style dance in a school show involving a white British audience. She problematizes not only the popular performativities of dancehall as it travels across transnational audiences, but also the apparent defense of homophobia that is implicit in Cooper's stance on Jamaican popular culture and her critique of non-Jamaican academic theorists.[21] While some academic commentaries on dancehall view it as "an affirmative expression of lower class/Black subjectivity and creativity" (including Cooper 2004 and Noble 2000), Noble here seeks to pursue a more complex account of dancehall's production and consumption across the discrepant postcolonial settings in which individuals negotiate power and enact "late modern freedoms." Noble's analysis ultimately questions "the eroticized body as a site of ontological authenticity and freedom" in contexts that mask the persistence of racism and class inequalities (Noble 2008: 224). In other words, we might ask, can a radical public politics of sexuality ever transform racist modes of citizenship and biopolitical governance? Can a radical sexual citizenship ultimately transform heteronormative, patriarchal, and racialized sexualities that have been defined, regulated, and deployed to control populations in both national and transnational arenas?

The argument for women's agency within the sexual cultures of the dancehall and ghetto feminism continues to be debated across national and transnational settings, further underlining the embroiling of sexuality within state practices and legal institutions. Patricia Saunders (2003: 114) offers a complex reading of ragga lyrics and sexual politics in Jamaica in which she agrees with the "claim that dancehall lyrics can indeed be read as an affirmation of black female sexuality in Jamaica, [yet] we cannot deny the very limited freedom women have in constructing their own sexuality, controlling their resources (their bodies and their labor), and certainly in protecting themselves from economic, political and physical violence."

Thus, in an alternative and more politically complex reading of women's sexual agency within the dancehall, she suggests that "the cultural, economic and discursive linking of gender and sexual politics needs to be considered in relation to nationalist politics and nationalist constructions of sexuality. . . . The construction of sexuality in some dancehall lyrics effaces women as social, political and sexual beings, producing a masculinized narrative of unified national identity. From this perspective, workers in the global marketplace, women and their bodies are constructed as having no identity (no face, just body parts, or units of labor) and are constructed as absent from their sexual experiences and the 'body politic' of the nation" (Saunders 2003: 114–15). Thus, national(ist) discourses of masculinity come to mediate public performances and popular discourses of appropriate male and female sexualities, and the "productivity" of women's work/sexuality is tied to the reproduction of masculinity, heterosexuality, and the nation. Saunder's reading of women's sexual agency demands that we also read their political agency and, above all, their capacity to "*determine the meaning of equality and freedom*" (Saunders 2003: 115). Thus, her analysis re-links the issue of sexual agency to the problem of citizenship and what I have described as sexual citizenship.

As in other cases of citizenship from below, such as those discussed in previous chapters, "Discourses of resistance also work to reinscribe hegemonic practices" (Saunders 2003: 114). In view of Saunders's argument, Thomas (2004: 256) also observes that it would behoove us to "make central the links between gender, sexual politics, and nationalist constructions of sexuality, which . . . have defined the contours of respectable citizenship." Citizenship, as I have already argued, is at bottom not only embodied but also sexual; citizenship from "the bottom up" is lived as sexual. It is here that we must reject Gilroy's (1995) lament over sexual expression as pseudo-freedom and instead attempt to identify the forms that racialized sexualities take as they intersect with gender and racial formations within national and transnational politics. Rather than imagining a return to an asexual vernacular culture in a purified public-political sphere of respectable citizenship, we would do better to consider how and why public sexualities are taking their current forms at this particular historical juncture. We should begin to ask what more positive forms they might take (and possibly are taking) to escape from the reproduction of hegemonic scenarios and scripts that are damaging to people's health and well-being. It is here that theorists of queer sexualities have made crucial contributions to furthering an analysis of sexual citizenship and erotic agency.

Black masculinity, as I have shown, was at stake in struggles for citizenship from below in post-slavery societies, where white domination rested on the erotic subjugation of black bodies. These historical legacies of emasculation, de-gendering, and denial of erotic knowledge to subjugated peoples continues to inform contemporary struggles for sexual citizenship. The performances of hypermasculinity within dancehall culture are one part of a wider field of black masculinities that also includes the highly stylized performances posed with such tension between the deadpan, "affectless masculinity" of the "gangsta" in hip-hop culture and the "composed hauteur" and "extravagant use of face" of the camp "diva" in queer black performative cultures (Rose 1994a, 1994b). In 2010–11, public opinion swirled around condemnation of the dance style known as "daggering" in Jamaica, in which a woman stands on her head with her legs splayed open as men on either side of her perform aggressive thrusting movements against her pelvis. What kinds of masculinity and femininity are being performed here, and what is their relation to the long history of post-slavery struggles for sexual citizenship that have been traced throughout this book? As the Jamaican dancehall scholar and blogger Agostinho Pinnock asks, "Why are poor, disenfranchised youth in the ghettoes of Kingston and elsewhere in Jamaica pushed to choreograph such explicit and provocative types of dance? Do these forms of entertainment have any implications for their real lives in a 'stratified' Jamaican society?"[22] And can we ask why foreign voyeurs are so interested in representing Jamaica through these forms of "excessive" sexuality, without resorting to a naturalization of nationality as an exclusionary mechanism to shut down debate?

Lorde linked her reading of women's erotic power to African goddesses such as Afrekete, Yemanje, Oyo, and what she calls the "warrior goddesses of Vodun," in "An Open Letter to Mary Daly" (2007 [1984]: 67). In a similar move, Cooper argues that the dancehall artist "Lady Saw's erotic performance in the dancehall can be recontextualised within a decidedly African diasporic discourse as a manifestation of the spirit of female fertility figures such as the Yoruba Oshun."[23] Oshun is described as "the personification of the Erotic in Nature. It is she who sits as Queen of the Fertility Feast," and her manifestation is linked to the queens who appeared in the Jamaican Myal and Revival movements of the post-emancipation period. Cooper also invokes the orisha Oya "as a model for the performance of female sexual identity in the African diaspora" because of her connections to masquerades, spectacle, and fearsome female power. In her reading of Lady Saw's lyrics and stage performance, Cooper concludes that "Lady Saw's brilliant lyrics, reinforced by her compelling body language, articulate a potent message about sexuality, gender politics and the power struggle for the right to public space in Jamaica." Her erotic disguise, according to Cooper, allows her and other outspoken dancehall women to "cut loose" from social constraints and to "speak subtle truths about their society," playing out erotic roles that may not be available for women to express in everyday life.[24] Yet what has not been raised is whether the performance of daggering or other aggressive expressions of heteromasculinity might be an equally fearsome and powerful spectacle of the power of Ogou, much like the Maroons and the sword-bearing citizens of previous chapters. This dance, too, is a mobile kinetics that speaks subtle truths about society, in which women as well as men are caught up in ambiguous performances of power.

In the face of structural violence and the ambiguities of power, I am struck by my own experience in Léogâne, Haiti, in the summer of 2010, where dance could be found everywhere in forms that explicitly combined elements of the sensual, the spiritual, and the political. In several different venues, the survivors of the earthquake could be found dancing for uplift, for sanctity, and for sheer pleasure. Young people gathered around sound systems playing Haitian kompa, salsa, or reggaeton or American hip hop, but they just as happily gathered to dance to the drummers playing traditional rhythms. Older women danced together to kompa at a Mother's Day community gathering, even pulling me into the dance. Racine Con, an African-roots dance troupe in Léogâne, whose young dancers were living in tents in the muddy fields, performed a beautifully choreographed suite of dances built on the gestures of the service to the lwa, accompanied by a double battery of six Vodou drums and a male lead singer. Later in the night, the children in the audience vied to dance to the drum, circling it tightly and competing in embodiment of its ecstatic rhythms.[25] Later in the year, rara bands made a comeback and protests over electoral politics were accompanied by singing through the streets. While most political analysts of current events in Haiti pay no attention to dance or music, all of these practices suggest the role of dance in forming community and upholding human dignity and hope, as well as expressing various forms of embodied power.

Erotic domination today continues to take the form of rules, norms, laws, and structures of inequality that force people to give up control over their own bodies, labor, time, space, movement, kin, and spirit. In conclusion, we can see emerging out of trans-Caribbean theorizations of sexual

citizenship, embodied freedom, and erotic agency a broad terrain of political struggle that encompasses the national, regional, and transnational
scales yet locates agency and activism in the body, in the spaces of collective
"work," and in the quotidian interactions between bodies in those erotically
charged spaces of work, dance, sex, and sacred service. As I have attempted
to show, Caribbean theorizations of erotic agency offer an approach that
can deal with colonial histories of enslavement and emancipation as flu-
ently and effectively as they deal with contemporary neo-imperial and
neocolonial contexts and resistance movements against them. Indeed, this
approach enables us to draw connections between the past and the present
in ways that may offer greater insight into both the continuities and the
transformations within racial/sexual politics over several centuries.

A more explicit queering of black and Caribbean feminist theory has
been central to the recognition of the importance of embodied freedom in
the post-slavery world, and it enables us to reconnect recent "queer theories" of sexual citizenship with the colonial histories of racialized and
sexualized embodiment that mark contemporary inter-embodiments. Finally, we can say that a "queer Caribbean" theoretical project is emerging
that has the potential to bridge traditions of Caribbean women's studies,
black feminist theory, and transnational queer studies, creating a promis-
ing direction for future political work. Such work will have to navigate the
confluences of national and transnational perspectives, sexual and economic relations, material and spiritual dimensions, and academic and
activist engagements. But many are already doing this work, and we have
much to learn from them. Public discussion of lesbian, gay, bisexual, transgendered, and other minority sexualities emerged first within Caribbean
fiction and literary studies (e.g., Glave 2008; O'Callaghan 1998), taking root
especially in diasporic locations, but have now become an explicitly queer
Caribbean theoretical position as articulated by Caribbean writers and
researchers in recent conferences held in the region.

Rather than focusing on (and taking at face value) the alleged "deviancy" of the forms of violently heteronormative gender performance and
hypersexuality expressed within dancehall culture, the more historically
grounded analysis of sexual citizenship and erotic agency that I offer in this
book allows for the contextualization of contemporary cultural practices
in wider histories of transnational political and economic struggles for
citizenship from below. This chapter has also tried to explicitly connect the
erotic powers of the dancehall to the contested histories of reproduction,
birth control, and population biopolitics that inform relations between the

Caribbean and the United States, which is both my own location and the location of many of these debates about popular culture. Rather than reaching any final judgment on anything so complex as an entire cultural arena of erotic politics, it would be wiser to conclude by noting the ambivalence of the cultural forms themselves, the embroilment of one's own positionality in critiquing anyone else's embodied politics of freedom, and the ultimately sensual, spiritual, and metaphysical dimensions of the bodily praxis of erotic agency and erotic knowledge.

Public forums for expressing and debating sexual citizenship—whether aural or scribal, musical or lyrical, bodily or spiritual—can perhaps best contribute to the development of erotic agency as protest against, and resistance to, the constrained heteronormative sexualizations and hierarchical racializations of citizenship in the post-plantation Americas. Erotic agency here encompasses not just sexuality but all forms of self-determination of one's own bodily relation to time, space, movement, labor, knowledge, kinship, and divinity. It is the larger life horizon in which existence flourishes. Erotic power returns us to the very forms of embodied freedom that those "emancipated" from slavery were struggling for, and that so often remain unfulfilled today, especially in the current conditions for millions of people living in Haiti. It returns us to the question not of freedom for whom, but of freedom for what? Pulsing beneath our consciousness, moving our feet, welling up from below, erotic agency works our bodies toward an expansive engagement with life, implying a more holistic locus of citizenship that reaches far beyond the state and its strictures of erotic subjugation in exchange for recognition as a citizen. This mobile kinetic embodiment of historical forces propels all of us toward a future in which we can still learn from the ancestral spirits of those who were moved by slavery to seek freedom in its fullest sense.

While citizenship in the form of participation in elections, the rule of law, and the protection of rights may be crucial in Haiti, Jamaica, and throughout the Caribbean right now, it is not sufficient. Citizenship from below, today, also demands the capabilities to exercise full human capacities: to live in a world that values each and every person and the sanctity of his and her bodies and minds; to be able to choose sexual partners without being subject to marginalization and social violence; to bring children into the world (if one so wishes) with an expectation to be able to raise them in safety; to inhabit a balanced ecological system in which humans, plants, and animals can coexist and sustain each other; and to engage in communal practices of dancing spirits into the world and delving musically beneath the material surface of the world (if one finds sustenance there). All of this and more is part of citizenship from below, and it is the future task of critical Caribbean historiography, sociology, and anthropology to recognize these fundamental dimensions of existence that have been largely written out of mainstream political histories of freedom. Only then will erotic agency and Caribbean freedom emerge as fully realized political, spiritual, and sensual embodiments of the free citizen and human being.

NOTES

INTRODUCTION

1 Franco Montalto, with Patrick Gurian, Michael Piasecki, and Mimi Sheller, "Supporting Haitian Infrastructure Reconstruction Decisions with Local Knowledge," April 2010–March 2011, NSF-RAPID Award no. 1032184.

2 In the case of oral histories, there are questions about who controls the production of such narratives in terms of staging, recording, translating, framing, and introducing interviews and getting them published. When non-elitist historiography of the region turned toward methods such as oral history, life histories, autobiography, and testimonial, they sought to foreground questions of agency in the creation of history and memory, arguing in favor of attention to verbal and nonverbal forms of popular culture and symbolic expression, with an admonition to listen to their polyvocality and silences (Isaacman 1993). This approach drew on forms of life history and self-narration as an ethnographic method (see, e.g., the seminal life history of a Puerto Rican sugar worker in Mintz 1960) but more recently has also been influenced by feminist methodologies (Brereton 1995; Chamberlain 1995).

3 This study is marked by my particular subjectivities as a Jewish American but Quaker-educated Philadelphian; a heterosexual but queer-friendly unmarried mother; a color-conscious but white-privileged global minority; a return migrant from the foreign shores of England; and what some Jamaicans perceptively called a "brown whitey."

4 See the IRN website at http://www.irnweb.org and discussion in *sx salon*, issue 6 (August 2011), available online at http://smallaxe.net/wordpress3/discussions/2011/08/ (accessed 12 September 2011).

1. HISTORY FROM THE BOTTOM(S) UP

1 For very valuable histories of Caribbean emancipation that nevertheless sidestep sexuality studies, see, e.g., Cooper et al. 2000; Dubois 2004a, 2004b; Hall 1992, 2002; Holt 1992; R. Scott 1985, 2005.

2 There is also a growing interest in the intersections of gender, sexuality, and race in studies of state formation and politics in Latin America and the Hispanic Caribbean (see, e.g., Balderston and Guy 1997; Briggs 2002; Findlay 1999; Guy 1990; Radcliffe and Westwood 1996; Stepan 1991, 2001), as well as in histories of slavery and emancipation in the United States (esp. Gilmore 1996; Glenn 2002; Hartman 1997; Spillers 1987; Wiegman 1995).

3 On women and slavery, see Beckles 1989, 1999; Bush 1990; Mair 1987, 2006; Mathurin 1974; Morrissey 1989. On gender and emancipation, see Momsen 1993; Scully and Paton 2005; Shepherd et al. 1995; *Slavery and Abolition*, vol. 26, no. 2. Elsewhere in postcolonial studies, historians have drawn on Foucault's notions of biopower (Foucault 1990 [1978], 1997) and of the disciplining of the body (Foucault 1995) within sites such as "the hospital, the asylum, the police station, the museum, and even the colonial archive itself" (Ballantyne and Burton 2005: 416). These histories have made the micro-histories of bodies and sexualities, intimacy and conjugality, more central to understandings of macro-histories of power and domination. Contemporary Caribbean ethnographies have more thoroughly explored questions of race, class, gender, ethnicity, and citizenship in the enactment of national public spheres and global relations (see, e.g., Freeman 2000; Khan 2004; Thomas 2004; Ulysse 2008; Williams 1991) and can provide some useful points of entry into rereading Caribbean histories.

4 Since the 1990s, studies of British imperialism have employed critical perspectives on gender and racial formation throughout the empire, bridging domestic and imperial histories (see, e.g., Burton 1994, 1997; Gikandi 1997; McClintock 1995; Pratt 1992; Stoler and Cooper 1997; Ware 1992), while historical studies of specific colonial societies have shown how processes of race(ing) and gendering uphold colonial power through the intimate relations between different bodies (C. Hall 1992; Holt 1992; Scully 1997; Stanley 1998; Stoler 1995, 2002).

5 More complex understandings of racial formation and the racial state are also called for. For too long, Caribbean historiography has been written as if black, white, Asian, and so on were simply pre-existing, and hence unquestionable, obvious categories of existence. They never are, as any effort to compare racial categories cross-nationally and over time will show. While anthropologists and sociologists have been sensitive to the social construction of race, historians of the Caribbean have only recently begun to examine the formation of racial boundaries as a contingent and contextual process (see, e.g., R. Scott 2000).

6 Third-wave historical sociology, according to Julia Adams and her colleagues (2005: 3), is grounded in classic sociological concerns with markets, states, and civil societies in the making of modernity but gives "heightened attention to institutions, theorization of agents and signification, gendered analysis, and rejection of Eurocentrism." Charles Tilly (1995: 369), whose work is characteristic of the second wave, defines citizenship as the "rights and mutual obligations binding state agents and a category of persons defined exclusively by their legal attachment to the same state." As one of the supervisors of my doctoral dissertation, Tilly influenced the historical and comparative approach I took in *Democracy after Slavery* (Sheller 2000). Yet the genesis of this book's concerns with gender, race,

and sexuality actually preceded that work and contemporaneously emerged on a kind of parallel track "below" the official thesis, into which I found it difficult to incorporate a deeper understanding of embodied freedom.

7   Bryan Turner (1993: 2–3) defines citizenship as "that set of practices (juridical, political, economic and cultural) which define a person as a competent member of society, and which as a consequence shape the flow of resources to persons and social groups," thus placing "the concept squarely in the debate about inequality, power differences and social class." Deborah Yashar (2005: 31) likewise points out that many studies of democratization in Latin America have ignored basic questions such as "What is citizenship? Who gets to be a citizen? And how is citizenship experienced?" Yashar develops the concept of "citizenship regimes" to refer to the three fundamental questions that pattern differing forms of citizenship: who has access to citizenship; what is the form of citizenship; and what is the content of citizenship rights (civil, political, and social).

8   Thus, we can say that the idea of citizenship historically has served to order, regulate, and even legitimate a number of social inequalities. "It is not only that citizenship regimes might fail to deliver on the promise of unified political communities, equal political rights, and standardized forms of interest intermediation," according to Yashar (2005: 52–53), "but they might also mask the local autonomies and deep social inequalities that already exist." I would argue further that citizenship regimes actually *produce* (and in some sense require) the "local autonomies and deep social inequalities" to which Yashar refers.

9   I refer to the poem "High Life" by Dorothea Smartt, who describes herself as a "Brit-born Bajan," which she performed at Lancaster University during the Annual Conference of the Society for Caribbean Studies in July 2004.

10 I borrow this tripartite "chord of freedom" from Orlando Patterson (1991: 4), but I have departed somewhat from his notion of "civic freedom," which he defines as "the capacity of adult members of a community to participate in its life and governance" to include a broader range of public practices of citizenship, as I discuss further.

11 Tracy Robinson describes Alexander's trilogy of essays that were first published between 1991 and 1997 as "the most striking feminist rendition of the predicates of Caribbean modernities: the violence of a heteropatriarchal state, the political freight of sex, and the precariousness of citizenship for certain postcolonial bodies" (Alexander 1991, 1994, 1997; Robinson 2007: 118).

12 It is notable that Lauren Berlant compares Americans' interest in the controversy over the Anita Hill–Clarence Thomas Senate hearings with "that perverse space between empathy and pornography that Karen Sanchez-Eppler has isolated as constitutive of white Americans' interest in slaves, slave narratives and other testimonials of the oppressed" (Berlant 1997: 241; Sanchez-Eppler 1988). Given the eroticization of domination and the sexualization of racial difference, the question of the collision between empathy and pornography must be central to any social-justice movement working on issues of subordination.

13 The tactic of speaking about sexuality in public has something in common with the vulgar oraliteracies and "low theory" championed by the Jamaican theorist

Carolyn Cooper. "These vulgar products of illicit procreation [found in Jamaica's sexually explicit oral cultures] may be conceived—in poor taste—as perverse invasions of the tightly-closed orifices of the Great Tradition" (Cooper 1993: 9), or, we might say, of the orifices and policed boundaries of national sexuality. Cooper develops the idea of oraliteracy—a form of literacy that intervenes in the written *langue* via the oral *parole*—by incorporating the more disreputable urban popular cultures of the dancehall to achieve what she calls "folking up theory."

14 Buju Banton's song "Boom Bye Bye" (1992) called for "a bullet in batty bwoy hed" and led to international boycotts of his music and the cancellation of some concerts (Skelton 1995). In 2004, Buju Banton was accused of involvement in a group attack on a gay man in Kingston, although he was acquitted in January 2006. These incidents helped to catalyze the international "Stop Murder Music" campaign led by the British organization OutRage!, which focused on a worldwide boycott of the dancehall lyricists who were promoting murder of "battymen" and "sodomites." See "Outrage! Dancehall Dossier," available online at http://www.soulrebels .org/dancehall/k_concerts.htm (accessed 23 September 2011). This led to an investigation by Scotland Yard of eight reggae artists for incitement to murder and the banning of the reggae musician Sizzla from entering the United Kingdom for a concert in November 2004. In February 2005, after dozens of concerts were canceled, a "deal" was reached between the dancehall industry and the gay, lesbian, bisexual, and transgender organizations that were involved in the campaign, in which the industry vowed to ban lyrics that incited anti-gay violence. Nevertheless, many of the artists involved quickly disavowed their apologies and broke promises that they would discontinue singing violent homophobic lyrics.

15 Human Rights Watch, "Hated to Death: Homophobia, Violence, and Jamaica's HIV/AIDS Epidemic," available online at http://hrw.org/reports/2004/jamaica 1104 (accessed 10 June 2009).

16 In April 2009, gay activists in San Francisco and New York called for a boycott of Jamaican products such as Red Stripe beer and Myers Rum, an action that was opposed by J-FLAG in an open letter dated 12 April 2009 pointing out that "Jamaica's deeply ingrained antipathy towards homosexuality and homosexuals is a social phenomenon that will not be undone by boycott campaigns or government dictate. It requires the painstaking effort of confronting the society and talking to social actors who can bring change in the way society sees LGBT people": see the websites at http://www.boycottjamaica.org (accessed 10 June 2009); http://www .ifbprides.org/ifbp_news_may_09_boycott.php (accessed 10 June 2009).

17 *Glass Closet: Sex, Stigma, and HIV/AIDS in Jamaica*, dir. Gabrielle Weiss, prod. Micah Fink, available online at http://pulitzergateway.org/the-glass-closet (accessed 23 September 2011).

2. QUASHEBA, MOTHER, QUEEN

1 An extensive body of work now exists on Caribbean women's lives under slavery, often with a focus on forms of "resistance," beginning with Lucille Mathurin Mair's groundbreaking doctoral research at the University of the West Indies in the

1970s, which only recently has been published (Mair 2006). See also Beckles 1989; Bush 1990, 1996; Gaspar 1996; Mair 1987; Mintz 1979; Morrissey 1989.

2 In the next chapter, I discuss more fully the interactions between the freed people of Jamaica who were of African descent (i.e., the vast majority of the population) and the smaller group of indentured workers who came from India starting in the 1840s. Racial categories in Jamaica in this period included "white," "black," "brown," and "coloured" and the ethnic labels "African" and "coolie." I use the terms "Afro-Jamaican" or "African Jamaican" to refer to both "black" and "brown" people, or those who would likely fit into one of those categories (such as "laborers" or "freedmen") and use the term "black" to refer to a self-conscious politicized racial identity among African Jamaicans.

3 The ode appears in Edwards 1801 and is discussed in Bush 1990: 11; Cooper 1995: 23.

4 Jamaica Archives, Saint Georges 2/18/6, Buff Bay Courthouse, General Slave Court, Summary Trial, 27 May 1828.

5 Indeed, this structural contradiction was recognized by Max Weber as a major factor in the transformation of the system of slavery in the Roman world (see Weber 1976: 54–55).

6 One dimension of this importance of the flesh is that themes of gendered and racialized bodily marking, scarring, and (re)appropriation have been central to black women's literature (Simmonds 1997).

7 In the United States, too, Northern middle-class women's "growing perception of the exploitation of slave women as a violation of the norms of true womanhood" fed antislavery activism and was popularized by publications such as Harriet Jacobs's *Incidents in the Life of a Slave Girl* (Fox-Genovese 1986).

8 Despite all of its contradictions for the slave (cf. Bush 1986), the role of mother also has had special resonance within Afro-Caribbean cultures. As Jean Besson (1993: 28) notes, "The significance of motherhood in conferring personal status among Afro-Caribbean women . . . is widely indicated in the regional literature." The honorific use of the title "Mother" in Caribbean and African American communities is discussed later.

9 *Morning Journal*, vol. 1, no. 14, 25 April 1838.

10 Similar incidents of protest among female workers, and nursing mothers especially, are known to have occurred on other islands (cf. Marshall 1977; Olwig 1985).

11 For similar justifications of women's protest, see Kafka 1997; Marshall 1977: 95; Olwig 1985: 33, 54.

12 Not only was Williams's account published in England, but it was read in the House of Lords by the antislavery advocate Lord Brougham, initiating an inquiry that eventually contributed to the early ending of the apprenticeship system. At the heart of Williams's charges were descriptions of the mistreatment of women, especially while pregnant or with infants. For an excellent contextualization and republication of this document, see Paton 2001.

13 *Morning Journal*, vol. 1, no. 115, 21 August 1838.

14 Ibid., no. 116, 22 August 1838.

15 Ibid., no. 187, 7 November 1838.

16 *Baptist Herald and Friend of Africa*, vol. 1, no. 5, 9 November 1839, 2.

17 Ibid., no. 2, 28 September 1839, 2.

18 Between 1838 and 1844, as Sidney Mintz (1958: 49) notes, "19,000 freedmen and their families removed themselves from the estates, bought land, and settled in free villages." With an average of five persons per family, this represented as many as 100,000 people out of the total 311,000 freed.

19 *Falmouth Post*, 12 June 1839.

20 Planters first struggled to control their organized labor force, then replaced it with more disoriented indentured workers from Africa and India, who were paid for at public expense, could be controlled more easily, and among whom men far outnumbered women (Schuler 1980; Tinker 1993). Although male indentured workers were supposed to be paid one shilling; women, 10 pence; and children, 6 pence, one missionary wrote in 1845 that the people were "so ill requited for their labor on the neighbouring Estates since the introduction of the Hill Coolies who work for 6 [pence] per day and their food, [that] they prefer laboring at their chapel" without any pay at all: G. Holland to Directors, Mt. Zion, 29 July 1845, LMS, box 5.

21 Letter by Eleanor Vickars, *Morning Journal*, 25 May 1842, and continued in another letter on 2 June 1842. Vickars mentions that her father was a deacon, and she may have been a relative of the Edward Vickars who ran for the House of Assembly in 1844 with the slogan, "Vote for Vickars, the Black Man" (Heuman 1981: 121).

22 Memorial of the Church at First Hill, Clarendon, 1845(?), LMS, box 5; Memorial of the Congregations at Dry Harbor and Claremont, Saint Ann's, encl. in Clark to Directors, 21 May 1845, LMS, box 5; Memorial of the Members of the Church assembling at Union Chapel, Davyton, Manchester, 30 December 1846, LMS, box 5.

23 Martin Young to Directors, 23 May 1847, WMMS, West Indies Correspondence, Jamaica; see also Edmondson to Directors, 4 May 1847, Rev. Henry Bleby to Directors, 8 May 1847, WMMS, West Indies Correspondence, Jamaica.

24 Like the WMMS, the BMS gradually eroded congregational democracy after 1845 in reaction to blacks' assertion of independence (Stewart 1992: 84, 148; see also Sheller 2000: chap. 5). It is unfortunate that Robert Stewart pays no attention to women in his otherwise excellent study. Diane Austin-Broos (1997) picks up the story of African Jamaican women's passionate and pervasive participation in religion but concentrates mainly on the twentieth century.

25 *Watchman*, vol. 1, no. 36, 31 October 1829.

26 On the participation of women in circle dances, public processions, and attacks on Obeahmen, see Banbury 1895: 22; Waddell 1970 (1863): 187–89. The revivalists of 1860–61 were described by one clerk of the peace as "principally women": Evidence of Beckford Davis, JRC, part 2, 520.

27 Rev. Walter Dendy to BMS, Salter's Hill, "Thirty-six Letters and Reports of Baptist Missionaries," 18 March 1862, NLJ, ms 817a; Evidence of Rev. George Truman, JRC, part 2, 415; Hillyer to Directors, Mt. Zion, 7 January 1861, LMS, box 8; Gardner to Directors, 23 February 1861, enclosing newspaper extracts, 18 February 1861, LMS, box 9; various enclosures in Eyre to Cardwell, 23 November 1865, in *Papers Relating to the Disturbances in Jamaica* 1866: no. 47.

28 W. Holdsworth to Directors, 23 October 1861, WMMS, West Indies Correspondence, Jamaica.

29 *Baptist Herald and Friend of Africa*, vol. 5, no. 33, 13 August 1844, 259. The overall female population in 1861 was enumerated as 6,251 white, 42,842 brown, and 179,097 black.

30 I will not rehash the reputation–respectability debate here, but see Austin 1984; Besson 1993; Wilson 1973. On "slack" women, cf. Cooper 1993. Most recently, Richard D. E. Burton (1997) argues for a more complex understanding of the reputation–respectability duality but does not abandon the emphasis on a *masculine* culture of play and opposition.

31 PRO, CO 142/1; *Watchman and Jamaica Free Press*, vol. 3, no. 4, 12 January 1831.

32 Despite Mintz's oft-cited belief that there is little evidence of women predominating in marketing before the emancipation of slaves in Jamaica (Mintz 1989: 211, 216), there are enough early references—some of which he cites—to "wandering higglers" (Lewis 1861: 41, from a visit to Jamaica in 1815–17, cited in Mintz [1974] 1989: 202–3), women selling their husbands' produce (Madden 1970 [1835]), and so on, to show that marketing was very much a women's activity even before emancipation.

33 A similar point has been made of the street vendors, peddlers, and washerwomen of San Juan, Puerto Rico, in the nineteenth century (Matos-Rodriguez 1995). Kingston was one of the great female-dominated trading centers of the colonial world.

34 *Baptist Herald and Friend of Africa*, vol. 1, no. 31, 3 June 1840. Mary Clarke ended up among the three women and six men sentenced to serve three months in prison for rioting against the police and soldiers who were called out to restore order; women were also prominent in several tax riots in the 1840s (Wilmot 1995: 286).

35 *Morning Journal*, vol. 1, no. 215, 7 January 1842. Similar resistance arose in Montego Bay when a drum known as a "Joe Wenda" was confiscated by a magistrate: ibid., no. 211, 1 January 1842.

36 Wilmot (1995: 288–89) has found evidence that, despite disfranchisement, women participated in election riots in Saint David's in 1851 and in Kingston in 1853.

37 Darling to Newcastle, 9 June 1859, with enclosures, government dispatches, PRO, CO 137/345.

38 Enclosures in Darling to Colonial Office, 25 March 1859, PRO, CO 137/344.

39 Darling to Colonial Office, 9 August 1859, enclosing Kitchen and Castle to the Governor's Secretary, 2 August 1859, PRO, CO 137/345.

40 Darling to Colonial Office, 10 November 1859, PRO, CO 137/346.

41 Although not directly mentioned here, the story is reminiscent of Nanny, the eighteenth-century Maroon leader who has been enshrined as a national hero of Jamaica. Women's oral histories preserve accounts of Nanny's victories over European armies, and she remains an important icon of female anticolonial leadership (cf. Besson 1993; Sistren Theatre Collective 1986).

42 Evidence of Louis Q. Bowerbank, Cardwell Papers, PRO 30/48/44.

43 JRC, part 2, 200; *County Union*, 17 October 1865.

44 Eyre to Cardwell, 7 August 1865, enclosing report of Custos John Salmon, PRO, CO 137/392.

45 Evidence of John Burnett, JRC, part 2, 229.

46 Evidence of James Britt, Volunteer, JRC, part 2, 178.

47 Evidence of Louis Q. Bowerbank.

48 Clark to Directors, 23 October 1865, LMS, box 9.

49 Morant Bay Rebellion: Contemporary Newspaper Cuttings, NLJ, MST 74, 23.

50 Bean to Phillippo, 26 January 1866, *Extracts from Correspondence of Edward Bean Underhill with Missionaries in Jamaica, 1864 to 1866*, BMS, 54.

51 Excerpt from *Lyons' Montego Bay Commercial Newspaper*, in Jamaica Committee 1866: 28.

52 *Gleaner*, 16 November 1866, "Extracts from Local Newspapers, 1866," NLJ, ms 1353.

3. HER MAJESTY'S SABLE SUBJECTS

1 A wide range of work is relevant, but one might begin with Fraser 1989; Landes 1988; Pateman 1988; Phillips 1991.

2 Others have explored the valorization of "manliness" and a discourse of "Christian Manhood" among certain post-emancipation communities in the United States (see, e.g., Becker 1997; Hartman 1997; Higginbotham 1993; Kelley 1996: 23, 65–66, 112–14; Raboteau 1997).

3 Even before slavery was abolished, the path to emancipation was different for men and for women. While men most often gained freedom as an incentive or compensation for military service (i.e., during the Haitian Revolution, the Latin American wars of independence, the U.S. Civil War, the Cuban Ten Years' War, or through service in the British West India Regiment), women were most often emancipated as a result of sexual relations with white men, usually after having worked as domestic servants within white households. Thus, for men freedom might be linked to a masculine identity forged in military service, which gave them a claim to citizenship, while for women, emancipation was more likely to be a private transaction lodged within an economic and sexual trade-off. For debates on historiography's valorization of armed liberation at the expense of women's "everyday forms of resistance," see Beckles 1989; Bush 1990; chapter 5 in this volume.

4 On Habermas's linkage of the private family and the political public, see Habermas 1989 (1962). For critiques of his uncritical approach to gender and his Eurocentric amnesia vis-à-vis the colonial world, see Cohen and Arato 1992; Emirbayer and Sheller 1999; Fraser 1989.

5 For an excellent discussion of these issues in South Africa, see Scully 1997.

6 Figures come from Confidential Jamaica: State of Affairs in Jamaica (1853), 97, Appendix A: Immigration and Sugar Return, Cardwell Papers, no. 6, PRO 30/48. See also Shepherd 1987: 173.

7 For example, a Wesleyan Methodist at Stoney Hill reported that after six months of instruction he had baptized a "captured African" man named Nelson, together with "the wife of his youth and the six children she had borne him in Africa," thus underlining the interest in keeping families together and instructing them toward Christian marriage: Letter of John Williams, 25 January 1840, WMMS, West Indies Correspondence, Jamaica, box 204.

8 Resolutions of a Public Meeting at the Baptist Chapel, Falmouth, 21 February 1840, in *Baptist Herald and Friend of Africa*, vol. 1, no. 17, 26 February 1840, 3. Although white missionaries directed these meetings and wrote up the resolutions and petitions, records of speeches given at such meetings indicate some degree of participation by the emancipated population. For further discussion of the use of such public texts in writing subaltern histories, see Sheller 2000: introduction, chap. 7.

9 *Baptist Herald and Friend of Africa*, vol. 1, no. 31, 3 June 1840.

10 Meeting of Baptist Western Union, Oracabessa, 2 July 1840, in *Baptist Herald and Friend of Africa*, vol. 1, no. 36, 8 July 1840, 1.

11 In taking as its motto "The Spirit of Liberty That Strikes the Chain from the Slave, Binds the Freeman to His Brother," the *Baptist Herald* extended a discourse of freedom pertaining specifically to a fraternity of men. It echoed the abolitionist motto, "Am I Not a Man and a Brother?" without any cognizance of the antislavery feminist appropriation "Am I Not a Woman and a Sister?" (see Sheller 2011a; Yellin 1989).

12 Letter signed by T.H.P.M., 4 July 1844, *Baptist Herald and Friend of Africa*, vol. 5, no. 28, 9 July 1844, 220.

13 As Walter Rodney (1981: 42) argued in regard to indentured women in British Guiana: "Discrimination against female indentured workers persisted because planters assigned women to the weeding gang and other low-paying jobs and because women were given less when they performed the same field task as men. Indeed, one of the backward characteristics of indentured labor was the employment of a significant proportion of low-paid women and juveniles—all constrained to undertake arduous and often undignified tasks in order to try and build the subsistence earnings of the family."

14 *Morning Journal*, vol. 10, August 16, 1847.

15 "Report of a Meeting of the Labourers, Hanover," *Morning Journal*, 6 December 1847, 2. The language used in the report is typical of some newspapers of the period, which tried to convey the oral form of Creole through various kinds of transcription. The class and racial distinctions implicit in this linguistic device are indicative of some of the implicit filters on access to a "public sphere," even for "free men." On the issue of class-inflected linguistic exclusions from public spheres, see Fraser 1989.

16 Apprehended Outbreak in the Western Parishes, 1848, enclosing report of T. F. Pilgrim, 6 July 1848, and Proclamation of Governor Charles Edward Grey, 14 July 1848, PRO, CO 137/299.

17 Darling to Colonial Office, 4 January 1859, Governor's Dispatches, enclosed in PRO, CO 137/343.

18 Darling to Colonial Office, 9 June 1859, enclosing two petitions from Rev. Charles M. Fletcher (of Rodney Hall Post Office, Saint Thomas in the Vale) to the queen and to the governor dated 8 March 1859 and signed by residents in Saint Thomas in the Vale, Saint Ann, Saint Mary, Saint Andrew, and Metcalfe, Governor's Dispatches, PRO, CO 137/345.

19 Darling to Colonial Office, 9 June 1859, enclosing Samuel Rennales, custos of Saint Thomas in the Vale, 7 April 1859, Governor's Dispatches, PRO, CO 137/345. Ap-

proximately 160 of the names on the petition are identifiable as women's names. The fact that they appear interspersed with men's names is unusual on a British petition, where men's petitions were usually separated from those from groups of "ladies."

20 Governor Darling to Duke of Newcastle, 8 September 1859, enclosing Henry Walsh to Darling, 1 July 1859, Governor's Dispatches, PRO, CO 137/346.

21 Governor Darling to Colonial Secretary, 9 August 1859, Governor's Dispatches, PRO, CO 137/345.

22 "Report on Special Sessions of the Peace Held at Court House, Montego Bay, to Inquire into Alleged Ill-treatment of Coolies," *County Union*, vol. 16, no. 26, 1 April 1864; Rev. Henry Clarke to Mr. Chamerovzow, 6 January 1866, in Jamaica Committee 1866: 31–34. Additional reports on the starvation, abuse, and deaths of indentured Indians are in Eyre to Newcastle, no. 97, 24 October 1862 (reporting on Clarke's allegations about the system of immigration published in the *Jamaica Guardian*, 6 October 1862), enclosing Clarke to Eyre, 16 October 1862; Eyre to Newcastle, no. 127, 23 December 1862, both in PRO, CO 137/368.

23 They also indicate that men were paid one shilling a day for heavy shoveling, while women lifted and carried for nine pence a day; boys got six pence; and girls got three pence. They also noted that many children were absent from school because they "were helping their parents to get in the ginger crop, the peeling and drying of the root requiring much labour of the women and children" (Harvey and Brewin 1867: 39).

24 Eyre to Cardwell, 5 July 1865, enclosing petition from African laborers in the parish of Vere, 29 May 1865, Governor's Dispatches, PRO, CO 137/392.

25 *Jamaica Watchman and People's Free Press*, 21 August 1865.

26 Evidence of William Anderson, JRC, part 2, 165.

27 See, e.g., petition from Saint Thomas in the East, 5 September 1865, in Storks to Cardwell, 1 February 1866, enc. 2, *Papers Relating to the Disturbances in Jamaica 1866*: part 3, no. 4.

28 The letter exists in the form of small handbills that were posted in public: copy of Underhill to Cardwell, 5 January 1865, PRO, CO 137/3.98, in NLJ, ms 106. For full discussion of the Underhill Meetings, see Sheller 2000: chap. 7.

29 Methodists also reported that many men could not obtain work, and when they did: "the remuneration is 1 [shilling] per day for a strong man, 9 [pence] for a woman, and 6 or 4½ [pence] for a boy or girl. Job work has for some time been substituted for day labor; but it is said that in many cases, the fields are longer, neglected, and the work greater, and the pay smaller than in former times. On some properties a few are employed throughout the year; but the masses are only wanted about eight out of the twelve months": Jon Edmondson to the Secretaries, Kingston, 20 April 1865, WMMS, West Indies Correspondence, Jamaica.

30 Eyre to Cardwell, 6 May 1865, no. 128, PRO, CO 137/391.

31 Eyre to Cardwell, private letters, 7 November 1865, 23 October 1865, Edward Cardwell Papers, August–December 1865, Correspondence with Governor Eyre, PRO 30/48/42.

32 Henry Taylor note, 8 June 1865, attached to Eyre to Cardwell (6 May 1865).

33 Evidence of Lewis Q. Bowerbank, 9.

34 On the Morant Bay Rebellion and its aftermath, see Heuman 1994; Sheller 2000; and chapter 4 of this book.

4. LOST GLIMPSES OF 1865

1 "Deaths in the Services," *British Medical Journal* 2, no. 3324 (13 September 1924), 488.

2 Gulland would have traveled with the Royal Warwickshire 6th Regiment of Foot, which was deployed to all the places that appear in the album: see "The Royal Warwickshire Regiment," available online at http://www.britisharmedforces.org/ i_regiments/warwickfus_index.htm (accessed 11 June 2011). The Second Battalion of the regiment apparently embarked for the West Indies on 4 March 1864 aboard the troopship *HMS Orontes*.

3 Adolphe Duperly first went from Paris to Haiti, then traveled via Santiago de Cuba to Jamaica, settling in Kingston in 1824 and establishing his photography studio in 1840. His sons Armand (1834–1909) and Henri Louis joined his business and kept it going after his death. Armand's sons Armand John Louis Duperly (d. 1903) and Theophile John Baptiste Duperly (d. 1933) continued the studio in Kingston, winning the gold medal in the Jamaica Exhibition of 1891. Henri Louis established a photography studio in Colombia in 1876, which was continued by his son Oscar. Two professional photographers directly descended from the family are still working today: Victoria Restrepo in Colombia (www.vrestrepo.com) and Beverly Duperly Boos in the United States (www.mangophotography.com): see Glory Robertson, "Some Early Jamaican Postcards, Their Photographers and Publishers," *Jamaica Journal*, vol. 18, no. 1, February–April 1985, 17; Macmillan 1909. Armand John Louis's death is reported in *The Gleaner*, 11 June 1903, 5, 11. I thank Leah Rosenberg for this information.

4 A second volume of *Daguerian Excursions in Jamaica* was planned but never published. See also Robertson, "Some Early Jamaican Postcards."

5 Some information on Duperly comes from *Art and Emancipation in Jamaica: Isaac Mendes Belisario and His Worlds*, exhibition catalogue, Yale Center for British Art and Yale University Press, New Haven, 2007. The National Gallery of Jamaica also presented an "abridged and amended" version of the exhibition, titled "Isaac Mendes Belisario: Art and Emancipation in Jamaica," in 2008. It featured the Jamaican loans to the original exhibition and additional loans from various Jamaican collections.

6 *Colonial Standard and Jamaica Dispatch*, 18 November 1865, quoted in David Boxer, "The Duperlys of Jamaica," *Duperly: An Exhibition of Works by Adolphe Duperly, His Sons, and Grandsons Mounted in Commemoration of the Bicentenary of His Birth*, exhibition catalogue, National Gallery of Jamaica, Kingston, 2001, 11.

7 Boxer, "Introduction," in *Duperly*, 2.

8 Although many historians report 500 people killed in total, some primary evidence indicates a cover-up of much higher numbers. For example, Lewis Bowerbank, the custos of Kingston, initially gave evidence that "the number of persons

officially reported to the Government as killed during the insurrections . . . was 2,010 This, I understand, included those shot down in open rebellion, as also those taken and executed": Edward Cardwell Papers, Extracts of Colonial Office Confidential Prints, 1865–66, PRO 30/48/44, Evidence of Lewis Q. Bowerbank, 8. Another document finds some merit in Commodore Sir Francis Leopold McClintock's report (dated 8 November) that on his arrival in Jamaica on 31 October, "he found that 300 had been hung and about 800 shot, chiefly by the Maroons—that arrests and court martials were still going on and that 1500 would be a low computation probably of the total loss of life": "The Number of Rebels Killed," draft marked "read to the Cabinet, 6 December 1865," in Edward Cardwell Papers, Extracts of Colonial Office Confidential Prints, 1865–66, PRO 30/48/44, 105–6. Not all of the original evidence was published, as it was considered too incendiary.

9   Excerpts from the *Colonial Standard*, 27 October 1865, in Jamaica Committee 1866: 23.

10   Joseph Hall, a black cooper held in the Morant Bay prison, testified that he and others were taken out each day to bury the prisoners executed the previous evening. When asked where the bodies were buried, he replied, "Some at the back of the burnt Court-house and some at the cross road": House of Commons, *Parliamentary Papers*, 1866 [3683–1], in *Minutes of Evidence and Appendix*, JRC, part 2, 242 (hereafter, PP JRC).

11   The naval hospital, begun in 1817, is an early example of cast-iron architecture. The prefabricated beams were shipped from England, and the building was still in use to shelter most of the population during the hurricane of 1951.

12   The HMS *Duncan* was a ninety-one-gun, first-rate line-of-battle ship launched in 1859 and commissioned on 6 January 1864 as the flagship of Vice-Admiral James Hope, North America and West Indies, commanded by Captain Robert Gibson. It gives a sense of the powerful gunships that were used in suppressing rebellions in the colonies, along with lighter corvettes, such as the HMS *Wolverine*. By April 1866, the HMS *Duncan* had been deployed to New Brunswick with seven hundred troops to put down an attempted Fenian "invasion" of Canada, so this photograph was taken before that date.

13   The underwater ruins have been designated a National Heritage Site by the Jamaican National Heritage Trust: see the photographs at "The Port Royal Project," available online at http://nautarch.tamu.edu/portroyal/archhist.htm (accessed 11 June 2011).

14   Cardwell to Eyre, 23 November 1865, House of Commons, *Parliamentary Papers*, 1866, *Papers Relating to the Disturbances in Jamaica*, part 1, dispatch 3, 242 (hereafter, PP *Jamaica Disturbances*).

15   For an important contemporary critique of Governor Eyre and the Colonial Office by a "Late Member of the Executive Committee in the Legislative Council of Jamaica and Late Custos of St. Catherine," see Price 1866.

16   Cardwell to Eyre, 1 December 1865, PP *Jamaica Disturbances*, dispatch 10, enc. 5, 249.

17   Eyre to Cardwell, 7 November 1865, PP *Jamaica Disturbances*, dispatch 22, enc. 43, 125–26.

18   In 1864, in a confidential report to Cardwell, Eyre described the opposition in the

House of Assembly as consisting of eight Jews (Andrew Lewis, George Solomon, Aaron Salom, Isaac Levy, David J. Alherga, Charles Levy, Robert Nunes, and Hiam Barrow), six "colored persons" (G. W. Gordon, Robert A. Johnson, John Nunes, Samuel Constantine Burke, Robert Osborn, and Daniel P. Nathan), and two racially unidentified, presumably white, men (Joseph Williams and Francis Lynch). The governor's correspondence frequently complains about the Jewish faction, which controlled many newspapers: March 1864, no. 98, 9 March 1864, Governor's Dispatches, PRO, CO 137/380.

19 Evidence of Sidney Levien and extract from *County Union*, 17 October 1865, PP JRC, 198–200; see also Heuman 1994: 152.

20 PP JRC, 198.

21 Nelson had already written from Morant Bay on 4 November, "I do not consider myself justified in arraigning these prisoners before a court-martial. My reason for thus doing so is—these prisoners all uttered the sentiments which are said to be seditious prior to the rebellion, and though I may have the power and authority under martial law (a power to myself very doubtful) yet it is a power I do not feel myself justified in exercising, and which I shall not exert unless I receive positive orders so to do": Nelson to Major-General Luke Smythe O'Connor, 4 November 1865, enclosed in Eyre to Cardwell, 8 November 1865, PP *Jamaica Disturbances*, dispatch 25, enc. 20, 157.

22 A similar sketch appears on the cover of Heuman's book (1994); the artist in both cases is unknown.

23 Evidence of James Britt, 178.

24 Letter of Rev. E. Palmer, Baptist minister of Kingston, quoted in Jamaica Committee 1866: 30–31. See also Heuman 1994: chap. 10.

25 Following criticism of his harsh actions during the suppression of the rebellion, Hobbs was examined by a board of medical officers and declared of unsound mind. Ordered back to England with his family in May 1866, he threw himself overboard and drowned (see Heuman 1994: 175–76).

26 Evidence of Henry Good, a white policeman, PP JRC, 30. According to Heuman (1994: 9–10), Price "was a political supporter of Baron von Ketelhodt [the principal magistrate] and also had close business connections with Rev. Herschell," both of whom were political opponents of G. W. Gordon. Although some in the crowd tried to protect Price, several women declared that he did not deserve to live because he had not paid them for work. On 1 November, a court-martial sentenced Justina (or Jessie) Taylor and Mary Ward to be executed for his murder.

27 Krista Thompson (2006) offers an excellent discussion of such photographic images of the poor and working classes. She includes postcard images created by the Duperly grandsons at the studio in Kingston from the 1890s into the early twentieth century, but she does not specifically discuss a link between the early photographic practices of Adolphe Duperly and later tourist imagery. The grandsons' photos continue to influence contemporary tourist imagery.

28 Eyre to Cardwell (6 May 1865).

29 Eyre to Cardwell, 20 October 1865, no. 251, PRO, CO 137/393; Evidence of Alexander Fyfe, PP JRC, 894. See also Heuman 1994: 131.

30 "The Outbreak in Jamaica," Spanish Town, February 9, 1866, in Morant Bay Rebellion: Contemporary Newspaper Cuttings, NLJ, 9.

31 See *Addresses to His Excellency, Edward John Eyre, Esquire* ([Kingston]: M. DeCordova, 1866), item 12.

32 Boxer, "The Duperlys of Jamaica," 13. Tom Cringle's Cotton Tree measured 18–20 feet in diameter and "was used as a directional aid on several maps and as the 100th milestone marker for Kingston": see the photograph and description at NLJ, "Tom Cringle's Cotton Tree, St. Catherine's, Jamaica," available online at http://www .flickr.com/photos/28320522@No8/2714886856 (accessed 15 July 2011). The tree collapsed on 18 January 1971.

33 "The Case of Mr. George William Gordon," House of Commons, *Parliamentary Papers*, 1866, JRC, part 1, *Report*, 31. On the printing and distribution of this handbill, see Major-General O'Connor to Governor Eyre, 16 October 1865, PP *Jamaica Disturbances*, dispatch 1, enc. 55, 33, and Provost Marshal [George D. Ramsey] to Captain Luke, 16 October 1865, PP *Jamaica Disturbances*, dispatch 1, enc. 58, 35.

34 Confidential print no. 2, October 1865, printed for the use of the Cabinet, Papers Relating to the Insurrection in Jamaica, PRO, CO 884/2, 23, quoted in Heuman 1994: 91.

35 Resolutions from the Public Meeting at Saint Ann's Bay, 29 July 1865, printed in *Jamaica Watchman and People's Free Press*, 28 August 1865. Garvey's presence at the July meeting is first noted in Sheller 2000: 238–39.

5. SWORD-BEARING CITIZENS

1 Régis Antoine (1978) demonstrates the feminization of the Antilles in French literature, as does J. Michael Dash (1997: 1) for Haiti, citing, for example, the work of Gustave d'Eichtal, who wrote in 1839 that "the black race seems to be the woman-race [la race femme] in the human family, as the white is the male race."

2 On black masculinity in relation to African American labor history, see Roediger 1991; Trotter 1990. For the Caribbean, the best starting point remains James 1963.

3 Parallels can also be seen in certain strands of the contemporary "manhood" movement and concerns with the "crisis of the black male" in America (cf. Connell 1995). On the making of Caribbean masculinities, see Edmondson 1999; Lewis 2003; Reddock 2004.

4 Latino/a studies has fueled a growing academic interest in analyzing machismo in contemporary Latin American culture, which is beyond the scope of, but related to, this study.

5 Otherwise exemplary works of Haitian political historiography that largely ignore gender include Dupuy 1989; Nicholls 1996; Plummer 1992; Trouillot 1990.

6 It is known that "the earliest archives in Haiti were destroyed in the time of President Boyer. Others were probably lost when the National Palace was blown up on December 18, 1869. It is believed that all of the existing government archives were destroyed by fire during the disturbance of September 22 and 23, 1883" (Logan 1941: 459).

7   I deliberately omit Haitian literature and poetry, since the kind of detailed analysis required of novels, poems, and plays would be beyond the scope of this work. For a partial bibliography of nineteenth-century literary sources, consult Nicholls 1996. A feminist interpretation of the "silencing" of Haitian women writers is in Chancy 1997.

8   On Haiti's isolation, see Logan 1941; Plummer 1992; Sheller 1999.

9   Constitution impériale d'Haïti, 20 May 1805, an II [Year 2 of Independence], art. 14, in Linstant 1851: 49; my translation.

10 The Phrygian bonnet, "traditionally worn by emancipated slaves in classical Rome," was adopted by French Jacobins as a symbol of the revolution (Burton 1993: 71). It had double significance in Haiti, where it meant both liberty for the republic and liberty for the slave.

11 A *vévé* is a ritual design, drawn in cornmeal, with a distinctive pattern that is associated with each *lwa*.

12 On the significance of Ogou, see Desmangles 1992; Hurbon 1995: 67, 74–75; Laguerre 1989; Nicholls 1996: 31–32. That many "possession performances" of Ogou involve the *lwa* mounting a woman (R. Burton 1997: 251) complicates any straightforward interpretation of this sword-bearing masculinity, a point to which I return later.

13 Much the same theme is articulated, although in different terms, in Trouillot 1990. See also Kelley 1996: 24–25, 229–33; J. C. Scott 1985. Richard Burton (1997: 254) also notes: "Vodou combines a theoretical egalitarianism . . . with an indelible propensity toward hierarchy, inequality, and authoritarianism in practice. Its pantheon of spirits . . . is structured along quasi-military lines."

14 As Jacqueline Jones (1985: 62, 66) points out of the postbellum United States, "Within the limited public arena open to blacks, the husband represented the entire family. . . . The political process, tainted though it was by virulent racial prejudice and violence, provided black men with a public forum distinct from the private sphere inhabited by their women folk."

15 "Hayti" is the name that was given to the French colony of Saint-Domingue after 1804; from 1807 to 1820, it was divided into a northern kingdom and a southern republic; from 1822 to 1844, it was united with the rest of Hispaniola (subsequently the Dominican Republic).

16 Quoted in *Pièces rélatives aux communications faites au nom du gouvernement français* 1816; my translation.

17 Quoted in *Royal Gazette of Haiti*, 4 January 1816, in Sanders 1816: 209.

18 Act 1, art. 1 of the Supreme Authority, in Sanders 1816: 128 (my translation; emphasis added).

19 "Narrative of the Accession of Their Royal Majesties to the Throne of Hayti" in Sanders 1816: 112.

20 Code Henri, Title 1, chaps. 1–2, arts. 19, 23, in Sanders 1816: vii, passim.

21 Mackenzie to Canning, 9 September 1827, *Communications Received at the Foreign Office Relative to Hayti*, no. 3, AN, CC9a.54.

22 Gustave d'Alaux (the pen name of French Consul-General Maxime Reybaud) cites several sources from the period to suggest that there were 25,000 men in the army

in a population of about half a million in the 1830s (or 700,000, including the Dominicans), three-fifths of which were thought to be women (d'Alaux 1851: 195). The unnamed writer "C. M. B.," who may be the writer Mark Bird, also refers to "65,000 soldiers, out of less than a million of people [in 1843]" (C. M. B. 1850: 117).

23 On poor soldiers and national guardsman, see Schoelcher 1843, 278; Report of 1825 CCC, AMAE, Les Cayes, 1825–31; Laguerre, 1993: 44–45.

24 Autobiography of James Hartwell (1840), Special Series, Biographical, West Indies box 588, WMMS, 40, 133.

25 "Des Sociétés Maçonniques en Haïti," *Le Républicain*, no. 9, 15 December 1836; my translation.

26 *Morning Journal*, 10 June 1842.

27 Ibid., 12–19 October 1842, 1; my translation.

28 *L'Eclaireur Haytien ou le parfait patriot*, no. 5, 3 September 1818, and no. 9, 8 November 1818; my translation.

29 *Le Manifeste*, vol. 1, no. 1, 4 April 1841, 1, signed E***H [probably Emile Hertelou]; my translation.

30 *Le Temps*, no. 1, 10 February 1842, quoted in Desquiron 1993: 1:191–92; my translation.

31 *Le Patriote*, [vol. 1], no. 1, 2 March 1842, in Desquiron 1993: 1:199; my translation. Emile Hertelou also responded to *Le Temps* and similarly defended the maturity of the Haitian people in *Le Manifeste*, no. 49, 6 March 1842, and no. 50, 13 March 1842. A year earlier, *Le Manifeste* also printed lengthy debates on the readiness of Haiti for a participatory democratic government (no. 1, 4 April 1841; no. 2, 11 April 1841; no. 26, 26 September 1841).

32 Charles Mackenzie to Canning, 6 September 1826, General Correspondence, PRO, FO 35/3.

33 Papiers du Admiral Charles Baudin; my translation.

6. "YOU SIGNED MY NAME, BUT NOT MY FEET"

1 This chapter draws in part from Sheller 2000.

2 Mintz calls "reconstituted peasantries" the slaves, indentees, maroons, and other runaways who became peasants "directly as a mode of resistance and response to the plantation system and its imposed patterns of life"; thus, their very existence attests to both agency and autonomy (Mintz quoted in Watts 1990: 506).

3 Haitian historiography commonly employs the terminology of *noir* versus *mulâtre*, or black versus mulatto, to describe the groups who were contending for power in the nineteenth century. I will also use these terms, but with the caveat that I understand these groupings as instances of "racial formation" in which particular forms of distinction (based not only on phenotype, but also on ancestry, class, status, language, literacy, and other markers) were used to draw *salient political boundaries* (cf. Omi and Winant 1994; Sheller 1999).

4 Though independent, Haiti was still highly vulnerable to the economic influence and military threats of France, Britain, the United States, and Spain. The French persisted in plans to recapture their former colony from the end of the Napoleonic

wars onward. Records from the Ministère de la Marine et des Colonies contain plans to reconquer "Saint Domingue" by force in 1814, 1817, 1819, and 1822, in addition to more explicit attempts to negotiate French sovereignty with President Pétion in 1816 and President Boyer in 1823. This culminated in the indemnification agreements of 1825 and 1838. Documents on these efforts appear in AN CC9a.47 and AN CC9a.50–52. Although France finally recognized Haitian independence in 1838, followed shortly thereafter by Britain, it still backed Dominican independence in 1844 and secretly negotiated for exclusive use of the port of Samana. The United States did not recognize Haiti until 1863, following Abraham Lincoln's Emancipation Proclamation.

5 One carreaux equals 1.29 hectares, or 3.33 U.S. acres.

6 Figures are from Knight 1990: 370; Trouillot 1993: 124; Consul-General Charles Mackenzie to the Earl of Dudley, 31 March 1828, *Communications Received at the Foreign Office Relative to Hayti*, no. 18, General Table of Exports from Hayti, 1789, 1801, 1818–26, AN, Séries CC9a.54 Saint-Domingue.

7 Wilmot Horton to Mr. Canning, 14 October 1826, enclosing memorandum of information from James Franklin, PRO, FO 35/1.

8 Charles Mackenzie to Earl of Dudley (31 March 1828).

9 Code Rural d'Haiti, 1826, AN, Séries CC9a.54 Saint-Domingue, art. 30.

10 "Loi concernant la police des habitations, les obligations réciproques des propriétaires et fermiers, et des cultivateurs," 20 April 1807, Year 4, art. 2, in Linstant 1851: 307–15.

11 On exports in this period, see Ardouin 1860: 9:53–64; Bonneau 1862: 38; Nicholls, 1996: 69.

12 Memorandum from James Franklin, enclosed in Horton to Canning, 14 October 1826, PRO, FO 35/1.

13 Article 185 of the Rural Code ensured that pregnant women could only be employed in light tasks and after the fourth month were not to work in the fields; women were to return to field labor four months after the birth of a baby, according to Article 186, but were given an extra hour off at the beginning and end of each day: Code Rural d'Haïti.

14 Mackenzie to Canning, 30 November 1826, *Communications Received at the Foreign office Relative to Hayti*, no. 1017 February 1829, AN, Séries CC9a.54 Saint-Domingue. See also Brown 1972 (1837): 281.

15 Code Rural d'Haïti; my translation.

16 See, e.g., discussion of European gender ideologies in Davidoff and Hall 1987; C. Hall 1992.

17 Mintz 1993, quoting J. B., "Notes of a Tour in Haiti," *Evening Post*, 53, 19 May 1854.

18 Mackenzie to Canning (30 November 1826).

19 On foreign creditors and women's indebtedness, see ibid.; Ussher to Foreign Office, 14 January 1843, PRO, FO 35/26; Mintz 1993.

20 *Le Patriote*, no. 49, 20 April 1843.

21 Letter of 29 March 1843, AN, Papiers du Admiral Charles Baudin.

22 Ussher to Lord Aberdeen, 2 May 1844, enclosing "Ordre du Jour" of J. Acaau, 23 April 1844, PRO, FO 35/28.

23 Ibid. Acaau's peasant dress also suggests the figure of the Vodou lwa related to agricultural work, Cousin Azaka, who appears as a peasant, in a straw hat, and protects the interests of the rural laborer (Hurbon 1995: 79, 99).

24 Bauduy to Secretaries, 24 May 1844, wmms, West Indies Correspondence, Haiti.

7. ARBOREAL LANDSCAPES

1 To pick up on the phallic sticks with which chapter 5 opened, and the playful orality of Carolyn Cooper's vernacular theory, one could write at length on the popular meanings of the terms "wood" and "bamboo" as innuendos for men's sexual prowess in common parlance and song throughout the Caribbean. Linden Lewis (2003) has explored some of these expressions of masculinity that are linked to symbolic resources concerned with reproduction, family, and subaltern cultural vitality more generally.

2 Even within Britain there is a longstanding divergence between "woodland" and "champion" landscapes, with the large open-field systems of the champion regions still characterized by "nucleated villages, with the houses closely clustering around the church or village green. In contrast, the settlement pattern of woodland regions still contains many isolated houses, and hamlets scattered amidst the [smaller] fields" (Williamson and Bellamy 1987: 13). These differing landscapes reflected intense social struggles over the control and enclosure of land.

3 George Lamming, *The Sovereignty of the Imagination* (Kingston: Arawak, 2004), 9, quoted in Trotz 2007: 74.

4 See Esther Figueroa, dir., *Jamaica for Sale* (film, Vagabond Media and Jamaica Environment Trust, 2009).

5 Madison Smartt Bell, "Mine of Stones: With and without the Spirits along the Cordon de l'Ouest," *Harper's Magazine*, January 2004, 56; Dan Merrefield, "The Tree," *Haiti Cheri*, no. 25, 1 September 2003, 1, available online at http://www .haiticheri.org (accessed 22 November 2004).

6 J. David Harden, "Liberty Caps and Liberty Trees," *Past and Present*, February 1995, available online at http://www.findarticles.com/p/articles/mi_m2279/ is_n146/ai_17249824/print (accessed 24 November 2004).

7 Jean-Bertrand Aristide, "Aristide Statement," 6 March 2004, available online at http://www.zmag.org/content (accessed 24 November 2004).

8 Woolridge to Directors, 2 August 1839, lms, box 2.

9 W. G. Barret to Directors, Four Paths, 15 August 1839, lms, box 2.

10 As also noted in Augusto 2009. See, e.g., Carney 2001; Carney and Voeks 2003; G. Hall 1992; McKittrick 2006; Warner-Lewis 2003.

11 It would also be very rewarding to use Caribbean landscape representation to interrogate and reexamine European or North American visual representations of the Caribbean. Haitian landscape painting of the twentieth century, for example, is replete with the "dream landscapes" of a proto-peasant world, depicted as terrestrial paradise, especially those by the Jacmel school. Trees also appear in religious allegorical painting such as those that once adorned the Holy Trinity Epis-

copalian Church, which collapsed in the earthquake, as well as many Vodou *hounforts* in Haiti (see Nadel-Gardere and Bloncourt 1986).

8. RETURNING THE TOURIST GAZE

The epigraph was translated from Haitian Creole by Jack Hirschman, in *Mute*, no. 23, 1999, 46.

1 On intra-Caribbean migrations, see Puri 2003.

2 See Nancy Leys Stepan's discussion of Louis Agassiz's use of photography in the 1860s to explore "the tropical body" in Brazil. She argues that the photograph was "a very powerful cultural representation in an era of scientific racism; [but] it was easy to forget that the anthropological outlook itself was a specific world-view, shaped by time and place and in turn shaping representations, and that many scientists recognized that the photograph itself was an unreliable document of the world" (Stepan 2001: 117–19). There is, of course, a close relation between the ethnological gaze, the ethnographic gaze, and the tourist gaze, and just as nineteenth-century photographs of "racial types" make us uncomfortable today, so does the gaze represented in the travel writing analyzed here.

3 These discourses echo earlier comments by Charles Kingsley in his popular travelogue/novel *At Last: A Christmas in the West Indies* (1873). For a good analysis of his work, see Wahab 2004. See also Edmondson 2003; Gikandi 1996.

4 I have analyzed this book more fully elsewhere (Sheller 2003). See also Gikandi 1996.

5 Greg Allen, "Haiti's Arts City Loses Much but Retains Vision," National Public Radio broadcast, 23 January 2010, available online at http://www.npr.org/templates/story/story.php?storyId=122877605 (accessed 17 January 2011). In the earthquake, Fosaj sadly lost its director, Flo McGarrell, a 36-year old from Vermont who had come to love Haitian culture. He was "born female," according to his mother, "but started transgender therapy and lived as a man."

6 Although negotiating quite different sets of embodied relations, I also found my body being read for the ways in which it disrupted local categories of distinction in Kingston while I carried out dissertation research there in 1994. I was clearly foreign since I was walking and riding the buses without the requisite "tuffness" that Gina Ulysse (2008) identifies as protective armor for women in public spaces. But I was also not deploying my body in ways that would map easily onto local systems of class and color differentiation. Thus, the commentaries of men hanging out on street corners revolved around where I was from and what color I was—my suntanned color fell slightly outside the range of whiteness (being called out sometimes as "brown girl" or "Coolie"), while my transgression of spatial boundaries and dress sense placed me as a class-privileged outsider. One street-corner debate finally resolved that I must be a "brown whitey," an interesting assessment of what has been described as a kind of "whiteness of a different color" (Jacobsen 1998).

7 See Ulysse's website at http://www.ginaathenaulysse.com/index_2.html (accessed 17 January 2011).

9. EROTIC AGENCY

1 According to Amnesty International's website (accessed 17 October 2011), sex between men is criminalized in all but two English-speaking Caribbean countries (the Bahamas and Turks and Caicos). Article 76 of the Jamaican Offences against the Person Act, for example, punishes the "abominable crime of buggery" with up to ten years' imprisonment with hard labor, while Article 79 of the same act punishes any act of physical intimacy between men in public or private with a term of imprisonment of up to two years and the possibility of hard labor. As for women who have sex with women, "Jamaican and Guyanese laws are silent on lesbianism, whilst in Trinidad and Tobago, Barbados and Saint Lucia, all acts of homosexuality are illegal." Such laws have led to a climate in which violence against gay men and lesbians has been tolerated, and in some cases perpetrated by the police. Homophobia and anti-gay attitudes are promoted both by the Christian churches and within popular culture, leading to an extensive transnational debate about Jamaican homophobia and the role of reggae dancehall artists in inciting anti-gay violence.

2 In addition to Jacqui Alexander's extensive body of work, which is cited elsewhere in this volume, see Glave 2000, 2005, 2008. See also Allen 2011; Francis 2010; Gill 2010; Silvera 1991; Smith 2011; Tinsley 2010; Wekker 1997, 2000, 2006.

3 I draw here on Bell and Binnie 2000; Bell and Valentine 1995; Binnie 2004; Grosz 1995; Probyn 1993; Puar 2002.

4 An argument made by Fraser 1992; Landes 1988; M. Ryan 1997; Warner 1993.

5 As has occurred in debates surrounding subaltern studies—namely, in some critiques of Gayatri Spivak—the relation between academics located "at home" (in India, say) and those located "in the diaspora" (in New York, London, or Toronto) is also at issue in the Caribbean. My own positioning outside the region also matters, of course, and in many ways affects the reception and reading of this work.

6 This kind of transnational approach to "cultural erotics" also draws on a significant body of work within Cuban history and literary criticism, which has focused on the erotics of Cuban nationalism (Behar 2000; Kutzinski 1993) and the cultural and political erotics of the Cuban diaspora (Ortiz 2007) and of black "self-making" (Allen 2011).

7 Stepan (2001: 112) points out the specific connection between black sexuality and reproduction of the social order: "Woman was by convention the reproductive sex, and thus was considered the key to the biological reproduction of the race and the nation. She was critical, that is, to the maintenance of the boundaries between races, by engaging or not engaging in sexual activity; equally, she was critical to transgressions of these boundaries through her ungoverned sexuality. Since the tropics were perceived as a place where the constraints of civilization were loosened, and the heat of the climate created an unbridled sensuality, 'tropical woman' was the sign of sexual excess and of the fatal disorganization that so threatened . . . racial order."

8 Beyond the Caribbean, literature, gender, race, sexuality, and questions of national

embodiment have been crucial to ongoing work in colonial history and postcolonial studies. It is clear that white colonial discourses connected Black sexuality with hypersexuality, deviance, and transgression. Sander Gilman's work on Saartje Baartman, the so-called Hottentot Venus, has been picked up on by many subsequent analysts to illustrate how primitive sexuality was located in African women's bodies in ways that have gone on to inform not only racist stereotypes but also Black popular culture (Gilman 1985).

9 Kamala Kempadoo (2004: 42) defines transactional sex as "sexual-economic relationships and exchanges where gifts are given in exchange for sex, multiple partnerships may be maintained, and an up-front monetary transaction does not necessarily take place." This is characteristic of certain forms of sexual exchange associated with tourism in the Caribbean (see Brennan 2004; Kempadoo 1999; Sanchez-Taylor 1999), but it also can be understood as deeply informing histories of sexual transactions in slavery and post-slavery societies, which involved many kinds of non-monetary exchanges for sex. It is important to recognize, however, that such relationships are not peculiar to the Caribbean or even to localities where sex work is common; they are just one form of a more general pattern of "the purchase of intimacy," including marriage, the sex trade, and the caring professions (Zelizer 2005).

10 This history is highly relevant to the biopolitics of reproduction today, in the sense of both sexual procreation and domestic labor. The ongoing nexus between international promotion of birth control and eugenics, on the one hand, and interracial transnational domestic service work, on the other, constitutes a crucial overlapping field in which black sexuality and citizenship continue to be pathologized while white sexuality and citizenship are protected.

11 Norplant is a form of contraception based on the insertion of silicone rods under the skin of the arm that slowly release a hormonal contraceptive for a period of five years. It is associated with a wide range of side effects and risks, including prolonged and heavy menstrual bleeding, and is the subject of major class-action lawsuits in the United States.

12 Interview with Rose-Anne Auguste, Coordinator of Klinik Sante Fenm Kafour Fey (Carrefoure Feuilles, Port-au-Prince), from my personal notes from Haiti Support Group Study Tour, 19–26 June 1996. Excerpts are also published in Arthur and Dash 1999: 133.

13 Another contested form of controlling black women's sexuality, fertility, and family formation is through incarceration in prison. A transnational movement of activists and prisoners analyzes the recent mushrooming of women's imprisonment in a number of countries as an outcome of the "prison-industrial complex" (Davis 1998b; Sudbury 2005). According to these analyses, there is "*a symbiotic and profitable relationship between politicians, corporations, the media and state correctional institutions that generates the racialized use of incarceration as a response to social problems rooted in the globalization of capital*" (Sudbury 2002: 61).

14 According to Gender Action, *The Haiti Gender Shadow Report*, 2010, available online at http://www.genderaction.org/publications/2010/gsr.pdf (accessed 15 February 2011), the crime of rape was integrated into the Penal Code of Haiti only in

2005, due to the efforts of the late Magalie Marcelin, a Haitian women's rights lawyer who perished in the earthquake. "Pre-earthquake Haiti already faced a high rate of domestic abuse towards women and girls," the report states. "In addition, 46% of all Haitian girls between the ages of 5 and 17 faced sexual abuse." See also Mark Schuller, *Unstable Foundations: Impact of NGOS on Human Rights for Port-au-Prince's Internally Displaced People*, 4 October, 2010, available online at http://ijdh.org/archives/14855 (accessed 27 January 2011).

15 Alan Lomax, *Haitian Diary: Papers and Correspondence from Alan Lomax's Haitian Journey, 1936–37*, comp. and ed. Ellen Harold, Estate of Alan Lomax under exclusive license to Harte Recordings, 2009, included in the *Recordings for the Library of Congress* box set.

16 Patterson's work was recently exhibited at the National Gallery of Jamaica but also appeared in the Ghetto Biennale in La Rue Grande, Haiti, in December 2009, in a show that was positioned "as a counter exhibition, disrupting conventional art scene exclusions, as well as a bold conversion of global power systems, centers of art production, and cultural transmission." She presented an installation of "flags" that brought her provocative "Gangstas for Life" iconography into dialogue with the spiritual splendor of the traditional Haitian Vodou flags or "drapos": see National Gallery of Jamaica blog, available online at http://nationalgalleryofjamaica.wordpress.com/2010/01/06/ebony-g-patterson/#more-414 (accessed 27 January 2011).

17 Ibid.

18 One might also compare the emergence of a genre known as Sissy Bounce in New Orleans as another branch of queer diasporic performance and sexual interrogation: see the Internet blog at http://blog.seanbonner.com/2010/03/29/sissy-bounce (accessed 27 January 2011).

19 Clearly, there is a continual effort by the music, film, and tourism industries to reprocess and repackage subaltern performances of sexual and racial difference for foreign consumption. All analyses of popular music as a form of resistance must negotiate the traps of commodification, sexualization, and privatization that beset the contemporary mass public (Warner 1993). Nevertheless, the approaches of Cooper, Davis, Kelley, Noble, and others suggest that a counter-public discourse of erotic autonomy and sexual agency might just subvert the "capture of sexualities."

20 See Agostinho Pinnock's interview with Afua Hall on "Spotlight Video: About Afreeka," available online at http://www.youtube.com/watch?v=I9iBztgrUqY (accessed 22 June 2009).

21 See also the critical discussion of Cooper's book *Sound Clash* (2004) in *Small Axe* 10, no. 3 (October 2006).

22 See the entry dated 11 June 2009 on the Internet blog http://rawpoliticsjamaicastyle.wordpress.com (accessed 22 June 2009), in which Pinnock describes the international media's new interest in this dance form and questions the voyeuristic "curiosity" about Jamaican popular culture.

23 Carolyn Cooper, "Lady Saw Cuts Loose: Female Fertility Rituals in the Dancehall," in Cooper 2004: 103.

24 In a rather different vein, Diane Austin-Broos describes Pentecostal experience in

contemporary Jamaica as an embodied rite. She writes about the "in-filling" of the body by the spirit and the forms of undulation and movement of those possessed by the spirit as a kind of erotically embodied experience: "Given the central place that dancing has as a mode of *jouissance* in Jamaican culture and given that Pentecostals cannot engage in any form of temporal dancing, these expressions of Holy Ghost possession, along with testimony and chorus singing, are the ones most instrumental in creating a eudemonic in the church" (Austin-Broos 1997: 144). This is in contrast to the "ethical rationalism" of European missions in which the "disciplines of the body not only repudiated the world of play and its carnival-esque aesthetic, [but] also sought to stifle in Jamaica an intense eudemonic of freedom which both transformed and re-embodied an African sense of joy in the world" (Austin-Broos 1997: 42). This raises the loaded question that I cannot fully explore here of whether the forms of embodied power within Pentecostalism are also expressive of a kind of erotic agency (which may be precisely why others such as Seventh Day Adventists disavow all dance).

25 These are all observations made during my stay in the summer of 2010 at Mon P'tit Village, a school in Léogâne run by the Neges Foundation, under the direction of Marie Yoleine Gateau-Esposito and James Philemy, whom I thank for their great hospitality.

MANUSCRIPT SOURCES AND ARCHIVES

England

Baptist Missionary Society Archives (BMS), Angus Library, Regents College, Oxford
WI/5 Jamaica Correspondence
Extracts from Letters Written by BMS Missionaries, bound vol., 1840–46

Public Record Office (PRO), London
Colonial Office (CO) 137, Original Correspondence of Jamaican Governors
Colonial Office (CO) 142/1
Colonial Office (CO) 884/2 Confidential Print, no. 2: Papers Relating to the Insurrection in Jamaica, October, 1865. Printed for the Use of the Cabinet, December 1865.
PRO 30/48/42 Edward Cardwell Papers: August–December 1865. Correspondence with Governor Eyre.
PRO 30/48/44 Edward Cardwell Papers: 1865–66. Extracts from Colonial Office Confidential Prints, Proceedings of the Jamaica Royal Commission of Enquiry, press cuttings, draft manuscript reports.
Foreign Office (FO) 35/1–35/29, General Correspondence, Haiti, 1825–44
Report of the Jamaica Royal Commission [JRC], parts 1–2 (London: G. E. Eyre and William Spottiswoode, 1866)

School of Oriental and African Studies, University of London
Wesleyan Methodist Missionary Society Archives (WMMS)
  West Indies Correspondence, Haiti, 1834–57
  West Indies Correspondence, Jamaica, 1838–65, boxes 195–99
Council of World Missions, London Missionary Society Archives (LMS)
  1837–69, boxes 2–9

France

Archives du Ministère des Affaires Étrangères (AMAE), Paris
Corréspondence Consulaire et Commerçial (CCC)
    Le Cap Haitien, 1825–56, 2 vols.
    Les Cayes, 1825–31, 1 vol.
    Port-au-Prince, 1825–1901, 13 vols.
Corréspondence Politique (CP), Haiti, 1838–44, vols. 8–12

Archives Nationales (AN), Paris
Colonies, Archives Ministerielles Anciennes
    Séries CC9a.47
    Séries CC9a.50–52
    Séries CC9a.54 Saint-Domingue
Papiers du Admiral Charles Baudin, Mission d'Haïti, 1837–38, Archives du Ministère des Marines, GG II.1

Jamaica

Jamaica Archives, Spanish Town
    General Slave Court
National Library of Jamaica (NLJ), Kingston

United States

Princeton University Library, Princeton, N.J.
    Alexander Dudgeon Gulland, photographic album of Jamaica, 1865, Graphic Arts Collection, Department of Rare Books and Special Collections

NEWSPAPERS

Baptist Herald and Friend of Africa (Kingston)
Colonial Standard (Kingston)
County Union, 1864–65 (Montego Bay)
L'Éclaireur Haytien ou le parfait patriote, 1818–19 (Port-au-Prince)
Evening Post (London)
Falmouth Post (Falmouth, Jamaica)
Gleaner (Kingston)
Jamaica Watchman and People's Free Press, 1865 (Kingston)
Le Manifeste, 1841–44 (Port-au-Prince)
Morning Journal, 1838–(Kingston)
Le Patriote (Port-au-Prince)
Le Républicain, récueil scientifique et littéraire, 1837 (Port-au-Prince)
Le Temps (Port-au-Prince)
Watchman and Jamaica Free Press, 1829–31 (Kingston)

PUBLISHED PRIMARY SOURCES

Addresses to His Excellency, Edward John Eyre, Esquire. 1866. [Kingston]: M. DeCordova.

d'Alaux, Gustave [Maxime Reybaud]. 1851. "La République dominicaine et l'empereur Soulouque." *Revue des deux mondes* 10, 193–210.

Ardouin, Beaubrun. 1860. *Études sur l'histoire d'Haïti,* 11 vols. Paris: Dezobry, Madeleien.

Auguste, Jules, Clément Denis, Arthur Bowler, Justin Dévost, Louis Joseph Janvier. 1882. *Les détracteurs de la race noir et de la république d'Haïti. Réponses à M. Léo Quesnel,* 2d ed. Paris: Marpon et Flammarion.

Banbury, Rev. T. 1895. *Jamaica Superstitions; or, the Obeah Book: A Complete Treatise on the Absurdities Believed in by the People of the Island.* Kingston: Mortimer De Souza.

Belisario, Isaac Mendes. 1837–38. *Sketches of Character, in Illustration of the Habits, Occupation, and Costume of the Negro Population in the Island of Jamaica.* Kingston: by the artist, 21 King Street.

Bird, Mark B. 1869. *The Black Man; or, Haytian Independence.* New York: n.p.

Bonneau, Alexandre. 1862. *Haïti: Ses progres, son avenir.* Paris: E. Dentu.

Brassey, Sady. 1885. *In the Trades, the Tropics, and the Roaring Forties.* London: Longman's, Green.

Brown, Jonathan. 1972 (1837). *The History and Present Condition of St. Domingue,* 2. vols., repr. ed. London: Frank Cass.

Bukeley, Owen T. 1899. *The Lesser Antilles: A Guide for Settlers in the British West Indies, and Tourists' Companion.* London: Sampson Low, Marston, Searle, and Rivington.

Charlevoix, Father Pierre-Francois-Xavier de. 1766. *A Voyage to North America; Undertaken by Command of the Present King of France, Containing . . . a Description and Natural History of the Islands of the West Indies Belonging to the Different Powers of Europe,* 2 vols. Dublin: John Exshaw and James Potts.

C. M. B. 1850. *A Glimpse of Haiti, and Her Negro Chief.* Liverpool: Edward Howell; London: Arthur Hall, Virtue & Company.

Davis, N. Darnell. 1888. *Mr. Froude's Negrophobia; or, Don Quixote as a Cook's Tourist.* Demerara: Argosy.

Day, Charles William. 1852. *Five Years' Residence in the West Indies.* 2 vols. London: Colburn and Co.

Day, Susan de Forest. 1899. *The Cruise of the Scythian in the West Indies.* London: F. Tennyson Neely.

Duperly, Armand. 1844. *Daguerian Excursions in Jamaica, Being a Collection of Views . . . Taken on the Spot with the Daguerreotype.* Kingston: Duperly.

Edwards, Bryan. 1801. *The History, Civil and Commercial, of the British Colonies in the West Indies.* 2 cols. London: John Stockdale.

Exquemelin, Alexander. 1684 (1678). *The History of the Bucaniers: Being an Impartial Relation of All the Battels, Sieges, and Other Most Eminent Assaults Committed for Several Years upon the Coasts of the West Indies by the Pirates of Jamaica and Tortuga.* London: Thomas Malthus.

Fletcher, Duncan. 1867. *Personal Recollections of the Hon. George W. Gordon, late of Jamaica*. London: Elliot Stock.

Harvey, Thomas, and William Brewin. 1867. *Jamaica in 1866: A Narrative of a Tour through the Island, with Remarks on Its Social, Educational, and Industrial Condition*. London: A. W. Bennett.

Hastings Jay, E. A. 1900. *A Glimpse of the Tropics; or, Four Months Cruising in the West Indies*. London: Sampson Low, Marston.

Hyatt, Pulaski F. (U.S. Consul, Santiago de Cuba), and John T. Hyatt (Vice-Consul). 1898. *Cuba: Its Resources and Opportunities*. New York: J. S. Ogilvie.

Jamaica Committee. 1866. *Facts and Documents Relating to the Alleged Rebellion in Jamaica, and the Measures of Repression, Including Notes of the Trial of Mr. Gordon*. Jamaica Papers no. 1. London: Jamaica Committee.

Janvier, Louis Joseph. 1886. *Les Consitutions d'Haïti, 1801–1885*. Paris: C. Marpon et E. Flammarion.

Kingsley, Charles. 1873. *At Last: A Christmas in the West Indies*, new ed. London: Macmillan.

Lepelletier de Saint-Remy, Romuald. 1846. *Saint-Domingue: Étude et solution nouvelle de la question haïtienne*. Paris: A. Bertrand.

Lewis, Matthew G. [Monk]. 1834. *Journal of a West-India Proprietor, Kept during a Residence in the Island of Jamaica*. London: John Murray.

Linstant, Baron S. 1851. *Réceuil général des lois et actes du gouvernement d'Haïti*, vol. 1. Paris: Auguste Durand.

Macmillan, Allister. 1909. *The West Indies Illustrated: Historical and Descriptive, Commercial and Industrial, Facts, Figures and Resources*. London: W. H. and L. Collingridge.

Madden, Richard. 1970 (1835). *A Twelvemonth's Residence in the West Indies, during the Transition from Slavery to Apprenticeship; with Incidental Notices of the State of Society, Prospects, and Natural Resources of Jamaica and Other Islands*, vol. 1, repr. ed. Westport, Conn.: Negro Universities Press.

Madiou, Thomas. 1985–91 (1847–48). *Histoire d'Haïti*, 8 vols., ed. Michèle Oriol, repr. ed. Port-au-Prince: Editions Henri Deschamps.

Niles, Blair. 1926. *Black Haiti: A Biography of Africa's Eldest Daughter*. New York: G. P. Putnam's Sons.

Papers Relating to the Disturbances in Jamaica and Further Papers Relative to the Disturbances in Jamaica. 1866. Parts 1–3. London: Harrison & Sons.

Paton, Edward Agnew. 1888. *Down the Islands: A Voyage in the Caribbees*. London: Kegan Paul, Trench.

Pièces rélatives aux communications faites au nom du gouvernement français, au Président d'Hayti par M. le Général Dauxion Lavaysse, deputé de S.M. Louis XVIII, Roi de France et de Navarre, enclosing "Procès Verbal des Séances du Conseil Général de la Nation, Cap-Henry, 1814." 1816. New York: Imprimerie Joseph Desnives.

Price, George. 1866. *Jamaica and the Colonial Office: Who Caused the Crisis?* London: Sampson Low, Son, and Marston.

Redpath, James, ed. 1970 (1861). *A Guide to Hayti*, repr. ed. Westport, Conn.: Negro Universities Press.

Report by the Central Board of Health of Jamaica. 1852. Printed by order of the House of Assembly. Spanish Town: F. M. Wilson.

Sanders, Prince, ed. 1916. *Haytian Papers. A collection of the very interesting proclamations and other official documents; together with some account of the rise, progress and present state of the kingdom of Hayti.* London: W. Reed.

Schoelcher, Victor. 1843. *Colonies étrangères et Haïti: Résultats de l'émancipation anglaise.* Paris: Pagnerre.

Stoddard, Charles Augustus. 1895. *Cruising among the Caribbees: Summer Days in Winter Months.* London: Kegan Paul, Trench, and Trubner.

Sturge, Joseph, and Thomas Harvey. 1838. *The West Indies in 1837.* London: Hamilton, Adams.

Van Dyke, John C. 1932. *In the West Indies: Sketches and Studies in Tropic Seas and Islands.* New York: Charles Scribner's Sons.

Waddell, Rev. Hope Masterton. 1970 (1863). *Twenty-Nine Years in the West Indies and Central Africa: A Review of Missionary Work and Adventure, 1829–1858*, repr. ed. London: Frank Cass.

Wilberforce, William. 1823. "An appeal to the religion, justice and humanity of the inhabitants of the British Empire on behalf of the Negro slaves in the West Indies, by William Wilberforce Esq. M.P." London: J. Hatchard and Son.

Williams, James. 1838. *A Narrative of Events since the First of August, 1834, by James Williams, an Apprenticed Labourer in Jamaica*, bound with Lord Brougham's Speech on the Slave Trade in the House of Lords, 29 January 1838. London: J. Rider.

SECONDARY SOURCES

Adams, Julia, Elisabeth Clemens, and Ann Orloff, eds. 2005. *Remaking Modernity: Politics, History, and Sociology.* Durham: Duke University Press.

Agamben, Giorgio. 1998. *Homo Sacer: Sovereign Power and Bare Life.* Stanford: Stanford University Press.

Agulhon, Maurice. 1981. *Marianne into Battle: Republican Imagery and Symbolism in France, 1789–1880.* Cambridge: Cambridge University Press.

Ahmed, Sara. 2000. *Strange Encounters: Embodied Others in Post-Coloniality.* New York: Routledge.

——. 2004. *The Cultural Politics of Emotion.* Edinburgh: Edinburgh University Press.

——. 2006. *Queer Phenomenology: Orientations, Objects, Others.* Durham: Duke University Press.

Aidoo, Agnes A. 1985. "Asante Queen Mothers in Government and Politics in the Nineteenth Century." *The Black Woman Cross-culturally*, ed. Filomina C. Steady, 65–77. Cambridge, Mass.: Schenkman.

Alexander, M. Jacqui. 1991. "Redrafting Morality: The Postcolonial State and the Sexual Offences Bill of Trinidad and Tobago." *Third World Women and the Politics of Feminism*, ed. Chandra Talpade Mohanty, Ann Russo, and Lourdes Torres, 133–52. Bloomington: Indiana University Press.

——. 1994. "'Not Just (Any) Body Can Be a Citizen': The Politics of Law, Sexuality, and Postcoloniality in Trinidad and Tobago and the Bahamas." *Feminist Review* 48, 5–23.

———. 1997. "Erotic Autonomy as a Politics of Decolonization: An Anatomy of Feminist and State Practices in the Bahamas Tourist Economy." *Feminist Genealogies, Colonial Legacies, Democratic Futures*, ed. M. Jacqui Alexander and Chandra Talpade Mohanty, 63–100. New York: Routledge.

———. 2000 (1994). "Not just (any) body can be a citizen: The Politics of Law, Sexuality and Postcoloniality in Trinidad and Tobago and the Bahamas." *Cultures of Empire: A Reader*, ed. Catherine Hall, 260–76. Manchester: Manchester University Press.

———. 2005. *Pedagogies of Crossing: Meditations on Feminism, Sexual Politics, Memory, and the Sacred*. Durham: Duke University Press.

Allen, Jafari. 2011. *¡Venceremos?: The Erotics of Black Self-making in Cuba*. Durham: Duke University Press.

Andrews, George, and Herrick Chapman, eds. 1995. *The Social Construction of Democracy, 1877–1990*. New York: New York University Press.

Anglade, Georges. 1982. *Espace et liberté en Haïti*. Montréal: Groupe d'Études et de Recherches Critiques d'Espace, département de géographie, Université de Québec À Montréal, and Centre de recherches Caraïbes de l'Université de Montréal.

Anim-Addo, Anyaa. 2011. "Place and Mobilities in the Maritime World: The Royal Mail Steam Packet Company in the Caribbean, c. 1838 to 1914." Ph.D. diss., Royal Holloway, University of London.

Anthias, Floya, and Nira Yuval-Davis. 1992. *Racialized Boundaries: Race, Nation, Gender, Colour, Class, and the Anti-Racist Struggle*. London: Routledge.

Antoine, Régis. 1978. *Les écrivains français et les Antilles: Des premiers pères blancs aux surréalists noirs*. Paris: G. P. Maisonneuve et Larose.

Aparicio, Frances R., and Susana Chavez-Silverman, eds. 1997. *Tropicalizations: Transcultural Representations of Latinidad*. Hanover, N.H.: Dartmouth University Press.

Arnold, David, and Ramachandra Guha. 1995. "Introduction: Themes and Issues in the Environmental History of South Asia." *Nature, Culture, Imperialism: Essays on the Environmental History of South Asia*, ed. David Arnold and Ramachandra Guha, 1–20. Delhi: Oxford University Press.

Arthur, Charles, and Michael Dash, eds. 1999. *Libète: A Haiti Anthology*. London: Latin America Bureau.

Ashcroft, Bill, Gareth Griffiths, and Helen Tiffin, eds. 2002. *The Empire Writes Back: Theory and Practice in Post-Colonial Literatures*, 2d rev. ed. London: Routledge.

Augusto, Geri. 2009. "'A World Only Partly Named': Knowledge of Plants for Therapeutic Interventions in the Early Cape Colony among the Free and Unfree." *Freedom: Retrospective and Prospective*, ed. Swithin Wilmot, xxxvi–lxxiv. Kingston: Ian Randle.

Austin, Diane J. 1984. *Urban Life in Kingston, Jamaica: The Culture and Class Ideology of Two Neighborhoods*. New York: Gordon and Breach.

Austin-Broos, Diane J. 1997. *Jamaica Genesis: Religion and the Politics of Moral Orders*. Chicago: University of Chicago Press.

Averill, Gage. 1997. *A Day for the Hunter, a Day for the Prey: Popular Music and Power in Haiti*. Chicago: University of Chicago Press.

Bakan, Abigail. 1990. *Ideology and Class Conflict in Jamaica: The Politics of Rebellion*. Montreal: McGill-Queen's University Press.

Bakhtin, Mikhail. 1984. *Rabelais and His World*, trans. Helene Iswolsky. Bloomington: Indiana University Press.

Balderston, Daniel, and Donna Guy, eds. 1997. *Sex and Sexuality in Latin America*. New York: New York University Press.

Ballantyne, Tony, and Antoinette Burton, eds. 2005. *Bodies in Contact: Rethinking Colonial Encounters in World History*. Durham: Duke University Press.

Bardaglio, Peter W. 1995. *Reconstructing the Household: Families, Sex, and the Law in the Nineteenth-Century South*. Chapel Hill: University of North Carolina Press.

Barnes, Natasha. 2000. "Body Talk: Notes on Women and Spectacle in Contemporary Trinidad Carnival." *Small Axe* 7, 93–105.

Barrett, Leonard. 1976. *The Sun and the Drum: African Roots in Jamaican Folk Tradition*. Kingston: Sangster's.

Barrow, Christine. 1998a. "Caribbean Masculinity and Family: Revisiting 'Marginality' and 'Reputation.'" *Caribbean Portraits: Essays on Gender Ideologies and Identities*, ed. Christine Barrow, 339–58. Kingston: Ian Randle.

———, ed. 1998b. *Caribbean Portraits: Essays on Gender Ideologies and Identities*. Kingston: Ian Randle.

Barthélémy, Gerard. 1989. *L'univers rural haitien: Le pays en dehors*. Port-au-Prince: Henri Deschamps.

Basch, Linda, Nina Glick Schiller, and Cristina Szanton Blanc. 1994. *Nations Unbound: Transnational Projects, Postcolonial Predicaments, and Deterritorialized Nation-States*. London: Gordon and Breach.

Becker, William H. 1997. "The Black Church: Manhood and Mission." *African-American Religion: Interpretive Essays in History and Culture*, ed. Timothy E. Fulop and Albert J. Raboteau, 177–200. New York: Routledge.

Beckles, Hilary. 1989. *Natural Rebels: A Social History of Enslaved Black Women in Barbados*. London: Zed.

———. 1999. *Centering Woman: Gender Discourses in Caribbean Slave Society*. Kingston: Ian Randle.

Behar, Ruth. 2000. "Post Utopia: The Erotics of Power and Cuba's Revolutionary Children." *Cuba, The Elusive Nation*, ed. Damián J. Fernández and Madeline C. Betancourt. Gainesville: University Press of Florida.

Beisel, Nicola, and Tamara Kay. 2004. "Abortion, Race, and Gender in Nineteenth-Century America." *American Sociological Review* 69 (August), 498–518.

Bell, David, and Jon Binnie. 2000. *The Sexual Citizen: Queer Politics and Beyond*. Cambridge: Polity.

Bell, David, and Gill Valentine. 1995. *Mapping Desire: Geographies of Sexualities*. London: Routledge.

Bellegarde-Smith, Patrick. 1990. *Haiti: The Breached Citadel*. Boulder: University of Colorado Press.

Berlant, Lauren. 1993. "National Brands/National Body: *Imitation of Life*." *The Phan-*

tom Public Sphere, ed. Bruce Robbins, 173–228. Minneapolis: University of Minnesota Press.

———. 1997. *The Queen of America Goes to Washington City*. Durham: Duke University Press.

Berlant, Lauren, and Elizabeth Freeman. 1997. "Queer Nationality": *The Queen of America Goes to Washington City*, 145–73. Durham: Duke University Press.

Berlant, Lauren, and Michael Warner. 2002. "Sex in Public." *Publics and Counterpublics*, ed. Michael Warner, 187–208. New York: Zone.

Besson, Jean. 1979. "Symbolic Aspects of Land in the Caribbean: The Tenure and Transmission of Land Rights among Caribbean Peasantries." *Peasants, Plantations, and Rural Communities in the Caribbean*, ed. Malcolm Cross and Arnaud Marks, 86–116. Guildford: University of Surrey Press.

———. 1984. "Family Land and Caribbean Society: Toward an Ethnography of Afro-Caribbean Peasantries." *Perspectives on Caribbean Regional Identity*, ed. Elizabeth Thomas-Hope, 57–83. Liverpool: Liverpool University Press.

———. 1992. "Freedom and Community: The British West Indies." *The Meaning of Freedom: Economics, Politics, and Culture after Slavery*, ed. Frank McGlynn and Seymour Drescher, 183–219. Pittsburgh: University of Pittsburgh Press.

———. 1993. "Reputation and Respectability Reconsidered: A New Perspective on Afro-Caribbean Peasant Women." *Women and Change in the Caribbean*, ed. Janet Momsen, 15–37. London: James Currey.

———. 1995. "Land, Kinship, and Community in the Post-Emancipation Caribbean: A Regional View of the Leewards." *Small Islands, Large Questions: Society, Culture, and Resistance in the Post-Emancipation Caribbean*, ed. Karen Fog Olwig, 73–99. London: Frank Cass.

———. 1997. "Caribbean Common Tenures and Capitalism: The Accompong Maroons of Jamaica." *Plantation Society in the Americas* 4, nos. 2–3, 201–32.

———. 2002. *Martha Brae's Two Histories: European Expansion and Caribbean Culture-Building in Jamaica*. Chapel Hill: University of North Carolina Press.

Bilby, Kenneth. 2005. *True-Born Maroons*. Gainesville: University Press of Florida.

———. 2011. "Picturing the Maroons in the Morant Bay Rebellion: Complicating the Imagery of Commemoration." *Princeton Library Chronicle* 72 (2), 574–83.

Binnie, Jon. 2004. *The Globalization of Sexuality*. London: Sage.

Black Public Sphere Collective, ed. 1995. *The Black Public Sphere: A Public Culture Book*. Chicago: University of Chicago Press.

Bloch, Marc. 1953. *The Historian's Craft*, trans. Peter Putnam. New York: Vintage.

Bogues, Anthony. 2009. "The 1805 Haitian Constitution: The Making of Slave Freedom in the Atlantic World." *Freedom: Retrospective and Prospective*, ed. Swithin Wilmot, 144–71. Kingston: Ian Randle.

Bolland, Nigel O. 1981. "Systems of Domination after Slavery: The Control of Land and Labor in the British West Indies after 1838." *Comparative Studies in Society and History* 23, 591–619.

———. 1991. "The Politics of Freedom in the British Caribbean." *The Meaning of Freedom: Economics, Politics, and Culture after Slavery*, ed. Frank McGlynn and Seymour Drescher, 113–46. Pittsburgh: University of Pittsburgh Press.

Bordo, Susan. 1993. *Unbearable Weight: Feminism, Western Culture, and the Body*. Berkeley: University of California Press.

Brennan, Denise. 2002. "Selling Sex for Visas: Sex Tourism as Stepping Stone to International Migration." *Global Woman: Nannies, Maids, and Sex Workers in the New Economy*, ed. Barbara Ehrenreich and Arlie R. Hochschild, 154–68. New York: Henry Holt.

———. 2004. *What's Love Got to Do with It? Transnational Desire and Sex Tourism in the Dominican Republic*. Durham: Duke University Press.

Brereton, Bridget. 1995. "Text, Testimony, and Gender." *Engendering History: Caribbean Women in Historical Perspective*, ed. Verene Shepherd, Bridget Brereton, and Barbara Bailey, 63–93. Kingston: Ian Randle.

———. 1999. "Family Strategies, Gender, and the Shift to Wage Labour in the British Caribbean." *The Colonial Caribbean in Transition: Essays on Postemancipation Social and Cultural History*, ed. Bridget Brereton and Kevin Yelvington, 77–107. Gainesville: University Press of Florida,

Briggs, L. 2002. *Reproducing Empire: Race, Sex, Science, and U.S. Imperialism in Puerto Rico*. Berkeley: University of California Press.

Brooks, Daphne. 2006. *Bodies in Dissent: Spectacular Performances of Race and Freedom, 1850–1910*. Durham: Duke University Press.

———. 2011. *Subterranean Blues: Black Women and Sound Cultures—from Minstrelsy through the New Millennium*. Cambridge: Harvard University Press.

Brown, Elsa B. 1995. "Negotiating and Transforming the Public Sphere: African American Political Life in the Transition from Slavery to Freedom." *The Black Public Sphere: A Public Culture Book*, ed. Black Public Sphere Collective, 111–50. Chicago: University of Chicago Press.

Brown, Karen McCarthy. 1991. *Mama Lola: A Vodou Priestess in Brooklyn*. Berkeley: University of California Press.

———. 1997. "Systematic Remembering, Systematic Forgetting: Ogou in Haiti." *African-American Religion: Interpretive Essays in History and Culture*, ed. Timothy E. Fulop and Albert J. Raboteau, 433–62. New York: Routledge.

Brown, Laura. 1993. *Ends of Empire: Women and Ideology in Early Eighteenth-century English Literature*. Ithaca, N.Y.: Cornell University Press.

Brown, Wendy. 1988. *Manhood and Politics: A Feminist Reading in Political Theory*. London: Rowman and Littlefield.

Browning, Barbara. 1998. *Infectious Rhythm: Metaphors of Contagion and the Spread of African Culture*. New York: Routledge.

Bryson, Norman. 1997. "Cultural Studies in Dance History." *Meaning in Motion: New Cultural Studies of Dance*, ed. Jane Desmond, 55–80. Durham: Duke University Press.

Buck-Morss, Susan. 2000. "Hegel and Haiti." *Critical Inquiry* 26, no. 4 (Summer), 821–65.

Burton, Antoinette. 1994. *Burdens of History: British Feminists, Indian Women, and Imperial Culture, 1865–1915*. Chapel Hill: University of North Carolina Press.

———. 1997. *At the Heart of the Empire: Indians and the Colonial Encounter in Late-Victorian Britain*. Berkeley: University of California Press.

Burton, Richard D. E. 1993. "'Maman-France Doudou': Family Images in French West Indian Colonial Discourse." *Diacritics* 23, no. 3, 69–90.

——. 1997. *Afro-Creole: Power, Opposition, and Play in the Caribbean*. Ithaca: Cornell University Press.

Bush, Barbara. 1986. "'The Family Tree Is Not Cut': Women and Cultural Resistance in Slave Family Life in the British Caribbean." *In Resistance: Studies in African, Caribbean, and Afro-American History*, ed. Gary Y. Okihiro, 117–32. Amherst: University of Massachusetts Press.

——. 1990. *Slave Women in Caribbean Society, 1650–1838*. London: James Currey.

——. 1996. "Hard Labor: Women, Childbirth, and Resistance in British Caribbean Slave Societies." *More than Chattel: Black Women and Slavery in the Americas*, ed. David Barry Gaspar and Darlene Clark Hine, 193–217. Bloomington: Indiana University Press.

Butler, Judith. 1990. *Gender Trouble: Feminism and the Subversion of Identity*. New York: Routledge.

——. 1992. "Contingent Foundations: Feminism and the Question of 'Postmodernism.'" *Feminists Theorize the Political*, ed. Judith Butler and Joan Scott, 3–21. New York: Routledge.

——. 2002. "Is Kinship Always Already Heterosexual?" *Differences* 13, no. 1, 14–44.

——. 2003. *Bodies That Matter: On the Discursive Limits of Sex*. New York: Routledge.

Butler, Judith, and Joan Scott, eds. 1992. *Feminists Theorize the Political*. New York: Routledge.

Calhoun, Craig, ed. 1992. *Habermas and the Public Sphere*. Cambridge: MIT Press.

Canaday, Margot. 2003. "Building a Straight State: Sexuality and Social Citizenship under the 1944 GI Bill." *Journal of American History* 90, no. 3, 935–57.

Carby, Hazel. 1986. "It Just Be's Dat Way Sometime: The Sexual Politics of Women's Blues." *Radical America* 20, no. 4 (June–July), 9–22.

Carney, Judith A. 2001. *Black Rice: The African Origins of Rice Cultivation in the Americas*. Cambridge: Harvard University Press.

Carney, Judith A., and Robert A. Voeks. 2003. "Landscape Legacies of the African Diaspora in Brazil." *Progress in Human Geography* 27, no. 2, 139–52.

Carpentier, Alejo. 1963. *Explosion in a Cathedral: A Novel*. Trans. John Sturrock. London: Gollancz.

——. 1967. *The Kingdom of This World*. London: Gollancz.

Center for Human Rights and Global Justice, New York University School of Law. 2011. "Sexual Violence in Haiti's IDP Camps: Results of a Household Survey" (March 2011). Accessed 27 September 2011 at http://ijdh.org/archives/18122.

Chamberlain, Mary. 1995. "Gender and Memory: Oral History and Women's History." *Engendering History: Caribbean Women in Historical Perspective*, ed. Verene Shepherd, Bridget Brereton, and Barbara Bailey, 94–110. Kingston: Ian Randle.

Chancy, Myriam J. A. 1997. *Framing Silence: Revolutionary Novels by Haitian Women*. New Brunswick: Rutgers University Press.

Charles, Carolle. 2003. "Popular Imageries of Gender and Sexuality: Poor and Working-Class Haitian Women's Discourses on the Use of Their Bodies." *The Cul-

ture of Gender and Sexuality in the Caribbean, ed. Linden Lewis, 169–70. Gainesville: University of Florida Press.

Chevannes, Barry. 1994. *Rastafari: Roots and Ideology*. Syracuse: Syracuse University Press.

——. 1998. *Rastafari and Other African-Caribbean Worldviews*. The Hague: Institute of Social Studies.

Clark, Anna. 1995. *The Struggle for the Breeches: Gender and the Making of the British Working Class*. Berkeley: University of California Press.

Clarke, Edith. 1957. *My Mother Who Fathered Me*, 2d ed. London: George Allen and Unwin.

Clarke, John H., and Amy J. Garvey. 1974. *Marcus Garvey and the Vision of Africa*. New York: Vintage.

Cliff, Michelle. 1996 (1987). *No Telephone to Heaven*. New York: Plume, Penguin Books.

Cohen, Jean, and Andrew Arato. 1992. *Civil Society and Political Theory*. Cambridge: MIT Press.

Collins, Patricia Hill. 1990. *Black Feminist Thought: Knowledge, Consciousness, and the Politics of Empowerment*. New York: Routledge.

——. 1994. "Shifting the Center: Race, Class and Feminist Theorizing about Motherhood." *Mothering: Ideology, Experience, and Agency*, ed. Evelyn Nakano Glenn, Grace Chang, and Linda R. Forcey, 45–65. New York: Routledge.

——. 1999. "Producing the Mothers of the Nation: Race, Class and Contemporary U.S. Population Policies." *Women, Citizenship, and Difference*, ed. Nira Yuval-Davis and Pnina Werbner, 118–29. London: Zed.

——. 2000. "It's All in the Family: Intersections of Gender, Race and Nation." *Decentering the Center: Philosophy for a Multicultural World*, ed. Uma Narayan and Sandra Harding, 156–76. Bloomington: Indiana University Press.

——. 2004. *Black Sexual Politics: African-Americans, Gender, and the New Racism*. London: Routledge.

Comaroff, John, and Jean Comaroff. 1991. *Of Revelation and Revolution*, Vol. I: *Christianity, Colonialism, and Consciousness in South Africa*. Chicago: University of Chicago Press.

——. 1992. "Medicine, Colonialism and the Black Body." *Ethnography and the Historical Imagination*, 215–33. Boulder: Westview.

——. 1997. *Of Revelation and Revolution*, Vol. II: *The Dialectics of Modernity on a South African Frontier*. Chicago: University of Chicago Press.

Comhaire, Jean L. 1955. "The Haitian 'Chef de Section.'" *American Anthropologist* 57, no. 3 (June), 620–24.

Connell, Robert W. 1995. *Masculinities*. London: Polity.

Cooper, Carolyn. 1995. *Noises in the Blood: Orality, Gender, and the "Vulgar" Body of Jamaican Popular Culture*. London: Macmillan.

——. 2004. *Sound Clash: Jamaican Dancehall Culture at Large*. New York: Palgrave.

Cooper, Frederick, Thomas C. Holt, and Rebecca J. Scott. 2000. *Beyond Slavery: Explorations of Race, Labor, and Citizenship in Postemancipation Societies*. Chapel Hill: University of North Carolina Press.

Cooper, Frederick, Florencia E. Mallon, Steve J. Stern, Allen F. Isaacman, and William Roseberry. 1993. *Confronting Historical Paradigms: Peasants, Labor, and the Capitalist World*. Madison: University of Wisconsin Press.

Cooper, Frederick, and Ann Laura Stoler, eds. 1997. *Tensions of Empire: Colonial Cultures in a Bourgeois World*. Berkeley: University of California Press.

Corrigan, Philip, and Derek Sayer. 1985. *The Great Arch: English State Formation as Cultural Revolution*. Oxford: Blackwell.

Cossman, Brenda. 2007. *Sexual Citizens: The Legal and Cultural Regulation of Sex and Belonging*. Stanford: Stanford University Press.

Courlander, Harold. 1960. *The Drum and the Hoe: Life and Lore of the Haitian People*. Berkeley: University of California Press.

Cresswell, Tim. 2006. *On the Move: Mobility in the Modern Western World*. New York: Routledge.

Cronon, William. 1983. *Changes in the Land: Indians, Colonists, and the Ecology of New England*. New York: Hill and Wang.

Darby, Wendy Joy. 2000. *Landscape and Identity: Geographies of Nation and Class in England*. Oxford: Berg.

Dash, J. Michael. 1997. *Haiti and the United States: National Stereotypes and the Literary Imagination*, 2d ed. Basingstoke: Macmillan.

Davidoff, Leonore, and Catherine Hall. 1987. *Family Fortunes: Men and Women of the English Middle Class, 1780–1850*. Chicago: University of Chicago Press.

Davis, Angela. 1981. *Women, Race and Class*. New York: Random House.

——. 1998a. *Blues Legacies and Black Feminism: Gertrude "Ma" Rainey, Bessie Smith, and Billie Holiday*. New York: Pantheon.

——. 1998b. "Race and Criminalization: Black Americans and the Punishment Industry." *The Angela Y. Davis Reader*, ed. Joy James, 61–73. Malden, Mass.: Blackwell.

——. 2003 (1981). "Racism, Birth Control, and Reproductive Rights." *Feminist Postcolonial Theory: A Reader*, ed. Reina Lewis and Sara Mills, 353–67. Edinburgh: Edinburgh University Press.

Dayan, Joan. 1995. *Haiti, History, and the Gods*. Berkeley: University of California Press.

de Certeau, Michel. 1984. *The Practice of Everyday Life*. Berkeley: University of California Press.

Defries, Amelia Dorothy. 1917. *In a Forgotten Colony: Being Some Studies of Nassau and at Grand Bahama during 1916*. Nassau: St. Martin's Press.

DeLoughrey, Elizabeth M. 2007. *Routes and Roots: Navigating Caribbean and Pacific Island Literatures*. Honolulu: University of Hawaii Press.

Desmangles, Leslie G. 1992. *The Faces of the Gods: Vodou and Roman Catholicism in Haiti*. Chapel Hill: University of North Carolina Press.

Desmond, Jane, ed. 1997. *Meaning in Motion: New Cultural Studies of Dance*. Durham: Duke University Press.

Desquiron, Jean, comp. 1993. *Haïti à la une: Une anthologie de la presse haïtienne de 1724 à 1934*, 2 vols. Port-au-Prince: n.p.

Douglass, Lisa. 1992. *The Power of Sentiment*. Boulder: Westview.

Dubois, Laurent. 2004a. *A Colony of Citizens: Revolution and Slave Emancipation in the French Caribbean, 1787–1804*. Chapel Hill: University of North Carolina Press.

——. 2004b. *Avengers of the New World*. Cambridge: Harvard University Press.

Du Bois, W. E. B. 1992 (1935). *Black Reconstruction in America, 1860–1880*, repr. ed. New York: Atheneum.

Dudink, Stefan, Karen Hagemann, and Anna Clark, eds. 2007. *Representing Masculinity: Male Citizenship in Modern Western Culture*. New York: Palgrave Macmillan.

Dudink, Stefan, Karen Hagemann, and John Tosh, eds. 2004. *Masculinities in Politics and War: Gendering Modern History*. Manchester: Manchester University Press.

Duncan, James. 1999. "Dis-Orientation: On the Shock of the Familiar in a Far-Away Place." *Writes of Passage: Reading Travel Writing*, ed. James Duncan and Derek Gregory, 151–63. London: Routledge.

Duncan, James, and Derek Gregory, eds. 1999. *Writes of Passage: Reading Travel Writing*. London: Routledge.

Dupuy, Alex. 1989. *Haiti in the World Economy: Class, Race, and Underdevelopment since 1700*. Boulder: University of Colorado Press.

Edelman, Lee. 2004. *No Future: Queer Theory and the Death Drive*. Durham: Duke University Press.

Edmondson, Belinda. 1999. *Making Men: Gender, Literary Authority, and Women's Writing in Caribbean Narrative*. Durham: Duke University Press.

——. 2003. "Public Spectacles: Caribbean Women and the Politics of Public Performance." *Small Axe* 13 (March), 1–16.

Edwards, Laura F. 1997. *Gendered Strife and Confusion: The Political Culture of Reconstruction*. Urbana: University of Illinois Press.

Eley, G. 1992. "Nations, Publics, and Political Cultures: Placing Habermas in the Nineteenth Century." *Habermas and the Public Sphere*, ed. Craig Calhoun, 289–339. Cambridge: MIT Press.

Emirbayer, Mustafa, and Mimi Sheller. 1999. "Publics in History." *Theory and Society* 28, 145–97.

Enloe, Cynthia. 1990. *Bananas, Beaches, and Bases: Making Feminist Sense of International Politics*. Berkeley: University of California Press.

Evans, David T. 1993. *Sexual Citizenship: The Material Construction of Sexualities*. London: Routledge.

Evans, Sara M., and Harry C Boyte. 1986. *Free Spaces: The Sources of Democratic Change in America*. Chicago: University of Chicago Press.

Fanon, Frantz. 1994 (1967). *Black Skin, White Masks*, trans. Charles Lam Markmann. New York: Grove.

Farmer, Paul. 2005. *Pathologies of Power: Health, Human Rights, and the New War on the Poor*. Berkeley: University of California Press.

Ferguson, Moira. 1992. *Subject to Others: British Women Writers and Colonial Slavery, 1670–1834*. New York: Routledge.

Fermor, Patrick Leigh. 1955 (1950). *The Traveller's Tree: A Journey through the Caribbean Islands*, repr. ed. London: John Murray.

Ferrer, Ada. 1999. *Insurgent Cuba: Race, Nation, and Revolution, 1868–1898*. Chapel Hill: University of North Carolina Press.

Fick, Carolyn. 1988. "Black Peasants and Soldiers in the Saint-Domingue Revolution: Initial Reactions to Freedom in the South Province 1793–94." *History from Below: Studies in Popular Protest and Popular Ideology*, ed. Frederick Krantz, 247–70. Oxford: Basil Blackwell.

——. 1990. *The Making of Haiti: The Saint-Domingue Revolution from Below*. Knoxville: University of Tennessee Press.

Findlay, Eileen. 1999. *Imposing Decency: The Politics of Sexuality and Race in Puerto Rico, 1870–1920*. Durham: Duke University Press.

Fischer, Sibylle. 2004. *Modernity Disavowed: Haiti and the Cultures of Slavery in the Age of Revolution*. Durham: Duke University Press.

Foucault, Michel. 1990 (1978). *The History of Sexuality*, Vol. I: *An Introduction*, trans. Robert Hurley. New York: Vintage.

——. 1991. "Governmentality," trans. Rosi Braidotti and revised by Colin Gordon. *The Foucault Effect: Studies in Governmentality*, ed. Graham Burchell, Colin Gordon, and Peter Miller, 87–104. Chicago: University of Chicago Press.

——. 1995. *Discipline and Punish: The Birth of the Prison*, trans. Alan Sheridan. New York: Vintage.

——. 1997. "The Birth of Biopolitics." *Michel Foucault, Ethics: Subjectivity and Truth*, ed. Paul Rabinow, 73–79. New York: The New Press.

Fox-Genovese, Elizabeth. 1986. "Strategies and Forms of Resistance: Focus on Slave Women in the United States." *In Resistance: Studies in African, Caribbean, and Afro-American History*, ed. Gary Y. Okihiro, 143–65. Amherst: University of Massachusetts Press.

Francis, Donette. 2010. *Fictions of Feminine Citizenship: Sexuality and the Nation in Contemporary Caribbean Literature*. New York: Palgrave Macmillan.

Francis, Wigmoore. 2003. "Nineteenth- and Early-Twentieth Century Perspectives on Women in the Discourses of Radical Black Caribbean Men." *Small Axe* 13 (March), 116–39.

Fraser, Nancy. 1989. *Unruly Practices: Power, Discourse, and Gender in Contemporary Social Theory*. Minneapolis: University of Minnesota Press.

——. 1992. "Rethinking the Public Sphere: A Contribution to the Critique of Actually Existing Democracy." *Habermas and the Public Sphere*, ed. Craig Calhoun, 109–42. Cambridge: MIT Press.

Freeman, Carla. 2000. *High Tech and High Heels in the Global Economy: Women, Work and Pink-Collar Identities in the Caribbean*. Durham: Duke University Press.

Gardiner, Judith, ed. 2002. *Masculinity Studies and Feminist Theory*. New York: Columbia University Press.

Gaspar, David Barry. 1996. "From 'The Sense of Their Slavery': Slave Women and Resistance in Antigua, 1632–1763." *More than Chattel: Black Women and Slavery in the Americas*, ed. David Barry Gaspar and Darlene Clark Hine, 218–38. Bloomington: Indiana University Press.

Geggus, David. 1996. "Slave and Free Women in Saint-Domingue." *More than Chattel: Black Women and Slavery in the Americas*, ed. David Barry Gaspar and Darlene Clark Hine, 259–78. Bloomington: Indiana University Press.

Giambelli, R. 1998. "The Coconut, the Body, and the Human Being: Metaphors of

Life and Growth in Nusa Penida and Bali." *The Social Life of Trees: Anthropological Perspectives on Tree Symbolism*, ed. Laura M. Rival, 133–57. Oxford: Berg.

Giddings, Paula. 1984. *When and Where I Enter: The Impact of Black Women on Race and Sex in America*. New York: William Morrow.

Gikandi, Simon. 1994. "Travel, Theory, and Englishness: Writing the West Indies in the Nineteenth-Century." *Nineteenth Century Contexts* 18, 49–70.

——. 1996. *Maps of Englishness: Writing Identity in the Culture of Colonialism*. New York: Columbia University Press.

Gilkes, Cheryl Townsend. 1997. "The Roles of Church and Community Mothers: Ambivalent American Sexism or Fragmented African Familyhood?" *African-American Religion: Interpretive Essays in History and Culture*, ed. Timothy E. Fulop and Albert J. Raboteau, 365–88. New York: Routledge.

Gill, Lyndon. 2010. "Transfiguring Trinidad and Tobago: Queer Cultural Production, Erotic Subjectivity, and the Praxis of Black Queer Anthropology." Ph.D. diss., Harvard University, Cambridge.

Gilman, Sander. 1985. *Difference and Pathology: Stereotypes of Sexuality, Race, and Madness*. Ithaca: Cornell University Press.

Gilmore, Glenda E. 1996. *Gender and Jim Crow: Women and the Politics of White Supremacy*. Chapel Hill: University of North Carolina Press.

Gilroy, Paul. 1991. *There Ain't No Black in the Union Jack: The Cultural Politics of Race and Nation*. Chicago: University of Chicago Press.

——. 1993. *The Black Atlantic: Modernity and Double Consciousness*. London: Verso.

——. 1995. "'After the Love Has Gone': Bio-politics and Ethno-poetics in the Black Public Sphere." *The Black Public Sphere: A Public Culture Book*, ed. Black Public Sphere Collective, 53–80. Chicago: University of Chicago Press.

——. 2000. *Between Camps: Nations, Cultures, and the Allure of Race*. London: Penguin.

Ginsburg, Faye, and Rayna Rapp, eds. 1995. *Conceiving the New World Order: The Global Politics of Reproduction*. Berkeley: University of California Press.

Glave, Thomas. 2000. *Whose Song? and Other Stories*. San Francisco: City Lights Publishers.

——. 2005. *Words to Our Now: Imagination and Dissent*. Minneapolis: University of Minnesota Press.

——, ed. 2008. *Our Caribbean: A Gathering of Lesbian and Gay Writing from the Antilles*. Durham: Duke University Press.

Glenn, Evelyn Nakano. 2002. *Unequal Freedom: How Race and Gender Shaped American Citizenship and Labor*. Cambridge: Harvard University Press.

Glissant, Edouard. 1989. *Caribbean Discourse: Selected Essays*, trans. J. Michael Dash. Charlottesville: University of Virginia Press.

Gmelch, George. 2003. *Behind the Smile: The Working Lives of Caribbean Tourism*. Bloomington: Indiana University Press.

Golden, Thelma, ed. 1994. *Black Male: Representations of Masculinity in Contemporary American Art*. New York: Whitney Museum of American Art.

Gombrich, Ernst. 1979. "The Dream of Reason: Symbolism of the French Revolution." *British Journal of Eighteenth-Century Studies* 2, 187–205.

Gopinath, Gayatri. 2005. *Impossible Desires: Queer Diasporas and South Asian Public Cultures*. Durham: Duke University Press.

Goucher, Candice. 2010. "The Memory of Iron: Forging the Black Atlantic." Paper presented at the Caribbean Studies Association Annual Conference, Almond Beach Village, Barbados, May.

Gould, Jeffrey L. 1990. *To Lead as Equals: Rural Protest and Political Consciousness in Chinandega, Nicaragua, 1912–1979*. Chapel Hill: University of North Carolina Press.

Grosz, Elizabeth. 1995. *Space, Time, and Perversion: The Politics of Bodies*. Sydney: Allen and Unwin.

Grove, Richard. 1995. *Green Imperialism: Colonial Expansion, Tropical Island Edens, and the Origins of Environmentalism, 1600–1860*. Cambridge: Cambridge University Press.

Guha, Ranajit, and Gayatri Spivak, eds. 1988. *Selected Subaltern Studies*. New York: Oxford University Press.

Gunew, Sneja. 2003. "The Home of Language: A Pedagogy of the Stammer." *Uprootings/Regroundings: Questions of Home and Migration*, ed. Sara Ahmed, Claudia Castañeda, Anne-Marie Fortier, and Mimi Sheller, 41–58. Oxford: Berg.

Guy, Donna. 1990. *Sex and Danger in Buenos Aires: Prostitution, Family, and Nation in Argentina*. Lincoln: University of Nebraska Press.

Habermas, Jürgen. 1989 (1962). *The Structural Transformation of the Public Sphere: An Inquiry into a Category of Bourgeois Society*, trans. Thomas Bürger. Cambridge: MIT Press.

——. 1998. "Deliberative Politics: A Procedural Concept of Democracy." *Between Facts and Norms*, 287–328. Cambridge: Cambridge University Press.

Hall, Catherine. 1992. *White, Male, and Middle Class: Explorations in Feminism and History*, Cambridge: Polity.

——. 1995. "Gender Politics and Imperial Politics: Rethinking the Histories of Empire." *Engendering History: Caribbean Women in Historical Perspective*, ed. Verene Shepherd, Bridget Brereton, and Barbara Bailey, 48–59. Kingston: Ian Randle.

——. 2000. "Introduction: Thinking the Postcolonial, Thinking the Empire." *Cultures of Empire: A Reader*, ed. Catherine Hall, 1–33. Manchester: Manchester University Press.

——. 2002. *Civilising Subjects: Metropole and Colony in the English Imagination 1830–1867*. Cambridge: Polity.

Hall, Douglas. 1959. *Free Jamaica, 1838–1865: An Economic History*. New Haven: Yale University Press.

——. 1993. "The Flight from the Estate Reconsidered: The British West Indies, 1838–1842." *Caribbean Freedom: Society and Economy from Emancipation to the Present*, ed. Hilary Beckles and Verene Shepherd, 55–63. Kingston: Ian Randle.

Hall, Gwendolyn Midlo. 1992. *Africans in Colonial Louisiana: The Development of Afro-Creole Culture in the Eighteenth Century*. Baton Rouge: Louisiana State University Press.

Hall, Stuart. 1999. "Whose Heritage? Un-settling 'The Heritage,' Re-imagining the Post-nation." *Third Text* 49 (Winter), 3–13.

Hallam, Elizabeth. 2000. "Texts, Objects, and 'Otherness': Problems of Historical Process in Writing and Displaying Cultures." *Cultural Encounters: Representing "Otherness,"* ed. Elizabeth Hallam and Brian V. Street, 260–83. London: Routledge.

Handler, Jerome. 1971. "The History of Arrowroot and the Origin of Peasantries in the British West Indies." *Journal of Caribbean History* 2 (May), 46–93.

Hansen, Miriam. 1993. "Unstable Mixtures, Dilated Spheres." *Public Culture* 5, 179–212.

Haraway, Donna. 1992. "Ecce Homo, Ain't (Ar'n't) I a Woman, and Inappropriate/d Others: The Human in a Post-Humanist Landscape." *Feminists Theorize the Political*, ed. Judith Butler and Joan Scott, 86–100. New York: Routledge.

Harding, Sandra. 1991. *Whose Science? Whose Knowledge? Thinking from Women's Lives*. Ithaca: Cornell University Press.

Harding, Vincent. 1981. *There Is a River: The Black Struggle for Freedom in America*. New York: Vintage Books.

——. 1997 (1969). "Religion and Resistance Among Antebellum Slaves, 1800–1860." *African-American Religion: Interpretive Essays in History and Culture*, ed. Timothy Fulop and Albert J. Raboteau, 107–53. London and New York: Routledge.

Harrison, Faye V. 2005. "Global Perspectives on Human Rights and Interlocking Inequalities of Race, Gender, and Related Dimensions of Power." *Resisting Racism and Xenophobia: Global Perspectives on Race, Gender, and Human Rights*, ed. Faye V. Harrison, 1–34. Walnut Creek, Calif.: AltaMira.

Hartman, Saidiya. 1997. *Scenes of Subjection: Terror, Slavery, and Self-Making in Nineteenth-Century America*. Oxford: Oxford University Press.

Hatch, Nathan O. 1989. *The Democratization of American Christianity*. New Haven: Yale University Press.

Henke, Holger, and Karl-Heinz Magister, eds. 2007. *Constructing Vernacular Culture in the Trans-Caribbean*. Boston: Lexington.

Henriques, Julian. 2008. "Sonic Diaspora, Vibrations, and Rhythm: Thinking through the Sounding of the Jamaican Dancehall Session." *African and Black Diaspora* 1, no. 2 (July), 215–36.

Herskovits, Melville J. 1964 (1937). *Life in a Haitian Valley*, repr. ed. New York: Octagon.

Heuman, Gad J. 1981. *Between Black and White: Race, Politics, and the Free Coloreds in Jamaica, 1792–1865*. Westport, Conn.: Greenwood Press.

——. 1994. *"The Killing Time": The Morant Bay Rebellion in Jamaica*. London: Macmillan.

Higginbotham, Evelyn Brooks. 1992. "African-American Women's History and the Metalanguage of Race." *Signs* 17, 251–374.

——. 1993. *Righteous Discontent: The Women's Movement in the Black Baptist Church, 1880–1920*. Cambridge: Harvard University Press.

Higman, B. W., ed. 1980. *The Jamaican Censuses of 1844 and 1861*. Kingston: University of the West Indies Press.

——. 1984. *Slave Populations of the British Caribbean, 1807–1834*. Baltimore: Johns Hopkins University Press.

——. 1988. *Jamaica Surveyed: Plantation Maps and Plans of the 18th and 19th Centuries*. Kingston: Institute of Jamaica.

——. 1995a. "Post-emancipation Historiography of the Leeward Islands." *Small Islands, Large Questions: Society, Culture and Resistance in the Post-Emancipation Caribbean*, ed. Karen Fog Olwig, 8–28. London: Frank Cass.

——. 1995b. *Slave Populations of the British Caribbean, 1807–1834*. Reissue. Kingston: University Press of the West Indies [Baltimore: Johns Hopkins University Press, 1984].

——. 2000. *Writing West Indian Histories*. London: Macmillan.

Hill, Robert A. 2010. "Redemption Works: From 'African Redemption' to 'Redemption Song.'" *Review* 43, no. 2, 200–207.

Hindess, Barry. 1993. "Citizenship in the Modern West." *Citizenship and Social Theory*, ed. Bryan Turner, 19–35. London: Sage.

Hintzen, Percy. 2001. "Rethinking Democracy in the Postnationalist State." *New Caribbean Thought: A Reader*, ed. Brian Meeks and Folke Lindahl, 104–24. Kingston: University of the West Indies Press.

——. 2002. "The Caribbean: Race and Creole Ethnicity." *A Companion to Racial and Ethnic Studies*, ed. David Theo Goldberg and John Solomos, 475–94. Oxford: Blackwell.

Hobsbawm, Eric J. 1964. *Labouring Men: Studies in the History of Labour*. London: Weidenfeld & Nicholson.

Holt, Thomas C. 1992. *The Problem of Freedom: Race, Labor, and Politics in Jamaica and Britain, 1832–1938*. Baltimore: Johns Hopkins University Press.

——. 2000. "The Essence of the Contract: The Articulation of Race, Gender, and Political Economy in British Emancipation Policy, 1838–1866." *Beyond Slavery: Explorations of Race, Labor, and Citizenship in Postemancipation Societies*, ed. Frederick Cooper, Thomas C. Holt, and Rebecca J. Scott, 33–59. Chapel Hill: University of North Carolina Press.

Honig, Bonnie. 1992. "Toward an Agonistic Feminism: Hannah Arendt and the Politics of Identity." *Feminists Theorize the Political*, ed. Judith Butler and Joan Scott, 215–37. New York: Routledge.

hooks, bell. 1981. *Ain't I a Woman: Black Women and Feminism*. Boston: South End.

——. 1990. *Yearning: Race, Gender, and Cultural Politics*. Boston: South End Press.

——. 1994. "Feminism Inside: Toward a Black Body Politics." *Black Male: Representations of Masculinity in Contemporary American Art*, ed. Thelma Golden, 127–40. New York: Whitney Museum of American Art.

Hoving, Isabel. 2002. "Remaining Where You Are: Kincaid and Glissant on Space and Knowledge." *Mobilizing Place, Placing Mobility: The Politics of Representation in a Globalized World*, ed. Ginette Verstraete and Tim Cresswell, 125–140. Amsterdam: Rodopi.

Hunt, Lynn. 1984. *Politics, Culture, and Class in the French Revolution*. Berkeley: University of California Press.

——. 1992. *The Family Romance of the French Revolution*. Berkeley: University of California Press.

Hurbon, Laennec. 1995. *Voodoo: Truth and Fantasy*. London: Thames and Hudson.

Inda, Jonathan X., and Renato Rosaldo. 2002. "Introduction: A World in

Motion." *Anthropology of Globalization: A Reader*, ed. Jonathan X. Inda and Renato Rosaldo, 1–34. Malden, Mass.: Blackwell.

Isaacman, Allen F. 1993. "Peasants and Rural Social Protest in Africa." *Confronting Historical Paradigms: Peasants, Labor, and the Capitalist World System in Africa and Latin America*, ed. Frederick Cooper, Florencia E. Mallon, Steve J. Stern, Allen F. Isaacman, and William Roseberry, 205–317. Madison: University of Wisconsin Press.

Jacob, Margaret C. 1991. *Living the Enlightenment: Freemasonry and Politics in Eighteenth Century Europe*. New York: Oxford University Press.

Jacobsen, Matthew F. 1998. *Whiteness of a Different Color: European Immigrants and the Alchemy of Race*. Cambridge: Harvard University Press.

James, C. L. R. 1963. *Black Jacobins: Toussaint L'Ouverture and the San Domingo Revolution*, 2d ed. New York: Vintage.

Jemmott, Jenny. 2009. "Marginality or Activism: The Black Male and the Family in Nineteenth-Century Jamaica." *Freedom: Retrospective and Prospective*, ed. Swithin Wilmot, 94–111. Kingston: Ian Randle.

Jones, Jacqueline. 1985. *Labor of Love, Labor of Sorrow: Black Women, Work, and the Family, from Slavery to the Present*. New York: Vintage.

Joseph, Gilbert, and Daniel Nugent, eds. 1994. *Everyday Forms of State Formation: Revolution and the Negotiation of Rule in Modern Mexico*. Durham: Duke University Press.

Kafka, Judith. 1997. "Action, Reaction, and Interaction: Slave Women in Resistance in the South of Saint-Domingue, 1793–94." *Slavery and Abolition* 18, no. 2, 48–72.

Kamugisha, Aaron. 2007. "The Coloniality of Citizenship in the Contemporary Anglophone Caribbean." *Race and Class* 49, no. 2, 20–40.

Kaplan, E. Ann. 1983. *Women and Film: Both Sides of the Camera*. New York: Methuen.

Keane, John. 1988. *Democracy and Civil Society*. London: Verso.

Kelley, Robin D. G. 1996. *Race Rebels: Culture, Politics, and the Black Working Class*. New York: Free Press.

——. 2002. *Freedom Dreams: The Black Radical Imagination*. Boston: Beacon.

Kempadoo, Kamala, ed. 1999. *Sun, Sex, and Gold: Tourism and Sex Work in the Caribbean*. Lanham, Md.: Rowman and Littlefield.

——. 2004. *Sexing the Caribbean: Gender, Race, and Sexual Labor*. New York: Routledge.

Khan, Aisha. 2004. *Callaloo Nation: Metaphors of Race and Religious Identity among South Asians in Trinidad*. Durham: Duke University Press.

Knight, Franklin. 1990. *The Caribbean: The Genesis of a Fragmented Nationalism*, 2d ed. New York: Oxford University Press.

Knowles, Caroline. 2003. *Race and Social Analysis*. London: Sage.

Koselleck, Reinhart. 1988. *Critique and Crisis*. Cambridge: Harvard University Press.

Kraemer, Ruth S., and Verlyn Klinkenborg, eds. 1996. *The Drake Manuscript in the Pierpont Morgan Library: Histoire Naturelle des Indes*. London: André Deutsch.

Kuhn, Annette. 1982. *Women's Pictures: Feminism and Cinema*. London: Routledge and Kegan Paul.

Kutzinski, Vera M. 1993. *Sugar's Secrets: Race and the Erotics of Cuban Nationalism*. Charlottesville: University of Virginia Press.

Lacerte, Robert K. 1975. "The First Land Reform in Latin America: The Reforms of Alexander Pétion, 1809–1814." *Inter-American Economic Affairs* 28, no. 4, 77–85.

Laguerre, Michel S. 1989. *Voodoo and Politics in Haiti*. New York: St. Martin's Press.

——. 1993. *The Military and Society in Haiti*. Knoxville: University of Tennessee Press.

Lambert, David. 2004. "Deadening, Voyeuristic, and Reiterative? Problems of Representation in Caribbean Research." *Beyond the Blood, the Beach, and the Banana: New Perspectives in Caribbean Studies*, ed. Sandra Courtman, 3–14. Kingston: Ian Randle.

Landes, Joan. 1988. *Women and the Public Sphere in the Age of the French Revolution*. Ithaca: Cornell University Press.

——, ed. 1998. *Feminism, the Public, and the Private*. Oxford: Oxford University Press.

Lao-Montes, Agustin. 2001. "Mambo Montage: The Latinization of New York City." *Mambo Montage: The Latinization of New York*, ed. Agustin Lao-Montes and Arlene Davila, 1–54. New York: Columbia University Press.

Larose, Serge. 1975. "The Haitian Lakou: Land, Family, and Ritual." *Family and Kinship in Middle America and the Caribbean*, ed. Arnaud Marks and Rene Romer, 482–512. Willemstad: Institute of Higher Studies in Curaçao.

Lefebvre, Henri. 1991. *The Production of Space*, trans. Donald Nicholson-Smith. Oxford: Blackwell.

Lewis, Linden, ed. 2003. *The Culture of Gender and Sexuality in the Caribbean*. Gainesville: University Press of Florida.

Lewis, Matthew G. 1861. *Journal of a Residence among the Negroes in the West Indies*. London: J. Murray.

Leyburn, James G. 1980 (1966). *The Haitian People*. New Haven: Yale University Press.

Lloyd, Genevieve. 1984. *Man of Reason: Male and Female in Western Philosophy*. London: Routledge.

Logan, Rayford. 1941. *The Diplomatic Relations of the United States with Haiti, 1776–1891*. Chapel Hill: University of North Carolina Press.

Lomax, Alan. 2009 (1936). "A Tour of Street Music—The Mascaron." *Haitian Diary: Papers and Correspondence from Alan Lomax's Haitian Journey, 1936–37*, comp. and ed. Ellen Harold. Estate of Alan Lomax. San Francisco: Harte Recordings.

Look Lai, Walton. 1993. *Indentured Labor, Caribbean Sugar: Chinese and Indian Migrants to the British West Indies, 1838–1918*. Baltimore: Johns Hopkins University Press.

Lorde, Audre. 1984. *Sister Outsider: Essays and Speeches by Audre Lorde*. Freedom, Calif: Crossing.

Lumsden, Joyce. 1987. "Robert Love and Jamaican Politics." Ph.D. diss., University of the West Indies, Mona, Jamaica.

——. 1995. "The People's Convention: Celebrating the Diamond Jubilee of Full Freedom in Jamaica." *August 1st: A Celebration of Emancipation*, ed. Patrick Bryan, 49–

54. Kingston: Friedrich Ebert Siftung and Department of History, University of the West Indies.

MacKinnon, Catharine A. 1989. *Toward a Feminist Theory of the State.* Cambridge: Harvard University Press.

Macnaghten, Phil, and John Urry, eds. 1998. *Contested Natures.* London: Sage.

———. 2000. "Bodies in the Woods." *Body and Society* 6, nos. 3–4, 166–82.

Mahabir, Joy Allison Indira. 2003. *Miraculous Weapons: Revolutionary Ideology in Caribbean Culture.* New York: Peter Lang.

Mair, Lucille Mathurin. 1987. *Women Field Workers in Jamaica during Slavery (The 1986 Elsa Goveia Memorial Lecture).* Mona, Jamaica: University of the West Indies.

———. 2006. *A Historical Study of Women in Jamaica, 1655–1844.* Kingston: University of the West Indies Press.

Mallon, Florencia E. 1983. *The Defense of Community in Peru's Central Highlands: Peasant Struggle and Capitalist Transition, 1860–1940.* Princeton: Princeton University Press.

———. 1995. *Peasant and Nation.* Berkeley: University of California Press.

Marshall, Woodville K. 1993. "Provision Ground and Plantation Labor in Four Windward Islands: Competition for Resources during Slavery." *Cultivation and Culture: Labor and the Shaping of Slave Life in the Americas,* ed. Ira Berlin and Philip D. Morgan, 203–20. Charlottesville: University of Virginia Press.

Marshall, Woodville K. 1993, ed. 1977. *The Colthurst Journal.* Millwood, N.Y.: KTO Press.

Martin, Emily. 1987. *The Woman in the Body: A Cultural Analysis of Reproduction.* Boston: Beacon.

Martinez-Alier, Verena. 1989. *Marriage, Class, and Colour in Nineteenth-Century Cuba,* 2d ed. Ann Arbor: University of Michigan Press.

Mathurin, Lucille. 1974. "A Historical Study of Women in Jamaica from 1655 to 1844." Ph.D. diss., University of the West Indies, Kingston.

———. 1975. *The Rebel Woman in the British West Indies during Slavery.* Kingston: African-Caribbean Publications.

Matless, David. 1998. *Landscape and Englishness.* London: Reaktion.

Matos-Rodriguez, Félix. 1995. "Street Vendors, Peddlers, Shop Owners, and Domestics: Some Aspects of Women's Economic Roles in Nineteenth Century San Juan, Puerto Rico (1820–1870)." *Engendering History: Caribbean Women in Historical Perspectives,* ed. Verene Shepherd, Bridget Brereton, and Barbara Bailey, 176–93. Kingston: Ian Randle.

Maurer, Bill. 1997. "Colonial Policy and the Construction of the Commons: An Introduction." *Plantation Society in the Americas* 4, nos. 2–3, 113–34.

Mauss, Marcel. 1992 (1934). "Techniques of the Body." *Incorporations (Zone 6),* ed. Jonathan Crary and Sanford Kwinter. Zone Books: MIT Press.

Maximin, Daniel. 1989. *Lone Sun.* Trans. from the French. CARAF Books. Charlottesville: University of Virginia Press.

McAdam, Doug. 1982. *Political Process and the Development of Black Insurgency, 1930–1970.* Chicago: University of Chicago Press.

McClintock, Anne. 1995. *Imperial Leather: Race, Gender, and Sexuality in the Colonial Context*. New York: Routledge.

McGlynn, Frank, and Seymour Drescher, eds. 1992. *The Meaning of Freedom: Economics, Politics, and Culture after Slavery*. Pittsburgh: University of Pittsburgh Press.

McKittrick, Katherine. 2006. *Demonic Grounds: Black Women and the Cartographies of Struggle*. Minneapolis: University of Minnesota Press.

Mehta, Brinda. 2004. *Diasporic (Dis)locations: Indo-Caribbean Women Writers Negotiate the Kala Pani*. Mona, Jamaica: University of the West Indies Press.

Mercer, Kobena. 1994. "Black Masculinity and the Sexual Politics of Race." *Welcome to the Jungle: New Positions in Black Cultural Studies*. London: Routledge.

Métraux, Alfred. 1972. *Voodoo in Haiti*. New York: Schocken Books.

Miller, Errol. 1987. *Marginalization of the Black Male*. Mona, Jamaica: University of the West Indies Press.

——. 1992. *Men at Risk*. Mona, Jamaica: University of the West Indies Press.

Mintz, Sidney. 1958. "Historical Sociology of the Jamaican Church-Founded Free Village System." *De West-Indische Gids*, nos. 1–2, 46–70.

——. 1960. *Worker in the Cane: A Puerto-Rican Life History*. New York: W. W. Norton.

——. 1979. "Slavery and the Rise of Peasantries." *Historical Reflections* 6, no. 1, 213–42.

——. 1989. *Caribbean Transformations*. New York: Columbia University Press.

——. 1993. "Black Women, Economic Roles, and Cultural Traditions." *Caribbean Freedom: Society and Economy from Emancipation to the Present*, ed. Hilary Beckles and Verene Shepherd, 238–44. Kingston: Ian Randle.

Mintz, Sidney, and Douglas Hall. 1960. "The Origins of the Jamaican Internal Marketing System." Publications in Anthropology no. 57. Yale University, New Haven.

Mohammed, Patricia. 1995. "The Negotiation of Gender Relations among Indian Men and Women in Post-indenture Trinidad Society, 1917–47." *Engendering History: Caribbean Women in Historical Perspective*, ed. Verene Shepherd, Bridget Brereton, and Barbara Bailey, 20–47. Kingston: Ian Randle.

——. 1998. "Towards Indigenous Feminist Theorizing in the Caribbean." *Feminist Review* 59, 6–33.

——. 2000. "'But Most of All Mi Love Me Browning': The Emergence in Eighteenth and Nineteenth-Century Jamaica of the Mulatto Woman as the Desired." *Feminist Review* 65, 22–48.

——. 2007. "Gendering the Caribbean Picturesque." *Caribbean Review of Gender Studies* 1, no. 1 (April), 1–27.

Mohammed, Patricia, ed. 2002. *Gendered Realities: Essays in Caribbean Feminist Thought*. Bridgetown, Barbados: University of the West Indies Press.

Mohanram, Radhika. 1999. *Black Body: Women, Colonialism, and Space*. Minneapolis: University of Minnesota Press.

Mohanty, Chandra Talpade. 1991. "Under Western Eyes: Feminist Scholarship and Colonial Discourse." *Third World Women and the Politics of Feminism*, ed. Chandra Talpade Mohanty, Ann Russo, and Lourdes Torres, 51–80. Bloomington: Indiana University Press.

Momsen, Janet H. 1988. "Gender Roles in Caribbean Agriculture." *Labour in the Caribbean: From Emancipation to Independence*, ed. Malcolm Cross and Gad Heuman, 141–58. London: Macmillan.

——, ed. 1993. *Women and Change in the Caribbean*. Kingston: Ian Randle.

Morgan, Jennifer L. 2005. "Male Travelers, Female Bodies, and the Gendering of Racial Ideology, 1500–1770." *Bodies in Contact: Rethinking Colonial Encounters in World History*, ed. Tony Ballantyne and Antoinette Burton, 54–66. Durham: Duke University Press.

Morisseau-Leroy, Félix. 1999. "Tourist." Trans. Jack Hirschman. *Left Curve*, 23, http://www.leftcurve.org/LC23webPages/felixpoems.html. Accessed 19 September 2011.

Morris, Aldon D. 1984. *The Origins of the Civil Rights Movement*. New York: Free Press.

Morrissey, Marietta. 1989. *Slave Women in the New World: Gender Stratification in the Caribbean*, Lawrence: University of Kansas Press.

Mosse, George L. 1985. *Nationalism and Sexuality: Respectability and Abnormal Sexuality in Modern Europe*. New York: Howard Fertig.

Nadel-Gardere, Marie-Jose, and Gerald Bloncourt. 1986. *La peinture haitienne/Haitian Arts*, trans. Elizabeth Bell. Paris: Editions Nathan.

Nagel, Joane. 2003. *Race, Ethnicity, and Sexuality: Intimate Intersections, Forbidden Frontiers*. Oxford: Oxford University Press.

Narain, Denise deCaires. 1998. "Body Talk: Writing and Speaking the Body in the Texts of Caribbean Women Writers." *Caribbean Portraits: Essays on Gender Ideologies and Identities*, ed. Christine Barrow, 255–75. Kingston: Ian Randle.

Narcisse, Carol, and Judith Wedderburn. 2009. "Unfinished Business: Ignored Voices." *Freedom: Retrospective and Prospective*, ed. Swithin Wilmot, 248–53. Kingston: Ian Randle.

Nelson, Dana D. 1998. *National Manhood: Capitalist Citizenship and the Imagined Fraternity of White Men*. Durham: Duke University Press.

Nettleford, Rex M. 1978. *Caribbean Cultural Identity: The Case of Jamaica, an Essay in Cultural Dynamics*. Kingston: Institute of Jamaica.

Nicholls, David. 1996. *From Dessalines to Duvalier: Race, Colour, and National Independence in Haiti*, 3d ed. London: Macmillan.

Noble, Denise. 2000. "Ragga Music: Dis/Respecting Black Women and Dis/Reputable Sexualities." *Un/Settled Multiculturalisms: Diasporas, Entanglements, Transruptions*, ed. Barnor Hesse, 148–69. London: Zed.

——. 2008. "Postcolonial Criticism, Transnational Identification, and the Hegemonies of Dancehall's Academic and Popular Performativities." *Feminist Review* 90, 106–27.

Northrup, David. 1995. *Indentured Labor in the Age of Imperialism, 1834–1922*. Cambridge: Cambridge University Press.

Nussbaum, Martha. 2006. *Frontiers of Justice*. Cambridge: Harvard University Press.

——. 2007. "Constitutions and Capabilities." *Harvard Law Review*, 121, 4–97.

O'Callaghan, Evelyn. 1998. "'Compulsory Heterosexuality' and Textual/Sexual Alternatives in Selected Texts by West Indian Women Writers." *Caribbean Portraits:*

Essays on Gender Ideologies and Identities, ed. Christine Barrow, 294–319. Kingston: Ian Randle.

Olwell, Robert. 1996. "'Loose, Idle, and Disorderly': Slave Women in the Eighteenth-Century Charleston Marketplace." *More than Chattel: Black Women and Slavery in the Americas*, ed. David Barry Gaspar and Darlene Clark Hine, 97–110. Bloomington: Indiana University Press.

Olwig, Karen Fog. 1985. *Cultural Adaptation and Resistance on St. John*. Gainesville: University of Florida Press.

——. 1997. "Caribbean Family Land: A Modern Commons." *Plantation Society in the Americas* 4, nos. 2–3, 135–58.

Omi, Michael, and Howard Winant. 1994. *Racial Formation in the United States from the 1960s to the 1990s*. New York: Routledge.

Ortiz, Ricardo L. 2007. *Cultural Erotics in Cuban America*. Minneapolis: University of Minnesota Press.

Ozouf, Mona. 1988. *Festival and the French Revolution*, trans. Alan Sheridan. Cambridge: Harvard University Press.

Parker, Andrew, Mary Russo, Doris Sommer, and Patricia Yaeger, eds. 1992. *Nationalisms and Sexualities*. New York: Routledge.

Pateman, Carole. 1988. *The Sexual Contract*. Cambridge: Polity.

Paton, Diana. 2004. *No Bond but the Law: Punishment, Race, and Gender in Jamaican State Formation, 1780–1870*. Durham: Duke University Press.

——. 2008. "Pronatalism, Amelioration, and Emancipation in the Anglophone Caribbean." Paper presented at the Atlantic Emancipations conference, 10–12 April, Philadelphia.

Paton, Diana, ed. 2001. *A Narrative of Events, since the First of August, 1834, by James Williams, an Apprenticed Labourer in Jamaica*. Durham: Duke University Press.

Paton, Diana, and Pamela Scully. 2005. "Introduction: Gender and Slave Emancipation in Comparative Perspective." *Gender and Slave Emancipation in the Atlantic World*, ed. Pamela Scully and Diana Paton, 1–34. Durham: Duke University Press.

Patterson, Orlando. 1973 (1967). *The Sociology of Slavery: An Analysis of the Origins, Development, and Structure of Negro Slave Society in Jamaica*. London: Granada.

——. 1991. *Freedom in the Making of Western Culture*. New York: Basic.

Peabody, Sue. 2005. "Gendered Access to Freedom: Manumission and Emancipation during the Ancien Regime and the Revolution." *Gender and Emancipation in the Atlantic World*, ed. Pamela Scully and Diana Paton, 56–78. Durham: Duke University Press.

Petley, Christer. 2004. "Flying Away and Grounds for Concern: Mobility, Location, and Ethical Discomfort in Researching Caribbean History form the UK." *Beyond the Blood, the Beach and the Banana: New Perspectives in Caribbean Studies*, ed. Sandra Courtman, 15–23. Kingston: Ian Randle.

Petras, Elizabeth M. 1988. *Jamaican Labor Migration: White Capital and Black Labor, 1850–1930*. Boulder: Westview.

Phillips, Anne. 1991. *Engendering Democracy*. University Park: Pennsylvania State University.

Plummer, Brenda. 1992. *Haiti and the United States: The Psychological Moment*. Athens: University of Georgia Press.

Povinelli, Elizabeth. 2006. *The Empire of Love: Toward a Theory of Intimacy, Genealogy, and Carnality*. Durham: Duke University Press.

Pratt, Mary Louise. 1992. *Imperial Eyes: Travel Writing and Transculturation*. London: Routledge.

Price, Richard. 1983. *First Time: The Historical Vision of an Afro-American People*. Baltimore: Johns Hopkins University Press.

Probyn, Elspeth. 1993. *Sexing the Self: Gendered Positions in Cultural Studies*. New York: Routledge.

Puar, Jasbir. 1999. "Transnational Sexualities and Trinidad: Modern Bodies, National Queers." Unpublished Ph.D. diss., Department of Ethnic Studies, University of California at Berkeley.

——. 2002. "Queer Tourism: Geographies of Globalization." GLQ 8, nos. 1–2, 1–6.

Puri, Shalini. 2004. *The Caribbean Postcolonial: Social Equality, Post-Nationalism, and Cultural Hybridity*. New York: Palgrave Macmillan.

Puri, Shalini, ed. 2003. *Marginal Migrations: The Circulation of Cultures within the Caribbean*. Oxford: Macmillan.

Puwar, Nirmal. 2005. *Space Invaders: Race, Gender, and Bodies out of Place*. Oxford: Berg.

Raboteau, Albert J. 1978. *Slave Religion: The "Invisible Institution" in the Antebellum South*. New York: Oxford University Press.

——. 1997. "The Black Experience in American Evangelicalism: The Meaning of Slavery." *African-American Religion: Interpretive Essays in History and Culture*, ed. Timothy E. Fulop and Albert J. Raboteau, 89–106. New York: Routledge.

Radcliffe, Sarah, and Sally Westwood. 1996. *Remaking the Nation: Place, Politics, and Identity in Latin America*. London: Routledge.

Ramsey, Kate. 2011. *The Spirits and the Law: Vodou and Power in Haiti*. Chicago: University of Chicago Press.

Reddock, Rhoda. 1985. "Women and Slavery in the Caribbean: A Feminist Perspective." *Latin American Perspectives* 44, no. 12, 63–80.

——. 1994. *Women, Labour, and Politics in Trinidad and Tobago, a History*. London: Zed.

Reddock, Rhoda, ed. 2004. *Interrogating Caribbean Masculinities*. Kingston: University of the West Indies Press.

Richardson, Diane. 1998. "Sexuality and Citizenship," *Sociology* 32, no. 1, 83–100.

——. 2000. *Rethinking Sexuality*. London: Sage.

Riley, Denise. 1995. *"Am I That Name?": Feminism and the Category of "Women" in History*. Minneapolis: University of Minnesota Press.

Rival, Laura., ed. 1998. *The Social Life of Trees: Anthropological Perspectives on Tree Symbolism*. Oxford: Berg.

Roach, Joseph. 1996. *Cities of the Dead: Circum-Atlantic Performance*. New York: Columbia University Press.

Roberts, Dorothy E. 1997. *Killing the Black Body: Race, Reproduction, and the Meaning of Liberty*. New York: Pantheon.

Robinson, Tracy S. 2000. "Fictions of Citizenship, Bodies without Sex: The Production and Effacement of Gender in Law." *Small Axe* 4, no. 7, 1–27.

———. 2003. "Beyond the Bill of Rights: Constituting Caribbean Women as Citizens." *Confronting Power, Theorizing Gender: Interdisciplinary Perspectives in the Caribbean*, ed. Eudine Barriteau, 231–61. Kingston: University of the West Indies Press.

———. 2007. "A Loving Freedom: A Caribbean Feminist Ethics." *Small Axe* 24 (October), 118–29.

Roderick, Ian. 1998. "Habitable Spaces." *Space and Culture* 1 no. 3, 1–4.

Rodney, Walter. 1981. *A History of the Guyanese Working People, 1881–1905*. Baltimore: Johns Hopkins University Press.

Roediger, David. 1991. *The Wages of Whiteness: Race and the Making of the American Working Class*. London: Verso.

Rose, Sonya. 2007. "Fit to Fight but Not to Vote?: Masculinity and Citizenship in Britain, 1832–1918." *Representing Masculinity: Male Citizenship in Modern Western Culture*, ed. Stefan Dudink, Karen Hagemann, and Anna Clark, 151–68. New York: Palgrave Macmillan,

Rose, Tricia. 1994a. "Rap Music and the Demonization of Young Black Men." *Black Male: Representations of Masculinity in Contemporary American Art*, ed. Thelma Golden, 149–57. New York: Whitney Museum of American Art.

———. 1994b. *Black Noise: Rap Music and Black Culture in Contemporary America*. Middletown, Conn.: Wesleyan University Press.

Roseberry, William. 1988. "Political Economy," *Annual Review of Anthropology* 17, 161–85.

———. 1994. *Anthropologies and Histories: Essays in Culture, History and Political Economy*. New Brunswick, N.J.: Rutgers University Press.

Ryan, James. 1997. *Picturing Empire: Photography and the Visualization of the British Empire*. Chicago: University of Chicago Press.

Ryan, Mary P. 1990. *Women in Public: Between Banners and Ballots, 1825–1880*. Baltimore: Johns Hopkins University Press.

———. 1992. "Gender and Public Access." *Habermas and the Public Sphere*, ed. Craig Calhoun, 259–88. Cambridge: MIT Press.

———. 1997. *Civic Wars: Democracy and Public Life in the American City during the Nineteenth Century*. Berkeley: University of California Press.

Sale, Maggie Montesinos. 1997. *The Slumbering Volcano: American Slave Ship Revolts and the Production of Rebellious Masculinity*. Durham: Duke University Press.

Sanchez-Eppler, Karen. 1988. "Bodily Bonds: The Intersecting Rhetorics of Feminism and Abolitionism." *Representations* 24, 28–59.

Sanchez-Taylor, Jacqueline. 1999. "Tourism and 'Embodied' Commodities: Sex Tourism in the Caribbean." *Tourism and Sex: Culture, Commerce, and Coercion*, ed. Stephen Clift and Simon Carter, 41–53. London: Pinter.

Saunders, Patricia. 2003. "Is Not Everything Good to Eat, Good to Talk: Sexual Economy and Dancehall Music in the Global Marketplace." *Small Axe* 13 (March), 95–115.

Schama, Simon. 1995. *Landscape and Memory*. London: Harper Collins.

Schuler, Monica. 1980. *"Alas, Alas Kongo": A Social History of Indentured African Immigration into Jamaica, 1841–1865*. Baltimore: Johns Hopkins University Press.

——. 1993. "Myalism and the African Religious Tradition in Jamaica." *Caribbean Freedom: Society and Economy from Emancipation to the Present*, ed. Hilary Beckles and Verene Shepherd, 295–303. Kingston: Ian Randle.

Schuller, Mark. 2010. *Unstable Foundations: Impact of NGOs on Human Rights for Port-au-Prince's Internally Displaced People*. Research Report, October 2010. http://ijdh.org/archives/14855. Accessed 27 September 2011.

Scott, James C. 1985. *Weapons of the Weak: Everyday Forms of Peasant Resistance*. New Haven: Yale University Press.

——. 1990. *Domination and the Arts of Resistance: Hidden Transcripts*. New Haven: Yale University Press.

——. 1999. *Seeing Like a State: How Certain Schemes to Improve the Human Condition Have Failed*. New Haven: Yale University Press.

——. 2009. *The Art of Not Being Governed: An Anarchist History of Upland Southeast Asia*. New Haven: Yale University Press.

Scott, Joan Wallach. 1988. "Gender: A Useful Category of Historical Analysis." *Gender and the Politics of History*, 28–50. New York: Columbia University Press.

Scott, Julius Sherard. 1986. *The Common Wind: Currents of Afro–Caribbean Political Communication in the Era of the Haitian Revolution*. Ph.D. diss., Duke University, Durham.

Scott, Rebecca. 1985. *Slave Emancipation in Cuba: The Transition to Free Labor, 1860–1899*. Princeton: Princeton University Press.

——. 1988. "Exploring the Meaning of Freedom: Postemancipation Societies in Comparative Perspective." *Hispanic American Historical Review* 68, 407–28.

——. 2000. "Fault Lines, Color Lines, and Party Lines: Race, Labor, and Collective Action in Louisiana and Cuba, 1862–1912." *Beyond Slavery: Explorations of Race, Labor, and Citizenship in Postemancipation Societies*, ed. Frederick Cooper, Thomas C. Holt, and Rebecca J. Scott, 61–106. Chapel Hill: University of North Carolina Press.

——. 2005. *Degrees of Freedom: Louisiana and Cuba after Slavery*. Cambridge: Belknap.

Scully, Pamela. 1997. *Liberating the Family?: Gender and British Slave Emancipation in the Rural Western Cape, South Africa, 1823–1853*. Portsmouth, N.H.: Heinemann.

——. 2005. "Masculinity, Citizenship, and the Production of Knowledge in the Postemancipation Cape Colony, 1834–1844." *Gender and Emancipation in the Atlantic World*, ed. Pamela Scully and Diana Paton, 37–55. Durham: Duke University Press.

Scully, Pamela, and Diana Paton, eds. 2005. *Gender and Emancipation in the Atlantic World*. Durham: Duke University Press.

Semmel, Bernard. 1962. *The Governor Eyre Controversy*. London: Macgibbon and Kee.

Sen, Gita, and Caren Grown. 1987. *Development, Crises, and Alternative Visions: Third World Women's Perspectives*. New York: Monthly Review.

Senior, Olive. 2005. *Gardening in the Tropics*. Toronto: Insomniac Press.

Sepinwall, Alyssa G. 2005. *The Abbé Grégoire and the French Revolution: The Making of Modern Universalism*. Berkeley: University of California Press.

Sheller, Mimi. 1997. "Sword-Bearing Citizens: Militarism and Manhood in Nineteenth-Century Haiti." *Plantation Society in the Americas* 4, nos. 2–3, 233–78.

——. 1998. "'Quasheba, Mother, Queen': Black Women's Public Leadership and Political Protest in Post-emancipation Jamaica, 1834–65." *Slavery and Abolition* 19, no. 3, 90–117.

——. 1999. "The 'Haytian Fear': Racial Projects and Competing Reactions to the First Black Republic." *The Global Color Line: Racial and Ethnic Inequality and Struggle from a Global Perspective*, ed. Pinar Batur-Vanderlippe and Joe R. Feagin, 283–301. Greenwich, Conn.: JAI.

——. 2000. *Democracy after Slavery: Black Publics and Peasant Radicalism in Haiti and Jamaica*. London: Macmillan.

——. 2003. *Consuming the Caribbean*. London: Routledge.

——. 2004. "Natural Hedonism: The Invention of the Caribbean as Tropical Playground." *Tourism in the Caribbean: Trends, Developments, Prospects*, ed. David Duval, 23–38. London: Routledge.

——. 2005a. "Acting as Free Men: Subaltern Masculinities and Citizenship in Postslavery Jamaica." *Gender and Emancipation in the Atlantic World*, ed. Pamela Scully and Diana Paton, 79–98. Durham: Duke University Press.

——. 2005b. "'Her Majesty's Sable Subjects': Citizenship and Subaltern Masculinities in Post-Emancipation Jamaica." *Political Power and Social Theory* 17, 71–100.

——. 2005c. "'You Signed My Name but Not My Feet': Paradoxes of Peasant Resistance and State Control in Post-Revolutionary Haiti." *Contesting Freedom: Control and Resistance in the Post-Emancipation Caribbean*, ed. Gad Heuman and David Trotman, 87–103. Oxford: Macmillan Caribbean.

——. 2007a. "Arboreal Landscapes of Power and Resistance." *Caribbean Land and Development Revisited*, ed. Janet Momsen and Jean Besson, 207–28. Oxford: Macmillan.

——. 2007b. "Work That Body: Sexual Citizenship and Embodied Freedom." *Constructing Vernacular Culture in the Trans-Caribbean*, ed. Holger Henke and Karl-Heinz Magister, 345–76. Boston: Lexington.

——. 2011a. "Bleeding Humanity: Anti-Slavery Sugar Boycotts, Gendered Embodiment, and Ethical Consumers." *Humanity* (Fall), 171–92.

——. 2011b. "Hidden Textures of Race and Historical Memory: The Rediscovery of Photographs Relating to Jamaica's Morant Bay Rebellion of 1965." *Princeton Library Chronicle*, 72 (2): 532–67.

Shepherd, Verene. 1987. "Depression in the 'Tin Roof Towns': Economic Problems of Urban Indians in Jamaica, 1930–1950." *India in the Caribbean*, ed. David Dabydeen and Brinsley Samaroo, 173–88. London: Hansib and University of Warwick.

——. 1994. *Transients to Settlers: The Experience of Indians in Jamaica, 1845–1950*. Leeds: Peepal Tree.

Shepherd, Verene, Bridget Brereton, and Barbara Bailey, eds. 1995. *Engendering History: Caribbean Women in Historical Perspective*. Kingston: Ian Randle.

Shiva, Vandana. 1989. *Staying Alive: Women, Ecology, and Development*. London: Zed.

Silvera, Makeda. 1991. "Man Royals and Sodomites: Some Thoughts on the Invisibility of Afro-Caribbean Lesbians." *Piece of My Heart: A Lesbian of Colour Anthology*, 14–26. Toronto: Sister Vision.

Simmel, Georg. 1997. *Simmel on Culture: Selected Writings*, ed. David Frisby and Mike Featherstone. London: Sage.

Simmonds, Felly Nkweto. 1997. "My Body, Myself: How Does a Black Woman Do Sociology?" *Black British Feminism: A Reader*, ed. Heidi Safia Mirza, 50–63. London: Routledge.

Sinha, Mrinalini. 1995. *Colonial Masculinity: The "Manly Englishman" and the "Effeminate Bengali" in the Late Nineteenth Century*. Manchester: Manchester University Press.

——. 1999. "Giving Masculinity a History: Some Contributions from the Historiography of Colonial India." *Gender and History* 11, no. 3, 445–60.

——. 2007. "Unraveling Masculinity and Rethinking Citizenship: A Comment." *Representing Masculinity: Male Citizenship in Modern Western Culture*, ed. Stefan Dudink, Karen Hagemann, and Anna Clark, 261–74. New York: Palgrave Macmillan.

Sistren Theatre Collective, with Honor Ford Smith. 1986. *Lionheart Gal: Life Stories of Jamaican Women*. London: Women's Press.

Skelton, Tracey. 1995. "Boom Bye Bye: Jamaican Ragga and Gay Resistance." *Mapping Desire: Geographies of Sexualities*, ed. David Bell and Gill Valentine, 264–83. London: Routledge.

——. 2004. "The Importance of Reflexivity in Caribbean Research: Thinking through 'Race,' Self, and Politics." *Beyond the Blood, the Beach, and the Banana: New Perspectives in Caribbean Studies*, ed. Sandra Courtman, 24–33. Kingston: Ian Randle.

Smith, Faith. 2007. "Crosses/Crossroads/Crossings." *Small Axe* 24 (October), 130–38.

Smith, Faith, ed. 2011. *Sex and the Citizen: Interrogating the Caribbean*. Charlottesville: University of Virginia Press.

Smith, Michael, and Luis Guarnizo, eds. 1998. *Transnationalism from Below*, Comparative Urban and Community Research Series, vol. 6. New Brunswick: Transaction.

Smith, Raymond T. 1973. "The Matrifocal Family." *The Character of Kinship*, ed. Jack Goody, 121–44. Cambridge: Cambridge University Press.

Smith, Rogers. 1997. *Civic Ideals: Conflicting Visions of Citizenship in U.S. History*. New Haven: Yale University Press.

Socolow, Susan M. 1996. "Economic Roles of the Free Women of Color of Cap Français." *More Than Chattel: Black Women and Slavery in the Americas*, ed. David Barry Gaspar and Darlene Clark Hine, 279–97. Bloomington: University of Indiana Press.

Somers, Margaret R. 1993. "Citizenship and the Place of the Public Sphere: Law, Community, and Political Culture in the Transition to Democracy." *American Sociological Review* 58 (October), 587–620.

——. 1994. "Rights, Relationality, and Membership: Rethinking the Making and Meaning of Citizenship." *Law and Social Inquiry* 19, no. 1, 63–112.

——. 2005. "Citizenship Troubles: Genealogies of Struggle for the Soul of the Social."

Rethinking Modernity, ed. Julia Adams, Elisabeth Clemens, and Ann Orloff, 438–69. Durham: Duke University Press.

Spelman, Elizabeth. 1990. "Gender and Race: The Ampersand Problem in Feminist Thought." *Inessential Woman: Problems of Exclusion in Feminist Thought*, 114–32. Boston: Beacon.

Spillers, Hortense. 1987. "Mama's Baby, Papa's Maybe: An American Grammar Book." *Diacritics* 17, no. 2, 65–81.

Spivak, Gayatri. 1988. "Can the Subaltern Speak?" *Marxism and the Interpretation of Culture*, ed. Cary Nelson and Lawrence Grossberg, 271–315. Urbana: University of Illinois Press.

Spurr, David. 1993. *The Rhetoric of Empire: Colonial Discourse in Journalism, Travel Writing, and Imperial Administration*. Durham: Duke University Press.

Stanley, Amy Dru. 1998. *From Bondage to Contract: Wage Labor, Marriage, and the Market in the Age of Emancipation*. Cambridge: Cambridge University Press.

Stanley-Niaah, Sonjah. 2004. "Kingston's Dancehall: A Story of Space and Celebration." *Space and Culture* 7, no. 1, 102–18.

——. 2008. "Performance Geographies from Slave Ship to Ghetto." *Space and Culture* 11, no. 4, 343–60.

Stanley-Niaah, Sonjah, and Donna Hope. 2009. "Canvasses of Representation: Stuart Hall, the Body, and Dancehall Performance." *Culture, Politics, Race, and Diaspora: The Thought of Stuart Hall*, ed. Brian Meeks, 218–48. Kingston: Ian Randle.

Stepan, Nancy Leys. 1991. *The Hour of Eugenics: Race, Gender, and Nation in Latin America*. Ithaca: Cornell University Press.

——. 2000. "Race, Gender, Science, and Citizenship." *Cultures of Empire: A Reader*, ed. Catherine Hall, 61–86. Manchester: Manchester University Press.

——. 2001. *Picturing Tropical Nature*. London: Reaktion.

Stern, Steve J. 1993 (1988). "Feudalism, Capitalism and the World-System in the Perpective of Latin America and the Caribbean." *Confronting Historical Paradigms*, eds. Frederick Cooper, Florencia E. Mallon, Steve J. Stern, Allen F. Isaacman, and William Roseberry, 23–83. Madison: University of Wisconsin Press.

Stern, Steve J., ed. 1987. *Resistance, Rebellion, and Consciousness in the Andean Peasant World, 18th to 20th Centuries*. Madison: University of Wisconsin Press.

Stewart, Robert J. 1992. *Religion and Society in Postemancipation Jamaica*. Knoxville: University of Tennessee Press.

Stinchcombe, Arthur. 1996. *Sugar Island Slavery in the Age of Enlightenment: The Political Economy of the Caribbean World*. Princeton: Princeton University Press.

Stitt, Jocelyn F. 2007. "Gendered Legacies of Romantic Nationalism in the Works of Michelle Cliff." *Small Axe* 24 (October), 52–72.

Stoler, Ann Laura. 1995. *Race and the Education of Desire: Foucault's "History of Sexuality" and the Colonial Order of Things*. Durham: Duke University Press.

——. 2002. *Carnal Knowledge and Imperial Power*. Berkeley: University of California Press.

Stoler, Ann Laura, and Frederick Cooper, eds. 1997. *Tensions of Empire: Colonial Cultures in a Bourgeois World*. Berkeley: University of California Press.

Sudbury, Julia. 2002. "Celling Black Bodies: Black Women in the Global Prison-Industrial Complex." *Feminist Review* 70, 57–74.

Sudbury, Julia, ed. 2005. *Global Lockdown: Race, Gender, and the Prison-Industrial Complex*. New York: Routledge.

Sutcliffe, David, and Carol Tomlin. 1986. "The Black Churches." *The Language of the Black Experience. Cultural Expression through Word and Sound in the Caribbean and Black Britain*, ed. David Sutcliffe and Ansel Wong, 15–31. Oxford: Blackwell.

Terborg-Penn, Rosalyn. 1986. "Black Women in Resistance: A Cross-Cultural Perspective." *In Resistance: Studies in African, Caribbean, and Afro-American History*, ed. Gary Y. Okihiro, 188–209. Amherst: University of Massachusetts Press.

Thomas, Deborah A. 2004. *Modern Blackness: Nationalism, Globalization, and the Politics of Culture in Jamaica*. Durham: Duke University Press.

Thompson, Edward P. 1966. *The Making of the English Working Class*. New York: Vintage.

Thompson, Krista. 2006. *An Eye for the Tropics: Tourism, Photography, and the Framing of the Caribbean Picturesque*. Durham: Duke University Press.

Tilly, Charles, ed. 1995. *Citizenship, Identity, and Social History*. Cambridge: Cambridge University Press.

——. 1999. *Durable Inequality*. Los Angeles: University of California Press.

Tinker, Hugh. 1993 (1974). *A New System of Slavery: The Export of Indian Labour Overseas, 1830–1920*, 2d ed. London: Hansib.

Tinsley, Omise'eke N. 2008. "Black Atlantic, Queer Atlantic: Queer Imaginings of the Middle Passage." *GLQ* 14, 2–3.

——. 2010. *Thiefing Sugar: Eroticism between Women in Caribbean Literature*. Durham: Duke University Press.

Titley, Gavin. 2005. "Accidental Cosmopolitanism: Connectivity, Insistence and Cultural Experience," Ph.D. diss., Dublin City University.

Tolia-Kelly, Divya. 2004. "Locating Processes of Identification: Studying the Precipitates of Re-memory through Artifacts in the British Asian Home." *Transactions of the Institute of British Geographers*, new series 29, 314–29.

——. 2006. "Mobility/Stability: British Asian Cultures of Landscape and Englishness." *Environment and Planning* 38, no. 2, 341–58.

Tolia-Kelly, Divya, and Andy Morris. 2004. "Disruptive Aesthetics? The Burden of Representation in the Art of Chris Ofili and Yinka Shonibare." *Third Text* 18, no. 2, 153–67.

Tomich, Dale. 1993. "Une Petite Guinée: Provision Ground and Plantation in Martinique, 1830–1848." *Cultivation and Culture: Labor and the Shaping of Slave Life in the Americas*, ed. Ira Berlin and Philip D. Morgan, 221–42. Charlottesville: University of Virginia Press.

Trotter, Joe William, Jr. 1990. *Coal, Class, and Color: Blacks in Southern West Virginia, 1915–1932*. Urbana: University of Illinois Press.

Trotz, Alissa. 2007. "Red Thread: The Politics of Hope in Guyana." *Race and Class* 49, no. 2, 71–79.

Trouillot, Michel-Rolph. 1990. *Haiti: State against Nation: The Origins and Legacy of Duvalierism.* New York: Monthly Review.

———. 1992. "The Inconvenience of Freedom: Free People of Color and the Political Aftermath of Slavery in Dominica and Saint-Domingue/Haiti." *The Meaning of Freedom: Economics, Politics, and Culture after Slavery,* ed. Frank McGlynn and Seymour Drescher, 147–82. Pittsburgh: University of Pittsburgh Press.

———. 1993. "Coffee Planters and Coffee Slaves in the Antilles: The Impact of a Secondary Crop." *Cultivation and Culture: Labor and the Shaping of Slave Life in the Americas,* ed. Ira Berlin and Philip D. Morgan, 124–37, 331–35. Charlottesville: University of Virginia Press.

———. 1995. *Silencing the Past: Power and the Production of History.* Boston: Beacon.

———. 2003. "North Atlantic Universals: Analytical Fictions, 1492–1945." *The South Atlantic Quarterly* 101 (4), 839–58.

Turner, Bryan. 1993. "Contemporary Problems in the Theory of Citizenship." *Citizenship and Social Theory,* ed. Bryan Turner, 1–18. London: Sage.

Turner, Mary S. 1982. *Slaves and Missionaries: The Disintegration of Jamaican Slave Society, 1787–1834.* Urbana: University of Illinois Press.

———. 1995. "From Chattel Slaves into Wage Slaves: A Jamaican Case Study." *From Chattel Slaves to Wage Slaves: The Dynamics of Labour Bargaining in the Americas,* ed. Mary S. Turner, 33–47. London: James Currey.

Ulysse, Gina Athena. 1999. "Uptown Ladies and Downtown Women: Female Representations of Class and Color in Jamaica." *Representations of Blackness and the Performance of Identities,* ed. Jean Rahier, 147–72. New Haven: Greenwood.

———. 2002. "Conquering Duppies in Kingston: Miss Tiny and Me, Fieldwork Conflicts, and Being Loved and Rescued." *Anthropology and Humanism* 27, no. 1, 10–26.

———. 2008. *Downtown Ladies: Informal Commercial Importers, a Haitian Anthropologist, and Self-Making in Jamaica.* Chicago: University of Chicago Press.

Urry, John. 1990. *The Tourist Gaze: Leisure and Travel in Contemporary Societies.* London: Sage.

Urry, John, and Jonas Larsen. 2011. *The Tourist Gaze 3.0.* London: Sage.

Vogel, Ursula. 1994. "Marriage and the Boundaries of Citizenship." *The Condition of Citizenship,* ed. Bart van Steenbergen, 76–89. London: Sage.

Wahab, Amar. 2004. "Inventing 'Trinidad': Colonial Representations in the Nineteenth Century." Ph.D. diss., University of Toronto.

Ware, Vron. 1992. *Beyond the Pale: White Women, Racism, and History.* London: Verso.

Warner, Michael. 1990. *Letters of the Republic.* Cambridge: Harvard University Press.

———. 1993. "The Mass Public and the Mass Subject." *The Phantom Public Sphere,* ed. Bruce Robbins, 234–56. Minneapolis: University of Minnesota Press.

———. 2002. "Publics and Counterpublics." *Public Culture* 14, no. 1, 49–90.

Warner-Lewis, Maureen. 2003. *Central Africa in the Caribbean: Transcending Time, Transforming Culture.* Kingston: University of the West Indies Press.

Watts, David. 1990. *The West Indies: Patterns of Development, Culture, and Environmental Change since 1492.* Cambridge: Cambridge University Press.

Weber, Max. 1976. *The Agrarian Sociology of Ancient Civilizations*, trans. R. I. Frank. London: New Left Books.

Wekker, Gloria. 1997. "One Finger Does Not Drink Okra Soup: Afro-Surinamese Women and Critical Agency." *Feminist Genealogies, Colonial Legacies, Democratic Futures*, ed. M. Jacqui Alexander and Chandra Talpade Mohanty, 330–52. New York: Routledge.

——. 2000. "Mati-ism and Black Lesbianism: Two Idealtypical Expressions of Female Homosexuality in Black Communities of the Diaspora." *The Greatest Taboo: Homosexuality in Black Communities*, ed. Delroy Constantine-Simms, 149–62. Los Angeles: Alyson.

——. 2006. *The Politics of Passion: Women's Sexual Culture in the Afro-Surinamese Diaspora*. New York: Columbia University Press.

Wiegman, Robyn. 1995. *American Anatomies: Theorizing Race and Gender*. Durham: Duke University Press.

Williams, Brackette. 1991. *Stains on My Name, War in My Veins: Guyana and the Politics of Cultural Struggle*. Durham: Duke University Press.

Williamson, Tom, and Liz Bellamy. 1987. *Property and Landscape: A Social History of Land Ownership and the English Countryside*. London: George Philip.

Wilmot, Swithin R. 1986. "Emancipation in Action: Workers and Wage Conflict in Jamaica, 1838–40." *Jamaica Journal* 19, 55–62.

——. 1995. "'Females of Abandoned Character'?: Women and Protest in Jamaica, 1838–65." *Engendering History: Caribbean Women in Historical Perspective*, ed. Verene Shepherd, Bridget Brereton, and Barbara Bailey, 279–95. Kingston: Ian Randle.

Wilmot, Swithin R., ed. 2009. *Freedom: Retrospective and Prospective*. Kingston: Ian Randle.

Wilson, Peter J. 1973. *Crab Antics: The Social Anthropology of English-speaking Negro Societies in the Caribbean*. New Haven: Yale University Press.

Wilson-Tagoe, Nana. 1998. *Historical Thought and Literary Representation in West Indian Literature*. Gainesville: University Press of Florida.

Winn, Peter. 1986. *Weavers of Revolution: The Yarur Workers and Chile's Road to Socialism*. New York: Oxford University Press.

Wolf, Eric R. 1969. Peasant Wars of the Twentieth Century. New York: Harper and Row.

——. 1982. *Europe and the People without History*. Berkeley: University of California Press.

Wynter, Silvia. 1971. "History and the Novel: Plot and Plantation." *Savacou* 5 (June), 95–102.

Yashar, Deborah. 2005. *Contesting Citizenship in Latin America: The Rise of Indigenous Movements and the Postliberal Challenge*. Cambridge: Cambridge University Press.

Yellin, Jean F. 1989. *Women and Sisters: The Antislavery Feminists in American Culture*. New Haven: Yale University Press.

Yelvington, Kevin. 1995. *Producing Power: Ethnicity, Gender, and Class in a Caribbean Workplace*. Philadelphia: Temple University Press.

Young, Iris Marion. 1990. *Justice and the Politics of Difference*. Princeton: Princeton University Press.

——. 1998 (1987). "Impartiality and the Civic Public: Some Implications of Feminist Critiques of Moral and Political Theory." *Feminism, the Public, and the Private*, ed. Joan B. Landes, 421–47. Oxford: Oxford University Press.

Young, Robert. 1995. *Colonial Desire: Hybridity in Theory, Culture, and Race*. New York: Routledge.

Zelizer, Viviana. 2005. *The Purchase of Intimacy*. Princeton: Princeton University Press.

Page numbers in italics refer to figures.

absences, from the historical record, 3, 13, 15, 218, 229

Acaau, Louis-Jean-Jacques, 181–83

Africans, liberated, 98

Afro-Creole nationalism, 240–41

"Afro-Creole" world, 160

Agassiz, Louis, 230

agrarian history, 32

Ahmed, Sara, 28, 92, 220–21

Aizan (lwa), 202

Alexander, M. Jacqui, 30, 224–25, 241–43, 245; *Pedagogies of Crossing*, 46

Amazons of Salnave, 184

"amelioration," 57, 60

Andrews, George, 162

Anglade, Georges, 177–78

Anthony, Susan B., 255

apprenticeship, 10–11, 53, 56, 59–67

arboreal landscapes, 14–15, 187–94, 197–201, 206

archives, 11, 85–86, 169. *See also* absences, from the historical record; silences, in the historical record

Ardouin, Beaubrun, 159, 163, 175, 179–80

Aristide, Jean-Bertrand, 203

Arnold, David, 189

arrowroot, 204

Auguste, Rose-Anne, 257–58

Augusto, Geri, 187

Austin-Broos, Diane, 67–68, 96

Baldwin, James, 38–39

Ballantine, Bill: "Maman Celie" (illustration), 231–33, *232*; "Photo Studio" (illustration), 214, *215*; "Voodoo Village," 231

"bass culture," 266–67

Beisel, Nicola, 53, 255

Belisario, Isaac Mendes, 116

Berlant, Lauren, 41–42, 251–52

Berlant, Lauren, and Elizabeth Freeman, "Queer Nationality," 260

Besson, Jean, 96–97, 191–92, 209

biomedicine, 251

"biopolitics," 26–27

biopower, 247–54, 282 n. 3

Bird, Mark, 159–60, 180

birth control, 247–48, 253–59, 301 n. 11

Birth Control Federation of America, Negro Project, 255

"black," the, 218–20

"black communism," 183–84

"blackness," 38–39, 134–36, 185–86

Bloch, Marc, 4, 167–69

blues, 263–65

body, the: disciplining of, 282 n. 3; in slavery, 251–54; and work, 267

Bogle, Paul, 123–24, 139

Bogues, Anthony, 89–90

Bolland, Nigel, "The Politics of Freedom in the British Caribbean," 5

Bouchereau, Telismon, 163

Boyer, General (later President) Jean-Pierre, 154–56, 159, 163–64, 172; defeat at Port-au-Prince, 181

branding, 54–55

Brassey, Sady, 222–23

Brathwaite, Kamau, 34

Brereton, Bridget, 96

Briggs, Laura, 256

Briscoe, Captain Joseph, 134

British abolition efforts, 58–59

Brooks, Daphne, 263

Brown, Jonathan, 177

Brown, Karen McCarthy, 151

Brown, Laura, 197

Bryson, Norman, 262

Buck-Morss, Susan, 169

Burton, Richard, 143–44, 150–52

Bush, Barbara, 55

Butler, Judith, 41

Bwa Kayiman, Haiti, mapou tree at, 201

Carby, Hazel, 264

Cardwell, Edward, 121–22

Caribbean Studies Association, 8–9

Caribbean subaltern groups, 91–92

caricatures, 54, 77, 176

carnival, 42–43, 268–69

Chapman, Herrick, 162

Charles, Carolle, 256–57

Christmas riots in Kingston (1842), 78

Christophe, King Henri, 153–54, 168, 171

churches, 11, 67–71; Baptist, 99–100; missionaries, 67–69; Native Baptists, 139; Pentecostal, 303 n. 24; women's political activities in, 67–74

citizenship, 9–14, 19–29, 52–53, 89–97, 132–33, 148–57, 161–65, 211; black, 186; embodied, 26–27; equalities of, 283

n. 8; erotic agency and, 30; exclusion from, 25–26, 142–43, 154–57; and freedom, 5–8, 100; and Freemasonry, 158–60; gendered, 13, 142–43, 145; language of, 239–40; masculine, 11, 111, 146–47; practices of, 283 n. 7; respectable, 275; sexual economies of, 237–38; and women's health, 258–59. See also sexual citizenship

Cliff, Michelle, No Telephone to Heaven, 192–93

Code Henri, 154–57

Code Rural (1826), 172–73; and pregnant women, 297 n. 13

coffee cultivation, 171, 174–75, 204

Columbus, Christopher, 194

Comhaire, Jean, 157

Cooper, Carolyn, 66, 270–71, 276–77

Cooper, Frederick, 211

corporeality, 42

counter-gaze, the, 225, 233–38

counter-publics, 11, 35–40

court cases, 56; against female apprentices, 60–62; on rent and wages, 65

courthouses, 11

Cousin Azaka (trickster figure), 182

"creole gaze," 234

"creole" speech, 37

Cresswell, Tim, 38, 45–46, 262

"daggering," 276–77

dance, 38, 267, 276–77

dancehall, 42, 44, 247, 261–70, 274–75, 278–79

Darfour, Félix, 162

Darling, Governor Charles, 103, 105–6

Davis, Angela, 254–55, 263–64

Day, Charles William, Five Years' Residence in the West Indies, 225–26

Day, Susan de Forest, 223

deforestation, 197

DeLoughrey, Elizabeth, 193

democracy, 175

Depo-Provera, 258–59

Desmond, Jane, 266–67

Dessalines, General Jean-Jacques, 149–51, *156*, 156–57, 171

de Tocqueville, Alexis, *Democracy in America*, 66

"deviancy," 278

difference, 28–29, 211–12, 223, 235–36

disgust, 221, 224, 226

domesticity, 74

domination, erotic, 277–78

douglas, 112–13

Drake Manuscript, 194–95

Dubois, Laurent, 89, 169, 207

Duncan, James, 218

Duperly family, 116–17, 291 n. 3

Dutty, Boukman, 149, 183

Duval-Carrié, Edouard, "Le Nouveau Familier," *156*, 157

Duvalier, François, 156

Edmondson, Belinda, 271–72

elections, 70–71, 279

enclosure system, in Britain, 198

erotic agency, 6, 16–17, 30, 47, 240–48, 260–61, 264–65, 277–80

"ethnoperformance," 237

eugenics, 247, 254–56

exclusion, 25–26, 154–56

executions, 83–84, 127, 292 n. 8, 292 n. 10

Eyre, Governor Edward John, 81, 83–84, 118, 128, 131; criticism of, 121–24; report on conditions in Jamaica, 109–10

family, the, 29, 50, 74, 107–12, 154; nuclear, 162–63; patriarchal, 94–97, 102–5, 112, 128–29; rhetoric of, 143, 148–50, 157–65

family land, 191–92, 204

femininity, 112, 240–41

feminism: campaigns of, 255; ghetto, 272, 274

Fermor, Patrick Leigh, *The Traveller's Tree*, 199–200

fertility, 247

Fick, Caroline, 171

Fischer, Sibylle, 169

flogging, 83–84, 127; of women, 53, 56, 58–60, 62

forests, 192–97. *See also* arboreal landscapes

Foucault, Michel, 26; *The History of Sexuality*, 248–54

Fox-Genovese, Elizabeth, 68

Francis, Wigmoore, 146

Franklin, James, 176

Fraser, Nancy, 36–37

freedom, 89–90, 92–93, 111, 184–86, 279–80; and citizenship, 5–8, 100; and control, 14; embodied, 9–10, 14, 19–24, 246–48, 261–70, 278–79; personal, 11, 58; queer Caribbean, 239–43

Freeman, Elizabeth. *See* Berlant, Lauren, and Elizabeth Freeman

Freemasonry, 158–60

Froude, James Anthony, *The English in the West Indies; or, The Bow of Ulysses*, 230

fruit trees, 204; in slave ownership, 207–9

Fyfe, Colonel Alexander, 116; and the Maroons, 133–34, *135*

gangsta, 269–70

Garvey, Marcus, 140

Garvey, Marcus Mosiah, 140

gaze, the, 15–16, 234; counter-gaze to, 225, 233–38; disruption of, 231; imperial, 216–17; returning of, 219, 221, 227–28, 235, 237–38; staring, 223; tourist, 212, 217

Geggus, David, 175–76

gender, 2, 11, 26, 29, 108, 143–48, 223

Geoghagan family, 82–83, 118, 127

Gikandi, Simon, 216–17, 220–21, 230–31

Gill, Lyndon, 245

Gilroy, Paul, 37, 267–68, 275

Glissant, Edouard, 34, 193, 200, 203, 216

globalization, 34–35

Gmelch, George, 235

goddesses, 276–77

Gombrich, Ernst, 202

Gordon, George William, 121–23
Goucher, Candice, 151
Grenada, U.S. invasion of, 243
Grey, Governor Charles Edward, 102
Guha, Ramachandra, 189
guidebooks, 218
Gulland, Alexander Dudgeon, 114–17

Haiti: civil war in (1805–20), 170; coat of
    arms of, 150–51; economic influences
    on, 297 n. 4; independence recog-
    nized, 297 n. 4; infantilization of, 163–
    65; liberal revolution in (1843), 180–
    82; position of women in, 175–80; U.S.
    occupation of, 230. *See also* Kingdom
    of Haiti; Republic of Haiti
Haitian earthquake (2010), 1–2, 4–5, 185–
    86, 233, 277
Haitian Revolution, 142–43, 166–71
Hall, Catherine, 59, 95
Hall, Douglas, 64, 204–5
Hall, Stuart, 217, 231
hangings, 83–84, 292 n. 8
Harris, Wilson, 193
Harrison, Faye, 236–37
Harrison, John, 196
Hartman, Saidiya, 19–20, 34–35, 50, 252,
    260, 268
Harvey, Thomas, 60–61, 84
Hastings Jay, E. A., 227–28; "Four
    Months Cruising in the West Indies,"
    200
hegemony, 32–33
Henriques, Julian, 266
heteronormativity, 40, 43, 45, 240,
    278–79
Heuman, Gad, 81–82, 118
Higman, Barry, 189–92
Hill, Robert A., 140
hip-hop, 267
history, 7–8, 31–35, 193; oral, 6, 281 n. 2;
    subaltern, 200–201; textual, 237–38
HIV/AIDS, 44–45
Holt, Thomas, 56, 60
homophobia, 43–47, 247, 284 n. 14

homosexuality, 40, 43–47, 241–42; crimi-
    nalized, 300 n. 1
hooks, bell, 240–41
houses of correction. *See* workhouses
Hurbon, Laennec, 151

identity, 193
immigration, 102–3, 105
indentured laborers, 11, 97–103, 106–7,
    112, 286 n. 20, 289 n. 13, 290 n. 22

Jacmel, Haiti, 233; "Artists at work in Jac-
    mel," *234*
Jacobs, Harriet, *Incidents in the Life of a
    Slave Girl*, 251–52
Jamaica Gay Freedom Movement, 9
Jamaica Royal Commission, on the Mor-
    ant Bay Rebellion, 117, 123–24
Janvier, Louis Joseph, 172
Jemmott, Jenny, 90–91

Kamugisha, Aaron, 211, 240–41
Kartel, Vybz, 270
Kay, Tamara, 53, 255
Kelley, Robin D. G., 75, 262
Kempadoo, Kamala, 55, 250–51, 262,
    267–68
Kincaid, Jamaica, 209
kinesthetic imagination, 38, 213, 262
Kingdom of Haiti, 153–54, 170–71
Kingsley, Charles, 200; *At Last: A Christ-
    mas in the West Indies*, 226
Kingston, Jamaica, 44–45, 72, 228, 266,
    272, 292 n. 8; population in 1844, 75;
    riots in, 78–80
Kingston Quarterly Meeting (1847),
    70–71
kinship, 51, 74, 96. *See also* family, the
Knowles, Caroline, 37

labor: disputes, 10–11, 49, 56–57, 61–67,
    171–72; division of, 175, 177–78; do-
    mestic, 29; history of, 31–32; re-
    productive, 29–30; rights, 51
Lady Saw, 276–77

Laguerre, Michel, 150

Lamming, George, 191

land, 15; distribution of, 173–75; ownership of, 153, 171

landscape painting, 198–99, 298 n. 11

landscapes, 197–201, 298 n. 2; of power,
206

Latin America, 185

latinization, 33

Lefebvre, Henri, 191, 205

Léogâne, Haiti, 180, 277, 303 n. 25

Lespinasse, Dumai, 161

Levien, Sidney, 123–24, *125*

Leyburn, James, *The Haitian People*, 168

"liberation flora," 187–88, 204

Liberty Trees, 201–4

limbo, 267

literature, 192–93, 216–17

Lomax, Alan, 239, 264–65

Lorde, Audre, 243, 276; "Uses of the
Erotic: The Erotic as Power," 244–45

Louverture, Toussaint, 149, 151, 161, 203;
"Chef des Noirs Insurgés de Saint
Domingue," *152*

Love, Robert, 86

Mackenzie, Charles, 164, 172

Madiou, Thomas, 149

Mahabir, Joy, 266, 268

Mair, Lucille Mathurin, 48, 53

Makandal, François, 149

mangroves, 200–201, 203

manhood, 103, 108, 146, 164–65

Manifeste de Praslin, 161–62, 180

Manigat, Leslie, 182

mapou tree, 201, 203

"*marchandes*," 177–80. *See also* market
women

marginality, men's, 91–92

market places, 78–79

market women ("higglers"), 76–77, 177–
80, 287 n. 32

Marley, Bob, "Redemption Song," 140

Maroons, 116, 119, 127, 133–37, *135*, 204,
287 n. 41

marriage, 66–67, 96, 107

Martha Brae, Jamaica, 208–9

masculinity, 111–12, 134, 142–47, 164–65,
240–41, 275–77; alternative, 90–93; in
dancehall culture, 269–70; forms of,
262; military prowess and, 148–57;
subaltern, 11–12

memory, 206, 213

Métraux, Alfred, 202

militarism, 142–43, 148–57, 170–71, 184–
85; government and, 149–50, 157–58

Minaj, Nicki, 43

Mintz, Sidney, 168, 174, 177–78, 204

mobility, 14, 166, 172–74, 247

Morant Bay, 124, 126–27

Morant Bay Rebellion, 12, 81–84, 117–20,
123–24; George William Gordon's involvement in, 121–23; leadership of,
126–27; Maroons' involvement in, 133–
37; martial law enforced, 119–20, 122–
23; Native Baptists and, 139; numbers
killed in, 292 n. 8; Sidney Levien's involvement in, 123–24; suppression of,
127–33; victims of, 117, 123–24, 128–30.
See also photograph album relating to
Morant Bay Rebellion

Morisseau-Leroy, Félix, "Tourist," 210,
212

Morris, Andy, 217

Morrissey, Marietta, 64

"Mother," 11, 51, 73–74

motherhood, 11, 29, 48, 51, 57–59, 87–88,
255–56; "othermothers" and, 87–88;
property and, 252

musical forms, 263–67, 272–75, 302 n. 19

Myal, 68; revivals (1842 and 1860–61),
72–73

Nanny (Maroon leader), 287 n. 41

Nelson, Brigadier-General Abercrombie,
123

Nettleford, Rex, 4

Newcastle, above Kingston, 120–21

Niles, Blair, "A Monkey on a Postcard"
(chapter title), 229–30

Noble, Denise, 261, 272–74
"noir" identities, 185
Norplant, 258–59, 301 n. 11
"nursing mothers" uprisings, 10–11

Obeah, 68, 72
Ogou/Ogou Feray, 150–51
Ozouf, Mona, 202

Paine, Thomas, "Liberty Tree," 203
palm trees, 194–95, 200–204
Paton, Diana, 34, 49, 54–55
Paton, Edward Agnew, *Down the Islands: A Voyage in the Caribbees*, 219–21
patriarchy, 11, 150, 158–60, 241. *See also* family, the: patriarchal
Patterson, Ebony, *Gangstas for Life* (installations), 269–70
Patterson, Orlando, 58, 91–92
peasantry, 32–33, 168–70, 173–75, 185
People's Convention, 86
performances, 9–10, 21–22, 41, 213, 216, 236–37; of citizenship, 12–13, 27–28
Pétion, President Alexandre (later Alexander), 154, 171
petitions, 70–71, 79, 101, 103–8
"petticoat rebellions," 10–11, 55–56
photograph album relating to Morant Bay Rebellion, 12, 114–17, 121–24, 133–37, 139–41; "Colonel Fyfe," *135*; "The Cotton Tree at the Cross Roads near Morant Bay," 137–39, *138*; "Execution of Rebels at the ruins of the Court House, Morant Bay," *126*, 126–27; "Grave of eighty rebels near Morant Bay, Jamaica," *119*, 119–20; "Morant Bay from the Harbour," 126; "Mr. Levine,—Tried by Civil Power and Convicted," 123, *125*; "Mr. Price, Murdered," *129*, 130; "Natives of Jamaica," 130–33, *131*; "Victims of the Jamaica Rebellion of 1865," 128–30, *129*
photography, 213, 228–30, 299 n. 2
picturesque, the, 115, 132, 205–6, 213, 217–19, 221

Pinnock, Agostinho, 276
Piquet Rebellion (1844), 13, 181–82
Piquets, the, 181–84
plantations, 61–67, 99–100, 171–72, 190–93, 204–5. *See also* labor
plants, 187–88, 194–96, 204
plot system, 190–93, 204–5
poetry performances, 236–37
political movements, 10–11, 32, 146–47, 213–14; women's roles in, 13, 48–51, 55–57, 75–76, 86–88
popular culture, 38, 45–46, 246–48, 260–61, 272; challenging the state, 49, 75–78; regulation of, 78–79. *See also* dance; musical forms
population control, 255–56, 259
Port-au-Prince, 185
Port Royal, 120
poverty, 1, 78–79, 107–10, 129–32
Povinelli, Elizabeth, 55, 239–40
public/private spheres, 11, 35–39, 40. *See also* family, the
public spaces, 11, 55, 75–78, 213–14
Puerto Rico, 146, 256
punishments, 53–56, 58–63, 83–84, 127, 292 n. 8, 292 n. 10, 301 n. 13
Puri, Shalini, *The Caribbean Postcolonial*, 112–13

"Quasheba," 10, 51, 54, 75; parody letter signed as, 85–86
"Queen," 11, 51, 73–74
queer subjects, 3–4, 8, 40, 113, 127. *See also* homophobia; homosexuality; sexuality
Quesnel, Léo, *Révue politique et littéraire*, 164–65

race, 2, 11, 29, 140–41, 212, 220–25, 230, 235, 240
Racine Con (dance troupe), 277
racism, 220, 230; scientific, 164–65
ragga, 272–75
Ramsey, Gordon, 127
Ramsey, Kate, *The Spirits and the Law: Vodou and Power in Haiti*, 46

Reddock, Rhoda, 77
reggae, 267
religion, 46–47, 49, 67–74. *See also* churches
reproduction, 29–30, 51–53, 87, 247–53, 300 n. 7; freedom of, 252–59, 301 n. 11; and production, 53, 57. *See also* birth control
Republic of Haiti, 154–57, 170–71
"repulsive," the, 221, 226
resistance, 10–11, 13, 16, 166–67, 181–82, 234; riots, 77–84, 105–6; strikes, 11, 65
revivalism, 69, 71
revolution, women's roles in, 180–86
Reybaud, Maxime, 183–84
Roach, Joseph, 37–38, 213, 268
Robinson, Tracy, 30
Roseberry, William, 33
"ruination," 192–93, 199
Ryan, Mary, 36

"Sable Venus" (ode to), 54
sacred tree, the, 137–41
Saint-Domingue, 173
St. John, Orford, "How to Behave in the Tropics," 231
Sale, Maggie Montesinos, 90–91
Salnave, President Sylvain, 184
Sanger, Margaret, 254–55
Sans Souci, 168
Saunders, Patricia, 274–75
Schoelcher, Victor, 159, 207–8
scientific racism, 164–65
Scott, James, 48, 78, 234
Scott, Joan W., 144
Scott, Rebecca, 63
Scully, Pamela, 5–6, 34
segregation, 230
sex tourism, 211, 233
sexual citizenship, 9–10, 16–17, 20–22, 45, 243–48, 271–80; and popular culture, 260–70; and the state, 40–42, 239–43
sexual economies, 55, 153, 225–27, 237–38
sexual violence, 58, 62, 259, 265, 270
Sexualities Working Group, 9

sexuality, 24–26, 29–30, 39–47, 73, 109–10, 240–42, 247–56, 301 n. 8; embodiment and, 37–39, 210–16, 250–51, 263
silences, in the historical record, 3–5, 13, 167, 169
silk cotton tree, 201, 203–4
Simmel, Georg, 212
Sims, Marion, 253
slackness, 42–43, 270–71
slavery, 10, 48, 53, 251–53
small plots, 204–5
Socolow, Susan, 176
Somers, Margaret, 20–21
Songz, Trey, "Bottoms Up," 43
soul music, 267
spaces, 14–15, 21–22, 189–92, 205. *See also* public spaces
Spillers, Hortense, 53, 252–54
spirituality, 15, 46, 206–7, 244–45, 276–77
Spivak, Gayatri, 5, 300 n. 5
Stanley-Niaah, Sonjah, 38
Stanton, Elizabeth Cady, 255
Stepan, Nancy Leys, 24, 199, 249
Stern, Steve, 185
Stitt, Jocelyn, 192–93
Stoddard, Charles Augustus, 224
Stoler, Ann Laura, 211
street protests, 11
strikes, 11, 65
Sturge, John, 60–61
suffrage, 160
sugar production, 171

textual histories, 237–38
Thomas, Deborah, 7, 272
Thomas, J. J., *Froudacity*, 230–31
Thompson, Krista, 228–29, 231; *An Eye for the Tropics*, 218
Tolia-Kelly, Divya, 206, 217
Tonton Macoutes, 156
tourism, 15–16, 200, 210–14, 217–18, 222–25; economy of, 234–35; local people and, 210–12, 219; sex, 211, 233, 301 n. 9; tensions of, 226–33; working classes and, 223–25. *See also* gaze, the

"transactional sex," 250–51, 256–57, 267–68, 301 n. 9

travel writing, 15, 197, 214–21; by women, 222–24

treadmills, 60, 62

trees, 15, 137–41, 187–89, 192–97, 200–209

Trinidadian Jamettes, 271

Trollope, Anthony, 95

Trouillot, Michel-Rolph, 3, 6, 167–68, 170, 174

Truth, Sojourner, "Ar'n't I a Woman?" 58

Turner, Mary, 63

Ulysse, Gina Athena, 236–37

Underhill, Edward Bean, 84, 109–10

Underhill Meetings (1865), 81, 108–10, 118, 140

unemployment, 80–81

Up Park Camp, Jamaica, 121

Urry, John, 212

U.S. Civil Rights Movement, 213

Ussher, Thomas Neville, 183

utilitarianism, 195–97

van Dyke, John, 218–19

Vastey, Pompée Valentin, Baron de, 146–47

violence, 1–2, 45, 54–55; sexual, 62–63, 259, 264, 270, 302 n. 14. *See also* executions; punishments

Vodou, 46, 183, 202, 206–7, 269–70

Vogel, Ursula, 66

wages, 64–67, 105, 107–8, 290 n. 23, 290 n. 29

Wahab, Amar, 198–99, 235

Warner, Michael, 40

warriors, popular images of, 148–53

West Indian Orientalism, 216

whiteness, 224–25

"whitening," 249

Wilmot, Swithin, 49, 56, 64–65

Wilson-Tagoe, Nana, 193

workhouses, 54, 60–62

working classes, the, 145–46, 223–25, 247, 256–59; and working children, 222

Wynter, Sylvia, 190

Yellin, Jean, 58–59

Young, Iris Marion, 40

MIMI SHELLER is a professor of sociology in the Culture and Communication Department and the founding director of the Center for Mobilities Research and Policy at Drexel University. She is the author of *Consuming the Caribbean: From Arawaks to Zombies* (2003) and *Democracy after Slavery: Black Publics and Peasant Radicalism in Haiti and Jamaica* (2000). She is founding co-editor of the journal *Mobilities*, as well as the editor (with John Urry) of *Mobile Technologies of the City* (2006) and *Tourism Mobilities: Places to Play, Places in Play* (2004), and editor (with Sara Ahmed, Claudia Castañeda, and Anne-Marie Fortier) of *Uprootings/Regroundings: Questions of Home and Migration* (2003). She is currently co-editing the *Handbook of Mobilities* and completing a book *Aluminum Dreams: Lightness, Speed, Modernity*.

Library of Congress Cataloging-in-Publication Data

Sheller, Mimi.
Citizenship from below : erotic agency and Caribbean freedom / Mimi Sheller.
p. cm. — (Next wave : new directions in women's studies)
Includes bibliographical references and index.
ISBN 978-0-8223-4934-1 (cloth : alk. paper)
ISBN 978-0-8223-4953-2 (pbk. : alk. paper)
1. Women—Caribbean Area—Social conditions.
2. Sexual minorities—Caribbean Area—Social conditions.
3. Power (Social sciences)—Caribbean Area. I. Title. II. Series: Next wave.
HQ1501.S47 2012
305.409729—dc23   2011041911

Printed in Great Britain
by Amazon